STEVE RICHARDS has been chief political commentator at the *Independent* since 2000, before which he was a BBC political correspondent and political editor for the *New Statesman*. He has also written for the *Guardian, Observer, Evening Standard* and the *TLS*. He presented *Despatch Box* on BBC 2 and *The Sunday Programme* on GMTV. He currently presents *Week in Westminster* on BBC Radio 4 and is a regular guest on the *Today* programme and *Newsnight*. In autumn 2010 he is writing and presenting a major series on Gordon Brown for Radio 4. He was named political journalist of the year in 2009 by the Political Studies Association.

WHATEVER IT TAKES

The Real Story of Gordon Brown and New Labour

STEVE RICHARDS

FOURTH ESTATE • *London*

First published in Great Britain in 2010 by
Fourth Estate
An imprint of HarperCollins*Publishers*
77–85 Fulham Palace Road,
London W6 8JB
www.4thestate.co.uk

LOVE THIS BOOK? WWW.BOOKARMY.COM

1 3 5 7 9 10 8 6 4 2

A catalogue record for this book is
available from the British Library

ISBN 978-0-00-732032-5

Typeset in Minion by G&M Designs Limited,
Raunds, Northamptonshire

Cover illustration © Norma Bar

Printed in Great Britain by Clays Ltd, St Ives plc

Mixed Sources
Product group from well-managed
forests and other controlled sources
www.fsc.org Cert no. SW-COC-001806
© 1996 Forest Stewardship Council

FSC

FSC is a non-profit international organisation established to promote the
responsible management of the world's forests. Products carrying the FSC
label are independently certified to assure customers that they come
from forests that are managed to meet the social, economic and
ecological needs of present and future generations.

Find out more about HarperCollins and the environment at
www.harpercollins.co.uk/green

To Barbara, Amy and Jake

CONTENTS

PREFACE

From the beginning the New Labour project was deliberately evasive. The term 'new', first used by Tony Blair on the day he became leader, was both an early clue to what was to follow and a red herring. Who could oppose a force that was new compared with one that was old? Most of us would prefer a new set of clothes to the older ones, at least until we find out more about what the clothes are like. But beyond a superficial attraction, where did the evasive adjective lead? The term was apolitical, like so many of the adjectives that were applied with such misleadingly feverish energy in the years that followed the emergence of New Labour.

The clue was the act of depoliticization. Newness was neither a quality on the left nor the right. The red herring was the notion that the adjective paraded with such a flourish conveyed clear direction, a party moving away from its past towards a 'new' future, forward not back, as the party put it in a slogan for the 2005 election. Blair relished the meaningless metaphor more than any other. 'I do not have a reverse gear,' he told his party conference in 2004. Actually he used that particular gear quite a lot, as all leaders do. But the image tells us nothing about the values of an individual or the party they lead.

The apolitical adjectives were not alone. Most of the rows that attracted so much intense attention for more than a decade were over issues relating to 'integrity', eruptions of 'temper' and personal rivalries. These were appropriately apolitical rows for the depoliticized decade. Debates about integrity can be staged about any public figure. They do not take us very far in discovering where these figures come

1

from and are trying to get to, beyond an uneasy sense that their adoption of an apolitical adjective in the first place was partly because they were not entirely sure where they were going as a political force either.

The subsequent internal divide within New Labour blurred further the original evasion. Suddenly in the mid-1990s there were Blairites and Brownites springing up from nowhere in large numbers. The noun became an adjective, the adjective a noun. I would not have been surprised if I had heard a cue on an interview programme along the lines of: 'Joining me now is the Blairite, Tony Blair.' Both adjectives were applied a thousand a times a day in attempts to shed light. Most of the time they obscured while purporting to clarify. Was a Blairite someone who was merely loyal to Tony Blair? Was a Brownite some-one who was personally loyal to Gordon Brown? Did a Blairite espouse a set of values and policies distinct from a Brownite's? If so, what were they?

The lack of clarification enabled the creators of New Labour to build up a big tent of support in the early years, as David Cameron and Nick Clegg sought to do when they formed their coalition after the election in 2010. Cameron and Clegg proclaimed a 'new politics', the ubiquitous fresh-faced adjective in place once more. New Labour. New Politics. The coalition was not a break with the past, but its echo.

Anyone could read more or less what he or she wished to into a project that claimed vaguely to be in the 'radical centre'. When New Labour was popular, support came from the right and left. But when it became unpopular there were unavoidably a thousand contradic-tory interpretations as to what had gone wrong. These post mortems were as foggy as the intentions of the original political project. As a result, the New Labour era remains one of the most misunderstood in modern times. Millions of words have been written on the subject already and yet the myths persist.

The role of Gordon Brown in the New Labour years is especially hazy and elusive. Like a central character in a whodunnit, his role and character seem obvious until we step back to question the assump-tions that shape our perceptions. In spite of the mountain of words written about him there are many unresolved questions. Here are some of thm, although others surface in the coming pages:

Why was Brown so seemingly poorly prepared for his period as Prime Minister when he had planned for his tenure at the Treasury like a military campaign?

Why did someone singled out by the highly demanding Peter Mandelson as 'media friendly' in the 1980s come to be regarded as a hopeless communicator by the time he became Prime Minister?

Why would some of Brown's staff have died for him, while other colleagues loathed him?

Why was Brown, so gripped by the need to address poverty and poor public services, the best friend of bankers and an ardent supporter of a light regulatory regime for the City?

Why did a Chancellor who made a fetish of being prudent and reducing borrowing take huge risks with the level of public debt towards the end of his tenure at the Treasury?

Why did Brown react quite so badly in 1994 to Blair securing the leadership, a reaction that determined so much that followed? After all, other highly ambitious politicians have failed to become leader and reacted more calmly.

Were the differences with Blair beyond fuming ambition and if so what were they?

What are the lessons for a party, any party, when two figures and their closest advisers seize total control?

How significant was the role of the media as Blair and Brown played out their dance?

How to explain a figure that claimed his Presbyterian father was his model and spoke of his moral compass yet presided over a paranoid court with close colleagues in fear of being briefed against and one of his oldest friends, Alistair Darling, claiming the 'forces of hell' were unleashed against him in the early autumn of 2008?

How was such a devoted bibliophile so contorted, dense and plodding when he wrote and spoke in public?

3

The questions accumulate and feed on themselves. One prompts another. The answers shed light not only on Brown's long career at the top of British politics, but on the entire New Labour project and on the challenges for the coalition government formed in the summer of 2010. In order to make sense of Brown's stormy premiership and the New Labour years that preceded it I begin where the seeds were sown, the summer of 1992.

For nearly two decades political journalism became largely defined by whether a writer was sympathetic to Tony Blair or Gordon Brown: 'Ah, that story about Brown dyeing his hair purple was written by Matthew Nice. That means it must have come from the Blair camp. Nice is a Blairite.' If a flattering story about Brown appeared, written by Kevin Nasty, there was a similar response: 'Ah, Nasty is a Brownite. It will have come from the Brown camp.'

The duopoly ruled the government, and although the duo was never as good at manipulating the media as it thought or had hoped, it came to determine the dynamics of political writing too. The result was a stifling form of journalism. Journalists are trained to detect relevance. Virtually all other institutions and individuals in politics had become irrelevant.

After Peter Mandelson's first resignation, or sacking, from the cabinet at the end of 1998 the journalist John Lloyd went for coffee at his house in Notting Hill. In effect Mandelson had been forced out of the government by Gordon Brown's close allies. A mournful Mandelson asked Lloyd whether he was close to Blair or Brown. Lloyd replied innocently that he knew and respected them both. Mandelson paused, looked up and declared: 'That's impossible. You're either on one side or the other.'

In spite of Mandelson's largely accurate declaration I remained in close contact with key figures in both the Blairite and Brownite courts. I also saw Blair and Brown regularly. The degree and range of contact was unusual. In most cases if a writer had access to one court there was little or no contact with the other. Throughout the era I kept closely in touch with both sides. This book reflects a range of conversations with Blair, Brown and other key figures from the early 1990s until the election in May 2010. The section on Brown's premiership also includes retrospective insights from those who worked with Brown, based on a series of interviews I conducted for a BBC Radio 4 series, broadcast in September 2010.

Over the New Labour years, and to my surprise, Brown came to interest me more than Blair. I am drawn to political performers, and from the early 1990s no one could perform like Blair, but gradually I came to realize that Brown was embarked on an enterprise of awkward, cautious, pragmatic nobility as well as a self-centred egotistical one in his hunger to become leader. I also discovered there was a marked ideological contrast between the two of them, one that has still not been properly explored and yet was at the heart of their inflammable reign.

In his rows over policy with Brown, Blair tended to take the kind of view that David Cameron and Nick Clegg would have done, which is one reason why their disputes are still highly relevant. They were big rows too, and the policy questions are still unresolved. Perhaps they are beyond resolution. What is the precise role of the state? How to deliver modern public services? What is the relationship between the state and markets? How much does a modern government need to tax and spend? What is Britain's relationship with Europe and the Euro? How best to respond to an epoch-changing global financial crisis? Is it possible to address the level of poverty in Britain in a way that does not in the end alienate affluent voters? The attempts to answer these questions will define the fate of governments and the main opposition parties too for decades to come. The coalition government asked all these questions again soon after its formation in 2010.

As they sought to address these questions, perceptions of Blair and Brown changed radically but in very different ways. Blair was idolized and then loathed by large parts of the media and the voters. Both were irrational responses. Views of Brown changed wildly over his career.

In 1992 Brown was on a high, appointed a youthful shadow chancellor, topping shadow cabinet elections and winning rave reviews in the media. By the summer of 1994 he was so unpopular that Tony

Blair became leader and Brown did not even dare to stand. When Labour won power in 1997 he was seen widely as a great reforming Chancellor, the chief executive of the government. After 11 September 2001, when Blair became a global superstar, Brown seemed doomed to play only a supporting role. Many influential columnists wrote off his chances of becoming leader. After his budget in 2003 he was hailed as a defining radical, almost single-handedly conducting a social democratic revolution. In 2004 his fortunes were at such a low ebb he was excluded even from the team planning the general election. At the beginning of 2005 he was so popular that Blair had to bring him back to the heart of the election campaign and promise that he would remain Chancellor after the election. Following the election victory his popularity slumped so low that polls suggested Labour would be even more unpopular when he became leader. In 2007 when he did become Prime Minister he was so highly rated that he was tempted to hold an early election. His decision not to do so touched off a sequence in which he became the least regarded prime minister since polls began. In the autumn of 2008 he bounced back as the country slid into recession. At the start of 2009 he became deeply unpopular again as the recession took hold. During the 2010 election, polls suggested that Labour would be slaughtered, coming third in terms of the votes cast. It came second easily, and for a few days afterwards there was a faint possibility that Brown would remain as Prime Minister. The oscillating perceptions are linked to the unanswered questions relating to Brown's wider career. Compared with Margaret Thatcher, John Major and, to some extent, Tony Blair, he was a more complex and elusive figure. Although he served as a Prime Minister for a shorter period than all three he was as significant because of the unique power he wielded in the Labour party when it became a formidable election-winning machine, an era in which he had almost complete control over economic policy.

This is how I saw them, the New Labour years. I focus on the under-reported policy developments as well as the soap opera. Both were significant and became connected. I do not believe that Blair was

'pro-reform' and Brown was 'anti-reform'. It was much more complicated and more interesting than that. By the end of his leadership, and
arguably at the beginning, Blair was a social and economic liberal, in
many ways closer to the Conservatives, leading a centre-left party that
he knew was in a different place from him. Brown was a timidly
cautious social democrat seeking to run a country that he feared was
in thrall to economic liberalism and instinctively Conservative. These
are the contortions that confused and distorted everything.

I look at the years through the prism of Brown's career because
there are more unanswered questions and mysteries than there are in
the extensively chronicled life of Blair. In my view both were misunderstood, but Brown more so. Two early books on Brown by Paul
Routledge and Robert Peston were part of the battle at the time with
Blair, acts of war. They became episodes in the story rather than
attempts at explanation. Elsewhere Brown's epic flaws have generated
a thousand headlines and several books, while his remarkably long
period in which he was virtually alone responsible for economic
policy is too easily dismissed or taken for granted. And yet if he, rather
than Blair, had left British politics in 2007, the Labour government
would have been left with a much bigger hole as it tried to come to
terms with the economy.

In the end Brown left five days after the 2010 election. But his exit was
not the predicted humiliation, and fleetingly he did what he had done
so many times before: he sought to do whatever it took to retain
power. For once he did not succeed, but the fact that he had the space
to try was in itself an appropriately epic coda to an extraordinary
career.

INTRODUCTION

Smiling determinedly and with transparent effort, Gordon Brown arrived at the election count in Kirkcaldy's Adam Smith College just after 12.15 a.m. on 7 May 2010. This was the day he was supposed to lose power for ever. Virtually every commentator in the land, as well as a host of cabinet ministers, had assumed for months and in some cases years that Brown would be gone on the Friday after the election, a leader burdened for the rest of his life by a terrible defeat.

As with virtually every episode in Brown's long career at the top of politics, assumptions formed with unswerving confidence proved to be wrong. Brown was not going anywhere other than Downing Street on Friday 7 May, and Labour was still more or less alive as a national force, suffering some terrible losses but also making a few unforeseen advances. The denouement of Brown's career was appropriately complex and ambiguous. Unquestionably Labour had been defeated at the election, yet no other party had won. Far from becoming immediately irrelevant in the early hours of Friday morning, Brown and his party were still clinging to power.

The days that followed were a compressed version of his highly charged, nerve-racking career, one marked by dashed hopes and moments of soaring optimism, fuelled by self-interest and altruistic ambition. As the votes were being counted Brown was a player again in the midst of historic turmoil. Typically his control over the levers of power was far from straightforward. For many years Tony Blair had stood in Brown's way. When Brown finally became Prime Minister he was for much of the time too unpopular and unsure of himself to take full control. Now David Cameron and Nick Clegg were preparing to pull levers too. Brown was used to this, always operating in a tiny amount of space and seizing moments when they arose. Politicians quite often act in the way they do because they have no choice. Great ones make the most of the tiny spaces.

To rapturous applause from supporters, Brown and his wife Sarah shook hands and embraced old friends as they awaited the declaration in his constituency. Here at least was mutually uncomplicated affection, local friendships arising from a shared passion for politics but not ruptured by rivalry and ambition at the very top.

Defeated leaders, or leaders on the verge of defeat, are brought to life by visits to their constituencies. Harold Wilson became less paranoid when he felt the affection of voters in Huyton, his seat in the North West of England. John Major was at once more relaxed when he headed for the comforting safety of his Cambridgeshire seat with one of the biggest majorities in the country. From the more troubling terrain of opposition Michael Foot and Neil Kinnock felt the same about their seats in Wales, where intense loyalty to them was at such odds with the raging disdain expressed elsewhere.

Brown always seemed to function on frighteningly narrow political terrain and he was already feverishly thinking through the likely outcome of the election result and considering his options. Behind his sincere and yet forced smile as he greeted old friends, he was calculating. Even now, as the votes were being counted in an election he had lost, he had options, or appeared to have them.

The Prime Minister had delayed his arrival long enough to contemplate the TV channels' exit poll and the inconclusive early declarations. He was exhausted after the campaign and the long, contentious years at the top, but was also energized, having slept in the late afternoon and eaten lamb stew for his dinner in an almost relaxed frame of mind.

The lull had not lasted for very long. Lulls never did in his career. Both the exit poll and the actual results pointed to a hung parliament. Although in the confused early hours there was unjustified scepticism about the exit poll, there was no doubt even then that, in terms of the share of the vote, the Conservatives had come first and Labour second. The Liberal Democrats were well behind in third place.

Brown had come second, but was still breathing as a leader and the Conservative leader, David Cameron, was in no position to claim victory. Brown had lost and won. A hung parliament presented possibilities. He had spent much of the campaign fearing that Labour would come third, a historic defeat and bleak personal humiliation. After the first televised debate when 'Cleggmania' erupted, Brown had told his closest ally, Ed Balls, that he would resign at once if the Liberal Democrats overtook Labour.

His speech at the count reflected the uncertainty. Normally he prepared speeches too thoroughly. This one was compiled speedily after brief telephone conversations with Peter Mandelson and Ed Balls once the exit poll had been broadcast at ten o'clock. The speech had a valedictory air and yet was not quite a farewell. Even now, seemingly doomed, Brown delivered words that had more than one purpose, as he had done for nearly two decades.

To a packed hall, Brown reflected the grey fuzziness of the results:

> The outcome of this country's vote is not yet known. But my duty to the country, coming out of this election, is to play my part in Britain having a strong, stable and principled government, able to lead Britain into sustained economic recovery and able to implement our commitments to far-reaching reform to our political system – upon which there is a growing consensus in our country.

Sarah Brown, tall and berry red in a bright coat, stuck like glue to her husband's side during the count, as she had done for much of the campaign. Standing on stage, nervously adjusting his jacket, Brown looked like a man desperate to fight on, even though the results were suggesting his career as a leader may be over.

Indeed the early part of his speech sounded as if he was taking his bow from the national stage:

Let me say to the people of this great constituency, there is no greater privilege than to serve in Parliament the people you have grown up with. Men and women you have gone to school with, whose children have also grown up here.

A few yards from here is the home in which I grew up as I was young. Immediately across the road from here is the church where my father preached and where I first began to learn about social justice.

And decades ago I learned here in Kirkcaldy something that has never left me – I learned what true friendship is.

And so many of us who meet first at school have been friends for life, and many of them are here tonight and I thank you for your unwavering support for me. For me personally, and also for your support for our cause.

This was Brown the human being making authentic references to his father and childhood friends. Both had sustained him through the years. Brown then turned to defend his record:

I'm proud of much that the Labour Government has achieved, the minimum wage, the child tax credit, the NHS renewed, more police officers, half a million children out of poverty, two million more jobs than in 1997.

Brown went on to offer more extensive thanks and a defence of his long period in power. No leader with a future ahead of him would focus so much on friendship and the past, but Brown left the door ajar.

In listing the government's achievements, and some of his own, he added at the end of each sentence:

That is what I have done … am doing … and continue to do.

His retrospective was accompanied by a defiant hint of future intent.

* * *

He and the Liberal Democrats were in agreement about the broad outlines of economic policy, and recently he had become an expedient, cautious supporter of electoral reform. He had become a convert in order to make the most of precisely these circumstances, a hung parliament.

Brown was waving goodbye and hinting that he might be willing to say hello one more time.

Soon after making his speech of conflicting messages Brown and his small entourage flew down to London. Election nights had always been highly charged for Brown even when Labour was winning landslides. In 1997 he had taken a similar flight in the early hours of an election morning wondering whether Tony Blair would give him the powers he sought. In 2001 he flew to London determined to force Blair to indicate his readiness to stand aside. In 2005 he made the short flight with a similar sense of angry resolution. Since 1997 the four post-election flights from Edinburgh to London for Brown had been troubled ones. Oddly, the short flight that took off at half past two in the morning on 7 May 2010 was the most positive. Although Labour was losing, Brown sensed he might be back in the game.

On his return to London Brown paid a brief visit to Labour's headquaters at Westminster. After thanking staff he spoke to Peter Mandelson, who had been in charge of the campaign, and who advised him to get some sleep. But already Brown was focused on the task ahead, as if the immediate past had not happened. He took notes ferociously, attacking his notebook, as he explored the new political situation. Mandelson had been watching the television coverage like a hawk, as well as appearing on various news programmes to declare with emphatic, mischievous charm that the election was a defeat for the Conservatives. Since Brown's leadership had turned into a form of hell he had turned to Mandelson as often as Blair had done after 1994. Both had a childlike dependence on a personality who displayed childish tendencies as well, although Mandelson had matured in recent years, keeping calm in the face of various media storms where once he would have erupted.

Famously, Brown had felt an irrational level of betrayal when Mandelson backed Blair in 1994, anger from which he never recovered and that led him dangerously astray. With Blair out of the way, Brown was able to purge his angry jealousy by having a similarly dependent relationship. At the end of long days as leader Blair used to proclaim: 'Get me Peter.' Tony was 'addicted' to Peter according to those who knew them both. Gordon had become an addict too, even though their relation in this final phase was still complicated, a potent mix of mutual doubt and intense relief that their old friendship had survived fourteen years of destructive enmity. Brown had invited Mandelson to become a cabinet minister in the autumn of 2008, an act that saved his leadership and highlighted how weak he had become. Together in yet another drama of uncertain outcome, on the Friday after an election they had jointly fought Mandelson told Brown that there was nothing he could do for a few hours, but the day ahead would be long. Sleep was best for now.

Uncharacteristically, Brown recognized that sleep was indeed a sensible option. He went to bed not knowing whether he was spending his final hours in Number Ten.

For others election night was sleepless. In particular the leader of the Liberal Democrats, Nick Clegg, was more or less staying awake through the night and into the next day. He had decisions to make, but was anyway in a state of mind not conducive to sleep as he was driven from his constituency in Sheffield to his home in Putney.

In the space of three weeks Clegg had twice been taken aback for wholly opposite reasons. During the campaign he and his wife Miriam had been shocked by the outbreak of 'Cleggmania', simultaneously exhilarated and slightly disturbed by the sudden switch from frustrated anonymity to indiscriminate adulation from voters and ferocious attacks from some newspapers. On the whole Clegg had been excited by the sudden transformation in his public status, but Miriam had her doubts about Clegg's political venture from the beginning, intelligently sceptical about the theatrical dimension in British politics. During the campaign they had become the theatre. Even a rock star has more time to prepare for fame than the Cleggs.

Still, at least the hysteria had hinted at historic opportunities, and then the results on election night dashed his soaring hopes. Having adapted to Cleggmania during the campaign, Clegg now had to come to terms with anticlimax. Against all expectations the Liberal Democrats were performing worse in terms of seats than at the last election. The final outcome was close to the one predicted by the prematurely derided exit poll. The Conservatives had won 307 seats, Labour was second with 258 and the Liberal Democrats had 57.

According to one of his close aides, Clegg made his crucial moves on the Friday morning while feeling 'shell-shocked' from recent events. Often leaders respond to setbacks by becoming more assertive. On a more epic scale this was how Blair reacted to the catastrophe in Iraq, more determined than ever to seize control of the domestic agenda in spite of failing when allowed to roam free in the explosive field of foreign affairs. Similarly Clegg was sobered by the disappointing results, but he was more single-minded rather than less.

Several times during the campaign Clegg had insisted that the party that came ahead of the others in a hung parliament had the first right to attempt to form a government. His formulaic answer was more flexible than it seemed in some respects. Clegg never specified whether the number of seats or votes would be more decisive. In the event this did not matter. The Conservatives had won more votes and seats.

He had also been careful to avoid any suggestion that the first attempt at forming a government was bound to be successful. At the same time he knew that momentum plays a big part in uncertain political situations. On the Friday morning he was determined to stick to his word and give the early cards to the Conservatives. At this point he had the full support of his influential mentor, Paddy Ashdown. Both agreed that the parliamentary arithmetic compelled them to let the Conservatives move first. Ashdown also agreed with Clegg on the Friday morning that whatever else had happened, Labour had lost the election, and that the Liberal Democrats' bargaining position was not as strong as they had hoped it would be. At this stage it had not crossed Ashdown's mind that a coalition with Labour

15

was feasible. Instead he was privately briefing journalists that the only options were a minority Conservative government or a Con/Lib arrangement.

With Brown still asleep in Number Ten, Clegg headed for his party's headquarters in Westminster. He made a short statement confirming his view that the Conservatives should be given the first chance to form a government. Clegg delivered the words without having any idea how David Cameron would respond. He was sticking with what he believed to be his only legitimate response to an election that the Conservatives had almost won. His more ideologically inclined predecessors would almost certainly have been less accommodating to the Conservatives, but Clegg was the party's first leader to be genuinely equidistant between the two other parties and in some respects closer to the Conservatives.

Soon after Brown emerged after a few hours' sleep, Mandelson briefed him on what Clegg had said. Both agreed that they still had cards to play. Labour had fought the election pledged to hold a referendum on electoral reform and to campaign in favour of a Yes vote. The Conservatives were opposed to electoral reform and were not at this point offering a referendum. Brown was especially resolute, more so than Mandelson. 'Clegg's party won't accept a deal with the Tories,' he repeated several times. They agreed Brown must make a statement, but one that was restrained. Mandelson told him: 'You must make clear that Cameron has every right to speak with Clegg first … appear gracious and prime-ministerial …'

Brown's subsequent intervention was perfectly pitched, making it clear that he was not deserting the stage but nor was he seeking to block others from taking over. In truth he had no power to block anyone, but Brown was almost enjoying a final challenge in which for him the stakes were not as high as they were for Cameron and Clegg. Either he would soon be released from the burden of power, or he would be the author of a breakthrough, a partnership between Labour and the Liberal Democrats. He would be making history once more.

The sweeping statement made outside Number Ten on Friday morning incorporated both scenarios:

With the outcome of the general election, we find ourselves in a position unknown to this generation of political leaders with no single party able to have a Commons majority and therefore have a majority government … I therefore felt that I should give you, and through you the country, my assessment of where we are. I do so as Prime Minister with a constitutional duty to seek to resolve the situation for the good of the country, not as the leader of the Labour party less than a day after the election.

This was both true and disingenuous. Brown was still the Prime Minister until an alternative could assemble adequate parliamentary support. Parts of the media attacked Brown for staying in Number Ten with a brutality that suggested the election campaign was still taking place, unable to stop kicking their victim even when there was no point in doing so. Brown had no choice but to stay put until the chaos of the election result had been resolved. But at the same time he was acting with the interests of the Labour party in mind, at least what he regarded as the party's interests.

First, it is well understood that we face immediate economic challenges that must be met. A meeting of the Euro Group is being held tonight to discuss Greece and other issues … On the critical question on the formation of a government that can command a parliamentary majority, I have of course seen the statements of other party leaders. I understand and completely respect the position of Mr Clegg in stating that he wishes first to make contact with the leader of the Conservative party … For my part I should make clear that I would be willing to see any of the party leaders, clearly should the discussions between Mr Cameron and Mr Clegg come to nothing, then I will of course be prepared to discuss with Mr Clegg the areas where there may be some measure of agreement between our two parties.

The statement cleverly conveyed a sense of business as usual, challenging the media and the voters to accept that Brown could still rule. More specifically he reminded Clegg and his party where they shared common ground.

Brown was almost exhilarated. On the Friday after the election no leader exerted full control. But he was more in control than he had been during what for him had been a wretchedly bleak campaign.

Brown had in common with Blair a capacity to focus on changing events with a forensic ruthlessness and sense of purpose. His first phone call on the Friday morning was to summon his Transport Secretary, Andrew Adonis, to Number Ten. Lord Adonis had been a close ally of Tony Blair's, and before that crucially he had been an active supporter of the SDP/Liberal alliance. He knew the Liberal Democrats better than anyone else in the cabinet. In yet another ironic twist Brown turned to Adonis, a figure he once viewed with suspicious hostility, in order to form a coalition with the Liberal Democrats, a concept he had viewed with horror while Blair was leader.

But on the Friday morning he was deadly serious, pulling prime-ministerial strings. The invitation to Adonis was testimony to his seriousness. He was working with Mandelson and Adonis, two figures who enthused about realignment on the centre left during the period that Brown was against any such transformation of the landscape, partly because he was not in charge to do the transforming.

For the first half of the election Brown had toured the country, captured on camera once or twice a day at a supermarket or at a school. In these bland locations he repeated the same message that 'he was looking forward to debating substance and not style'. That was more or less it. Mandelson had controlled the campaign in London, holding press conferences with vivacious, combative wit. Brown had been reduced to the role of King Lear, travelling from place to place with his entourage, stripped of real power within his party and beyond while those wild allies he had trusted and admired for their strategic insights were banished from the centre. Brown's wily old press secretary, Charlie Whelan, was explicitly told by Mandelson he would not be welcome at Labour's headquarters in Westminster. One of Whelan's successors, Damian McBride, was working for a school in north London, in political exile. Even Ed Balls had been reduced to a marginal role during the campaign. Each of them was bursting with ideas about how Labour could win and how Brown could be projected more effectively, but they were rarely heard since Mandelson and Alastair Campbell, also back at the heart of the operation, were not inclined to listen to any of them.

The Prime Minister's futile tour and the absence of those who had served him with unswerving loyalty highlighted one of the great tragic ironies of Brown's career. Brown had ached to replace Blair, but he proved far more powerful when he was Chancellor than as Prime Minister, and nowhere was his loss of authority more vividly exposed than during the campaign. In the 2001 and 2005 elections he and his entourage held absolute sway at the party's headquarters, determining strategy and calling the tunes. During the unseasonably cold late spring of 2010 Mandelson pulled the levers in London as Brown toured pointlessly.

Now the election was over he was quite unexpectedly playing a familiar role, doing whatever it takes to stay in the game. By the early afternoon his space to manoeuvre became even more constrained. David Cameron issued his response to Clegg and Brown. His speech was a work of art, a collaborative act of political genius that had been carefully prepared in advance. From early spring Cameron had recognized that he might not win an overall majority, having been confident of doing so a few months earlier. During the Conservatives' conference in the autumn Lord Ashcroft, the party's controversial donor and strategist, had told him he would win an overall majority of seventy. Some of Cameron's advisers thought the prediction was too pessimistic. But the Conservatives' support had fallen after their policies came under fleeting scrutiny at the start of the year. More fundamentally Oliver Letwin, an influential ally who had regular access to Cameron, was convinced that politics had changed and no single party could expect to win substantial victories again. Even when polls were predicting a big Tory lead, Letwin expected a tiny majority or none at all.

Letwin and a few others around Cameron were surprisingly relaxed about a political situation in which the Liberal Democrats might be a permanent third force of some national significance. They were convinced that Clegg and several other senior Liberal Democrats were much closer to them than to Labour, particularly in their critical attitude towards the state. This was by no means a universally shared view in Cameron's circle, and their pre-election objective had been to take as many seats as possible from Clegg's party. Nonetheless a common theme in their political discussions was that the Liberal Democrats under Clegg were potential allies, and not at all a party of the centre left.

In the light of the inconclusive results, the conflicting motives of Cameron and his inner circle came together. Cameron and his shadow chancellor, George Osborne, were instinctively more tribal than Letwin, but they had watched in awe as Tony Blair had threatened to destroy their party for ever by forming a big tent that included an army of non-Labour supporters in informal alliance. They also recalled more vividly Brown's fleetingly successful attempt to do the same when he became Prime Minister in 2007. A Tory MP defected to Labour and several non-Labour ministers joined the government. Brown had a soaring honeymoon as he strayed outside party boundaries. In spite of their massive majorities Blair and Brown cleared the path for the extraordinary events that followed the 2010 election, a politics of multi-layered calculation amidst proclamations of new and partially intended purity, the so-called new politics.

Whatever the definitions applied to their approach, Cameron and Osborne had chosen politics as their vocation in order to rule. They were fascinated by the choreography of politics, ways to win and the dark routes that led to defeat. On the whole they were perceptive readers of the rhythms. On this occasion they were titanic composers, recognizing an opportunity in their failure to win an overall majority. In his speech delivered early on Friday afternoon in Westminster, Cameron acknowledged that his party had fallen short of a majority and invited Clegg to form a coalition:

One option would be to give other parties reassurances about certain policy areas, and then seek their agreement to allow a minority Conservative government to continue in office without the country constantly facing the threat of its government falling ... But there is a case for going further than an arrangement that simply keeps a minority Conservative government in office. So I want to make a big, open and comprehensive offer to the Liberal Democrats. I want us to work together in tackling our country's big and urgent problems: the debt crisis; our deep social problems; and our broken political system.

At his first prime-ministerial press conference a few days later in the garden of Number Ten, held with Clegg standing beside him, Cameron gave the impression that it was only in their joint conversations that the two of them had agreed a coalition was the best option. It was clear, however, that this was what Cameron wanted the outcome to be before he had exchanged a single word with Clegg. The rest of his statement was a spectacular act of seduction in which he retained a strong grip on a potential coalition while appearing to let go, almost recklessly so:

Let me explain my thinking. First, it is right and reasonable to acknowledge of course that there are policy disagreements between us, many of which were highlighted in those television debates. To fellow Conservatives who have fought and campaigned and worked so hard to achieve the massive advance we have made in this campaign, I want to make it clear that I do not believe any government should give more powers to the European Union.

I do not believe that any government can be weak or soft on the issue of immigration which needs to be controlled properly. And the country's defences must be kept strong. I also believe that on the basis of the election result we have achieved, it is reasonable to expect that the bulk of the policies in our manifesto should be implemented.

Cameron gave no ground on these three big themes and on one other, his belief that spending cuts should be implemented within weeks. But then he put into public form the thrust of private conversations that had reverberated around his office over recent years:

> But across our two manifestos, there are many areas of common ground, and there are areas where I believe we in the Conservative Party can give ground, both in the national interest and in the interests of forging an open and trusting partnership.
>
> We share a strong desire to make opportunity more equal in this country, and I recognize the high priority that the Liberal Democrats have given to the proposals for a pupil premium in our schools.
>
> We agree with this idea, it is in our manifesto too, and I am sure we can develop a common approach that recognizes the urgency that the Liberal Democrats have attached to this proposal.
>
> The Liberal Democrats in their manifesto have made the achievement of a low-carbon economy an absolute priority and we support this aim. I'm sure we can agree a common plan to achieve it.
>
> The Liberal Democrats have also made proposals to reform our tax system. We both agree that Labour's jobs tax, as the Liberal Democrats manifesto puts it, 'is a damaging tax on jobs', and we would seek to reverse it.
>
> It has always been an aspiration for the Conservative Party to reduce taxes, especially on those who earn the least, and we are happy to give this aim a much higher priority, and to work together to determine how it can be afforded.
>
> We share a common commitment to civil liberties and to getting rid, immediately, of Labour's ID cards scheme. On our political system we agree with the Liberal Democrats that reform is urgently needed to help restore trust – and that reform must include the electoral system.

The statement out-Blaired Blair in evasive clarity. Cameron was being direct in arguing the patriotic case for stable government at a time of economic crisis. Genuinely he could see common ground with Clegg. And yet he did not concede much in spite of the magnificently generous tone. On Europe and cutting the deficit there were no concessions. In some other policy areas the two parties were already in agreement. At this stage Cameron hardly moved on electoral reform. One of his early objectives as leader had been to undermine the Liberal Democrats. Now he sought to embrace them, but in a way that might prove over time more lethal than his early attempts to stride on to their terrain.

The reaction to Cameron's statement of the two other players in this dance could not have been more different. Brown watched in Number Ten feeling more combative than at any point during the campaign. When Cameron proposed a review on electoral reform Brown recognized at once the echoes from 1974, when Ted Heath offered Jeremy Thorpe a speaker's conference on the issues after no party secured an overall majority. Thorpe rejected the meaningless concession. Brown exclaimed: 'They can't accept this … Cameron's given nothing on electoral reform … He's given them nothing at all.'

Brown was largely right, but with one massive qualification. Cameron was inviting the Lib Dems into government with an emphasis on their shared wariness of the state.

In striking contrast to Brown's scepticism, Clegg was excited by Cameron's offer. By then he had already in his own mind ruled out more or less the possibility of doing a deal with Labour, so the only options he perceived were a minority Conservative government or a more formal arrangement. Since becoming leader Clegg had deliberately kept his distance from Cameron and had no idea how to weigh up the motives behind the statement. Following Blair's journey in opposition Cameron had sought to make overtures towards Clegg as Blair had done with Ashdown. Clegg had shown no interest. He was irritated by the media's soft treatment of Cameron and jealous of the attention that he had attracted as leader of the opposition. The leader of the third party was also deeply suspicious of claims that Cameron had genuinely modernized his party. Nonetheless he had always found Cameron personable, whereas he could not bear dealing with Brown.

One exchange with Brown in particular had remained in Clegg's mind. The two of them had been discussing a book and getting on reasonably well. Clegg then merged the friendly discussion into one about party politics. Brown changed within a nanosecond from the engaged, enthusiastic bibliophile to the rigidly controlled tribalist. Clegg felt it was like talking to a different person, and in some ways it was. Brown could become unnecessarily defensive when engaging with political opponents and switch personality accordingly. Clegg was so shocked that he was convinced, wrongly, that Brown would be incapable of making the leap to multi-party politics.

Shortly after making his statement Cameron spoke to Clegg on the phone and reiterated the degree to which the offer was sincerely made. They agreed that negotiations between the two sides should begin.

Clegg's negotiating team signalled clearly which way he was heading. David Laws had been wooed several times by the Conservatives in the hope he would defect. Danny Alexander was in effect Clegg's representative. Chris Huhne was part of the generation of Liberal Democrats that yearned for power, and had told friends before the campaign that it would be impossible for the Liberal Democrats to make a deal with Labour if the government had lost its overall majority. Although instinctively more of a social democrat than Laws and Clegg, he had made the leap towards working with the Conservatives before a single vote had been cast. He wanted power.

In Number Ten power was an issue too. Two forces came together on the Friday afternoon, a Blairite–Brownite assumption that Labour should do whatever it took to retain power and the ultra-Blairite hunger for realignment on the centre left. Brown, Balls, Ed Miliband, Alastair Campbell and Peter Mandelson had been conditioned to fight for power, having been removed from it for so long in the 1980s and 1990s. At the same time Adonis in particular had yearned for realignment on the centre left. All of them were dreaming with different reasons and varying degrees of enthusiasm of a Lib/Lab coalition. At one point over the weekend Mandelson joked that 'Andrew has been waiting since 1906 for this moment to arrive.' They were not giving up now. In spite of Brown's public words earlier that he understood the right of Cameron and Clegg to seek agreement, Mandelson and Campbell urged Brown to speak to Clegg that evening in order to make clear that he was deadly serious about a Lib/Lab coalition.

Late on Friday afternoon Brown and Clegg spoke, each of them exhausted and instinctively wary of the other. Clegg did not welcome the call, regarding it as a diversion when the talks with the Conservatives had not properly begun. Brown's people-management skills were dreadful even when he had enjoyed a good night's sleep. Rarely in his career had he prevailed by intoxicating charm. His preferred approach was to put a relentless, unswerving case complete with warnings about the consequences of moving in a different direction to the one he had espoused. With Clegg, he tried his best in his formulaic opening: 'Nick, how's it going … have you had much sleep?' But the polite formalities were brief.

Quickly Brown made clear that Labour would offer a referendum on electoral reform as its top priority. A Lib/Lab coalition would be united in its support. To Brown's annoyed dismay, Clegg showed limited enthusiasm. He told Brown that he thought there were insuperable obstacles in terms of the parliamentary arithmetic and political legitimacy if the parties that came second and third formed a government, but he acknowledged the Lib Dems had more in common with Labour than the Conservatives. The two were speaking blindly, having spent the preceding hours acquiring wholly different mindsets. Clegg had been enthused by Cameron. Brown had become increasingly excited by his conversations with Adonis in particular about a Lib/Lab coalition. Characteristically, Brown did not give up, pointing out to Clegg that his party would find it far easier working with Labour. To Clegg's sleepless fury Brown suggested that the Lib Dems would not tolerate an arrangement with the Conservatives, especially when Labour was holding out the historic chance to change the voting system. Brown could not hide his frustration. He never could, whether in cabinet meetings, in one-to-one sessions with Blair, or during long-winded international gatherings. For a calculating politician, Brown was also surprisingly transparent.

As far as Clegg was concerned Brown had been too transparent. One of Clegg's team briefed the BBC that the call had been bad-tempered. Evidently they wanted to signal to their party that a route towards Labour was fraught with difficulties. If Clegg had felt instinctively more solicitous towards Brown he would have controlled his annoyance. He did not bother to do so.

At which point the media, a pivotal element in the entire New Labour saga, played its part in one final decision. Since the early hours of Friday morning some newspapers had screamed that Brown appeared determined to 'squat' in Number Ten. In fact until a new government could be formed he had a constitutional duty to remain in place. But in order not to look like a trespassing obsessive, Brown left Number Ten on the Saturday morning to spend the weekend in his constituency. Briefly he left the heart of the government's operation when there was still much to do, not least in speaking to Labour MPs about the plans for a coalition. He did spend much of his time on the Saturday when he was in Scotland speaking to union leaders in order to get their support for what he was doing. He still had a hold of a sort over them. No union leader spoke out against a Lib/Lab coalition in the days that followed.

While Brown spoke to union leaders, Adonis contacted his friends in the Liberal Democrats, those with whom they had discussed for years the possibility of realignment. His conversations with Ashdown were especially fruitful. Adonis argued with his engaging modest conviction – an approach to politics and journalism that had captivated Roy Jenkins more than a decade earlier – that the parliamentary arithmetic did not rule out a Lib/Lab coalition. With patient persistence he pointed out that a Lib/Lab government would have 315 seats compared with 306 for the Conservatives. Although this was not an overall majority it was safe to assume that the assorted nationalists would not bring down the coalition in alliance with the Tories. Adonis made it clear that Brown was not necessarily proposing a 'rainbow coalition' with several other minority parties, as the media continued to report, but a Lib/Lab government that would rule at least long enough to introduce electoral reform.

Ashdown started to sway towards such an arrangement. Three other former leaders, Ming Campbell, Charles Kennedy and David

Steel, also indicated privately or in Steel's case publicly that they would prefer an arrangement with Labour. Adonis also had considerable influence on Tony Blair. Brown had spoken to Blair on the Friday and noted his scepticism about the feasibility of a Lib/Lab coalition because of the parliamentary arithmetic. Over the weekend Blair became more supportive of the idea.

In every frenzied conversation involving Adonis, Mandelson and senior Liberal Democrats, the position of Brown was raised as an overwhelming obstacle. Clegg had stated during the campaign that he could not do a deal with a defeated Brown. Over the weekend Ashdown told Adonis the same. A close ally of Clegg's, Neil Sherlock, who had spent as many hours as Adonis contemplating a realignment on the centre left, also made it clear that no deal could be done with Brown continuing for any length of time as Labour's leader. Vince Cable spoke directly to Brown several times over the weekend. The two were old friends. Cable retained a certain limited respect for Brown and the two of them shared a fair amount of common political ground, at least in relation to economic policy. He gave a much stronger indication than Clegg that he would prefer to work with Labour, an appetite heightened perhaps by the fact that he was not part of the Liberal Democrats' negotiating team and had in Brown's view been deliberately marginalized by Clegg. At one point Cable told Brown: 'Emotionally I'm closer to Labour.'

Cable's final call to Brown was at six in the morning on the Monday. He told him that his departure was an essential condition to a deal. This was not expressed as an ultimatum. Cable knew that Brown was willing to resign in order to facilitate a deal. His call was merely confirmation that in order to open the door for serious negotiation a public declaration was necessary. Clegg had made the same point in his discussions with Brown, although he had not promised that negotiations would open as a result.

Brown took no persuading. Adonis, who had never worked closely with him, least of all in an atmosphere of nerve-racking intensity, was impressed and surprised by his resolute determination. Brown was ready to announce his resignation and had informed Clegg of his willingness to do so in a one-to-one meeting on the Saturday morning. The only issue was over precisely when. Cable had suggested the key moment would be after the meeting of Liberal Democrat MPs that would take place early on Monday afternoon.

Brown met Clegg again at the Commons on the Monday morning and was even more direct: 'Policies are not the issue between us – we are agreed on most issues. I am sure we could form a Progressive Alliance between us. I genuinely believe it could work ... If it increases the possibility of forming a Progressive Alliance, I am prepared to stand aside as Labour leader.'

While Brown, Campbell and Mandelson composed a statement late on Monday morning, the group they regarded as their ace card, Clegg's MPs, expressed concern at a formal deal with the Conservatives at their private meeting. The nature of the discussion at the meeting of the Liberal Democrats' parliamentary party focused less on what the negotiating team had brought back from their discussions with the Tories and more on the need to find out what Labour had to offer as an alternative route. Several MPs, including their former leader, Sir Ming Campbell, argued that realignment on the centre left had been the party's great mission and this was not the way to bring it about. Clegg replied openly wondering whether the reservations were generational, and to some extent geographical, with a lot of the concerns coming from older Scottish Liberal Democrats.

The meeting broke up with an announcement that the negotiating team would seek 'clarification' on some issues with their Conservative counterparts. The term was a euphemism that allowed the two wings of the Liberal Democrats to play for time. As far as David Laws was concerned, clarification related to a few minor details in relation to the pupil premium, a policy that united both parties. The social democratic wing had growing hopes that in the space still left a deal could be reached with Labour.

At which point Brown played his card. Those who were with him as he prepared to announce his resignation were struck by his calm. Brown could erupt angrily over trivial matters and remain focused when the political temperature reached boiling point. Speaking outside Number Ten, he seemed fleetingly to have changed the dynamics of British politics once more:

> Mr Clegg has just informed me that while he intends to continue his dialogue that he has begun with the Conservatives, he now wishes also to take forward formal discussions with the Labour Party. I believe it is sensible and it's in the national interest to respond positively … There is also a progressive majority in Britain, and I believe it could be in the interests of the whole country to form a progressive coalition government … I would however like to say something also about my own position. If it becomes clear that the national interest, which is stable and principled government, can be best served by forming a coalition between the Labour Party and the Liberal Democrats then I believe I should discharge that duty, to form that government, which would in my view command a majority in the House of Commons in the Queen's speech and any other confidence votes. But I have no desire to stay in my position longer than is needed to ensure the path to economic growth is assured and the process of political reform we have agreed moves forward quickly. The reason that we have a hung parliament is that no single party and no single leader was able to win the full support of the country. As leader of my party I must accept that that is a judgement on me. I therefore intend to ask the Labour Party to set in train the processes needed for its own leadership election.

This was becoming the equivalent of an epic centre court final at Wimbledon, with Brown the veteran competing against two younger, rising stars. Brown had responded to Cameron's statement on Friday with one that was crafted with the same level of political artistry, a stunning return to Cameron's beautifully played stroke. Yes, Brown would be going. No, he would not be going quite yet – an echo of Blair's resignation statement in September 2006. Brown had highlighted two priorities, the economy and political reform. He was looking for a graceful exit, one that would bristle with historic possibilities as he left in place a progressive coalition, but he was realistic enough to realize that he could play no part in the medium-term future. He had recognized this, or almost had, for a long time.

After Brown's statement some of the key figures in Number Ten rushed out to proclaim the new progressive opportunity. Adonis, Douglas Alexander (who never really believed that this was a progressive opportunity) and Alastair Campbell toured the studios to put the case for a Lib/Lab coalition. Brown sat back and watched, his career almost over whatever happened next.

What did happen next revealed quite a lot about Clegg, his favoured Liberal Democrats and parts of the Labour party. The first meeting between Labour's negotiating team and the Lib Dems' equivalent had been fairly informal on the Saturday afternoon. Labour's team consisted of Adonis, Mandelson, Balls, Ed Miliband and Harriet Harman. During that meeting they sensed that the Lib Dems were moving towards Labour. Mandelson was certain throughout that they were playing Labour along to get more from the Conservatives, but the others dared to wonder, and with mixed feelings, whether they were about to begin a fourth term in partnership with the Lib Dems. Before the cabinet meeting on the Monday afternoon, Balls was with Brown when he got another call from Clegg. By that point Clegg appeared to be moving fast towards Labour. He said to Brown that Labour and the Liberal Democrats were the two progressive forces and were therefore natural partners. By late Monday afternoon Brown and Balls were briefly convinced that a deal was on. Early on Monday evening Brown chaired his final cabinet meeting. No one knew for sure that this would be the end. Quite a few assumed now that Brown would be Prime Minister until the autumn. Brown also thought for a few hours this was likely.

No cabinet minister spoke out overtly against a Lib/Lab coalition, although several had intense private doubts, in particular Jack Straw. Brown talked through the situation with considerable enthusiasm showing none of the bad-tempered lack of patience he could display when chairing cabinet meetings in less tempestuous times.

The Labour and Lib Dems' negotiating teams met immediately after the cabinet, so quickly that ministers had no time to discuss in advance what they would be willing to concede. In the event they offered to move at least as far as the Conservatives, especially in the area of civil liberties, a policy area where the government had acquired a ragbag of policies, adopted for reasons of neurotic insecurity rather than principled machismo. The policies had never been fully supported by anyone on Labour's negotiating team. Perversely, a sticking point in the discussions was Labour's commitment not to start cuts in public spending until the following year. Even though the Lib Dems had argued for the same policy in the election campaign, David Laws was now insisting that immediate cuts should be part of the package. Chris Huhne also called for immediate legislation on the Alternative Vote followed by a wider referendum on other options for electoral reform. Even Adonis was taken aback at such a prospect. Huhne suggested 'this would be an experiment in an experimental coalition'. Although Labour's team was much more wary after this meeting, they assumed that Clegg was sincere in his willingness to do a deal and agreed to meet again on the Tuesday morning. Labour's team also proposed a separate meeting between Cable and Alistair Darling.

Hungry for power almost as an end in itself, Cameron and Osborne rushed out a new offer in response to Labour's moves, a referendum on the Alternative Vote. This was the same as Labour was offering in relation to electoral reform, although Labour was committed to campaigning for the change whereas the Conservatives were opposed. The duo had spent the last four years seeking a route to power, changing economic policy on the basis of the latest focus-group findings and proclaiming their party's modernization without changing many of the assumptions and polices that they had inherited. Cameron and Osborne opposed voting reform, but their desire for power meant they did not hesitate to make the offer.

Their move was decisive. When Clegg got the news, a few minutes before it was released to the media, his mind was more or less made up. He wanted to do a deal with the Conservatives and take part in a formal coalition. He had never had much doubt. Later Clegg was hailed for his ruthless negotiating techniques, but he did not have to try very hard. Both sides were desperate for a deal and at times he had been genuinely torn, not least because Ashdown had moved some distance over the weekend towards Labour, and his other former leaders – Charles Kennedy and David Steel – had always been keener on a deal with Labour.

But Clegg was reaching a firm decision on Monday evening and acquired ammunition from former cabinet ministers David Blunkett and John Reid who led the charge against a Lib/Lab coalition. Reid spoke out passionately against an arrangement. In fact Labour was not proposing a formal arrangement with the SNP, only with the Lib Dems, but Reid was not one to allow details to intervene. Blunkett was far more perceptive and his opposition carried more weight. The left of the Labour party started to speak out as well. On the other side Cameron faced similar problems with the right of his party, but Clegg had found his soulmate, two pragmatic leaders bound by their hostility towards the state and their capacity for polite, almost apolitical negotiations.

The dynamics revealed much about Labour's diminished hunger for power. Reid and Blunkett had been cabinet ministers. Straw had served in the cabinet from 1997 to the very end. If they had been eager for their first ministerial posts their reaction to the result might have been very different. Sated personal ambition played a part in the cries within Labour against a Lib/Lab coalition.

On the Tuesday morning Brown and Clegg had one further meeting, but Labour's negotiating team sensed they were being played along. The Lib Dems had briefed misleadingly that Labour's team had been aggressive in the negotiations, especially Ed Balls. Adonis, no natural ally of Balls, was adamant that Balls behaved politely throughout. Labour's team sensed trouble, assuming the briefing was aimed at showing Ashdown and others that they had tried but faced immovable objects. Brown, who had been in some ways the most enthusiastic for a coalition, moved from high hope on Monday night to pessimism by Tuesday morning. Still he clung to a shred of optimism. At midday, hours before his resignation, he had a phone call with Sir Ming Campbell, spelling out in detail how the mechanisms were in place for a Lib/Lab coalition and how he had prepared for the appointment of Lib Dems in senior departments.

During a phone call with Brown early in the afternoon Clegg was evasive. 'Look, I'm not in a position to give you a definitive answer,' he told Brown. 'I want to continue to speak to both sides. Coalition talks take a long time in other countries. There's nothing unusual about this. Why the hurry?'

Brown responded: 'The country will not understand if this ambiguity continues. The public needs certainty and we must provide an answer.' He issued one last plea to Clegg: 'I am convinced this is the right time to create a Progressive Alliance. I know the electoral arithmetic is difficult but I think there is a way round that.'

Clegg fudged again: 'I still want to go on talking to both sides.'

Brown struggled to hide his frustration as he replied: 'I have to go the Palace soon. If you are not prepared to commit yourself you have to tell me. Now.'

Clegg: 'I will call you back in five minutes after I've talked to my advisers.'

After Brown put the phone down, he discussed his next move with Mandelson, Campbell, and old cabinet allies Ed Balls, Ed Miliband and Douglas Alexander. They knew it was over. One observer noted: 'We all agreed it could not go on any longer … It was obvious Clegg wasn't serious about doing a deal. He was using it so he could go back to Cameron and get more out of him. We didn't have the numbers and the Labour Party just wouldn't wear it.'

Brown had made one big mistake in the four days. He had failed to summon Labour MPs for an early meeting in order to keep them fully informed. As a result they felt excluded and ignorant and began to express public wariness to a deal. Seen widely as a Labour tribalist, Brown had given little thought to the tribe as he planned a realignment on the centre left more dramatic than any plan contemplated by Tony Blair. By Tuesday mid-afternoon Brown knew that there would be no deal: he would be out of power within hours.

After three years of erratic, frail authority he decided to seize full control of his departure, with the help of Mandelson and Campbell, the great choreographers and manipulators of the New Labour era. As was often the case with the misunderstood duo, they were motivated by humane considerations as they planned a final move. Politicians are human beings, as fearful of public humiliation as anyone else. They had helped ease the way for a small army of ministers. Now the game was over for Brown, for them and for Labour. They wanted to help Brown to leave with dignity. Brown spent much of the day writing letters to friends and colleagues, thanking them for their support, a generous gesture made with no ulterior motive.

Brown also wrote the final version of his farewell speech, including a reference to his own personal failings, although others had encouraged him to part with a hint of humble self-awareness. With Sarah, Mandelson arranged the perfect visual departure in which finally their two sons John and Fraser would join them in the public eye as they left Number Ten for the last time, a humanizing image that had eluded Brown when he sought to cling to power.

In one final phone call Clegg had begged Brown to stay on for a little longer while he resolved what to do. Brown refused at first and then appeared to waver a little. Mandelson grabbed a card and wrote in big bold letters: 'No More Time!' He ostentatiously placed the card in front of Brown. There was no more wavering. Brown had also spoken to Blair again on the phone, explaining that he had given up hope of a deal. One way or another they were all there at the end as they had been at the beginning, Blair, Brown, Campbell and Mandelson. For all the mighty rows and fallings-out, they almost needed to be there for those final moments. When Mandelson had resigned from the cabinet for the first time he turned to Brown to help him compose his resignation letter even though Brown and his allies had brought about his downfall. Although Blair had kept Brown out of Number Ten for as long as possible, Brown turned to him for advice in his final days and Blair was happy to offer it.

Brown completed his call to Clegg insisting he had already decided to see the Queen to resign. 'I can't go on any longer, Nick, I'm going to the Palace.'

A resigned Clegg replied: 'If that's your decision …' Brown said: 'It is.' He called Sarah and his sons John and Fraser to his office, hugged his Downing Street team and walked out of Number Ten with his family for the last time.

Before leaving he uttered the only speech he had given for more than two decades that had no complicated calculations behind it, no move on a chessboard:

Only those that have held the office of prime minister can understand the full weight of its responsibilities and its great capacity for good.

I have been privileged to learn much about the very best in human nature and a fair amount too about its frailties, including my own.

Above all, it was a privilege to serve. And yes, I loved the job not for its prestige, its titles and its ceremony – which I do not love at all. No, I loved the job for its potential to make this country I love fairer, more tolerant, more green, more democratic, more prosperous and more just – truly a greater Britain.

In the face of many challenges in a few short years, challenges up to and including the global financial meltdown, I have always strived to serve, to do my best in the interest of Britain, its values and its people.

And let me add one thing also. I will always admire the courage I have seen in our armed forces.

And now that the political season is over, let me stress that having shaken their hands and looked into their eyes, our troops represent all that is best in our country and I will never forget all those who have died in honour and whose families today live in grief.

My resignation as leader of the Labour Party will take effect immediately. And in this hour I want to thank all my colleagues, ministers, Members of Parliament. And I want to thank above all my staff, who have been friends as well as brilliant servants of the country.

Above all, I want to thank Sarah for her unwavering support as well as her love, and for her own service to our country.

I thank my sons John and Fraser for the love and joy they bring to our lives.

And as I leave the second most important job I could ever hold, I cherish even more the first – as a husband and father.

Thank you and goodbye.

The last sentence was uncharacteristic in its stark clarity. Brown swept out of Downing Street for the last time, leaving behind a political situation of tantalizing possibilities and dangers for those that had acquired or sought to acquire power. It was an appropriate parting gift from a complex political figure who had breathed the politics of opportunities and dangers ever since he had climbed close to the top when he became shadow chancellor in 1992. There had been no break after that until the cold Tuesday evening in May when he said goodbye. From the summer of 1992 he had been doing whatever it took to secure power and act with expedient principle. He had been doing so even in his final few days. Suddenly the tiny space in which he strode had shrivelled to nothing. No options remained any more.

ONE

Trust

The high stakes and unpredictable outcome of the five days after the 2010 election campaign were so familiar for Brown that the sequence was almost a repeat, like the latest episode of long-running US television series where the plot and characters remain the same. Only the context had changed. Brief opportunities were seized and misjudgements made. Expedient hunger for power mingled with a vision of a new progressive consensus. In the final episode Brown failed to deliver, but he took his bow in a dignified manner and left behind a party that held enough seats to mount a serious challenge in the future.

He was more successful in the earlier phase of the long-running drama. The first episode in the series began during the summer of 1992, when Brown was made shadow chancellor. All the classic character failings were in place, along with the underestimated strengths of guile and conviction, a rare combination. Most politicians who possess intense conviction tend to display innocence when it comes to the street-fighting arts. Those who glory in their deviousness often lack conviction, coming to regard the scheming as an end in itself.

Politics moves so quickly that the day before yesterday is easily forgotten. I was constantly surprised how even some Labour MPs had only scant recollection of Brown's role as shadow chancellor, but it was his performance in this far-off period that made me realize that some of the allegations made against him when he became Prime Minister – in effect that he was useless and short-sighted – made little sense. His role in the early years was immense, more important in policy terms than Blair's.

Between 1992 and 1994 Brown began to rewrite left-of-centre economic policy making while navigating his way around the complex politics of Britain's humiliating withdrawal from the Exchange Rate Mechanism. In both cases he moved Labour to a position of heightened popularity but made himself deeply unpopular. Every day the political temperature was high for him, yet he was more than a decade away from the unbearable heat of becoming Prime Minister.

The decline in popularity over these two years was a steep fall. In the summer of 1992 Brown was on one of his highs, having been a star performer during the previous parliament when he regularly topped the annual shadow cabinet poll, an election in which only his fellow Labour MPs had the vote. The poll was seen as highly significant and those that came top were inevitably regarded as potential future leaders. I recall seeing Robin Cook emerge from a meeting that had announced the shadow cabinet results in 1987. He was pale and had aged around twenty-five years in the space of half an hour. I asked him what was the matter. He could not speak. Shortly afterwards I found that he had been voted off the shadow cabinet, the equivalent of being sent to Siberia.

On the whole the media too rated Brown highly in 1992. Politicians and journalists had witnessed the quick-witted oratory in the Commons and the command of a brief. Every newspaper had assumed he would secure the most senior post in the shadow cabinet and saw his elevation when it came as a signal of serious intent for Labour. He was forty-one when he became shadow chancellor, his girlfriend Sheena Macdonald was a glamorous TV interviewer and presenter. There was little talk then of his introverted eccentricities, although those who knew him well were aware of them. The orthodoxy at the time from across the political spectrum was that Brown was a formidable and charismatic politician. That changed from the summer of 1992.

One of the reasons why Brown's reputation fell dramatically between the summer of 1992 and the spring of 1994 is easy to discover: he became shadow chancellor. It is the fate of shadow chancellors to be unpopular. Most ambitious politicians yearn for the post in the doldrums of opposition. Their hunger is irrational. The post destroys reputations.

By virtue of the job shadow chancellors must appear economically credible, serious figures capable of making tough choices. They are also part of a team seeking to win an election and therefore cannot say anything that risks alienating too many voters. The few who are successful combine the appeal of a reassuring accountant and the skills of a political artist. Ultimately they must frame an economic policy that is able to withstand intense scrutiny from the media and political opponents. As a further complication shadow chancellors must devise policies in ways that are consistent with their party's principles even though their party will have recently lost an election espousing policies on which those principles were based.

A popular shadow chancellor is a contradiction in terms. There is a long list of shadow chancellors who held the job for a relatively short period. A much smaller number move up to become a chancellor of the Exchequer.

In Brown's case he was embarking on an exercise that required the stamina of the marathon runner, though he did not know at the beginning that he would be a shadow chancellor for five years and Chancellor for more than ten. Such a time span, fifteen years of being responsible for Labour's economic policy, is the equivalent of running several marathons in the desert. Many a talented politician would have fallen by the wayside long before.

The unusual demands of the job are highlighted by the fate of Brown's highly gifted predecessors and Tory successors who failed to meet the tough criteria. After Labour's 1983 landslide defeat the newly elected deputy leader, Roy Hattersley, became shadow chancellor but opted with relief for the relative safety of Home Affairs four years later after the party lost again. Hattersley admitted later that even by the 1987 election campaign there were some questions in television interviews about the party's 'tax and spend' policies he could not answer without contradicting his leader, Neil Kinnock: 'Instead I took the only course available to me ... I attacked the interviewer.' Hattersley was a more experienced politician in 1983 than Brown was in 1992. Four years were more than enough for him.

John Smith took over from Hattersley in 1987. He was respected and popular with the wider electorate but also failed to come up with policies that had a broad appeal.

The pattern of failure continued on the other side. After their 1997 defeat Conservative shadow chancellors also struggled to make their mark. They came and went more often than Conservative leaders, which was saying something during this period of identity crisis for the party. Francis Maude, Michael Portillo, Michael Howard and Oliver Letwin performed the role without coming up with popular, credible policies as the Conservatives lost three elections in a row. None of them enjoyed the experience particularly or emerged with his reputation enhanced. In some cases perceptions of their political expertise diminished considerably. Even the nimble-footed and astute George Osborne was the subject of intense internal and external criticism. For much of the 2010 election campaign he was hidden away, regarded as a liability.

Osborne discovered as other shadow chancellors had done before him that jealous rivals expressed a lofty disdain. But it did not fall on rivals to square the circle. They could pop in and out of the debate on economic policy, proposing a tax cut here or a spending rise there. They were under no obligation to paint a wider picture, one in which all the inconvenient sums added up. If they had done all the sums they would have been unpopular too.

The critics have an easy role as members of a loud disgruntled chorus. After the summer of 1992 the chorus around Brown soon became loud and large. It never went away. None of them realized, or were willing to acknowledge, the scale of the task that he faced. The context was unremittingly bleak. Soon after losing the 1992 election Neil Kinnock read a biography chronicling his arduous nine-year leadership. He sent a note to the author that concluded with a single exuberant and yet despairing sentence: 'What a bloody way to spend my forties!' There was no election win to compensate for the bloody, stressful battles that Kinnock had fought courageously for nearly a decade. By 1992 Labour's commitment to unilateral nuclear disarmament had been dropped – a cause to which Kinnock was once passionately committed. Labour no longer advocated withdrawal from Europe. Kinnock had sought to be business-friendly. The party had seen off the once potentially fatal threat of the SDP and had purged the left-wing Militant Tendency from its ranks. It had been neurotically careful not to propose sweeping tax rises, ones so punitive that they might reduce the pay packets of relatively low earners. It had agonized over spending plans and made only limited pledges. In some ways it was the slicker party in the field of presentation. Still Labour lost, miles behind the Conservatives in terms of votes.

A fortnight after the 1992 election Labour's National Executive Committee met for the post-mortem at the party's headquarters in Walworth Road, a mile or so away from Westminster. The internal pollsters reported that the party had lost above all for a single reason: it was not trusted to run the economy. In spite of all Kinnock's reforms, voters still assumed that Labour would tax and spend recklessly. There had been no enthusiasm for the Conservatives, but a much greater fear of Labour's economic policies. This would be Brown's challenge as shadow chancellor.

As he embarked on his thorny ascent Brown operated as a solo player and all of the traits that would come out later were evident, albeit in a lower key. One of his early advisers was Neal Lawson, who joined Brown in the summer of 1992. Lawson was beginning his own distinct journey leftwards. Later he was the founder of Compass, a group that challenged the pragmatic expediency of both Blair and Brown:

> Gordon didn't operate with a group of people who knew his mind. There were individual conversations, like hands of a clock he would have a talk with someone for an hour and then move on to the next. There was no collective conversation. Each of us was aware of bits of his thinking, but he held all the cards himself. It was frustrating as the only person who knew the whole strategy was Gordon. It was in his head, but never discussed with all of us in a group.

41

Brown never changed his approach. A wary insecurity meant that he was not at ease in large group discussions, even when he was Prime Minister in Number Ten. He was a hopeless people manager, unable to notice if there was a sense of divisive paranoia in his court. His idea of teamwork was a one-to-one session with his closest colleague, Ed Balls. Soon a lot of the team would turn against him on this basis alone. But in 1992 Brown had a clearer idea of what was required to win trust for an economic policy than anyone else in the Labour party.

At the broadest level, the outlines on an otherwise dauntingly blank canvas, he had a plan that went along these lines: make a public argument with the widest possible appeal while preparing policies more discreetly that were still rooted on the left of centre. He became so persistent as a public narrator that few noticed what was happening below. In embryonic form, this was his version of New Labour.

Although Brown wrote more books and articles than any other senior political figure of recent times, his key beliefs were rarely spelled out. He chose to be deliberately evasive because in his view a wide coalition of support could only be built around vague concepts such as 'courage' or 'Britishness', more of those apolitical themes that defined the public face of New Labour. He did not believe that a country that had voted for a Conservative government in four successive elections was ready for candid arguments about higher public spending, tax rises to pay for it and redistribution. He still did not believe it was ready for candour after Labour had won three elections. There is plenty of evidence to suggest that he was correct. In 1992 the assumption was even less contentious.

Brown never used the term 'left-of-centre', preferring the less threatening and vague 'progressive' to describe his politics. Some of his motives and objectives were almost entirely hidden in a haystack of words aimed at reassuring potential doubters about what he was doing. One of those who worked closely with him in opposition and in government says:

Gordon believed that quite often he could accomplish radical acts, but sometimes he felt able to make the case for them only once the acts had been implemented. Sometimes he did not want to say too much in advance. To take one example he redistributed quite extensively without making the case overtly for redistribution, because he felt that voters would regard such a term with fear, associating it with Labour in the 1980s. But once the controversial policies, such as tax credits and discreet increases in public spending, had been implemented and middle England or the media was not raging, he would make the case for them.

The sequence does not seem particularly significant now, but it was revolutionary at the time. What had happened previously was that Labour shadow chancellors would make a general argument for tax rises, only to be slaughtered for it in much of the media and in opinion polls. By the time they came up with the detailed policies they had lost the argument.

An informative early guide to Brown's values and approach is his biography of John Maxton, the left-wing Scottish Labour MP who helped to light up Westminster in the 1920s and 1930s. The book is revealing for the distant authorial voice that makes the case for expediency over impotent idealism.

Brown joked in the introduction that the book was 'twenty years in the making'. He studied Maxton as a student at Edinburgh University in 1967, then wrote a PhD thesis about Scottish politics in the 1920s, and finally published the biography in the mid-1980s when he was an ambitious Labour MP. By the time of publication he was already calculating how closely he wished to be associated with the book's subject, a Labour MP who never ruled. Even the publication of a book became an act of pragmatic idealism.

Brown described the scenes, evoked the personalities and told the story. But as an author he kept himself out of it, conveying neither enthusiastic approval nor the opposite. By the time the book was published in 1985 he was already developing his ambiguous public voice.

Quite often in the years to come, when he wanted to convey his own views he would do so under the protective clothing of somebody else, so that no one was quite sure where precisely Brown stood on highly charged matters. Many people, from the banker Sir Derek Wanless to President Obama, were to play the role of a shield for Brown as he implemented controversial policies. He never dared to rely on his voice alone, one that would be exposed to the howls of a thousand reactionary voices in response. His first shield was Maxton.

Brown noted that Maxton had suffered the 'condescension of posterity', but did not make entirely clear whether he believed the verdict was undeserved: 'The Independent Labour Party which he dominated for twenty years dwindled eventually to nothing, even as his audiences grew larger. But at the height of his powers, in the 1920s, he threatened to change the whole course of politics by offering British socialism a third way between Labour gradualism and communism.' He went on to acknowledge that the failure to implement Maxton's ideas 'foreshadowed the failure of a whole generation of British politicians to solve the problems of unemployment and poverty'.

This is the nearest Brown gets to intervening personally, with the implication that the task of left-of-centre politicians was to find a way of addressing unemployment and poverty, his two lifelong obsessions, by getting to a position where they could make a practical difference.

Towards the end of the book he also dared to offer an interpretation of Maxton's beliefs that was close to his own:

Cold bureaucratic state socialism held no attractions for him. For Maxton, the only test of socialist progress was in the improvement of the individual and thus the community. Greater educational opportunities would not only free exceptional people to realize their exceptional talents but allow common people to make the most of their common humanity, and ordinary people to realize their extraordinary potentials.

In the years to come, especially when he was Prime Minister, the essence of his philosophy remained firmly in place. Like Maxton he was in politics above all to help people to fulfil their potential, and he associated education, training and work as the way in which this would be brought about.

He developed this theme most openly in a lecture he delivered to Charter 88 just before the 1992 election, when he was free more or less to express what he felt. Later he often cited the talk as evidence of a sustained commitment to constitutional reform, but the words are more interesting as a clear evocation of his long-standing views about the relationship between governments, markets and individuals, the contentious theme that was to dominate both his own political career and Tony Blair's. He stated clearly in the lecture that: 'The 1979 settlement abandoned responsibilities for individual well-being that government had discharged on behalf of the community because it was now assumed that these could be left to the individual and the marketplace.'

Brown put forward an alternative interpretation: 'Individual well-being is best advanced by a strong community backed up by active and accountable government.'

He was still a sceptic about markets. He always had his doubts, but soon he would hold markets less critically because they would fill his Treasury's coffers with much-needed cash. But even then, before the 1992 defeat, in case there was any nervousness about an assertion of active government he made clear: 'Community need not be a threat to individual liberty but can assist the fulfilment of it … So the growing demand of individuals is that they should be in a position to realize their potential, to bridge the gap between what they are and what they have it in them to become.'

After Labour's defeat in 1992 the chances of his ever getting the opportunity to achieve his overriding objectives seemed about as slim as they were for Maxton in the 1920s and 1930s. Not surprisingly therefore, the outcome of the 1992 election reinforced Brown's caution and pragmatism.

For the five years preceding 1992, Brown had been part of Labour's agonized gyrations over its 'tax and spend' policies, an area they all of them entered like walkers with a fear of heights approaching the edge of a cliff.

When he was a youthful shadow chief secretary to the Treasury Brown had vetoed any proposed increases in public spending, knowing that explaining how they would be paid for was an almost impossible and vote-losing task. He was not alone. His successor in that role, Margaret Beckett, was at least as vigilant. 'If any of my colleagues propose a spending increase I will just say "no",' Beckett told journalists as the 1992 election came into view. Beckett was still widely seen as an irresponsible left-winger at the time.

Meanwhile at the top of the party Kinnock and Smith limited precise spending commitments to increases in pensions and child benefit. In his famous shadow budget launched amidst a ceremonial pomp that inadvertently exposed deep insecurity about the party's standing, Smith had outlined in detail how the commitments would be paid, for, spelling out why most voters would pay less tax. Voters were far from thrilled and the Conservatives had a ball projecting Smith's shadow budget as the equivalent of the Communist Manifesto.

After the 1992 election Brown concluded that Labour could not enter another election where its plans for taxing and spending were the central issue, or any issue. The conclusion seemed fairly obvious in the light of a fourth election defeat, although it was by no means universally shared within the Labour party.

More important, it was not clear where such a conclusion would lead, and addressing the implications can be a nightmare. David Cameron and George Osborne discovered the problems in opposition when they sought to do the same in reverse and pledged to stick with Labour's spending levels. They made the grand announcement and could not follow it through. Within eighteen months they had dropped the commitment.

In Brown's case the dilemma was clear. What would be the purpose of a supposedly centre-left government if it could not put the case for higher spending and redistribution? What would members of the shadow cabinet promise if they could not offer increased investment in Britain's declining public services? There was an obvious danger in being stuck mouthing a perverse political message: 'This Conservative government is not investing enough and we will not invest enough either. Vote Labour. Thank you and good night.'

There were no obvious answers to the questions, and yet Brown had to find them or risk entering another election in which Labour would be slaughtered over 'tax and spend'. He had to find a way of taxing and spending without taxing and spending.

As they gathered in his chaotically untidy office in One Parliament Street after he had been made shadow chancellor, Brown told his small team of advisers: 'We've got to work from first principles towards policies.' At this early stage Brown possessed a central insight, one that he clung to like a lifeline as he sought to address his 'tax and spend' conundrum. The insight was defensively pragmatic and highly significant. He resolved to make the main dividing line with the Conservatives more emphatically one between competence and incompetence, a divide without an ideological dimension, neither a left or right issue, another New Labour attempt to depoliticize the public debate.

Such ambition appears desperately narrow and puny, not least when Brown faced a Conservative government in the early to mid-1990s that was to display confused incompetence on a spectacular scale, as if John Major and his unruly MPs had volunteered to dance to his tunes. But determined expediency was a drastic break with Labour's immediate past. It was the starting point of a cautious revolution, one that was to prove at least as demanding as more romantic crusades.

Not only does an opposition have to prove that the government is a poor manager of the economy, it must convince voters it would be a more effective administrator. This seemed almost impossible in the summer of 1992 after Major had won an election partly by conveying a sense of reassuring steadiness and Labour had lost on the grounds that it offered the rockiest of rides.

The strategic decision also demanded a steely self-discipline from Brown. It is more fun and easier going to play the romantic politician in opposition. Wielding no power leaves speeches, declarations and positioning as the only means of definition. For Labour politicians, clear and attractive definition had tended to come from intoxicating images of better-funded public services and promises of redistribution from rich to poor. Brown resolved to project competence alone.

As part of his pragmatic insight Brown recognized that Labour's reputation in relation to economic policy was so low that a single word out of place risked another election defeat. If a member of the shadow cabinet uttered a word that implied a rise in public spending the newspapers would leap and Labour's reputation as a reckless party would be further reinforced. Therefore he made clear from the beginning to his shadow cabinet colleagues that no such word should be uttered.

Brown's forbidding approach to any public utterance was a source of many of his problems for the rest of his career in two key areas, relations with colleagues and the projection of his own image in the media, further examples of how the seeds of his undoing were sown at the very beginning.

With a determined possessiveness, he claimed the economics terrain as his alone and voluntarily tied himself up in chains as a public figure, comfortable from now on only with carefully rehearsed, formulaic answers and statements. In later years Brown was criticized widely for his stilted public performances, the contorted sentences and the humourless, repetitive relentlessness of his messages. They are partly explained by the fact that he carried the burden of presenting Labour's economic policy from 1992, justifiably worried about saying anything that would lose the party another election. In opposition parties have only words for ammunition. Brown was always terrified of a verbal explosion that would blow apart the fragile edifice. He was neurotically fearful, and could have displayed more deftness in interviews, but the pressure was immense and on a scale not faced by his carping colleagues.

Although he took this approach to extremes, both in his standing guard on the terrain and in his own over-rehearsed speak-your-weight-machine presentational style, there was a mountain of evidence to back up his judgement that ruthless self-discipline was required.

To take one example of many from Labour's immediate past, in the build-up to the 1992 election there had been a calamitous spat between Kinnock and Smith over taxation policy, exposing differences between the two of them and conveying, accurately, that Labour's taxation policy had not been fully thought through. This was after years in which both had resolved to get it right, assiduously determined to demonstrate that Labour's sums did add up and in ways that should not alarm most voters.

Kinnock and Smith had not cleared the ground first. What was tax for? What was a politically acceptable level of tax? Were there other ways of raising money other than those that led to electoral dead ends? In the absence of a clear and common purpose, leading figures went off-message, incurring a media onslaught. By contrast Brown sought at first an underlying clarity and was determined that only he would do the clarifying.

A powerful lesson emerges from the experience of Labour's long exile in opposition, and from the Conservatives' confused approach to tax and spend when they were out of power. Leaders must decide what messages they want to convey before embarking on the task of policy making. Brown understood what was required, but such an unbending approach to the public presentation of economic policy alienated other shadow cabinet colleagues almost immediately.

At the very least they yearned to roam a little into economic policy – terrain that took them to the heart of politics. If they tried, Brown would slap them down. In the end they gave up trying. In effect this meant Brown had a near-monopoly over Labour's economic policy from 1992, and certainly by 1994 when Blair became leader. Gradually his colleagues ceased to even think, let alone to speak, about the central area of policy making for any political party. While Brown's iron will meant that Labour's 'gaffes' in relation to the economy no longer dominated media coverage, there was also a deadly negative consequence. The atrophy of thought across large sections of the Labour party started when Brown became shadow chancellor. By

2007 as the party sought out potential leadership candidates other than Brown it discovered that there were none, partly because most of the obvious alternative choices had no experience of economic policy, not even of debating it in the privacy of cabinet meetings. From 1992 Labour produced only half-formed politicians, none of them giving much thought to the policy area that defined what was possible in every other field.

There was though a positive consequence: a single message was conveyed ruthlessly for years in an era when the media was on the lookout for contradictions and inconsistencies. This was the period when political journalists bemoaned the politics of the straitjacket and leapt when anyone loosened the knots.

From the summer of 1992 the shadow cabinet were silenced as Brown took his case to the media. Brown could see a headline a mile off, good and bad. He was fascinated by the running orders of television news bulletins. When he bumped into a BBC Political Correspondent in the mid-morning at Westminster his first question would be: 'What are you leading on at one o'clock?' If the exchange took place in the afternoon he would ask the same question of the forthcoming six o'clock news. When I saw him for a coffee on one occasion when he was Chancellor we passed a TV screen reporting the main leader's speech from Charles Kennedy at the Liberal Democrats' conference. It was twenty past one. Brown said without pausing: 'That's quite low down the bulletin. He'll be disappointed he's not higher up. The Liberal Democrats are still not seen as a serious force in the media, are they?' He was days away from a big IMF conference in the US, but was interested in where the Liberal Democrats managed to be in the running order of a news bulletin.

Brown had a fascination beyond professional interest in the way the media worked, one that he passed on to Blair after they became colleagues in 1983. It was not just the TV bulletins and the newspapers. In opposition Brown was up listening to *News Briefing* on the BBC, a programme that went out earlier than the *Today* programme, even earlier indeed than *Farming Today*. He had read the newspapers before most of his colleagues had woken up. More than any politician I have met, including David Cameron and George Osborne, who were accused of being obsessed with public relations, Brown followed the media the way a music critic listens to a concert.

In the early phase of his period as shadow chancellor he was a ubiquitous figure, appearing especially on television news bulletins with an absurd regularity, showing his naivety by assuming that ubiquity is the same as quality. Brown thought nothing of scrapping his plans to attend a football or rugby match in Scotland on a Saturday afternoon if there was a chance of going to a studio in Edinburgh or Glasgow to deliver a fifteen-second sound bite for the news bulletins. Brown was aware of the ratings for all the bulletins, which ones mattered and which did not. If one of his colleagues, say Robin Cook or David Blunkett, appeared on the Saturday teatime bulletins he was furious as he knew it got the highest audience of the week. Even when he was Prime Minister he wanted to be on TV more, complaining to his staff when he was not featured on the bulletins. Sometimes he would contrive an entire event in order to appear on TV as Prime Minister. Like so much else, a habit of neurotic self-projection began in 1992.

He knew also of the power of the Sunday newspapers in setting the agenda for the rest of the week. Brown was the recipient of many leaks from the Treasury and political editors of Sunday newspapers were offered documents that appeared to place the Conservative government in a bad light on an almost weekly basis. Quite often they were of limited significance, but Brown pushed them hard, working around the clock to expose any weaknesses in the government, especially in relation to spending plans or the higher taxes that it was being forced to implement.

His pell-mell hyperactivity did his party some good, as he managed to generate a range of superficially damning stories about the Conservative government. But his persistence led some political editors to doubt his judgement and sense of proportion. In addition to being so careful about his every public utterance, Brown quickly lost a significant dimension of his public personality. He became so controlled that his other slightly more ebullient side disappeared from public view and from the view of his colleagues. Before becoming shadow chancellor he had been a vivacious and witty speechmaker in the House of Commons and on platforms. Controlled ubiquity was his new theme. It was his answer to the anarchic chaos of the 1980s, and no one had a better one.

Before Brown had a chance to develop his public narrative in the media he was tested by a historic event. The unusual summer political calm in 1992 obscured a growing economic crisis. The leader of the Liberal Democrats, Paddy Ashdown, described the situation with a prophetic insight in an article for the *Guardian* written in the month that Brown became shadow chancellor:

> There is a curious feeling of slack water in British politics, almost of stagnant water. You know the tide is going to start moving sometime and some people say they have never known a period like it … all of us are sitting with our fingers in the water saying which way is it going to move?

The tide was propelled by Britain's membership of the Exchange Rate Mechanism. Over the summer Britain's membership became the subject of even greater controversy than it had been before, with many economists from across the political spectrum arguing that it was strangling any hopes of recovery. Some Labour MPs and left-of-centre columnists in particular saw a striking political opportunity: call for withdrawal and blame the Tory government for joining in the first place, a double whammy to counter all the double whammies that the Tories had deployed against Labour.

There was a problem with this approach. Labour had enthusiastically supported Britain's membership of the ERM. Indeed the support had defined its more 'modern' approach to Europe and economic policy making. As a result Brown faced his first big awkward decision as shadow chancellor. Should he make the case for Britain to leave the ERM or at least to realign sterling within the ERM? In theory at least this would have placed Labour in a strong position if Major was forced to withdraw.

Still young and relatively fresh, Brown was more capable of thinking several moves ahead on a political chessboard than later in his career. By the autumn of 2007 it became fashionable to argue that he was a clumsy, short-sighted strategist. That was not the case early on in his career, and only became so when he faced an avalanche of events and opponents towards the end. His approach to the ERM issue is an early example of Brown taking the lead and landing his party in a fruitful place at the end of the sequence.

Brown sensed and feared that calling for realignment or withdrawal from the ERM would lead to taunts that Labour was still the same unreformed and reckless supporter of devaluation. So he did not call for such a move. This was not an easy decision to reach. John Smith's closest allies and a substantial number of Labour MPs, including a section of the shadow cabinet, wanted him to make the call.

Instead he chose precisely the opposite course, seeking to make a virtue out of consistency and through being an 'opponent' of devaluation. Repeatedly he declared on those teatime TV bulletins: 'Devaluation was not our policy at the last election, is not our policy now and will not be our policy at the next election.'

As ever, Brown's calculations were multi-layered and were to come up repeatedly in the coming years in different circumstances. Indeed the ERM controversy serves almost as a template of contorted and yet in the end highly effective Brownite tactical thinking.

First, he was determined to signal a break with Labour's past. Previous Labour governments had been almost fatally derailed by enforced devaluations. He was not going to be a shadow chancellor calling for another humiliating devaluation. Second, he was worried about being on the wrong side of the argument with the Conservative government. He thought wrongly that John Major would prevail and that sterling would stay in the ERM. He feared the claim that while the Conservatives had patriotically defended the currency the same old Labour party was talking down the pound. Third, he wanted to show that Labour was robust enough to meet the disciplines of being a member of the ERM.

The issues changed, but those three factors recurred again and again in Brown's career as he went about taking pivotal decisions: a fear of Labour's past, an exaggerated alarm that the Conservatives, not Labour, would end up on the patriotic side of the argument, and a hunger to show that Labour was now the ruthlessly disciplined party. When some Labour MPs accused him of being the Iron Shadow Chancellor, with its echoes of Thatcher's Iron Lady, Brown was delighted. Even if it alienated some in his party, such a label ticked the boxes as far as he was concerned. In 1992 he was pleased to be compared with Thatcher. In 2007 as Prime Minister he invited Thatcher to tea, another echo. Like the bankers, Thatcher formed another protective layer. His politics could not have been more different from hers, but he hoped to appeal to voters and newspapers that revered Thatcher.

Even the Lady was used as a false trail.

In the late summer of 1992 Euro-sceptic members of the shadow cabinet fumed over what they were witnessing. Here was a Conservative government heading for a terrible crash pursuing a policy that was being fully supported by Labour's shadow chancellor.

Superficially their view appeared to be vindicated on 16 September, one of the most highly charged days in modern British politics, when the government was forced to pull out of the ERM after several attempts to prop up the pound by putting up interest rates to comically frightening levels. With mixed emotions Brown watched from his office in Westminster as a drained but privately relieved Norman Lamont made a statement as Chancellor to confirm the new government policy. Some of Brown's allies at the time did not know why the shadow chancellor was not more damaged by what had happened. 'I don't know how Gordon got away with it. He supported the policy that had led to the government's humiliation.'

On one level Brown did not get away with it as the anger of some shadow cabinet colleagues grew. But Brown's cautiously defensive

approach was vindicated almost at once. After the ERM debacle opinion polls showed that support for Major's government had slumped.
The Conservatives were never ahead in the polls again up until the
1997 election and well beyond. Labour had gained politically without
taking the risk of being attacked as the party that talked down the
currency, an onslaught that would have left Brown especially exposed
if the enforced devaluation had not taken place and if, as was possible,
Britain had stayed in the ERM.

Brown's expedient doggedness in the late summer and early
autumn was not especially dignified and carried its own risks. His
stance was the first example of another Brownite phenomenon, bold
caution. Brown had been bold because he had taken the risk of alienating a significant section of his party that wanted a realignment of
the pound or withdrawal from the ERM on opportunistic or ideological grounds.

One of the persistent allegations against Brown was that he was
pathetically afraid of taking on his party, an odd claim, seeing that
there was nearly always some section of his party raging against him.
Influential members of the shadow cabinet fumed in private and
some trade union leaders did so publicly. Smith was not thrilled either
at Brown's unyielding stance. Brown also lost the chance of having an
easy hit against the suddenly fragile Conservative government. He
stuck to his course.

It was during this period, the late summer of 1992, that significant
internal criticism against Brown became part of the permanent background noise in politics. Shadow cabinet members in particular,
already far from thrilled at being told that they could not say anything
that implied a spending proposal, found catharsis in private conversations with journalists and each other. After the Labour conference in
1992 one of the party's rising stars, Mo Mowlam, said to a group of
journalists: 'Sell shares in Gordon. He's blown it.' That was three
months after Brown had been made shadow chancellor. Mowlam was
far from being the most hostile of his colleagues.

But while his willingness to challenge his colleagues' more superficial calculations showed signs of political courage, Brown had been

cautious as well. He had adopted the stance for reasons of fear rather than conviction, a terror of being associated with devaluation. On this occasion his bold caution proved to be highly fruitful. Very quickly Brown was able to exploit the Conservatives' discomfiture as he developed his overriding pragmatic idea, that Labour must make the public battle one of competence rather than ideology.

This is when his embryonic public narrative merged with the immediate political crisis. In an emergency debate in the Commons shortly after the ERM debacle, Brown began his campaign to reverse the normal battle lines over which party could be trusted, the familiar divide that had destroyed Labour in the recent general election:

> The Conservatives ran a general election campaign on the slogan 'You Can't Trust Labour' and has now shown its complacently unworthy of trust. The party that has already been for years the party of unemployment and of poverty is now the party of devaluation ... Ministers who continued to hold responsibilities now cannot command respect. They may hold office for five years, but after five months have lost the authority to govern. They have failed the country and will never be trusted again.

Brown had begun the task of turning politics on its head. Trust! Trust! Trust! At the Labour conference in his first speech as shadow chancellor he adopted the same theme: 'They said you can't trust Labour. Let every billboard around the country tell the truth: you can never trust the Tories.'

In 2007 on becoming Prime Minister Brown looked back to 1992 and resolved again to restore trust in Labour after Iraq, the non-existent weapons of mass destruction and perceptions of spin. He was nowhere near as nimble as he had been in this early episode.

In November he launched Labour's Campaign for Recovery, in which he delicately dumped the proposals and the thinking behind the shadow budget, an audacious move, as his new leader, John Smith, had famously presented it and still stood by most of the policies that had been rejected by voters.

When Brown moved boldly he always looked for cover, whether from Thatcher, a banker or a business leader. On this occasion he used the ongoing economic crisis for protection, announcing that in the light of the recession: 'We are not proposing to raise tax and national insurance at this stage' – two propositions in the shadow budget dropped. While Smith looked on with a supportive wariness, he had begun the difficult process of wiping the slate clean.

At the same time Brown had hit upon a popular tax, raising the prospect vaguely of a one-off tax on the privatized utilities, the booming monopolies that were making profits so high that many voters and parts of the media were demanding a punitive response. At this point he had not done the detailed work, but the idea was another example of Brown being ahead of the game. Putting up income tax had, it seemed, become a fatal vote loser for Labour. But what if there were popular taxes to raise revenue? One element of the party's conundrum would be partially solved.

Cathartic and emphatic messages about 'tax and spend' were Brown's main priority as he sought to reassure voters that the party could be trusted. In his first year as shadow chancellor his speeches were peppered with these sound bites:

'We will only spend what we can afford to spend ...'

'We do not tax for its own sake ...'

'We don't spend for its own sake.'

He sprayed the phrases around like bullets from a gun. The following year he fleshed out some more detail, declaring that Labour was not against wealth and would scrap its plan for a new 50 per cent inheritance tax. In August he outlined what he called the new economic agenda. As part of it he declared he would contemplate cutting taxes and had dropped specific spending plans. He stated that: 'From now on Labour believes in creating the necessary wealth to fund the social benefits we demand.' Such statements were cited to prove that Brown had become a Thatcherite by 1992. Look more closely and he was still demanding social benefits and had announced a new tax. But he was clearing the ground.

Brown was so gripped by the need to convey a reassuring message that he was furious when Smith announced suddenly in the middle of his largely lethargic campaign to introduce one member one vote for leadership elections in 1993 that Labour would introduce a minimum wage. In mutually supportive discussions with his close allies Tony Blair and Peter Mandelson, Brown fumed: 'We haven't prepared the ground ... business leaders will turn against us ... we shouldn't have made the announcement like this ...'

Brown was always obsessed with clearing the ground, but what policies to put in place once he had pulled up the weeds? To some extent the answer to that question came in the autumn of 1993, when Brown appointed Ed Balls as his main adviser.

The shadow chancellor was not a trained economist. He was a politician to fingertips and understood from a political perspective what he wanted to achieve. The 28-year-old Balls was already a substantial economist, having studied economics at Oxford and Harvard, where he had worked closely with Bill Clinton's Treasury Secretary, Larry Summers. When they met, Balls was a leader writer on the *Financial Times* and a committed Labour supporter. The highly political Brown and the innovative, fresh-thinking, left-of-centre economist were close to being a perfect match. At their best the two of them were a creative force that swept all before them. At their worst they could work each other up into a paranoid fury as they pursued factionalized political strategies that often rebounded on them.

Balls taught Brown about economics, fleshing out the shadow chancellor's political ideas. Brown gave Balls some shrewd lessons on the art of politics, even if he also exposed him to some more destructive ones as well.

Balls had started to work informally for Brown from September 1992 after the trauma of the ERM crisis. As a leader writer for the *Financial Times*, often he did not have to be in the office until midday, so he would go in to see Brown at Westminster in the mornings. They had met at various gatherings, parties and conferences, but it was only after September 1992 that Balls was a regular visitor. Typically of Brown, sometimes he would be intensely demanding, making contact with Balls four times a day. Then the young journalist would hear nothing for weeks. Nonetheless when they did meet, Brown showed a willingness to listen and engage that defied the caricature of defiant, arrogantly introverted aloofness. Balls told Brown for example that he had been wrong to support the government's membership of the ERM, not for tactical reasons but in terms of economic policy. Balls had felt that the ERM had been a straitjacket that stifled the economy. In a pamphlet for the Fabians written shortly after Britain's exit, he argued that the economy had to be in much more robust shape before a British government could rejoin the ERM. Challenging a fair amount of Labour orthodoxy, he called for 'a credible and predictable macroeconomic framework which can deliver economic stability combined with government measures to promote growth and full employment ... only then can the UK hope to avoid a third destructive boom and bust cycle ...'

As part of that framework Balls put the case for Bank of England independence: 'freed from debilitating market doubts about the government's anti-inflationary resolve, a Labour chancellor would be free to concentrate on many other aspects of policy'. The persistent references to 'boom and bust' in Balls's pamphlet became a Brownite theme, dangerously so as it was to turn out when the economy went into deep recession in 2008, although the causes and consequences were different from those referred to in Balls's pamphlet. There was no space for nuance in 2008, no scope for explaining that they were referring to a different type of 'bust'.

Brown was fascinated by Balls's ideas. They seemed to address the dilemmas that he faced. He yearned for a stable framework, or at least the perception of one, so that he could focus on his other objectives without worrying that the economy or the currency was about to collapse. The youthful Balls had ideas about how to build the stable architecture, and yet like Brown he was also committed to tackling unemployment and poverty. In interviews later Balls described himself openly as a socialist, a rare admission in New Labour circles and not a term used by Brown. Keynes was one of Balls's heroes, long before the economist became more fashionable after the credit crunch in 2008.

When Peter Mandelson briefed the *Sunday Times* in September 1994 that New Labour's economic policies marked 'the death of Keynes', Balls was distraught and made sure that a counter-briefing took place in which all talk of Keynes's demise was dismissed as nonsense. This was the first direct spat between Balls and Mandelson, typically personal animosity mingled with profound ideological differences. At the time only the animosity attracted attention, as if they were all characters in a soap opera without a principle between them.

In economic matters Balls was supremely confident and Brown was not. After all there were not many economists in their twenties with close contacts at the top of the then glamorous Clinton administration and who had written a daring Fabian pamphlet that seemed to offer a new direction for left-of-centre politics. His arrogance and ruthless loyalty to Brown were characteristics much commented upon in the years to come. But Balls was a less confident public performer, and he was driven by principle and conviction as much as by a yearning for his master to become Prime Minister. In the following years there was much analysis inevitably of the Blair/Brown partnership and Blair's relationship with his press secretary, Alastair Campbell and with Peter Mandelson. The Brown/Balls relationship was equally important. In terms of policy development Balls was the third-most important figure in the New Labour hierarchy after Blair and Brown.

In spite of the age gap, the conflicting views at that point on Europe, and their differing backgrounds, the bond was not surprising. Together Brown and Balls watched closely the development of economic, social and welfare policies under Clinton. Arising from their joint passion, Brown and Balls began work on a Welfare to Work scheme and hailed a 'new deal' for the unemployed. At the same time, with the 1992 election always on his mind Brown stepped up his main political mission, proving that it was the Tories who could no longer be trusted on tax and spend.

At the start of 1994 he pointed out that taken together, direct and indirect tax was higher than under the previous Labour government. Brown spelt it out: 'These figures destroy the Conservatives' only political claim. Never again can they say they are the party of low taxation.'

Not surprisingly quite a few Labour party members worried about such protestations. 'Are we going to replace the Conservatives as the party of low taxation?' shadow cabinet members asked in private with growing despair. Brown's plans were subtler than that, but he was happy for the question to be raised, such was the need to purge the electorate's anxieties.

Some feared he was moving rightwards at an alarming speed. The normally highly perceptive David Blunkett observed to me despairingly in the autumn of 1992: 'Gordon is a monetarist.' Blunkett had been made shadow health secretary and wanted to say at least a few comforting words about Labour being committed to higher spending. Brown forbade it. Blunkett was left condemning the Tories' lack of investment without any obvious follow-up. He was furious.

While Blunkett detected Thatcherite orthodoxy, some of Brown's colleagues saw him as one of the vaguely defined 'modernizers'. As far as the angry John Prescott was concerned Brown was one of the 'beautiful people' preoccupied by television and other media appearances, not so much a Thatcherite as a celebrity mouthing banalities. Prescott's anger serves as a reminder that in 1992 Brown was seen as a media star, so apparently at ease with the medium that he was despised by those who also wanted to make the occasional appearance on television.

In his first two years as shadow chancellor Brown had made substantial progress on three different fronts. He had started to change the terms of the debate about trust and competence, although he was being helped more than he dared to realize by the implosion of the Conservative government. He had moved Labour on from the era of the shadow budget, even though this was the source of considerable tension with John Smith. By the early summer of 1994 it was Brown who was the one who was tough on spending and attacking the Tories for putting up taxes. Equally important work was being done behind the scenes to ensure that if Labour won next time it would be more than just a competent echo of the tired, divided

Conservative administration, with welfare to work, a windfall tax, a minimum wage and new training schemes being devised.

But between the summer of 1992 and 1994 his party noticed only Brown's noisy attempts to ditch perceptions about tax and spend. Shadow cabinet members, MPs and some party members took his protestations at their surface value. As a result, in the summer of 1993 his oscillating career hit its deepest low yet, a mere twelve months after he had been widely seen as Labour's big star.

Brown feared he had become so unpopular in the party that he would lose his seat on the National Executive Committee. He and Blair had only stood for election for the party's so-called governing body the year before. In August and early September 1993 in the build-up to the elections for the NEC, Brown lapsed into gloom, telling colleagues that the party did not understand what he was trying to do. He imagined a nightmare situation where he was voted off the Committee in the full glare of the party conference, humiliating him personally and sending out a signal that Labour was not ready to reconsider its vote-losing economic policy: here was someone who wanted to be the party's next leader who could not even win an election to a committee. He brooded excessively in the summer of 1993, telling Blair often over this period how tough it was making Labour electable and becoming personally unpopular.

I was invited to Brown's office on the Thursday before the Labour conference in which the result of the election would be announced. He was in a terrible state, slumped on his chair, clothes crumpled as if they had been lived in continuously for a decade, baggy-eyed. It was the first time I realized what a physically transparent politician he was. He exuded gloomy fearfulness, this time over the NEC results. 'The media doesn't understand what I'm trying to do,' Brown told me, without fully explaining what it was that he was trying to do.

When Brown felt under pressure, especially when he thought he was being misunderstood, he was capable of behaving abominably. There was no restraint, no sense of what was acceptable behaviour. On one tense occasion in the build-up to the NEC elections Blair walked into Brown's office at Westminster with a young adviser. Brown was kicking the wastepaper bin around the office in frustrated fury, having read a critical article in a newspaper. As Brown was giving the poor bin another kicking Blair looked at his adviser and placed his finger to his head, indicating his partially amused despair at Brown's loss of control and suggesting that he was bonkers.

The bin kicking in 1993 was an early example of his eccentric self-absorbed thoughtlessness. Two young advisers, closer at the time to Blair than Brown, Derek Draper and Tom Happold, helped Brown solicit support for his vulnerable candidacy of the NEC. They worked into the night on the shadow chancellor's campaign, stuffing envelopes and contacting potential supporters. In the end Brown was re-elected, although the level of his support dropped from the year before.

Afterwards a relieved Brown sought to show his appreciation by inviting Draper and Happold out for lunch. Both were thrilled, as the shadow chancellor was already acquiring a reputation for neglecting some of those who had put themselves out on his behalf and for being socially graceless. To their bewildered disappointment Brown took them to a local Italian near Westminster, where he gulped a bowl of spaghetti in near-silence and returned quickly to his office. Such behaviour meant it was easier for people to become Blairites rather than Brownites, even if their politics were closer to Brown.

The NEC election in the summer and early autumn of 1993 had been traumatic for Brown. Clearly he feared that if he had been voted off the NEC he would never have recovered. It was his first experience of hostile perceptions at a national level, after rising to the top of the Labour party and performing well in shadow cabinet elections.

Evidently the role of shadow chancellor was taking its toll. He was making progress on his original impossible conundrum, to devise an economic policy that was fair without taxing and spending, but he was doing so in ways that were making him intensely unpopular within his party, even if they were helping to make Labour more credible. The lack of positive support made him angry and depressed, two emotions that helped to fuel his further unpopularity, a familiar sequence in Brown's later career.

In 1993 he would have been more traumatized still if he had known as he struggled with his unpopularity that in a year's time there would be a vacancy for the party's leader.

TWO

Dangerous Assumptions

Politicians and journalists enjoy speculating about possible future leaders. The speculation can be fun, mischievous, or highly significant, sometimes a combination of all three. Who will lead next? In the early to mid-1990s the question was asked persistently in relation to the Conservative party and its leader, John Major. Potential candidates in the cabinet struck poses, conscious that they might be called upon to shaft their precarious leader or to take part in a contest if a vacancy arose. Attention was focused in particular on the ambitions of Ken Clarke, Michael Heseltine and Michael Portillo.

Yet it was the Labour party that made a change suddenly. The suddenness was the key, determining the course of events for another decade at least.

No one was ready for John Smith to die when he did. Between July 1992 and the early summer of 1994 there was a universally held assumption that Smith would lead his party into the next election. The assumption is the most important factor in understanding the high politics of Labour in these seemingly subdued two years and the reaction of almost violent intensity from Brown when he realized he was not going to be the successor. During these years the Conservatives were exhausted by government and yet energized by factional rows over almost everything. Labour was complacently calm, sleepwalking, as one anxious MP put it.

Smith was a new leader, popular within parts of his party and to some extent with the broader electorate. He combined the reassuring presence of a country solicitor with an egalitarian resilience that seemed willing to take on disapproving voters in England. He was a lively performer in the Commons, witty and sure-footed. Most important of all, he possessed a serene self-confidence.

Smith's press secretary, David Hill, who went on to work for Tony Blair, told me he had seen such unflappability in only one other senior politician, President Mitterrand, a Socialist who had won elections in France against what seemed to be the prevailing mood of the times. Hill was not spinning on behalf of his leader. He meant it and he was right. Blair, Brown and their impatient allies recognized the complacency that such self-confidence could induce. They were less ready to acknowledge that Smith possessed a sense of perspective and proportion when seemingly overwhelming crises erupted.

The key to Smith's calm was that, unlike so many of his confused and bewildered colleagues, he had been a minister. Smith was in the cabinet for the final phase of Jim Callaghan's government up to 1979. Power did not seem so elusive and mysterious for a Labour politician who had experienced it. For everyone else around him, power seemed as awesomely distant as the moon.

Before Smith secured the leadership his name topped any poll of potential leaders by an intimidating margin. Not surprisingly, after he won the 1992 leadership contest by a landslide, there was no feverish, highly charged speculation between politicians and political journalists over who should lead Labour in the immediate future. Such musings would have been fantastical. Not even the most attention-seeking columnist sought to make waves by asserting that Labour would have a new leader by the mid-1990s. He or she would have attracted derision rather than attention.

There were, as there always are, predictions in newspapers about future leaders. Those forecasts focused on Gordon Brown and, with an increasing intensity, Tony Blair. With accidental and mischievous timing, a flattering profile of Blair appeared in the *Sunday Times* on the day after Smith had been elected. Amidst the glowing prose and rock star-like photographs spanning several pages, the writer, Barbara

Amiel, suggested that Labour should have opted for Blair as its leader rather than Smith.

Such words can have an intoxicating impact on the subject of the profile, on his or her admirers, and on the media that feeds on speculation about potential leaders, but the timing on the weekend Labour had elected a new leader meant that her flattery did not fuel questions about a sudden change. It would have made no sense: 'Smith wins by a landslide! It's time for Blair!' The *Sunday Times* had thrown the equivalent of a tiny pebble into a calm sea.

Blair had hit upon a third way in nurturing his profile: articles about his leadership qualities at a time when there was no serious speculation about the top job. He became a potential leader when there was apparently no chance of becoming an actual leader in the near future. This was a dream contrivance, as a profile can build quietly and without too much destructive intensity.

No one accused Blair of making a destabilizing bid for the leadership. Instead there was a polite hum of approval around him and low-level doubts about Brown, who continued to alienate colleagues with his single-minded possessiveness over economic policy and his introspective rudeness. In their different ways both of them could cope with this polite approval, these negative whispers. They could get on with their lives and more or less sustain their own political friendship.

The hyperactive shadow chancellor read with irritable wariness the glowing profiles of Blair, but he was playing a much longer game, assuming that when there was next a leadership contest he would be established as the senior figure who had transformed Labour's economic policy. He had topped shadow cabinet polls. He had been an acting shadow chancellor and now held the senior post permanently. He assumed he was in a different league to his friend, partly because he was. Even during this period Brown assumed that Blair would be a supremely important colleague when he himself became leader.

How closely Brown and Blair worked together between 1992 and the early summer of 1994 is illustrated by their quick responses in the immediate aftermath of Labour's fourth defeat. Their instincts were to meet up without delay and decide how they should respond to the latest electoral calamity. They gathered several times over the post-election weekend at the home of the Newcastle MP Nick Brown, later to be identified as one of Brown's closest confidants, the personification of a 'Brownite', scheming loyally for his man against Blair. In this more delicately harmonious phase he was now a junior partner in the joint Blair/Brown post-election dance. Peter Mandelson joined them too, wondering what should happen next.

What Blair thought should happen next is part of the early New Labour mythology. During their exhausted and yet curiously energized exchanges over those dark days in April 1992, Blair urged Brown to stand for the leadership. For a brief period Blair was intensely persistent. An adviser to Brown who witnessed one exchange when the two of them had returned to Westminster the following week says: 'They almost came to blows on it. Tony was adamant about it. He really wanted Gordon to stand.'

Here was an early example of Blair forming a simplistic view about a situation and then acquiring a conveniently passionate conviction. On a far grander scale he displayed precisely the same characteristics in relation to Iraq more than ten years later. By 1992 Blair's political character was taking shape.

Brown thought briefly about standing for the leadership, agonized a little given the persuasive force of his friend, his own intense ambition and his tendency to agonize over everything, and then sensibly decided not to do so. Several people who knew both of them well at the time suggest that it was when Brown made what appeared superficially to be a cowardly decision that Blair wondered for the first time whether his older friend was suited for the top job. Did he really have the drive and courage to seize the day? Brown's apparent dithering in 1992 was cited privately by several of Blair's aides in the summer of 1994 when their man did go for the leadership as a contrast to Brown's 'failure' to do so two years earlier.

The dynamics of this fleeting moment of imprecise ambition are important. The exchanges and the calculations are emblematic of much that was to follow – the awkward dilemmas, the gestures of mutually well-meaning and disingenuous support, the careful positioning and the rest. They were all playing their part as early as 1992, and already Blair rather than Brown was proving to be an inadvertently masterful choreographer.

Blair wanted a so-called 'modernizer' to lead the party, or at least become deputy leader, at such a precarious moment and assumed with a slightly self-interested and yet genuine sincerity that Brown should be the man. Often for Blair convenience and conviction marched together as a monolithic force. At this point in 1992 he had an almost exaggeratedly high regard for Brown, reflecting his unusually generous attitude to big political figures anywhere. He tended to view anyone from the past or present who had been successful in winning elections with excessive awe, whether from the left or the right. Here was another apolitical New Labour characteristic from the Blairite perspective, an admiration for winners. When he first became Prime Minister he lavished indiscriminate homage on virtually any foreign leader on the basis that he or she had won an election. Every now and again in this early phase Blair told friends that he considered Brown to be a strategic genius. He would carry on making this flattering observation for quite a few years to come, although emphatically not by the end. In the darkness of 1992 part of Blair thought unequivocally that Brown should stand for the leadership and that if he did so he would win, at which point Labour could modernize with the two of them at the top.

But Blair was capable of being disingenuous while he was being sincere, a baffling, contradictory combination that gave him his distinct genius. Without quite realizing it, but almost doing so, he was urging his friend to incur a humiliation. Brown would have lost a leadership contest in 1992. When Kinnock stood down Smith was the clear favourite to win. As Brown told Blair, the only way he could enter the race would be with the objective of destroying Smith, exposing him ruthlessly as a vote loser, out of touch with voters. This would have been destructive, risky and an act of betrayal to someone who was still, in spite of the growing mutual mistrust, a close friend.

Probably Smith would still have won, but as a damaged leader and with Brown looking fruitlessly reckless.

Brown was not being pathetically cautious, but simply wise in recognizing that this was not the moment to stand against a soaring favourite who happened to be a friend and who would make him a powerful shadow chancellor. Brown calculated that as shadow chancellor he would have a fair amount of influence over economic policy, although part of Blair's strident advocacy was based on a concern that Smith would stick with the policies associated with the shadow budget. He repeated to Brown several times: 'If you want freedom to change the economic policies you need to be leader, and not the shadow chancellor below a leader who was responsible for those economic policies.' Blair had managed almost to define the situation as one in which Brown had acted weakly in accepting the role of shadow chancellor.

The angry exchanges over the leadership also proved that Blair regarded Brown still as the senior partner after the 1992 election. There was no talk of Blair standing as the candidate. Brown suggested that Blair might stand for the deputy, but their joint assumption was that only one would go for the top job: Brown.

The dynamics of their relationship pointed in that direction. When senior journalists went to see Blair up until the early summer of 1994 and their conversation veered on to complex matters of policy, Blair quite often told them: 'Speak to Gordon about that one.' Blair had witnessed at closer quarters than anyone else how Brown had risen suddenly to the challenge of becoming a stand-in shadow chancellor when Smith had a heart attack in 1988. He had taken part in a legion of conversations in which Brown cut through the seemingly impenetrable complexities of positioning and policy making. Quite often, like the journalists, Blair had been to see Gordon about that too. On this basis, a shared political past, their common assumption in 1992 was that Brown would be leader.

When the two of them worked in a cramped office at Westminster after the 1983 election Brown talked often to Blair about the media, how to frame a speech with a single message in mind, targeting newspapers, different bulletins. Briefly Brown had been a BBC producer in Scotland. He did not understand the rhythms of news anywhere near as well as he liked to think, but he knew more than his new colleague. Blair shared his fascination with the relationship between politics and journalism and had already written several articles for newspapers and the *New Statesman* magazine, but he began his parliamentary career as more of a novice. Soon Blair became the dazzling communicator, but Brown arrived at Westminster understanding more clearly that dealing with the media was a form of political art.

Together they watched bulletins, commenting on the ineptitude of Labour's presentation. Nearly always at this stage Brown led the conversation. 'The message is wrong ... that will alienate most voters ... we will be savaged for this tomorrow in the papers.' Blair noted admiringly that Brown was nearly always proved right in his analysis of how the media would report Labour's initiatives. Brown was also writing speeches, putting out press releases at first mainly aimed at the Scottish media long before he was on the front bench. He was also completing his biography of Maxton. He arrived with contacts across the Labour party. Throughout the 1980s Brown was not the senior and weightier figure by a tiny margin, but by a significant distance.

This was also Peter Mandelson's view at the time. No wonder both Brown and Blair were excited by the arrival of Mandelson as Labour's Director of Communications in the mid-1980s. Soon after his appointment Brown and Blair noticed an improvement in the way Labour's message was projected, especially on television bulletins, but also in the largely hostile newspapers. Their conversations became a little more upbeat and positive as they watched TV reports with the intensity of a director watching an edit of a new film. 'That's a better backdrop ... Neil [Kinnock] is much clearer ... the papers will like that ... it's good it's so high up the running order.' They both knew who had made the difference. Brown assumed that Mandelson, as well as Blair, would be an important figure when he fought a leadership contest at some future unspecified date.

But then on the morning of 12 May 1994 John Smith died suddenly of a heart attack. He had been leader for less than two years. His death transformed the political situation in lots of different ways.

Almost certainly if Smith had continued to lead Labour he would have won the forthcoming election and would have been a more rooted, solid prime minister compared with the insecure and media-obsessed Blair and Brown. How long England and its media would have tolerated a Scot with egalitarian instincts and outdated communication skills is much harder to predict, but for a time at least there probably would have been a clearer sense under Smith that the centre left had prevailed in an election than there was when New Labour and its big tent of support seized their ambiguous moment in 1997. It is also possible that Blair, Brown and some others might have grown in government under Smith, gaining ministerial experience and acquiring more political self-confidence by the time there was another vacancy at the top. Smith would have had the sense and resilience to let his cabinet breathe a little. Instead Blair and Brown moved into power with no ministerial experience. They had not watched at close quarters while a prime minister and chancellor handled the economy or, crucially, interpreted sensitive intelligence. They had no idea what it was like to run a big spending department.

Smith was complacent about the narrow appeal in England of a Labour party dominated still by activists from local government and the trade unions and he underestimated comically the ways in which political parties needed to adapt to the modern media. Suddenly the path was clear for half-formed politicians neurotically determined to purge their party of its past without being entirely sure about what should follow their cathartic moves.

Within minutes of Smith's death it was clear that from Brown's perspective the sudden vacancy for the leadership could not have arisen at a worse time. Virtually all Brown's public statements on economic policy had been aimed at the wider electorate and not at the Labour party members who would have a vote in the contest. In contrast Blair's reputation was soaring at a point when there were questions whirling around the media and in sections of his party about how Labour could appeal to resistant voters in England.

In his biography of Brown, Robert Peston argues that the shadow chancellor could have won a contest against Blair if he had decided to stand in 1994. Paul Routledge makes the same case in his earlier biography, the first written about Brown. Routledge put the argument with such intensity that his book became the cause of a decisive split between Blair and Brown when they were in government.

Although misplaced, this was the determined view of Brown's closest allies, who urged him to step forward and exploit his stronger base in the party. They were deceiving themselves out of loyalty to Brown and a sudden wariness about what Blair would do if he became leader. In the real world an unstoppable momentum was propelling Blair towards the leadership on the day of Smith's death. It did not take the scheming of Peter Mandelson or of anyone else. The broadcasting outlets and newspapers exploded with voices from the Labour party and beyond arguing that Blair should be the next leader. Opinion polls of Labour voters and the wider electorate conveyed the same message. In effect Blair was unofficial leader by the evening of Smith's death.

The suddenness of the changed situation gave Brown and his entourage no time to acclimatize. This is a partial justification for the delusional, self-absorbed and clumsily brutal response to the soaring rise of Blair. Obviously Brown was shocked and upset that a close friend had died. Equally obviously he wondered about what would happen next politically. There was a part of him that assumed Mandelson and Blair would be in touch at some point during the morning to discuss his candidacy for the leadership – another mistaken assumption. There were discussions, but none conducted on the certain basis he would be the candidate supported by the other two.

Brown's sense of betrayal was immediate, intense and irrational. Most ambitious politicians are able to accept defeat, or what in this case was an implied defeat, in a leadership contest and get on with their careers fairly calmly. Even the hungriest recover quickly. Michael Heseltine had wanted to be prime minister since his student days at

Oxford. After failing to win in 1990 he settled down to the less glamorous mission of finding an alternative to the poll tax as John Major's Environment Secretary. The nearest this big, complicated, exuberant and shy figure achieved to his ambition was standing in for John Major at Prime Minister's Question Time.

Brown could not settle down, and did not do so for another thirteen years. When he realized that Blair would wear the crown, his response was extraordinary. In a way that combined an insecure sense of entitlement, frustrated ambition, wilful competitiveness and, importantly, an underestimated principled conviction, Brown went about securing ownership over the future direction of the party and its policies as compensation. He assumed the role of leader in waiting the moment the new leader was elected. In the depths of his despair during those defining early summer weeks of 1994, Brown hit upon his own third way. He would not stand for the leadership but he would seek to lead. He would follow his third way with a constant resilience until he finally became leader in 2007.

Brown's frustrated personal ambition and his factionalized feuding in the years that followed have already filled shelves of books. One of his concerns has received less attention, but it partly explains why he responded in the way he did. It relates to Brown's assessment of Blair and of what he might do if he was left unchecked as leader. Publicly Brown has rarely hinted at his views of Blair. Away from his inner court he was discreet in private as well, but as early as 1994 he had genuine worries about what Blair would do to the Labour party and the country at a rare moment of heightened political opportunity. Brown's critics will argue that it was very convenient for him to discover principled concerns to justify what they regard as his acts of treacherous betrayal, but in being so doggedly, selfishly determined, Brown unquestionably saved the new leader from himself at certain points and also secured the freedom to be, sometimes, a reforming chancellor. Of course at the same time Brown also pioneered the famously destructive factionalism of which he was a victim as much as Blair, but there was some important purpose behind the manoeuvring which was not fully explored at the time or since.

With some evidence to justify his views, Brown had come to regard Blair as a superficial policy maker, more interested in process than in the building up of detailed policies with the aim of reaching specified objectives. He feared that Blair regarded policy decisions as little more than symbols to help him produce changes in the political choreography, and that it was the shape and pattern of politics that interested him. In Brown's view Blair would be excited by a policy that showed Labour had 'changed'. He would be less interested in the implementation of policies in the hope of achieving measures that brought about social justice, or higher levels of investment in public services. He had seen no evidence that Blair was gripped by the issues that interested him: economic policies, reforms that helped to address poverty and created the structures that gave even the poorest the chance to fulfil their potential, Brown's subterranean narrative and the reason why he was in politics.

In his obdurate disdain, Brown underestimated the potential importance of Blair's fascination with choreography, the possibility of progressives uniting in some form of anti-Tory force to shape a 'century for radicals' as Blair called it, and also in an entirely different context the scope for change in Northern Ireland. But he had a sound cause for concern. The divide between them was not so much at this stage one of left and right, but between the superficial, inexperienced policy maker and one who had begun to reshape Labour's economic policies with specific social objectives in mind. Blair's close allies argued then and continued to argue that it was Brown who was the short-term headline grabber, the figure who acted solely for his own interests and ambition. He was more than capable of acting in this way and became even more capable in his later years, but at this stage of their respective careers Brown was delving deep into economic policy making. Blair was floating nearer the surface, showing a forensic concern about the need for Labour to change and scrapping policies that had been so electorally harmful. But Blair had no view on economic policy. He knew what he was opposed to – the old 'tax and spend' policies advanced by Labour – but was less clear what he was in favour of in ways that marked a difference with the Conservatives.

Indeed there never was a 'Blairite' economic policy. The ubiquitous adjective was never applied even by ardent admirers to the key policy area, the one that drives everything else.

Brown's main aim in the build-up to their famous meeting at the Granita restaurant in Islington in May 1994 was to make sure he had control over the policies he cared about and input into decisions that related to the highly charged choreography, including front-bench reshuffles, relations with other parties and electoral reform. Contrary to mythology he did not go to the Islington restaurant seeking a deal over when Blair would hand over the leadership to him. Apart from anything else he was by then a traumatized and battered politician. He knew high politics could never be planned so neatly. Indeed he was living through a traumatic period that demonstrated how easily assumptions and ambitions could be blown apart by an unexpected event. By the time of Granita he had already received a commitment from Blair that as leader he would back him as the successor.

As far as Brown was concerned the meeting was about control. In particular he was worried about what Blair might say or do as leader on taxation and welfare reform. He lived in genuine and not opportunistic fear that Blair would make a speech, for example, that ruled out increasing the overall burden of taxation without thinking through the longer-term consequences and in a way that would have wrecked Brown's medium-term plans to raise taxation stealthily in order to pay for improvements in public services. He arrived at Granita seeking political space for himself and a degree of ideological incarceration for his young friend who was about to become a mighty leader.

During their relatively brief dinner at the Islington restaurant Brown was broodingly determined. Blair sought to be solicitously accommodating. Ed Balls joined Brown for the first course, almost as if Brown could not bear to enter the restaurant alone. He needed a protective layer to deal with his new friend for the first time in a transformed situation in the way he needed protection when implementing discreetly a left-of-centre policy. Suddenly Blair was the potential

76

leader and near-certain prime minister. Brown was negotiating for the runner-up's consolations.

Brown found it almost unbearable, even though Blair gave him everything he asked for. There was no small talk and no laughter. Brown made his demands and insisted that they be formalized. Blair said he would be happy to do so and added casually as an extra layer of reassurance that he would want to be leader for ten years at the most. He became expansive on the subject. No one should do it for as long as ten years. He had talked about it with 'Cherie and the kids'. He would be in the pressure cooker for less than ten years.

Later Cherie was furious when she realized that Brown had taken this as a commitment, a pledge. 'Why did you tell him that?' she asked Blair more than once that summer and over the next decade. Quite unnecessarily, Blair made the timing of his departure an issue even before he had been elected leader.

A briefing paper was drafted immediately after the meeting by Peter Mandelson. It stated that Blair was committed to Brown's 'fairness agenda – social justice, employment opportunities and skills'. In a copy obtained by the *Guardian* in May 2003 Brown had scrawled across one sentence 'has guaranteed this will be pursued', an acid intervention that suggested Brown had doubts about Blair's commitment to his ideas, and an early sign of the ideological tension that was to erupt fully during Labour's explosive second term in power. A transaction had taken place between the two of them, and it was over policy.

There was no formal agreement over the timing of any handover, but during the 2001 election campaign the television executive and close friend of Blair's Barry Cox gave me his assessment of the forthcoming second term: 'Tony is relaxed about the outcome of the election. This time he knows he is going to win with a fairly big majority. But he is really worried about Gordon. When Gordon realizes that Tony has no intention of going in less than ten years he knows Gordon will explode. He is not sure how to handle it.'

The casual reassuring aside made unnecessarily in the summer of 1994 had become a trap for Blair and a lifeline for Brown as ambition ate away at him. But the essence of the Granita deal lay deeper. Brown's main concern was not about precisely when Blair would stand down, although he seized on Blair's remarks about the length of time he envisaged doing the job and clung to the words with a neurotic ardour for years to come. Brown went to Granita with more immediate ambitions. The deal was about the balance of power between them.

This notorious meeting was even more important than mythology suggests. Already it has been the subject of a TV drama and formed the centrepiece of many accounts of the period. The exchanges were more epic than even the fictional drama conveyed. In the space of an hour and a half Blair made commitments that Brown chose to regard as carved in tablets of stone. In the years that followed Brown would exclaim regularly to his inner court in relation to Blair: 'He's broken the Granita deal!', especially when Blair instigated a cabinet reshuffle without consulting him.

Why did Blair give away so much in 1994 at a point when he was walking on water, widely regarded as the next prime minister before he had even won the leadership contest, easily the most lauded politician in the United Kingdom?

According to his close courtiers at the time there were many thoughts whirling around Blair's mind. He knew Brown wanted the leadership more than he did and that he had turned previous assumptions on their head. In negotiations Brown could be intimidating at the best of times. This was Brown's worst of times. It was a testament to Blair's growing steeliness that he was able to withstand the onslaught at all. Above all, though, Blair needed Brown. The shadow chancellor was the key architect in terms of economic policy. Take him out of the equation and Labour would be left without a strategy for the economy. In addition, and importantly at this stage, Blair admired how Brown had revised the party's policies. He was content to give him wider powers because he assumed they were thinking along similar lines.

Looking back many years later, a Brown ally noted that both men were desperately naive in assuming that any arrangement between the two of them could be formalized: 'Tony Blair should never have given Gordon Brown what he asked for and Gordon Brown should never have believed that he would get it.' But the Brownite ally also pointed out the context: 'In the spring of 1994 we didn't know there would be three terms of a Labour government. We were in opposition. We had not won an election. Modernization hadn't begun. We were not sure what kind of party it would become. We didn't know whether or not we would win the next election or when it would be.'

Here were two ambitious politicians, used to losing elections, mapping a precarious path that might have led to another election defeat or to a victory fairly soon. Both were on the pessimistic side even when polls were pointing to a landslide in the build-up to 1997. They had no idea they would be taking this agreement into power with massive majorities. For Blair the deal became an irksome ball and chain. For Brown it was a source of destructive hope.

For both it was also unavoidable. Although he would still have won, Blair did not want to fight a contest against Brown any more than Brown wanted to take on Blair. Their venture was too fragile, too dependent on a projection of assertive, and to some extent illusory, self-belief rather than actual deeply held confidence. It would not have survived a battle between the tentative co-architects. They thought Labour might lose the next election if only one of them stood. They feared even more the destructive impact of a public duel between them.

The deal at Granita was necessary for both of them even though it was a way of avoiding hard choices. Neither of them had to define clearly what they stood for and where they differed as a result of Granita. New Labour was born formally in an Old Labour backstage deal, an agreement that allowed it to escape clearer public definition. If there had been a contest between them, both would have been compelled to highlight the main difference: *Brown stood to the left of Blair*. Both would rather have died than have engaged in such a revealing battle. They preferred to be submerged in the comfort of apolitical terms and never engage in a candid public dialogue about where they stood in relation to each other.

For a party seeking to govern, the dynamics were more extraordinary, two individuals dividing up the spoils as if no other figure or institution mattered. That was the point. On this the lofty assumptions of Blair and Brown were right. They were taking over a party and they could choose to act as they wished.

One of Brown's defining characteristics in public and in private was that he never stopped. Monumental setbacks came and went. Triumphs were passing moments before he moved on to the next challenge. I have met few politicians with such relentless stamina. Tony Benn was another who kept going in the face of defeat, often to the fury of his colleagues. Margaret Thatcher was another, but she was more sustained by political highs. There are not many. In February 2010 Brown spoke to the interviewer Piers Morgan about dealing with 'pain' in his life, but said that he always 'fell forward', a revealing phrase. In a life punctuated by almost unbearable pain he was speaking specifically about the summer of 1994 when he lost out on the leadership to Blair.

After Brown announced that he would not stand for the leadership he did not skip a beat before planning with his small group how he would shape the next phase.

The resolutions made by Brown over this crucial period were a reflection of his complex personality and came to give it sharper definition over the next decade. To some extent they shaped the debate within the Labour party, or at least at the top of New Labour, which was where the only debates were permitted to take place.

First Brown resolved to take full control over economic and welfare policy as had been discussed at Granita. As the economy and welfare touched upon virtually all aspects of domestic policy, he was making an unprecedented resolution. No other shadow chancellor had sought or acquired such spectacular dominance.

For Brown this was the weighty compensation that occasionally lifted his summer gloom. In spite of his friendship with Smith, Brown never knew for sure how much space he enjoyed in relation to economic policy. Now he knew. The terrain was his alone. Even in this, the sunnier uplands of his thoughts, Brown harboured doubts. His press secretary, Charlie Whelan, told me in the autumn of 1994 : 'Gordon knows Tony won't always give him this power. It's bound to change.' But Brown was determined to make it as difficult as possible for Blair to drop his guarantee. As far as he was concerned this was a permanent commitment.

Brown's small team, already introverted, became much more insular after the summer of 1994, almost as a collective act of defiance, like mourners gathering to protect for ever the one who has been left behind. Together they had been through the trauma of betrayal as they irrationally saw it. As far as they were concerned their leader was Brown. Their man, a natural leader, had made the sacrifice of not standing for leadership, elbowed aside by a figure who was a relative lightweight. From now on, and with a greater intensity than before, they worked for Brown and viewed with raging suspicion the activities of those who were closer to Blair.

Until this point there had been no 'Brownites' or 'Blairites'. It was Brown's response to the leadership trauma that invited those imprecise labels. He needed a court although he was not king. Indeed he needed one because he was not king. As some of his closest allies admitted many years later, Brown's response at least in this respect was 'immature'. That is a mild description. Brown was childlike in his need to have 'his' people around him as an alternative court to Blair's.

In particular, and famously, Mandelson became an enemy. Brown could not fully understand why Blair had let him down. He did not even try to understand Mandelson's reasons for supporting Blair. When Brown sensed early on that Mandelson was not fully behind his candidacy he lapsed into fuming despair and wrongly spied his fingerprints on every front-page news story that favoured Blair. The two of them did not have a civil, relaxed conversation again until Brown became Prime Minister. Like many others Mandelson became a 'Blairite' first and foremost because Brown would have nothing to do with him. Up to the early years of the Labour government Mandelson rather nobly told journalists that Brown was the only leader to replace Blair 'in spite of all the obvious problems with Gordon', but as far as Brown and his entourage were concerned there was not a millimetre of space for rapprochement of any sort. Soon Mandelson ceased to make even the qualified case for Brown as successor.

The divide was to have profound practical implications, the first example of New Labour's capacity to become utterly dysfunctional. Blair's dependence on Mandelson and Brown's unyielding hostility meant that from the start there were two separate empires. The arrangements were always bizarre, but especially so during the 1997 election campaign. One senior figure who worked in the party's Millbank headquarters says: 'On one level it is a miracle we won that election. Peter and Gordon were supposed to be running the campaign but they did not talk to each other. They worked on either side of the main newsroom. Gordon was openly contemptuous of anyone who worked with Peter. It was unbelievable.'

The divide was even greater during the 2001 campaign, although Mandelson had a much lower profile. By then anyone in the Blairite court was sidelined by Brown. New Labour was widely praised for its professionalism, especially when it came to winning elections. But the professionalism was accompanied by the amateurish trappings of a feud.

The choreography of the divide in various buildings was highly significant and destructive, not least when Brown and his entourage took over Number Ten in the summer of 2007, marginalizing those who had worked for Blair when they might have learnt invaluable lessons about how to run the Downing Street machinery. They chose not to learn.

The formation of the Brownite court was not solely the equivalent of an emotional, cathartic scream. It had one important function. The courtiers and their king were seeking ways of prevailing over the more rootless Blair, knowing that no other individual or institution in the newly servile party was big enough to do so. Their court became the Resistance, the only form of accountability in a party that had lost the will or nerve to scrutinize the leadership. This became increasingly important in government.

Another important consequence that arose from the summer of 1994 was to have a profound impact on Brown's political reputation. The shadow chancellor was determined not to play the political martyr any more than was absolutely necessary in the future. In ways that his internal enemies continued to underestimate, he would still take tough decisions in relation to the economy, ones that sections of his party would not like. But he would also make sure that he was identified with the more immediately popular policies as well. Often in the years that followed Brown alienated colleagues through claiming association with popular policies and disappearing when there was a crisis of any sort. Angry ministers suggested that Brown was a coward who could not cope with trouble. Columnists closer to the Blairite court compared him to Macavity the mystery cat, nowhere to be seen when the going got tough.

Brown viewed the situation from a different perspective. He had taken all the knocks transforming Labour's economic reputation and had lost out on the leadership. He would continue to take them in the future, but from the summer of 1994 onwards he wanted to be more directly associated with palatable policies as well, and he was not going to go out of his way to defend Blair at all times, especially when he disagreed with the policies being pursued. Already he felt a martyr. There were limits to his martyrdom, not least because he wanted to be in a better place the next time a vacancy for the leadership arose. He did not want to be caught out again. In effect his leadership campaign began on the hot summer's day he stood aside for Blair in 1994.

Brown's failure to secure the leadership, the crushing of misguided assumptions, had one final consequence. The loss drove Brown into acts of treacherous collusion. With a ruthless precision and transparent lack of subtlety he chose to be friendly with those frontbenchers who had their doubts about Blair. Already he was watching carefully, sniffing out potential allies on the front bench and in the media for the struggles ahead and when the time arrived for the next leadership contest. Before long there would be 'Brownite' journalists as well as 'Brownite' MPs, a distinction that led to even more 'Blairite' journalists in response.

During the run-up to the 1997 election Brown became friendly with Clare Short, someone who was popular in the party at the time, seen as principled but expedient enough to dance to New Labour's tunes. Brown recognized that as a leading figure on the centre left, Short would be a useful ally in a future leadership contest and possibly in some of the internal battles he knew he would be fighting over policy.

In July 1996 Short gave a dramatic interview to me that marked the end of the New Labour truce, one in which every member of the shadow cabinet had paid public homage to Blair. Feeling sore after a reshuffle in which she was demoted, Short condemned the 'people in the dark' behind Blair, arguing that the likes of Mandelson and Alastair Campbell were bringing out the worst in Blair, giving the impression that Labour had changed, when it had not. She described the idea that the party had changed as 'a lie'. When the interview was published it led every news bulletin and was the main front-page news story in every newspaper. Mandelson alerted Blair and Campbell, who were both on holiday. In Blair's absence Mandelson had been put in charge of the party machine. He warned senior party workers: 'This interview could lose us the election!' Alert to every danger he added: 'She's broken the spell.' With typical mischief he then went on to ask me what time of day she had given the interview. I told him it was mid-afternoon the week before. 'Exactly ...' he replied with a knowing smile, implying that Short was drunk. She was not. She knew what she was doing, attacking Blair's leadership without attacking Blair directly.

Only one shadow cabinet member knew about the interview in advance. Over a glass of wine one evening at Westminster, Short told Brown what she had said and told him that there would be trouble. There was a pause after which Brown replied cheerfully: 'Well I will be up in Scotland when it is published and will be out of it. Leave it to Mandelson to sort out!'

Nonetheless the level of disloyalty at this point is easily overplayed. Brown sought always to be co-leader and to be in a strong position as the leader in waiting, and yet he shared Blair's hunger to win the next election. Their project to modernize Labour was about to be implemented. They had talked for years, now they had the power to act unimpeded. Brown was never, even at his angriest, a wholly destructive force. Part of him was always calculating how Labour could win, what needed to be said and done to challenge the Conservatives who he never forgot were the main opposition. In one of the many twists in the complex range of intense relationships at the top of New Labour, Brown helped to write Blair's victory speech in 1994. Here is Philip Gould, someone who was to become a 'Blairite', reflecting on Brown's commitment to the wider cause:

> Anyone who doubts GB's stoicism should have seen him late on the evening of 20 July 1994 the day before Blair was officially declared leader. Tony's acceptance speech was not finished and Gordon was working on it in his office in Millbank. If you want to know what real loyalty is it is this: Gordon Brown late in the evening, cursing, muttering, arms flailing as he punched words into the computer, writing the speech that just a few weeks earlier he believed he would be making himself.

It seemed entirely natural to Brown to keep on working for the bigger victory. It was often written of him that he was neurotically, furiously obsessed about Blair being leader. Often it was the opposite extreme. He almost forgot that Blair was in charge. Shortly after the 1997 election Brown produced a document on economic policy. Ed Balls told him that Blair wanted to write the introduction. Brown looked genuinely surprised as well as annoyed. 'Why does he want to do that?' he asked Balls. The adviser had to remind the Chancellor that Blair was the Prime Minister.

In their private exchanges Brown continued to behave as if he rather than Blair was the senior figure, not as a conscious act of dominance but because that was what came naturally to him. In the spring of 1996 I was in Brown's office one morning when his phone rang. Brown picked up the receiver and rattled off a series of instructions about how to handle Prime Minister's Question Time scheduled for that afternoon. 'If Major says that ask him why he had not acted earlier ... If he did act earlier ask him why it made no difference ... No, don't go in that direction ... We will get him on incompetence ...' After a few abrupt exchanges he put the phone down. I could hear Blair's voice on the other end seeking advice, but after the call Brown did not tell me who it was. He never showed off to journalists about the influence he wielded (in contrast to Mandelson, who in company would announce when Blair was on the line before he picked up the receiver) and was nearly always discreet about what he thought of Blair. But he was quite capable of showing his fuming impatient disdain directly to the leader, almost choosing to forget that Blair had leapfrogged over him.

The period between 1994 and 1997, the nervous march towards power, is pivotal in understanding the strengths and weaknesses of New Labour and the differences at this stage between Blair and Brown.

From the beginning the two of them and their close allies were all that mattered. The rest of the shadow cabinet had no more than walk-on parts, and some of them were lucky even to get that rather unflattering role. The most graphic demonstration of their subservience arose at the launch of Labour's 'Road to the Manifesto' document in 1996. When Blair, Brown and Margaret Beckett (the token woman who did not speak a word during the press conference) walked on to the stage the rest of the shadow cabinet stood to applaud. They were the audience, in some ways more passive observers than some of the highly influential political journalists who were also at the event.

Blair was a spectacularly successful leader of the opposition, engaging, focused, self-disciplined. His genius was to make defensively pragmatic leadership seem like a great radical crusade, although the contrast was bound to fuel disillusionment later when ecstatic voters began to take note of the fearful pragmatism.

In one particular area Blair's task was easier than Brown's. Blair inherited a large number of policies from Smith's leadership. They ranged from a commitment to hold a referendum on electoral reform for the Commons to the introduction of a minimum wage. Blair's main role was to revise some policies, drop others and make sense of them all to a largely right-wing media grown disillusioned with John Major's government. He also sought to prove that his party had changed with his successful campaign to scrap Clause Four of Labour's constitution and in his close dealings with the leader of the Liberal Democrats, Paddy Ashdown. This was an immense task, but one based largely on inherited policies.

Blair could compartmentalize his time ruthlessly, a great strength. In the build-up to the 1997 election, over one short recess he examined every policy in detail to analyse whether it could withstand the scrutiny of an election campaign and made changes if he concluded it could not. The controversial proposal to offer a referendum on the introduction of a Scottish parliament arose from this important exercise. Blair returned to Westminster and told his aides: 'I just can't see how we can argue that our election victory can be regarded as a mandate for such a precise and historic change ... and how can we offer a referendum on the Euro on the grounds that it is a constitutional matter when we're not offering one on a new parliament?' In opposition Blair was alert to any inconsistencies in policy. In power coherence and consistency became more challenging. When David Cameron became leader of the Conservative party in 2005 he and his allies, in their emulation of New Labour, assumed that the earlier project flourished largely through spin and presentation. They were wrong. It was partly a product of forensic policy examination.

But Brown went one stage further in policy making, his distinct achievement. He did not only have the task of revising existing policies, but of raising a whole new sructure on that ground.

After Blair became leader, Brown's liberating torment was evident at virtually every political event, free to develop economic policy while his former junior partner basked in leadership. In September 1994 Blair and Brown spoke at a gathering of business leaders held at the National Film Theatre on the South Bank, an appropriately artful backdrop for a significant act of political repositioning.

The two of them arrived together in the leader's official car. When the car halted close to the NFT Blair strode out in front with an authoritative verve to greet the organizers, leaving Brown and Whelan to walk sheepishly several yards behind. Brown looked almost baffled by Blair's assertion of leadership. I asked Whelan how Brown felt on occasions like this when Blair was so demonstratively the man at the helm. Whelan was capable of candour. 'Gordon bloody hates it. Of course he does.'

But Blair was keeping to his guarantee. Brown had the space to do what he and his small team wanted. At the NFT Brown proclaimed the first of his famous dividing lines. There would be many more such divides to come, but this was the one that started to address 'tax and spend', the issue on which Labour lost elections. Brown declared that 'Old Labour was a party of high taxation and high spending. New Labour will be the party of fair taxation and productive spending.' In the speech he argued that the Conservatives had wasted public money on failed policies that had led to a lot of 'unproductive spending', not least on social security payments that arose unavoidably when the economy was under-performing.

In his first big statement on economic policy since the death of Smith, Brown had framed the public debate with political cunning. In effect his pitch was once more focused on the managerial divide between competence and incompetence. He argued that the Tories had been incompetent and therefore had no choice but to waste money on unproductive spending. Labour would be competent and therefore have more money to use for vaguely defined productive spending. The divide was aimed at exposing the Tories and purging any lingering sense that Blair and Brown would tax and spend recklessly. It was also perfectly timed. The economy was starting to grow. The recession had passed. Whichever party won the next election, there would be money for 'productive spending' and less need to spend so much on welfare payments. It was also at this conference that Brown hailed the 'endogenous growth theory' in which policies that promoted openness, competition, change and innovation would promote growth. Balls had inserted the theory without wondering whether his audience or the wider public would have a clue what was meant. Blair would not have been so complacent. In fact it meant a lot as far as Brown was concerned, as he sought ways to achieve growth so that he would not need to raise taxes in ways that he feared would lose Labour elections.

Such was the uncritical euphoria around the leadership of Blair at the time that virtually no one in the media asked too many questions about what precisely the distinction would be between fair and high taxation. Some might have argued that 'high' taxation on the wealthy was a fair means to raise some much-needed cash, but few bothered making that case in the buzz of the changing political situation. Within the Labour party the only divide that seemed to matter was a conveniently chronological one between the past and the present, the old and the new.

A few weeks later at Labour's conference Brown developed the other side of his argument, one that would sustain him for fourteen years and had been his main theme when he wrote Maxton's biography:

> The big idea is people's potential. The big idea is that people have big ideas, huge talents, overlooked abilities, and it is by liberating people's potential that we build the dynamic market economy we need.

A dynamic market economy would provide the cash that would give less wealthy people the chance to fulfil their potential. As they fulfilled potential they would contribute to a booming economy.

This was the Brownite/New Labour accommodation. It would dance with the City in order to achieve left-of-centre goals. The dance came to a shattering end eventually, but in the mid-1990s, with public services in a dire state and much higher taxes close to being a political taboo, there was no other pre-election route available. The context was Labour's defeat in 1992. Those who voted in the 1992 election are as much to blame as Brown. The voters and those who mediate politics for them are big players in the New Labour story. We are the ones who define how much space political leaders have. It is the only power we possess.

In January 1997 Brown stunned his interviewer, James Naughtie on the *Today* programme, by declaring that under Labour there would be no changes to the top or basic rate of income tax for an entire parliament and that a newly elected Labour government would stick to the Conservatives' spending plans for two years. It was an extraordinary moment, so unexpected that the programme's editor kept to schedule and ended the interview on time instead of giving the obviously startled Naughtie time to explore the implications.

Still there was plenty of time for exploration. Later that day Brown delivered a speech to accompany the announcement:

> We want to send the clearest possible signal that we want to encourage employment and work, not penalize it ... because we want to encourage work, and after 22 tax rises since 1992 which have hit hard-working families, I want to make clear that a Labour government will not increase the basic rate of income tax. It is because we understand the importance of work that there will be no return to penal marginal rates at the top.

In the build-up to the announcement Brown's instinct had been to propose a new top rate of tax for very high earners, a policy he finally implemented in very different circumstances when he was Prime Minister. Whelan told journalists this would happen when Labour was first elected: 'We have got to do something to show we are Labour.'

Neurotically conscious of Labour's extreme vulnerability in relation to tax, Blair was determined to block Brown. In the autumn of 1996 when they were battling over the issue, Blair's press officer, Tim Allan, offered an article to the *New Statesman* under the name of the Labour MP Kim Howells, arguing that a top rate would not raise any additional revenue and would alienate some middle-England voters. Here was an early example of Blair being sometimes willing to challenge Brown over economic policy. He prevailed on this one and later

Brown was to concede that Blair had been right. It was a concession rarely made in the years to come.

The publicly declared policy on 'tax and spend' was widely hailed at the time as a masterstroke. The newspapers were reassured. The Conservatives were thrown into even more disarray. Labour's lead in the polls soared. And yet the seemingly bold announcement encapsulated the timid narrowness of Blair/Brown's short-term ambitions. Like so much else that was projected as bold, it was cautious. By the start of 1997 the Conservative government was falling apart, giving Labour more scope than Blair or Brown had dared to realize.

By accepting spending limits that the Conservative Chancellor, Ken Clarke, had described as 'eye-wateringly tight', Brown and Blair had little scope to challenge the Tory government on the funding of public services. They were not planning to invest very much either, so they could make no case about the lack of investment, the great hidden issue of British politics in the 1990s. Instead they conveyed the false impression that with the addition of a few pennies here and there, public services would be transformed. From a practical perspective it meant that desperately needed investment in public services was postponed to a point of even greater crisis at the turn of the century. Such was the euphoria around Blair that voters were convinced: the NHS would be saved and schools rebuilt without having to spend any more money.

When Brown became Chancellor he seemed awesomely powerful, the mighty figure in the Treasurer who was co-leader of the government. He was powerful in relation to the Prime Minister, but in terms of policy he had deliberately made himself the least powerful chancellor in modern history. He had no control over interest rates, no power to put up income tax, and for two years no authority to increase overall public spending. When he became shadow chancellor he chose to become constrained in what he said. As Chancellor he tied himself in chains so that voters, the financial markets and the media knew he could not be recklessly free.

But always with Brown, at least in this phase of his career, the subterranean narrative was the driving force. There was a degree of

thought-through purpose behind the extreme prudence. In his revealing book, one of the most important in the bulging New Labour bibli-
ography, the former Treasury Minister Geoffrey Robinson described
what motivated Ed Balls in his policy making. Robinson could have
as easily been writing about Brown:

> Important though his contributions were in economic terms, his deep
> concern on poverty, redistribution and fairness in society will be seen
> as more important in due course. Those issues are what motivate him.
> Getting the economics right is just the means to do something effective
> about them.

Robinson in the early years was a key policy maker in Brown's team.
He was a great admirer of Brown's but enthused even more about
Balls, recognizing in the youthful adviser an unusual talent for linking
strategy to complex detail in ways that could re-establish Labour's
credibility with business leaders while staying rooted firmly in the left
of centre. Robinson was pointing towards the big difference between
Brown and Blair.

For the remaining years in opposition Brown spent a lot of time on
policy detail, an arduous and unglamorous task, but the most important part of the politician's repertoire. Blair worked on existing ones
or got others to do so – devolution was one that demanded considerable work. David Miliband described the process to me as bomb
proofing, ensuring that every single policy presented in the forthcoming campaign was credible and part of a coherent narrative. In the
build-up to the 2010 election David Cameron and George Osborne
showed less interest in policy detail. When Cameron was asked how
he planned to implement his tax cuts for married couples he insisted
that the details would come later. Blair and Brown were not allowed
such lenience.

Brown asked Geoffrey Robinson to work on refining the Private
Finance Initiative. Once Brown and Blair had cordoned off their tax-
raising options they had to look elsewhere for ways of investing in
Britain's decaying hospitals. The Private Finance Initiative became

one option, hugely controversial and expensive but arguably unavoidable. Hospitals were built or improved in the early years of the Labour government through the PFI. They would not have been built otherwise in the timid 'tax and spend' climate of the times. Later many columnists on the left and right condemned the use of PFI, but again few among them would have supported a Labour manifesto in 1997 advocating tax rises to pay for new hospitals. Once again, culpability for the extravagantly wasteful PFI is widespread. We wanted new hospitals. We did not want to pay for them.

Later Robinson and Balls worked closely on the details of the one-off windfall tax on the profits of the privatized utilities, Brown's popular tax. Over time New Labour's critics saw only spin in virtually everything that Blair and Brown announced. It was always more complicated than that, and the hard grind that prepared for the one-off tax is a good example of the other side of the story.

A former chairman of Jaguar Cars, Robinson was a wealthy Labour MP who, when he was in London, lived in a suite at the Grosvenor House Hotel overlooking Hyde Park. He also owned glamorous homes in Tuscany and the South of France. One evening in October 1994 Robinson bumped into Brown during a vote in the Commons and told him how impressed he was at the way the shadow chancellor had handled the leadership issue. With an uncharacteristic candour Brown admitted he had not had much choice in the matter. The two talked for some time about the political situation. In every campaign since his mid-teens Brown was ruthlessly alert to potential useful allies. He recognized that Robinson's links with business would be extremely useful. Robinson also understood economics and had practical experience in business. Soon they became close allies. Robinson worked even more closely with Balls.

Robinson arranged for the accountants Arthur Anderson to prepare the details of how a windfall tax would be implemented and the likely level of revenue that would flow from the measure. The hired specialists showed in considerable detail how the tax could raise £6 billion to finance a 'welfare to work' programme and improve some hospital buildings. The ultra-cautious Brown insisted that they aim only for £5 billion and did not make excessive claims about what it could achieve. Separately Balls worked on other discreet revenue-raising measures.

In the early spring of 1997, shortly after Brown had played his 'tax and spend' ace on the *Today* programme, the shadow cabinet member Michael Meacher declared in an interview with a naive candour: 'We have ruled out increases in income tax but there are plenty of other taxes we could put up.' When he read the interview Brown was livid: inadvertently Meacher could have brought down with a single sentence the entire fragile tax-and-spend edifice. Meacher was right. Balls and Ed Miliband were looking in detail at other ways in which a Labour government might find some cash.

The media was so excited about Meacher's comments that he chose to hide in his shed in order to escape the attention of journalists on his doorstep. On his mobile phone, surrounded by gardening equipment, he expressed his bewilderment to friends: 'I did not break with party policy,' he declared.

That was precisely the point. Meacher had given away too much about party policy. From that moment the decent well-meaning left-winger was doomed. Although a member of the shadow cabinet, he was not appointed to the cabinet in 1997. His punishment extended way beyond exile in his shed.

Apart from his search for a few stealth taxes, Balls was preparing for prudence, the stability from which he and Brown could pursue some limited social democratic objectives. It was during this period that Brown concocted his famous golden rules in which he would borrow for investment only over the economic cycle and would ensure that public debt was held at a 'stable and prudent level'. The rules became famous for being implemented rigidly at first, manipulated in times of some difficulty and then spectacularly cast aside in the autumn of 2008. They played an important part, though, both in conveying a sense of trust in the early years and in providing a framework.

The fiscal rules were another reason why Labour won in 1997 with the biggest landslide since the Second World War and also with the widest range of self-imposed constraints. Business leaders were reassured. Voters who had dismissed Labour in 1992 as reckless tax-and-spenders were able to support the party. Tory-supporting newspapers could hardly believe their luck. They could back Labour and still have a government seemingly committed to the orthodoxies of recent years.

Labour won power bound hand and foot to prudence.

Albeit heavily manacled, Brown had made his Herculean leap. In the space of five gruelling years he had more or less achieved what appeared to be impossible when he became shadow chancellor. Assisted by the exhausted, divided Conservative government and the broad appeal of Tony Blair, he had made Labour appear the more competent party in relation to the economy.

Brown remained the ultimate student politician, basing his activities and approach on the many successful campaigns he led at Edinburgh University when he was always leader of a small gang, scheming and campaigning around the clock. There was an unconscious macho swagger as the group gathered in the evening, often in Robinson's suite of rooms at the Grosvenor House Hotel. They watched football together on TV and reviewed where they stood politically over a beer at the end of the day.

Robinson described the roles well. Whelan could be gregariously charming over a cigarette and a glass of wine. He cultivated political editors and columnists who were or would become closer to Brown's cause than Blair's. He acted as he saw fit, but did so with Brown's approval. Brown always stood by him. Brown expected loyalty as a matter of course, but always reciprocated, taking assiduous care to promote and protect allies, more so than Blair, who was relatively casual and careless in his treatment of political friends. Whelan was not to last long in power, but others from a similar mould followed. Brown saw politics as a noble battle, but he took the fighting more seriously than any other contemporary politician. Sometimes the fights were necessary, occasionally they were acts of assertiveness, a substitute for Blair's powers of patronage, and often they were merely habitual, the ugly side of Brown's politics.

There was never a pause in the fight, even on the night of Labour's landslide election win in 1997. The Conservatives had been defeated overwhelmingly, but for Blair and Brown the real battle had only just begun. It was between themselves, a clash of ambition, ideology and strategic will that could never be submerged even when the duo had cause to celebrate glorious victories.

THREE

Cautiously Bold

On election night in May 1997 most of the country seemed to be dancing the night away, or at least staying up to watch the election results, cheering joyfully when Tory cabinet ministers fell. Even some of those who did not vote Labour, most of the electorate, succumbed to the mood quickly. Polls showed that Labour's popularity soared once the votes had been cast. By the summer and autumn of 1997 the party was breaking all records in terms of opinion-poll leads, suggesting that some of those who had supported the Conservatives in the election or who had not voted were also enthused.

The mood was too excitable, at odds with the ambiguous nature of a limited turning point. Labour had achieved an unprecedented landslide, but it was based on a cautious incremental programme. The result was historic, but not the manifesto that produced it. The year 1997 was not a watershed like 1945 or 1979, with elections that heralded deep, almost revolutionary change as governments shaped and followed the zeitgeist of their times. For varying and contradictory reasons voters had put in place a government resolved to show that it was different from previous Labour administrations and in some ways in tune with the orthodoxies that had shaped the previous eighteen years of Conservative rule. 'We were elected as New Labour. We will govern as New Labour,' Blair declared pre-emptively outside Number Ten as he arrived for the first time as Prime Minister.

*   *   *

By 1997 Brown's reputation was rising again in the Labour party and beyond. He had travelled his first full circle: hailed as a formidable reformer in 1992, he was seen that way again as he headed for the Treasury. The phase in between, when he was so unpopular he would not have won a contest in a parish council, had passed. It would soon return. There were other circles to complete, but as Labour returned to power most newspapers and his party recognized the contribution he had made to the landslide. At any rate they cheered the public narrative, the emphasis on prudence and stability.

On this night in May 1997 Brown relished the fact that an electoral barrier had been overcome, but straight away there were more battles to be fought. According to his close allies he felt no sense of euphoria on election night. The victory was a brief pause before the next stage of the eternal political journey. There were pressing problems on his mind and he wanted them sorted fast.

From election night onwards this was the battle as Brown saw it. He had stamina, resilience, limitless willpower, the strength to threaten near-fatal trouble for the government if he chose to do so. Blair had the mighty powers of prime-ministerial patronage. In theory at least Blair could appoint and sack who he wished.

As Chancellor Brown had no equivalent powers, at least in terms of ministerial appointments. In theory at least, like the rest of the government he was dependent on the patronage of Blair. All he had to cling to was the so-called Granita deal and the fact that he had a plan for the economy whereas no one else in the government, Blair included, had given any significant thought to economic policy. Brown had not let them, but his possessiveness remained an easy excuse on their behalf to abstain from deep thinking on the subject.

In the early morning of 2 May Brown briefly joined the celebrations at the Royal Festival Hall. Revealingly, the jubilation was fuelled by disbelief. Along with several other journalists, I had a ticket for the event and soon after arriving bumped into David Miliband, dancing along to 'Things Can Only Get Better', Labour's anthem for the campaign. Seeing Miliband on the dance floor was quite a shock, but his words were more revealing. He looked up and joked: 'I am sure we will all wake up in the morning and find that the Tories have won again.'

From the start there was a collective fear that they were dreaming. The fear never died. They could not quite believe that the Tories were no longer an invincible force. From the beginning nearly all of them felt like impostors disturbing the natural order of things. Already those at the top of New Labour had acquired a reputation for arrogance, but the opposite was closer to the truth. In their insecurity they were never arrogant enough in imposing or even articulating an alternative vision after eighteen years of Conservative rule.

The insecurity persisted. I recall one social gathering on a Saturday evening in north London halfway through Labour's second term after the party had won another landslide in 2001. Those around the dinner table included a cabinet minister, the owner of an independent TV production company, two newspaper columnists and an influential economist. Along with the cabinet minister nearly all those around the heaving dinner table were Labour supporters at a time when the government had been in power for several years. The question of the evening was: How do we get a progressive consensus when the right is so powerful in Britain? Even when the left of centre wielded considerable power it did not dare to recognize the changed situation, or at least the potential for change.

In 1997, alone of the shadow cabinet, Brown had been able to choose his Treasury team and inform them in advance which ministerial jobs they would be taking up. Geoffrey Robinson for example informed Ian Hargreaves, his editor at the *New Statesman*, that Brown had made him Paymaster General long before the general election had even been called.

They huddled together in a corner of the Royal Festival Hall for an hour. One of those who knew members of the inner court well described the gloomy mood. 'They were bad times for Gordon and his senior allies. They weren't celebratory because of what was going on behind the scenes, the battles with Tony.' Those battles included who would be appointed to the cabinet and the roles of Brown's senior courtiers.

There was also another twist at the Royal Festival Hall, additional cause for the introspective tension on what should have been a night of celebratory euphoria. In fact it was the voters who were euphoric. Senior New Labour figures who had waited eighteen years for such a moment were miserable. Shortly after Brown arrived Cherie Blair marched up to him and accused him of being disloyal to her husband. According to one onlooker she exclaimed, 'You can't accept Tony won the leadership can you?' The same observer claimed she was 'staggeringly rude'. This was to become a pattern. In the winding corridors that connected Numbers Ten and Eleven Downing Street Cherie would challenge Brown whenever she got the chance. In contrast to her husband's calmer manner, she could not resist a cathartic blast.

Brown's wife, Sarah, was also the occasional victim of sharp and sometimes insensitive onslaughts from Cherie. The two wives could not have been more different in personality, although they had similar experiences of following a career and bringing up families at the centre of power. Cherie was outgoing and had a famously skittish exuberance. She had been wary of Brown from the 1980s when he shared an office with Blair. Brown was not part of their social circle in Islington and there were no common ties between her and him beyond politics. Her wariness deepened after 1994 when she saw how he reacted to Blair's victory in the leadership contest. She expected loyalty to 'my husband'. In his own way Brown assumed quite genuinely he was displaying a form of loyalty, at least to the Labour party, which is why he was taken aback whenever Cherie went for him. He was always surprised to discover that people felt angry or upset by his behaviour, an uncanny lack of self-awareness.

Sarah was more introverted than Cherie and avoided confrontation in any form. Her background was in marketing and she had met Brown when working on various projects for the Labour party where she also advised on PR for the *New Statesman*. They started going out when Brown was shadow chancellor. Those who knew her well were never entirely sure whether her more retiring personality was moulded by shyness or aloofness. Either way, Sarah did not go for open confrontation. Sometimes Cherie did.

Someone who knew the Browns well says: 'Gordon and Sarah took it personally when Cherie attacked them. She said horrible things – things that got in your head.' On more than one occasion Sarah was reduced to tears following an exchange with Cherie. Tony witnessed some of the outbursts and according to Brown's allies appeared to be embarrassed by them. If he was, he chose to do nothing about them. The outbursts continued for the next decade and extended to other members of the Brownite entourage, especially to Ed Balls. Cherie loathed Balls, perhaps as much as she loathed Brown.

Given the degree to which power in this particular government resided in the hands of two individuals, any event or relationship that reinforced the divide between them tended to have further ramifications. Brown's self-absorbed and immature response to the 1994 leadership drama sowed the seed for the creation of Brownites and Blairites. Cherie's aggressive loyalty to Tony fuelled the factionalism. Gordon and his inner court felt under attack from Cherie at times, and that, in a strange and destructive way, vindicated their need to form a separate court in the first place.

As far as they were concerned Brown and his inner court were to remain as distinct as they had been in opposition. They were not to be swamped by senior civil servants at the Treasury, the machinery of government or the clamouring ambitions of those more closely identified with Blair. The separation was not just an act of ambitious vanity, although this was a factor, but arose from a sense that they had a plan, a clear direction in which they wanted the government to move. They were not sure whether it would work, or whether Blair and his entourage would be supportive, but they intended to attempt it.

After a few hours' sleep Brown went to see Blair briefly in Number Ten. The two of them walked alone in the garden on an unusually hot and sunny day for early May. The two of them were at the top of the government, buttressed by the biggest majority since the Second World War – quite a leap from the dingy office they shared at the start of their parliamentary career in 1983 and from the last Labour government that collapsed eighteen years earlier with no majority at all.

But both of them were businesslike. In markedly different ways both Blair and Brown had a rare capacity to focus on what needed to be done in any circumstance and to cut themselves off from some of the noisy distractions of politics. In the years that followed, outsiders who worked on projects with both of them, or one of them separately, tended to notice this quality more than any other, and were pleasantly surprised by their insight. They had read in the media endless cynical assessments about the duo, and then came face to face with their ability to compartmentalize and think with clarity even in the thick of a thousand other crises and internal rows.

On the Friday after the election Brown discussed briefly the logistics of his planned bombshell announcement about the independence of the Bank of England. Blair moved on to an issue that he and his press secretary, Alastair Campbell, had discussed separately and intensely on several occasions. He pressed again for Brown to sack his press secretary, Charlie Whelan.

The suggestion revealed much about the new and inexperienced government that was the source of much euphoric hope around the country. Most obviously Blair wanted Whelan sacked because he regarded him as a loose cannon, capable of firing on colleagues as much as on the opposition. But Blair's concern went beyond Whelan's unpredictable behaviour. He and Campbell had resolved to make the presentation of policy as central as its implementation. Campbell was explicit about this in a statement he delivered to departmental press offices in the first full week of power. Blair and Campbell had watched and benefited from the chaotic management of news under the Major administration. They were determined to control the message centrally, and their desire to do so was not a marginal issue but at the heart of Blair's thinking about how he would be Prime Minister. Not surprisingly therefore, Campbell was keen to have Whelan out of the way in order to prevent conflicting messages emerging from Number Ten and the Treasury.

Later Blair and Campbell were to admit that in the early months – and arguably years – in office they retained the mindset of opposition, almost mistaking a favourable media report on an initiative for the successful implementation of policy. But their focus was not as trivial at it might appear to be. They recognized the power of the media in shaping the perception of a government and considered the need for a coherent message to be one of the new administration's main objectives.

There was also another reason for Blair placing Whelan at the top of his prime-ministerial hit list. He wanted to break up Brown's separate court. As far as Blair was concerned there was room for only one Prime Minister – a perfectly reasonable line to take, not least from the person who happened to reside in Number Ten. Blair knew that if he did not make a move right away it would be too late and a pattern would be established in government that followed what had happened in opposition with an alternative power base at the Treasury.

Predictably Brown was resistant, and Blair did not push it hard either, claiming that his concern was solely one about the government having a clear message. Alert to any attempt at challenging his empire, Brown saw in this move a first attempt to put him in his place. Blair had a press secretary, but apparently he was not allowed one. Brown regarded the suggestion as an attempt by Number Ten to seize control of the media agenda, whereas he had every intention of making his own distinctive mark in that area.

The quick exchange between two exhausted individuals in the immediate aftermath of a historic victory was tense, fuelled by mutual suspicion, and yet as they addressed issues related to internal factionalism they also managed briefly to discuss a historic policy as they geared up to make the Bank of England independent. There were to be many more such exchanges, angry, awkward, media-obsessed and humourless, although both of them possessed a sharp, humanizing sense of the ridiculous.

Two questions arise from their first exchange as rulers in a landslide government. Why did Blair not insist on getting his way – an echo of his weakness at Granita? Was Brown justified in refusing to become in effect a mere cabinet minister without his own courtiers around him?

The answer to the first question is fairly straightforward. In spite of his towering popularity, Blair did not feel strong enough to antagonize Brown, nor at this stage was he inclined even to try. He knew they had to find a way of working together and was not going to blow the relationship apart on Day One. He thought it was worth giving the future of Whelan a try partly because he wanted to send a signal to Brown that he was on his case and would not tolerate divergent briefings, but he never expected Brown to give in.

The answer to the second question is more complicated. On one level Brown's determination to have his own people working for him rather than for Blair or for the government as a whole was self-indulgent, divisive and grandiose. Yet as a new Chancellor he was under immense pressure to prove that Labour could be trusted to run the economy, a challenge almost as great as the one facing Blair as the incoming Prime Minister. In addition Brown was pioneering economic policy single-handedly. Only his immediate entourage understood his distinct New Labour strategy: a reassuring public narrative and the implementation of some social democratic policies by stealth. He needed them. In such a context he was justified in having his people around him even if their subsequent behaviour vindicated Blair's concerns.

Their meeting lasted little more than half an hour. Soon Brown left Blair's small empire in Downing Street and headed for his mighty institution in Whitehall. When Brown arrived at the Treasury he was greeted by 200 cheering civil servants. Those who were settling in at Number Ten watched warily as Brown was met by a noisy euphoria. Some of them suspected Whelan of orchestrating the move to convey a sense that here was an alternative centre of power with its own emperor. Whelan denied this, pointing out that he would have been in no position in advance to instruct senior Treasury officials to act in a certain public way. Yet the symbolism was striking. Blair had been cheered into Number Ten earlier in the day. Brown had been cheered into the Treasury. The two of them were operating from different centres now, with their own distinct resources.

Brown's reputation remained high in the early years of the government partly because he had worked out a detailed plan that he more or less kept to. As John Prescott joked privately in the early autumn of 1997, most of the government had 'hit the ground reviewing'. There were hundreds of policy reviews instigated as an alternative to policy making. Prescott had certainly launched several in his grand, newly created, dysfunctional Department of Transport, Environment and the Regions, otherwise known as the department with responsibilities that interested neither Blair nor Brown. Misguidedly the duo had no interest in transport, even though so many voters needed to travel. On this Prescott was way ahead of them. But they gave him no space to move in.

As a whole the government conveyed a deceptive impression of hyperactivity, but much of the ministerial energy was sapped by their instinct to kick decisions into the long grass.

In contrast, Brown started to implement policies in ways that gave the otherwise tentative administration much-needed momentum. Indeed one of the lessons of Brown's tenure at the Treasury is that the policies that sprang from arduous preparation in advance tended to endure while those announced more superficially, with the aim of outmanoeuvring the opposition or buttressing his own position, quickly fell apart. Brown's experience proved that hard work behind the scenes on making policy nearly always pays off. Superficial initiatives usually rebound on their political creators. Towards the end he became more attracted to the superficial.

Brown's early policy making after the 1997 election also challenges another of the main accusations made against him by his internal opponents and the Conservatives. Soon Blairites accused Brown of being too cautious and lacking political courage. They felt this passionately and with sincerity. They were not making it up in an attempt to find artificial causes for their disdain. But they were wrong.

It is true that Brown could be paralysing in his caution over day-to-day decisions. His ministerial critics witnessed many examples of disproportionate hesitancy. They drew too sweeping a conclusion from the dithering, failing to recognize the bravery of Brown's longer-term objectives, probably because economic policy was cordoned off from the rest of the government. Brown's critics had not been allowed to interfere with, or debate, the programme for the economy, so they took what happened more or less for granted.

This was highly unusual. Normally economic policy was the main subject of internal debate within a government. In the 1970s at least half the cabinet had firm and conflicting ideas. During the early 1980s the debate between wets and dries in Margaret Thatcher's first government was over economic policy. John Major's government was torn apart by disagreements over the Euro, partly an economic matter. Under New Labour Brown did economic policy, bestowing on the rest of them the luxury of taking growth for granted while they explored other ideas – such as 'choice' in public services – on the assumption that as if by magic plenty of money would be available for their schemes.

In the early years Brown was bold in two respects. He showed a determination to challenge Treasury orthodoxy and some of the powerful individuals in the mightiest Whitehall department. That took quite a lot of courage from someone with no previous ministerial experience of any kind. Second, some of the policies involved considerable risks, although they were risks of a very limited kind.

Balls had written a detailed paper on the Bank's independence as early as 1995, gripped by the need as he saw it 'to sort out the Bank'. He was a powerful persuader. During a meeting with senior Labour strategists in March 1995 he put the case strongly that in a global market: 'There is little any national government – and particularly a Labour government in a small country like Britain – can achieve by manipulating interest rates in the short or medium term. Stability and credibility are all.'

That was the aim: to acquire a reputation for stability and credibility in order to gain the freedom to act in other areas, such as increasing public spending, without being swallowed alive by the markets, business leaders and the media, the fate of previous Labour governments.

In May 1995, Brown gave a strong public hint about the direction in which he was heading. In a speech he spoke of the need to 'remove the suspicion that short-term party-political considerations are influencing the setting of interest rates'. As a Chancellor he would 'consider whether the operational role of the Bank of England should be extended beyond its current advisory role in monetary policy making'. He praised the 'openness of debate and decision making which occurs in the US and the internal democracy of decision making of Germany's Bundesbank and the targets set by the New Zealand government'. We journalists should have guessed which way he was heading.

Balls tried to combine the best of these international models in his proposals. In his 1995 paper he argued that the monetary policy committee should decide interest rates, the Bank's regulatory role should be hived off and the Chancellor should appoint the monetary policy committee and set the inflation target. That is what happened in 1997.

To their credit, and much more closely than Blair and his policy-making allies, the Brownites were concerned with the issue of accountability: which institution was accountable to whom?

It was the source of many rows between Prime Minister and Chancellor and is at the heart of virtually every debate in relation to the delivery of public services. To take an example from Cameron's preparations for power, in the build-up to the 2010 election the Conservatives held a series of energetic seminars on their plans for what they called a post-bureaucratic age. But they hit upon a problem: if the state withdraws and allows smaller groups such as co-operatives or housing estates to run their affairs, to whom are the smaller groups accountable? There was no clear answer, and quite often by the end of their seminars the Conservatives had appointed ten thousand new bureaucrats to run their post-bureaucratic age.

In the case of the Bank, free to act on his own in the luxurious space of opposition when few were following what he was up to, Balls addressed the issue of accountability in relation to independence with considerable skill, giving away power but ensuring that ultimately the elected Chancellor pulled the strings in terms of appointments and setting the overall objectives of the Bank.

Although Balls had been advocating the radical move since at least 1995, it was only on the final Monday of the 1997 election campaign that Brown confirmed he would implement the policy. He returned to London from his constituency and headed straight for the comfort of Geoffrey Robinson's suite at the Grosvenor House Hotel. Apparently speaking as if he had a thousand other thoughts on his mind, he told Balls he had decided to make the Bank independent as his first big policy announcement. Balls and Robinson assumed, probably accurately, that his diverted air was more to do with the fact that he could not quite believe what he was saying. The two of them sought out Balls's 1995 paper and got down to work in the remaining few days of opposition.

The speedy, ruthless manner in which the deed was done was part of the political bravery. There was no one else in the 1997 cabinet, including Blair, who would have been qualified to make such a sweeping change in relation to the Bank, or would have dared to do so. The new Prime Minister was wholly supportive of the move, but that is slightly different from making it.

Brown decided in the final weekend of the campaign not only to go ahead with the move, but to do so straight away. He realized that there would be only one real opportunity to act from a position of perceived strength, and that was at the very beginning. Any time after that and critics would detect the move as a sign of weakness, a sense that a Labour government was failing again.

In order to prevail on this and other matters, Brown and Balls were ready to take on the mighty mandarins if they had to. Balls met the Permanent Secretary, Sir Terry Burns, once a week for six months before the election, an assiduous cultivation. But he and Brown were suspicious of Burns, regarding him as someone who had been too 'cliquey' with Nigel Lawson and Ken Clarke, two long-serving Conservative chancellors. They were ready to form their own allies within the Treasury against the Permanent Secretary.

Balls sensed that Burns in particular felt a personal investment in the previous Tory strategy for the economy, but moved quickly to assert his – and therefore Brown's – authority. Quickly Balls acquired other allies in the Treasury. There was Steve Robson, the architect of railway privatization, who was according to Brown's allies 'at daggers drawn' with Burns because of various battles in the past. Another senior official, Nigel Wickes, had fallen out with Burns. Soon Gus O'Donnell joined them at the Treasury. O'Donnell had been John Major's press secretary, but such was his unthreatening demeanour and calm authority that he moved effortlessly to serving the Labour government. His love of sport helped too. O'Donnell talked football and cricket with Major when the Prime Minister was in the depths of gloom. He calmed down Brown sometimes with a talk about football of which Brown had an encyclopedic knowledge and could recite team sheets from decades ago.

There was a pattern forming. Wherever Brown and his inner court went they formed a faction, making alliances with a few trusted figures. The factions were partly defined by a perception that enemies lurked all around. In terms of the Labour party the Blairites were their main enemy. The Brownites extended political friendship to those who shared their grievances, worries and desire to prevail. In the Treasury Burns was seen as an obstacle to progress, along with a few other senior officials who appeared to form an allegiance with the long-serving Permanent Secretary. So the Brownites became closer to those officials who shared their doubts about Burns.

At times they had an exaggerated, destructive sense of the barriers placed in front of them, the enemies that had to be addressed, and the alliances they needed against common enemies. Once more the criticism was often made of Brown and Balls, in the media and beyond, that their politics were fuelled by an insecure paranoia.

There was something in the charge, but like the other criticisms about Brown's caution and cowardice it tended to ignore the wider context. In this case they were entering the Treasury with a series of radical plans, unsure whether they would have the support of the Prime Minister and for different reasons the Permanent Secretary. They were in a critical position, one that needed to be reinforced by ruthless politics and an acute awareness over who they could trust. Brown's reliance on a few close allies and the lack of people-management skills that accompanied such introverted dependency became a much bigger and less excusable flaw when he was Prime Minister. As a Chancellor determined to impose an agenda on a doubtful Prime Minister, he needed a faction and would have found one forming even had he sought – as he did not – to avoid such divisiveness.

In 1997 Brown was determined to break through resistance from the Treasury and to some extent transform its role. In the run-up to the election he published in draft form a new mission statement for the Treasury. As well as low inflation and sustainable growth he made the reduction of poverty an explicit objective for the department. According to one of Brown's allies the impact inside the Treasury was 'massive'.

Senior officials took mission statements seriously. The inclusion of poverty as an issue meant they had to make room for new dimensions, analysing more closely the consequences of their policies on the least well off. The same applied to Brown's focus on public services. Treasury officials did not have to only decide the sums for each department, but had to focus relentlessly also on agreed outcomes, on how the money was going to be spent, and over longer timescales, in an attempt to avoid the short-term frenzy of the annual public spending round. This was quite a leap for officials brought up on the need to balance books or adapt to an imbalance in the books. Brown wanted the Treasury to be more creative. He was pioneering a cultural revolution in the department while giving away conventional powers such as the setting of interest rates.

Brown was perceived as anti-reform when he had reformed the Treasury, a department intimidating in its determined conservatism. The debate should have been about what constituted appropriate reforms. But from 2001 Blair framed another apolitical debate: 'Reform or anti-reform'.

On the Sunday after the election Brown gave Burns the shock of his career when he handed over a letter in which he outlined on what terms he was giving away the power to set interest rates. The letter reflected Balls's interwoven layers of accountability, stating that 'the monetary policy of the Bank of England will be to deliver price stability (as defined by the government's inflation target) and without prejudice to this objective to support the government's economic policy including its objectives for growth'. Brown retained the powers to appoint the Governor and members of the monetary policy committee, obviously an extremely important form of patronage, although limited in the sense that Brown could not be seen disturbing the natural order of things too greatly in terms of appointing close allies. Brown set the inflation target at 2.5 per cent, with explanations demanded if the figure was significantly above or below that limit.

As part of their factionalized thinking, Brown and Balls also had doubts about Eddie George, the Governor of the Bank, whom they were empowering with their new policy. These doubts were more than reciprocated when Brown told George a few days later that the Bank would lose its role of monitoring the financial health of banks. As part of a period of frenetic early activity, on 18 May Brown announced that a newly established Financial Services Authority rather than the Bank of England would become the new independent regulator for the City.

The separation of powers became the subject of intense controversy more than a decade later when the scale of risks being taken by banks was disastrously revealed. Because of the epoch-changing recession that began in 2008, the establishment of the FSA became a ticking time bomb. In his party conference speech in the autumn of 2008 the Conservative leader David Cameron argued that it was this act more than any other that had led to the catastrophic regulatory failures. By the spring of 2009 the focus became more intense as several banks verged on bankruptcy, admitting that they had taken too many risks. What was the regulator doing? Why did Brown remove the powers from the Bank of England?

The questions whirled noisily around, the volume rising as some of those who had furiously disapproved of the move at the time spoke up claiming vindication more than a decade later. For Brown the questions became a form of torture in the winter of 2009.

But like the related policy to make the Bank independent, the new separation of powers was implemented more subtly than the chorus of retrospective indignation allowed in 2009. Because the policy had been thought through in opposition and had not been thrown together to chase a media headline, the complex issues of accountability, and which body answered to whom, had to some extent been addressed. Brown and Balls appointed two deputy governors of the Bank, one in charge of monetary policy, the other a link between the Bank and the new regulator, the Financial Sevices Authority. There was always a formalized link between the two bodies. It was too easy for the Bank to complain later that it had been sidelined.

In addition the Bank of England had been a poor regulator, presiding over several high-profile collapses in the 1980s and 1990s, including Johnson Matthey, BCCI and Barings. The new structure was not in itself responsible for the colossal errors in regulation that were to continue for the next decade.

As in his abrupt dealings with Burns, Brown had shown courage in his approach to Eddie George. In removing the Bank's regulatory powers Brown could easily have provoked a sensationally high-profile resignation. Indeed, George fleetingly contemplated a dramatic departure and almost admitted as much in public.

Brown was often underestimated and overestimated simultaneously. The verve with which he seized the moment in 1997 was seriously underplayed by his internal critics at the time and subsequently. But the degree to which he was being heroically radical was overstated in the days that followed his announcement of the Bank's independence and since.

The entire sequence was aimed at securing trust. The move was a defensive one and not an act of swaggering radicalism. Brown's introductory comments at the press conference in which he revealed the policy were perfectly judged to attract favourable comment from Labour's new friends in the media and in the financial markets. He declared: 'This is the time to take the tough decisions we need for the long-term interests and prosperity of the country. We will not shrink from the tough decisions needed to deliver stability for long-term growth.'

There was much talk at the time from both Brown and Blair about tough decisions that they were taking, as if they were revolutionaries in a hurry. The theme of Blair's first speech to Labour's conference as Prime Minister a few months later was 'hard choices'. In fact the government was postponing or avoiding a whole range of genuine tough choices, while giving the impression of boundless courage. Claiming to make those choices while avoiding them was the first New Labour conjuring trick in government.

In his final year as Chancellor Brown told me, at a point when Blair had ceased to be trusted by many voters after the war in Iraq, that the government 'needed to win political trust in the same way we were trusted with the economy after the Bank of England independence. We gave the Bank powers in order to be trusted and not for any fundamental economic reasons.'

The defensive motives behind the Bank's independence applied also to Brown's equally famous 'fiscal rules', another manacle, this time constraining Brown's freedom to borrow and spend. But like the other seemingly masochistic constraints this was also a flexible shackle.

In one of the early books to be written about Brown, *The First Year in Power*, Balls explained the broader thinking behind his famous fiscal rules. His candour made no waves at the time and yet his words are revelatory in retrospect: 'Left-of-centre governments need to favour tough fiscal policy because from time to time if economic crises occur you may have to relax that. But you have to build up the credibility and the means to do so.'

This is an important insight into the nervy thinking behind the self-confident façade. Balls admitted that the rules were the equivalent of a defensive formation for an insecure football team playing away from home. They were a necessary protective barrier for left-of-centre governments that were not trusted by mighty markets. But from the very beginning Balls accepted that there might come a time when the rules would not be applied. In 1997 he contemplated breaking the rules as he hailed their significance.

When Brown started to break the rules a few years later all hell broke loose. But here was Balls preparing the ground from the very beginning.

Brown's budgets were prepared, shaped and reshaped as if they were works of political art. They were a combination of the highly political and densely technical. To some extent all budgets are that, but Brown's outstripped his predecessors' in the scale of his political and technical ambition. His budgets were aimed at what would normally be regarded as a conflicting range of audiences, from traditional Labour voters to the CBI, from the Labour-supporting *Daily Mirror* to the *Daily Telegraph*. They were designed to sidle past the sometimes beady and cautiously conservative eyes of Tony Blair and to trick the Conservatives into moving further to the isolated right. For Brown they were great showpiece events, the occasions on which he sought to impose his evasive personality on the country, but in ways that left large parts of his personality elusive. His budget was punctuated with phrases about 'the people's priorities' and the need to act 'for the many and not the few'. 'Prudence for a purpose' was one of several constantly repeated slogans.

The importance Brown attached to the budgets as political ritual and as a means of framing and adjusting economic policy was seen at once when he effectively announced there would be two budgets a year. The pre-budget report, delivered usually in November, was a smart innovation, in effect giving Brown cover to make new policies without having to suddenly announce emergency mini-budgets, a device associated with his Labour predecessor, Dennis Healey.

Preparations for each budget changed in terms of scale as the range of policies expanded from the narrowly defined ambitions of the early years. More officials and organizations became involved. But the working principles were unaltered. Brown was the strategist outlining to his advisers what he wanted to achieve in terms of political and economic impact. Balls was more immersed in the policy detail, informing senior officials at the Treasury what he wanted. As one official told Blair's biographer, Anthony Seldon: 'Brown and Balls were the Treasury.' Ed Miliband was involved in some precise policy preparation and in writing significant sections of the budget. In the early years Geoffrey Robinson was also heavily involved in policy detail. Whelan's job was to brief the media, which he did with considerable skill in the build-up and the aftermath of early budgets. Balls and Miliband would also brief journalists, usually the growing army of political columnists. Presentation was central to the project.

The run-up to Brown's first budget in July 1997 was chaotic, yet so effectively choreographed that the same routine was followed for all the many successors. On the day before the event there were two different budget speeches, one prepared by the Chancellor's speech writer in the Treasury. The other had been written late into the previous night by Gordon Brown. The speech from the Treasury official had no political message, the ultimate sin as far as the Brownites were concerned, but contained all the measures that Brown was planning to implement. Brown's speech dealt with none of the measures, but communicated powerful political messages. He was being prudent for a purpose. He was following the people's priorities. The two Eds – Balls and Miliband – spent much of the day putting the two together, while Brown despaired that the inclusion of technicalities slowed down the speech. In the end Brown was told he could not go near a computer to make any further changes.

But the preamble to the July 1997 budget set a course. The influential strategist for the Democrats in the US, Bob Shrum, arrived around nine days before the budget to join the small team. Brown and Balls met Shrum on a visit to the US in 1995 and were excited by his interest and what seemed to them like an instinctive sense for what worked well politically. They sat together in Brown's main office, Brown at the computer typing furiously, Shrum working with a slide projector which would project what Brown was typing on the screen. The two Eds and a small number of other trusted advisers would be doing the final detailed work on policy in a separate room.

There was a final ritual, more nerve-racking than it need have been. The Treasury prepared a one-paragraph summary on each of the budget decisions. Brown had to finally sign them off by ticking each one. Half jokingly and half fearfully he would look up as he reflected on each proposal and ask: 'Do we have to do this?' The tick followed.

What were the aims of all this intense work, and were the objectives achieved? There are two conflicting interpretations from those inside the government during Labour's first term. In the autumn of 1997 Balls told me that Brown's overriding objective was to 'rehabilitate the politics of tax and spend'. This was a bold claim to make at the time, and even in retrospect it seems like a counter-intuitive ambition. At the time Brown was sticking to the previous Conservative administration's extremely tough public spending limits and was pledged not to increase the income-tax rates, levels that were relatively generous for the affluent compared with equivalent countries in Europe. But Balls was adamant that this was the plan. First he said they needed to secure the trust of the media, the electorate and influential business leaders.

He also told me of another obstacle. They had to get the proposals past Tony Blair who – according to Balls – was resistant to tax rises and yet quite often demanded increases in spending. Brown regarded his exchanges with Blair on economic policy as exhausting, fruitless and unenlightening. Quite often Brown returned from discussions with Blair about the budget to declare angrily: 'He wants me to cut taxes and increase public spending.' Right from the start, he and his inner court resolved to give away as little as possible, even to the Prime Minister.

In contrast to Balls's claim, Brown's critics were convinced that there was no such coherent plan to rehabilitate 'tax and spend' and that quite often the Chancellor was the roadblock to necessary public-spending increases. Some former cabinet ministers bear the scars to this day of their attempts to prise much-needed cash out of the Treasury.

Both versions have some truth in them. At first Brown blocked virtually all requests for increased cash, leaving ministers more or less impotent in their new departments. In some ways Blair was more alert to the urgent need for more cash, but it is also the case that he responded negatively to any proposed increases in tax that would have raised the revenue for more spending.

Brown did raise some cash from his so-called stealth taxes, but most of the income was spent on repaying government debt – part of what Brown and Balls regarded as the necessary groundwork in order to win the approval of the media and voters to raise public spending substantially.

Ministers in spending departments and users of public services were paying the price of Labour's long-standing reputation as reckless taxers and spenders. Brown and his inner court were also functioning in a media environment almost universally hostile to increases in public spending. Some newspapers might have supported Labour in the 1997 election, but they were rooted firmly on the right in terms of economic policy. They influenced the approach of the BBC and to some extent the attitude of Tony Blair as well. This is no trivial point. Few voters watch politics in the raw as it happens. Even on a budget day the audience size for the speech itself is tiny. By definition the media mediates politics. Brown was seeking to move economic policy very slightly leftwards against a media environment that cried out loud at any sign he was doing so. He was excessively patient in making his moves, and he allowed some public services to deteriorate further, but by the time he started to increase public spending substantially he was at least trusted to do so.

In the meantime Brown sought to balance the books. He was the Chancellor who was prudent for a purpose, a clever slogan that enabled the media to cheer the prudence as Labour MPs clung to their hopes about the purpose. In his first budget Brown removed the tax credit on pensions, immediately raising £5 billion. Later this was billed as a 'raid on pensions', but with pension funds booming and the government enjoying an unprecedented honeymoon there was little fuss when the announcement was made.

His debut budget was fairly pedestrian but Brown followed up with another budget in March 1998. The Chancellor managed to redistrib-ute a fair amount of cash to families on lower income without uttering the word 'redistribution', which he considered rightly to be a term that alarmed many voters who feared their money was being recklessly spent on those who did not necessarily deserve it. The transfer of cash came about via the working family tax credit, in which £5 billion was redirected to 1.5 million families on low income. Brown also found cash to cut Corporation Tax, giving him the ammunition to argue that it was Labour and not the Conservatives who were the party of business. More quietly he doubled stamp duty on expensive houses and stealthily increased a few other taxes that did not have the poisonous potency of the untouchable income tax. Income tax he left unaltered as promised, but the two budgets taken together had nonetheless raised quite a lot of cash through the so-called raid on pensions and big rises in stamp duty.

Yet few complained. That was because Brown was capable at his peak of being a great political artist in a way no other cabinet minister could match. Blair was equally assiduous in wooing the media, but normally he espoused policies that right-wing newspapers supported as a matter of principle. Brown managed to implement some more recognizably left-of-centre policies and yet for a time he still got the support of the media.

The *Daily Telegraph* on the day after the spring budget in 1998 summed up the discreet achievement. On its front page the headline screamed 'Brown Spares Middle Class. Budget Boom For Families, Savers And The Low Paid'. A euphoric Charlie Whelan looked up when he read this front page and described it as perfection. He exclaimed to members of the inner circle: 'We had to milk the middle classes and yet we get this bloody brilliant headline.' The rest of the newspapers were equally euphoric, reflecting the skilful guile with which Brown had navigated the hugely complex politics of economic policy for a left-of-centre government.

Inevitably parts of the media became suspicious as to how Brown was producing his conjuring tricks. The political impact of Brown's artistry was also ambiguous. Although the Conservative newspapers raved, some of Labour's traditional voters were starting to twitch nervously, a nervousness echoed at ministerial level. They also bought the spin that had been aimed at securing the approval of right-wing newspapers. The then junior minister Peter Hain observed in an interview with me that the government risked 'gratuitously alienating' its core vote. In 1999 the Defence minister, Peter Kilfoyle, resigned on the grounds that the government was failing to pay enough attention to traditional voters, a move that provoked a classic New Labour response, first deployed by Brown at a subsequent cabinet meeting. Brown argued that 'the entire country is our core constituency'. Blair used the phrase in a speech a short time later.

Hain's characteristically well-timed intervention, Kilfoyle's resignation and the Blair/Brown response highlighted the fragile basis on which New Labour was formed. No left-of-centre party could win an election in Britain by adopting an approach that suggested there was a 'core vote' somehow separated from the rest of the country that merited special favours, as Kilfoyle implied. A successful approach must be more holistic and inclusive than that. But the Blair/Brown desire to please nearly everyone in the bulging big tent was equally doomed to disappoint. There were too many contradictory aspirations and opinions: tax cutters; public spenders; pro-Europeans and Euro-sceptics and virtually the entire political spectrum crammed inside the marquee. The same applied when the Liberal/Conservative coalition was formed in May 2010, one example of many when the Cameron/Clegg era began as an echo of the recent past rather than a break from it.

Blair sought to navigate a third way in policy terms, a position that lay to the right of his own party and slightly to the left of the Conservatives. In some policy areas Brown sought to be more radical by stealth. But Robin Cook highlighted the problem with stealthy radicalism when he argued in a series of speeches during Labour's first term that many of his poorer constituents thought that the tax credits were a technical change introduced by the Inland Revenue. They had no idea that their additional money had any connection with government.

The early years also exposed a big gap in Brown's repertoire. He had given much thought to 'tax and spend', competition policy, welfare reform, Europe, and redistribution. In relation to all of them he had been inventive in terms of the revisionist policies and political projection. But he had given little thought to the politics of ownership. On ownership he was as complacent as Blair about the need for radical change.

Yet ownership is at the heart of government. Thatcher privatized and gave tenants the right to buy their council homes. Her approach to ownership formed her revolution. In 1945 the Labour government seized ownership of major industries and created the NHS. Neither Blair nor Brown took a view on ownership. As a result Brown made several calamitous errors. The biggest was the introduction of a Public Private Partnership for the decaying, increasingly unreliable London Underground. The policy revealed Brown's lack of any clear sense as to when the private sector worked well in the delivery of essential services and when it did not, a tendency to assume that any private deal would be better value, and a small-minded determination never to concede to political enemies, in this case Ken Livingstone, the aspiring Mayor of London who wanted to raise the much-needed investment by other more sensible means. The PPP scheme was enthusiastically brought to fruition by the senior civil servant Steve Robson, who had been one of the architects behind the privatization of the railways. It proved to be a costly disaster, and was scrapped when some of the private companies failed to deliver the promised improvements in spite of a massive injection of public funds. It was one of several ventures where the state, the taxpayer, took all the risks while inept private companies acquired any profits. In this case the government could not let the Underground close if any of the private companies failed.

Who is responsible for the delivery of what? This was a fundamental question in British politics in the late 1990s. New Labour never had a clear answer. Brown was not remotely interested at first in changing the arrangements for the privatized railways, even though their costly decline was powerful ammunition for a left-of-centre government to put the case for other forms of ownership. This was an unusually insecure and timid administration, and even venturing into the politics of ownership was a step too far. At no point in the early years did Brown challenge the model of ownership he inherited from the previous long-serving Conservative administration. Only amid the storms of the second term did he seek clearer definition, and that was in the midst of a blazing internal row about the future of the NHS.

There was much talk among Blair's and Brown's advisers and in Number Ten about the frustrations of power, the difficulty of getting things done. But that was partly because they were too scared to act. In many policy areas they did not want to change very much. As far as Brown was concerned, even in those areas where he was daring he did not want to change the terms of the public debate.

In his early years he was quietly daring in relation to public spending, redistribution and asserting his authority over the Treasury. He was silent on ownership. Most of the noise arose from his relationship in power with Blair.

FOUR

Personalities and Policies

The relationship between a prime minister and a chancellor is always a determining force, but in the government that was formed in 1997 it was more or less all that mattered. The emotional spasms, the explosive silences, the mutual feuding were of overwhelming importance because the dominance of the duo in the government and their party was total.

In any previous phase of Labour's history the factionalized uproar would have counted for less. In the 1970s and 1980s there was a range of leading players who had authority because of the views they represented, the strength of their internal support and force of personality. Harold Wilson's close courtiers fell out with each other in epic rows, but Wilson had other factors to take into account – the might of the party's National Executive Committee, the titans around his cabinet table, a restless parliamentary Labour party. Frontbenchers had their own bases. They clashed over ideas, strategy and direction. They were cheered on as they did so.

The public divisions and the persistent allegations of weak leadership in an unruly party explain why Blair and Brown seized total control, but in doing so they moved from one extreme to another. After 1997, Blair and Brown made the decisions. The rest of the front bench played no more than walk-on parts. The parliamentary party was largely docile and ignored. The National Executive Committee was little more than an administrative sideshow. The party conference was a few days of controlled theatre. They ceased to be part of the story. But when Brown fell out with Blair that was a big story, the running backdrop to the precarious, defensive, vaguely defined New Labour project. They fell out so often that it was more of a novelty when they were working harmoniously.

Shortly before he died I had a glass or two with Roy Jenkins. He noted almost sympathetically: 'It must be difficult for political writers now. You have only Blair and Brown.'

The soap opera mattered. Journalists wrote so much about Blair and Brown because the muscular battle was significant. A slight from one to the other was the equivalent in a previous era of a heroic and multi-layered battle culminating in a highly charged drama at a conference on a stormy seafront. There were none of the normal checks and balances of politics, least of all parliament, where Labour had won a landslide. Brown was the check on Blair, and to some extent Blair was a check on Brown. There was always the media of course. The media was a check on both of them. But in the elected arena they called the tunes.

The soap-opera dimension, the feuds, the shouting matches, the frustrated ambition, was compelling but in the end not as important as the related disputes over policy and the art of making policy. The chaotic resolution of policy disputes touched voters' lives. The back-stabbing and the devious scheming touched the lives of those who found they had a knife in the back.

Nonetheless this soap opera determined the context in which policy was agreed. There were some early significant episodes and one in particular that changed everything.

Up until the start of 1998 the relationship between Blair and Brown stuttered along awkwardly. Brown had been free to develop economic policy more or less unimpeded. He feared this would not last and that his strategy of stealthy change would be blocked by Blair, but it was the clumsiness of his entourage that brought about a hasty change in the dynamics of power. They made the almost impossible task of reforming Britain against the wishes of the Prime Minister and parts of the media much harder than it needed to be.

From January of Labour's first full year in office the relationship between Blair and Brown deteriorated. This time it was Blair who changed from his largely tolerant and empathic attitude to Brown's dogged, moody insularity.

From the summer of 1994 Brown had set his course by instinct. He coped with his supposedly subservient role in relation to Blair not by obsessing about his junior friend becoming leader, but by almost forgetting who was leader and who was not.

In a limited way, and to the frustration of his allies, Blair went along with Brown's view of their relationship. As a mighty Prime Minister enjoying a long and golden honeymoon, Blair had given away a lot of power to his Chancellor. A symbol of Blair's willingness to defer on economic matters came at the very beginning. Normally the Prime Minister chairs the cabinet committee on economic policy. Blair announced that Brown would take the chair.

Brown was subsequently given an extraordinary amount of space to prepare his first budget, with Blair occasionally asking what would be in it as if he were almost a bystander. Brown had been allowed to appoint his Treasury team with no questions asked and had been consulted about other dispositions. As far as Blair was concerned he had delivered more or less everything that Brown had wanted. Partly because of this, he had clung to the hope that their relationship might become more harmonious.

Blair gave up being optimistic with the publication of a biography of Brown by the journalist Paul Routledge at the beginning of 1998. The book was a trigger that transformed their relationship permanently. Blair saw it as an act of war and became more assertively aggressive towards Brown from its publication onwards. It marks an important episode in the relationship and also highlights the clumsy way Brown chose to promote his personal cause. More significantly, the change meant that the policy battles grew more intense, loud and angry. Blair became much more reluctant to concede ground. Ferociously competitive, Brown responded by being even more determined to prevail.

Routledge was an old friend of Whelan's and the two of them worked closely on his biography of Brown. The book commanded the headlines for days with its claims that Blair had broken a deal with Brown when he stood for the leadership in 1994.

Routledge argued that even though Blair betrayed Brown by standing for the leadership, the shadow chancellor could still have won but had stood aside for the sake of party unity, fuelling a Brownite fantasy. There was much more to the biography than that, but inevitably with the wounds still raw from the drama of 1994 this was the section that made the front pages.

The responses were more potent because Brown's close allies had cooperated fully with the book. Even Brown had indicated overt approval by agreeing to be interviewed. It looked like a crude attempt by Brown and his courtiers to undermine Blair and project their man once more as the lost and martyred leader. To some extent that was the purpose of the clumsy operation.

Not surprisingly therefore, the book's publication was seen as an unprovoked act of war by an unusually furious Blair, who was in Japan at the point when the revelations were raising the roof back home. Blair's fury was fuelled by the even greater anger of his press secretary, Alastair Campbell, who erupted when he received faxes of the front pages in his hotel in Tokyo. At one point Campbell sent a text to Charlie Whelan with the menacing words: 'You've had it this time … wait till I get back.' Whelan showed the text to journalists as if it was a badge of honour.

As usual with the Brownite entourage and their internal machinations, the impact of the book had not gone to plan. Brown had hoped with spectacular naivety that his strong sense of political purpose would emerge from Routledge's narrative, that he would become less of a caricature. Whelan envisaged a range of positive headlines about his boss and some damaging ones for Blair. Neither of them thought how a book so closely associated with the inner court would look from the outside. To many commentators it looked like an unnecessary desperate act of aggression, an attempt at self-aggrandizement from a figure who should be getting on with running the economy.

Blair was baffled by Brown's aggression and apparent determination to revisit the scenes of previous battles. He had been working on the assumption that Brown was the only obvious successor and in the meantime was a powerful Chancellor. Was that not enough?

Later in the same week someone close to Blair spoke to the *Observer*'s columnist Andrew Rawnsley. In the course of a long conversation the source famously described Brown as someone with psychological flaws. Rawnsley referred to this in his column and a sharp-eyed editor sniffed another volcanic news story. The *Observer* put the claim on the front page and the internal warfare escalated another notch. Brown and his close allies were convinced that Campbell was the source. It was certainly not unusual for Campbell to speak to Sunday columnists on a Friday morning, especially at points of high drama. If it was Campbell he was making a legitimate point. Brown had a perverse tendency to let his entourage work in ways that damaged him and nobody else.

But now it was the Brownites' turn to explode. Whelan, who had a sense of the ridiculous even as he was fighting his side of the battle, noted: 'We can't have someone in Number Ten briefing that the Chancellor is bonkers. It's fucking madness.'

As usual in these eruptions over non-policy issues, misunderstandings and cockups fuelled the growing sense of mutual mistrust. The decision by Brown and his friends to cooperate on a book was a reasonable one. As Whelan put it at the time: 'The Prime Minister has had two books on him, Prescott has a book about him, so has Cook. Why can't the Chancellor have a book written about him?' There was a spate of books during the heady years when Blair and his senior ministers were at the height of their popularity. Almost inevitably they became part of the internal tension. In such a context it is not surprising that Brown was keen to get his side of the story across, not just about the leadership, but his background and ideas. Blair was enjoying a spectacularly good media at the time, with several newspapers making a distinction between the leader and the rest of the government.

Indeed Brown was particularly worked up about Rupert Murdoch's newspapers, *The Times* and the *Sun*, which he felt were fawning on Blair while being unfairly critical of him. Whelan told me in the

127

spring of 1998: 'These newspapers are not pro-Labour. They are pro-Blair, which is a completely different matter.' Whelan revealed that during this period Brown was so furious about the broader media coverage of the government that he momentarily considered slapping VAT on newspapers. Instead he chose to woo them even more assiduously and started to approve of them or loathe them less when he got more positive coverage.

The first sign of Blair's new aggressive approach towards his old friend was the summer reshuffle in 1998, an event of traumatic significance for Brown. In the build-up to the reshuffle Brown waited to be consulted. As far as he was concerned that was part of the Granita deal: the two of them would work together on ministerial changes.

This time there was no consultation. Instead Blair went to Chequers with his closest advisers from Number Ten to plan the reshuffle, an act of prime-ministerial assertion that made Brown deeply uneasy. Brown was always fired up by reshuffles, more vividly aware of his ultimate powerlessness than at any other point in the political year, which Campbell fuelled by briefing the papers that Brown was not invited to the Chequers gathering.

From Blair's perspective the reshuffle was a glorious act of provocation, a response to the Routledge book and the sniping that had followed it. He moved an ally into the Treasury with Steve Byers becoming Chief Secretary. He took the Brownite Nick Brown away from the powerful base of being Chief Whip and promoted Peter Mandelson to Trade and Industry, the other main department connected with economic policy.

Most newspapers interpreted the move correctly as Blair asserting his authority over Brown. Instead of being slightly alarmed at such potentially fractious interpretations, Blair's close ally and friend Anji Hunter exclaimed aloud as she read the newspapers in Number Ten that they were 'the best front pages for Tony since we won the election'. The relationship had slipped into one about headlines, territory and reputations. Brown was culpable for acting clumsily. Had he been told in advance that a book would produce headlines about how Blair had betrayed him in 1994 he almost certainly would have had the sense to pull back, knowing that it would be counterproductive. But he let his team keep fighting, and Blair fought back.

After that summer reshuffle the briefly despairing Brown agreed with Hunter's excited verdict, but such a setback reinforced his determination to reassert his power in the government. Brown and his small group of allies never gave up and refused to let any crisis or negative coverage sway them from their various missions for very long. Balls, Whelan and the courtiers followed suit.

Soon internal opponents complained that Brown and his entourage had destroyed them politically. That was too easy an excuse. The truth was that the entourage had greater determination and political willpower, attached to a slightly more coherent sense of what they sought to achieve in power. They would not have survived without both.

The most dramatic example of their persistence in relation to the ongoing soap opera was the destruction of Peter Mandelson. Again the chosen instrument was a book. Once more the author was Routledge.

This time the impact was even more dramatic than the previous book's. Routledge revealed that Mandelson had taken a loan from his colleague Geoffrey Robinson while both of them were in opposition in order to buy a house in Notting Hill. Mandelson had not revealed the details of the loan to his Permanent Secretary, even though the department was investigating some of Robinson's business arrangements. Mandelson was forced to resign in the frenzy just before Christmas in 1998. His own insecurity and vain evasiveness had played their part in his downfall, but it was the Brown camp that had fired the shots.

Once more there was for Brown considerable collateral damage. Robinson, a close colleague, was also removed at the same time as Mandelson. After Christmas Blair finally prevailed and Brown agreed to Whelan's departure. Brown had gained little from the entire body-strewn affair other than an even grimmer reputation for being unforgiving in his vindictiveness. When the focus briefly changed to the policy battles, many commentators saw only Brown's fuming ambition and took Blair's side.

How much was Brown directly responsible for the malevolent scheming, and why did it take place? These are key questions asked often by supposed ministerial victims and by journalists who sometimes received astonishing information and views from Brown's close allies, but not from the Chancellor himself. The answer is complex, and varied to some extent from incident to incident. On one level Brown was wholly responsible for the scheming, conspiratorial, paranoid, self-pitying culture that sometimes pervaded his court. Most practically he could have stopped some of the manoeuvring, but instead encouraged an atmosphere where permanent conspiracy and scheming were part of the scenery, as natural and inevitable as wild rain on the Cornish coast. For Brown it was a necessary part of politics, remaining alert at all times to slights or more overt challenges, seeing off perceived enemies, deploying trusted allies to do what they regarded as necessary in order to prevail. He had functioned like that ever since being a young politically active student, and then rising up the Scottish Labour party in the 1980s. But his alertness to political dangers had sharpened since 1994 when Blair became leader.

For someone often accused of lacking charisma, Brown had the capacity to arouse total and sincere loyalty in those who worked for him. Some of them, and they were tough characters, would have placed themselves in front of an oncoming car if they thought that would save their master. They saw in Brown a commitment to social justice, a zest for life, a restless humane intelligence, a compelling tonal range that he showed to few others. They shared his sense of grievance that he did not become leader and worked around the clock to make up for it. When he became angry they did not wonder about his emotional balance. They became angry too.

Brown calculated that the likes of Whelan and, later, Damian McBride were invaluable allies, and that is why he did not want to ditch them. They were smart in particular at wooing the political editors of Conservative-supporting newspapers on behalf of Brown. Fighting an unofficial leadership contest and introducing some social democracy by stealth, for Brown that cultivation was worth a lot. He never realized the degree to which casual aggression alienated an army of potential supporters.

While Brown and Blair shared many assumptions at this early stage in power, there were also significant contrasts in the most substantial policy areas. Sometimes they reflected conflicting philosophies. Often they were a product of different approaches to making policy, with Blair tending still to skate on thin ice but capable of brilliantly presenting a narrative, while Brown delved several layers deeper, more aware of the consequences of superficially appealing policies, but unable often to present his version with the same convivial ease.

Nearly always Blair was portrayed as the more ambitious in what he hoped to achieve in policy terms. The opposite was the case. Precisely because of the scale of his ambition Brown chose not to articulate it too openly in case he was hammered by parts of the media. In contrast Blair's genius was often to ride with the prevailing currents, echoing the views of the most powerful newspapers, and yet presenting his actions as the more daring. This divide grew much wider in the second term.

The first and most fundamental difference between the two of them related to 'tax and spend', the thorniest policy area of them all, which Brown had been addressing obsessively since he became shadow chancellor in 1992. In opposition Brown and Blair were more or less in agreement. Labour's reputation for spending and taxing had to be ruthlessly purged. On this Brown had resolved to do whatever it took, with Blair's full support.

But crucially, Brown and Balls had not become opposed, as a matter of principled conviction, to taxing and spending. In contrast Blair was convinced fundamentally that taxes should fall and public-spending issues as far as they existed could be addressed through other means, vaguely defined. As part of the rootless complexity of his nebulous position, Blair was capable of changing his view on the question suddenly and dramatically, not least when it became much clearer to him that the dire state of public services was becoming an overwhelming issue in the media. This is what happens when rootless

131

politics is almost a driving principle. Convenient flexibility can lead to a chaotic lack of direction. The Liberal/Conservative coalition formed in the summer of 2010 displayed similar characteristics, although arguably Cameron and Clegg had no choice but to be flexible in the light of the indecisive election result. Blair and Brown were working with a landslide majority.

In both cases their slightly conflicting aspirations were stifled in timidity. Brown was convinced at this stage for example that a Labour government could never make an overt case for a rise in income tax. Yet he was furious when shortly before the Labour conference in 1998 Blair gave a revealing interview to the *Independent* newspaper in which he insisted that he saw the reduction of taxation as a 'key' objective and argued passively 'there is a long-term trend away from higher tax rates'.

On reading an interview in which Blair appeared to make such sweepingly definitive assertions about the virtues of low taxation, Brown worried that he would be further hemmed in by pressure from Blair and the media to cut taxes. But as part of his long-term attempt to be trusted in relation to taxing and spending there were times when Brown opted to cut taxes, and he made much of it when he did so. Here was an early, familiar contortion: Brown fumed when Blair spoke of tax cuts and then went on to cut some taxes. The indignation was part jealousy, but more importantly about control. Brown did want to put up taxes, but discreetly. He feared Blair was a tax cutter without discretion.

It was Brown who flared again when Blair admitted openly and sensibly that the burden of tax had risen under Labour towards the end of the first term. Blair could do little else. The burden had risen. There was no getting away from it. But Brown feared such an admission might be fatal. He preferred to equivocate in public on such matters.

They danced awkwardly in relation to tax and spend, like suspicious partners feeling their way towards an as yet unspecified denouement. The bigger difference between them at this stage had more to do with clarity of objectives. Brown was clearer, but because he had allowed his tormented ambition to be the main narrative in media and political circles, few noticed at the time or have since.

The second area over which they differed was welfare reform. This was one of many policies that Blair had spoken of with an upbeat boldness, making much of his intention to implement 'radical reform' without being very precise about what he meant to do. In advance of the 1997 election Blair had talked vaguely about the need to modernize welfare. The term 'modernization' was as conveniently flexible as 'radical' and 'bold'. It could mean more or less anything at all. In terms of detail, Labour had Brown's 'welfare to work' and not much else.

Blair was more excited by the symbolism of radical policies than by the arduous detail of implementation. This was the character trait that drove him inexorably towards Iraq, where boldness was proclaimed and the details left unexamined. Welfare reform was an early template.

In opposition Blair had theatrically told his shadow welfare ministers to 'think the unthinkable', but he did not really want them to do so, rather he wanted to be seen asking them to do so. One of his first acts as Prime Minister was to visit a council estate. In advance the visit was briefed to the media almost as a revolutionary act in itself. To the fury of the political editors who attended the visit and who had advised their bosses in advance that a major story would follow, Blair had nothing much to say.

This did not stop him playing the symbolism card. He made the social security minister Frank Field a privy councillor, when he formed his first government, to show that he was serious about reform. Field had ambitious plans that were also very expensive. Brown was opposed to the proposals on those grounds alone and had already established closer ties with the social security secretary, Harriet Harman, who had been his choice for the top job. Slowly Blair also turned against Field's ideas when he realized they would not reduce the social security budget in the short term.

The unresolved internal debate had several related themes. Could benefits be more effectively targeted or should they have universal application? Should there be a degree of compulsion in getting people back to work, and what form should the punitive dimension take? More generally, what were the best ways of turning a passive welfare culture into a more constructive one?

In spite of the incoherent mess in relation to welfare reform Blair announced a series of 'Welfare Roadshows' to be staged in the early part of 1998. Once more the emphasis was on the glitzy presentation rather than the policies to be implemented. In fact as the almost meaningless Roadshows got under way Field's very green Green Paper was being watered down to the point where it did not say very much at all. For a week before its publication in the spring of 1998, Field had extensive tuition from Alastair Campbell and his main press officer, Martin Sixsmith, on how to answer questions without making any commitments. Later the former BBC correspondent Sixsmith fell out spectacularly with the so-called Downing Street spin machine, but he was an enthusiastic participant for a short time.

As well as announcing the Roadshows, to Brown's fury just before Christmas 1997 Blair declared that he was going to get a grip on welfare policy and chair a special new committee on welfare reform. On the weekend before Christmas he made a speech in his Sedgefield constituency in which he gave the apparently significant announcement of his chairmanship. But once more Blair was concerned to give the impression of decisive leadership rather than having a particularly clear sense of what form the leadership should take. The committee met a few times and agreed on very little before it quietly ceased to function. The silent demise was in marked contrast to the Downing Street-orchestrated fanfare that had accompanied the announcement of its creation.

There were several reasons for the chaos, and they applied more widely to transport, local government, public service reform and Britain's relationship with Europe. Neither Blair nor Brown had agreed in advance what they wanted to achieve or how precisely they would go about it. In particular Blair was much more cautious than his declamatory style suggested.

Brown, although cautious, moodily uncooperative and possessive, had a greater sense of non-theatrical clarity over what was possible and how it could be achieved in relation to welfare reform. When the government's welfare policy was at the height of frenzied disarray, with Harriet Harman and Frank Field refusing to speak to each other at the Department of Social Security, Labour MPs threatening to rebel, and nearly everyone unsure what the government meant by hailing 'radical welfare reforms', Brown gave an uncharacteristically clear interview to me in January 1998. By this point most of his public statements were moodily obtuse, but sometimes he conveyed a clarity that reflected his capacity to focus when he chose to do so.

> First we must ensure there is work for those who are capable of working. My ambition is to move towards full employment, and that is something we can achieve as we move towards the next century.
>
> Second, work must pay. The minimum wage is absolutely crucial to this. The minimum wage is not only right in principle, but makes possible other changes. We are investigating the expansion of the working families tax credit and I think it is possible to do far more with child care. We are also looking at changes to the national insurance system.
>
> Third, those incapable of work: we need to make sure their requirements are met and that will mean increases in public spending to help them ...

Here was Brown warming to his theme, the war on poverty. There were many questions raised and some of the answers remained elusive. As late as 2008 Labour was still publishing welfare reform White Papers. But for an early inexperienced government that was lapsing into chaos behind the scenes, this interview represented the closest anyone had got to coherence. Brown did get near to reaching the technical definition of full employment. He started to use his tax credits to reward work. The minimum wage compensated a little more generously those on very low pay. Gripped always by the need to target resources more effectively, he saw to it that those incapable of work, such as the poorest pensioners, started to receive substantial

increases in income. Sometimes this had disastrous political consequences, such as when the basic state pension was raised by only a few
pence. Brown could be so focused on one element of his project that
he ceased to deploy his erratically alert political antennae at all. But
on the whole he followed the principles outlined in the interview,
although getting all those 'capable' of working to do so was fraught
with political and practical difficulties and impeded also at times by
a lack of will from Brown.

Quite often when Brown had the time and space to think aloud
with Ed Balls and Ed Miliband he would choose to agonize about the
politics of poverty over any other policy area. Could tackling inequality be made a priority without falling into what he feared would be
vote-losing traps in relation to taxation? Was it possible to mobilize a
coalition of broad support to tackle domestic poverty in the way that
there was now wide backing to address global poverty? These questions kept on recurring in discussions with the inner court. Some of
his closest allies reflected at the time that this was the big difference
with Blair. 'Tony never gives a thought to poverty', one of them
observed to me. 'Gordon agonizes about it all the time.'

The superficial origins of Blair's supposedly historic pledge to
abolish child poverty highlighted the degree to which his thoughts
were fleeting at best. The Prime Minister made the striking commitment as part of his Beveridge Lecture delivered in March 1999. Brown
knew nothing about it in advance.

During a period in which there was much talk about the disillusioned core vote, Campbell had warned Blair that the party's traditional supporters and the Labour-supporting *Daily Mirror* were
getting restless with the government. This was mid-term, the period
described by Brown naively as the 'post-euphoria pre-delivery phase'.
It was naive because it implied that delivery was just around the
corner, when it was still miles away.

Campbell told Blair that he needed a good news story from the
speech, not the normal stuff about 'radical welfare reform'. Brown's
closest allies were convinced that Campbell came up with the idea
that Blair should promise to abolish child poverty and briefed it to the

Mirror in order to get a positive front-page story. There had been little advance policy preparation.

The speech had the desired impact. The *Mirror* reported the pledge extensively. Left-of-centre columnists were ecstatic. The pledge got a deafening cheer at every subsequent Labour conference. Blair was typically cunning. He offered no precise definition of child poverty and announced a time span that extended to a period when he would be safely out of power.

Back at the Treasury there was the familiar exhalation of fuming breaths from Brown and his entourage when they heard out of the blue the news about Blair's commitment. Balls and Miliband calmed Brown down by pointing out that the pledge provided cover now for their agenda: whenever Blair complained about the tax credits and other anti-poverty initiatives coming from the Treasury they could cite the need to reach the target of abolishing child poverty.

Brown's mood lightened. He could see too that in a search for a headline Blair had cleared a path for the policies that he had been pursuing in a highly cautious and tentative way. Brown felt more emboldened to weave his elaborate, significant, but erratically administered tax credits into his subsequent budgets. He had a poverty target to meet. Whenever he got the chance he would include a reference to the government's 'historic' pledge to abolish child poverty. He inserted the grand adjective deliberately to annoy Blair. If Blair had paused in advance he would have realized that his pledge provided the green light for more tax credits, a policy over which he was deeply sceptical. But he was poor at making connections, at thinking through how sweeping proclamations might point to a precise policy direction.

The Labour government was criticized with some justification by commentators on the centre left, and later by David Cameron with cunning mischief, for failing to address widening levels of inequality. The criticisms became especially intense when the scale of the bankers' inordinate greed became an overwhelming theme in the recession that began in 2008, although the critics did not explain how a more punitive approach towards the bankers would have financed an effective package to help those at the bottom. In fact Brown's measures did narrow the gap between the low-paid and those on the average wage levels, and poorer pensioners were much better off as a result of his measures.

Schemes such as Sure Start also assisted families on low incomes, offering practical help to parents and their children in a range of ways. When Brown visited Sure Start centres he returned to the Westminster soap opera on an endearing high. 'If we achieve nothing else it would have been worth it for the work some of these centres are doing,' he told friends. For Brown such visits were a vindication of his decision to choose politics as a vocation, unlike his father, who had sought to serve through the Church.

Another momentous row between Blair and Brown in the first term was fluid and chaotic, symptoms of their declining relationship and causes of even deeper mistrust in the future. The eruption related to investment in public services, a consequence of their initial pragmatism over the bigger theme of 'tax and spend'. Typically evasive at different points in the row, Blair and Brown swapped sides several times. Who was in favour of increased spending? Who was against? It was not always easy to tell.

Both Blair and Brown were complacent about the dire position. In 1999 Blair told me that he had been slow to recognize what had been partly a hidden emergency in relation to public services, or at least one that did not capture the imagination as vividly as the 'winter of discontent'.

Blair only became fully aware of the decrepit state of the NHS when some newspapers started to scream about what was going on. The annual bout of winter flu became a major national news story because some hospitals were unable to cope. In itself this was enough to make Blair twitch. One of his most famous lines in the 1997 election was that a vote for Labour would save the NHS. After the first couple of years in power it still needed saving.

The media's influence peaked when the much-respected Labour peer and doctor Robert Winston gave an interview to the *New*

Statesman describing the gruesome experience of his mother at a hospital, in which he argued that Britain's hospitals were in a worse state than those in Poland and the government had to decide whether or not it was willing to invest and reform. His interview was a front-page story in several newspapers, including the *Daily Mail*, which had also separately run a highly effective campaign calling for better pay for nurses.

Brown had noted the stories but was working on an assumption that he had a long-term strategy for increasing public spending on the NHS. He saw no reason to make any immediate intervention in the light of the media frenzy. Although obsessed with the media, he had now also acquired a Treasury mindset, looking towards budgets and pre-budget reports to punctuate and shape the agenda. He became less aware of the need for a government sometimes to respond more quickly, and not only when his next financial statement was due.

With a much wider brief, Blair had retained the mindset of opposition, where both he and Brown felt the urge to respond to the news cycle almost hour by hour. Brown acquired the same mindset again when he became Prime Minister, with disastrous consequences. Two factors drove Blair to announce famously on David Frost's Sunday morning programme in January 1999 that the government would reach the average EU spending on the NHS. One of them related directly to his relationship with Brown. Blair's health adviser, Jonathan Hill, had alerted him quite rightly to the focus Brown was placing on tax credits in the forthcoming budget rather than on more money for the NHS. Such was Blair's fraught relationship with his Chancellor that he decided that he had no choice but to bounce Brown into making a big spending commitment. More immediately, Blair sought a headline that would counter the damaging front pages about the state of hospitals under his government. Growing into an accomplished news manager, he recognized that a commitment to reach the EU average would be a story to transform the debate.

Blair achieved both objectives. Brown had no choice but to start finding the money immediately. The dynamics of the story changed.

Would the Tories support the commitment? With predictable folly they opposed the move.

Equally famously, Brown burst out into one of his most volcanic eruptions, phoning Blair and telling him that he had 'stolen my f——ing budget'. Brown had some cause for anger. It was extraordinary for a prime minister to make a massive spending commitment without consulting his chancellor. Blair had also not given a moment's thought as to where the money would come from. That pressure would bear down at once on Brown. Blair had also acted with a speed that was so excessive that his own staff had not been warned of a policy announcement of mammoth proportions. Jonathan Hill spent the day on the phone to journalists explaining what had happened, but he had only found out through watching the Frost programme.

This was a superficial way to govern, echoing the sudden announcement that child poverty would be abolished. At least that pledge spanned twenty years. The one relating to the NHS demanded immediate action. Brown often declared to his entourage 'Tony never reads the papers', referring to the detailed policy documents that, in contrast, the Chancellor would study with excessive intensity. Such a significant policy shift should have been the product of considerable discussion between the two of them and others, not least over how it would be paid for.

Yet Brown was also culpable. Because he was so protective of his budget plans and so reluctant to discuss even with Blair precisely what he was doing, the supposedly mighty Prime Minister had reason to despair of advance discussion. Blair was also correct in his assessment of the crisis. Even former Conservative health secretaries admitted privately that Blair was right and that the NHS needed an immediate injection of cash.

But what followed highlighted the fluidity of the ideological and tactical dispute between the two. Brown did begin to scale the funding mountain, starting in his following budget, an almost comical document of two halves. The first was a highly technical outline of an expansion of tax credits, and then glued on at the end was the first phase of NHS increases. Any reader could see the joins. The first half was Brown's original budget. The second was Blair's after his Frost interview.

Towards the end of the first term Brown recognized that further improvements to the NHS could only be achieved by a substantial tax rise. There was no other way to raise the money to reach European levels of spending. This daunting recognition was to lead to the boldest move the government made in its thirteen years of power. At that point it was Blair who began to feel uneasy, an inevitable consequence of making a pledge without having thought through the means. But if a tax rise was necessary – and Blair was far from sure it was necessary – that would be a matter for the second term once the election was safely out of the way.

Bizarrely there was one policy area over which there was almost open admission of disagreement, and yet both of them were in almost the same position. This was the question of relations with the Liberal Democrats, and indeed of the way that leaders related to their own party.

Blair's alliance with the leader of the Liberal Democrats, Paddy Ashdown, was forged in opposition but had continued in power. Ashdown's diaries show that after the 1997 election Blair saw more of him in one-to-one sessions than he did most of his cabinet ministers. The two of them were drawn together by a mutual fascination and some common interests, a prelude to Cameron and Clegg. Because of his fascination with Blair Cameron had been an avid read of Ashdown's diaries, where the Labour leader is the dominant character.

Ashdown was one of those political leaders whom Blair genuinely admired. I have noted already that when Blair admired someone he displayed a generosity of spirit that is rare at the top of politics, openly acknowledging their strengths and sometimes forming an excessive admiration. In Ashdown he quickly recognized a fellow energetic leader with a capacity to think beyond orthodox boundaries. It was Ashdown who had first raised the possibility of a political realignment in a courageous speech delivered shortly after the 1992 election, long before Blair came to lead the Labour party. On a much smaller canvas, Ashdown was willing to take on and challenge his party, parts of which seemed to prefer the purity of isolated opposition to the opportunity of working in government.

Some experienced onlookers were convinced that the gullible Ashdown was brilliantly manipulated by Blair. The former minister Gerald Kaufman noted with glee that Ashdown had been taken for the 'biggest ride in British politics for a very long time'. Some senior Liberal Democrats agreed with this assessment. But the reality was more complex. After Labour's series of election defeats in the 1980s and 1990s Blair had little faith in his party as an electoral force on its own, even after the 1997 victory. Influenced heavily by Roy Jenkins, Blair made several speeches in opposition about how the split on the centre left between Labour and the Liberal Democrats had allowed the Tories to dominate the twentieth century.

Blair felt no great tribal attachment to Labour. He insisted passionately in private 'I am not a Tory', but he never followed up this proclamation with 'I am Labour.' He continued to contemplate after 1997 some sort of arrangement with the Liberal Democrats. His first move was to establish a cabinet committee to review constitutional reform that included Liberal Democrats. William Hague, the Tory party's youthful leader, watched with awestruck horror. He told me at the time that he feared Blair had a plan to destroy the Conservative party and how he felt an immense sense of relief when the Labour leader ditched his promise to hold a referendum on electoral reform. Hague became an enthusiastic participant in the negotiations with the Liberal Democrats in the immediate aftermath of the 2010 election, relishing the drama being played out in reverse.

In one of their private discussions Blair told Brown of his plans for a cabinet committee with the Liberal Democrats. Brown said he would have nothing to do with it. 'You'll never guess what he is going to do now,' Brown despairingly told his court in the Treasury. 'He's setting up a cabinet committee with Ashdown.' Once more it was Balls who calmed Brown down, insisting that the move would not go anywhere and that John Prescott would be even more apoplectic.

Blair was acting more or less on his own, leading to a widespread assumption that he was the promiscuous player and Brown the lost leader of his tribe. But in this case the boundaries were not so neatly defined. Even at the height of his relationship with Ashdown, Blair was an opponent of electoral reform for the Commons. He once admitted it accidentally during an interview with me in July 1995 when negotiations with Ashdown were at a delicate phase – a rare moment when Blair's mask slipped slightly in public. Asked whether he was against proportional representation he admitted fleetingly that he was.

Ashdown's diaries also show that Blair was fairly open with the Liberal Democrat leader about his longer-term intentions. He sought a merger and not a partnership with the third party. A few years later Blair told me that he thought it would have been 'quixotic' to have formed any coalition in 1997 in the light of the landslide, but he had given it serious consideration.

Brown's ambiguities were less widely discussed because it was more straightforward and arguably in his short-term advantage to place him in the tribal box. But he was as obsessed as Blair about pitching a big tent of support and therefore wooed the non-Labour media – which was most of the press – with as much intensity as Blair.

He was careful to build up rapport with business leaders and could be careless in his dealings with trade union leaders. Contrary to the mythology that he cultivated the trade unions, he could be thoughtlessly rude when meeting them. John Edmonds, the leader of the GMB, declared angrily during the early years of the Labour government that Blair was more openly attentive during their meetings compared with the ostentatiously dismissive Brown. The Chancellor was also candid with them in his opposition to big pay rises in the public sector. He was more direct with the unions, and not always wooing them as his critics suggested.

Brown was also beginning to realize that political parties were in decline and that activism was taking new forms, mainly in the form of single-issue pressure groups. These thoughts were to develop in significant ways during Labour's second and third terms. Brown was as tribal as his reputation suggested. Blair was not quite as politically promiscuous as he was seen at the time of his leadership.

In these early years the government was more popular than any previous administration since polling began. Yet on many fronts it lacked direction and purpose, surviving on the good will of a still excited electorate and media, although both were beginning to have their doubts.

The first term was one of the most evasively enigmatic in recent political history. On one level the list of achievements was striking and substantial. Blair presided over a constitutional revolution. Scotland acquired a parliament, Wales an assembly and London a mayor. At first Blair struggled to adapt to his own policies as he sought unsuccessfully to impose Labour candidates in London and Wales. But he failed in his attempts and the new settlement started to have profound policy consequences, a congestion charge in London and in Scotland an entirely different approach to the funding of universities and social care. Devolution played its part in the Northern Ireland peace process. An assembly in Belfast was part of a pattern and not an anomaly. Blair's role in the peace process was heroic in terms of energy, focus and preparation before coming into office in 1997. He and David Blunkett, his education secretary, began a relentless assault on low standards in some schools. 'Education, education, education' Blair had declared were his three priorities. But the follow-up sound bite that his concern was 'standards not structures' revealed the limits of his ambition. To some extent the structures inevitably determined the standards.

Blair also began his most sustained revolution, in communicating with voters. His presence was around the clock, compared with the occasional glimpses voters had caught of John Major and Margaret Thatcher. Blair set the tone for his entire premiership when on her death he described Princess Diana as 'the people's princess'. He managed to speak for Britain or an important part of it. He tried to do so repeatedly. Before long he was holding regular prime-ministerial press conferences and appearing on television and radio programmes acting almost as a commentator on his own government.

Most of Blair's initiatives, although important and challenging, could have been instigated by a leader from any part of the political spectrum, which is why some voters on the centre left became disillusioned with the government fairly quickly. They blamed Brown as much as Blair, but Brown was embarking on an economic plan that had distinct ambition, big increases in public spending and redistribution through a range of credits and the minimum wage, and targeted expenditure on poorer areas, and gradually his ambition took shape.

Patience was required and voters are impatient, sometimes with good cause. They had put up with poor public services for a long time, and yet in the first term New Labour spent relatively less than John Major.

There are several lessons from a period in which the government had acres of political space and wasted some of it. Government based on the tight control of two individuals can be as chaotic as when there is a wider accountability and a greater number of people and institutions involved. Blair and Brown had assumed that if they weakened all the unpredictable bodies capable of challenging leaders they would have a quieter life at the top, after all the noise in the 1970s and 1980s. They became the noisy alternative.

In opposition, if policy decisions are avoided they become harder to make in government. Blair and Brown had not decided in advance what they wanted to do in relation to the level of public spending, welfare reform and the Euro. Not surprisingly they still were not sure when they faced the draining complexities of power.

Another key lesson is that a new government often enjoys almost indiscriminate good will from the media and the electorate. The benevolent context means that if the government makes mistakes it will get away with them. The early phase is when a government has the space to take risks. Blair and Brown were careful not to take too many, kicking the Euro and electoral reform into the long grass. Blair proclaimed his radicalism. Brown hailed his prudence. Blair was being cautious. Brown was being stealthily bold. Most of the time the media wanted to celebrate the mesmerizing honeymoon. Whatever happened, New Labour got the thumbs up. The tables changed within a few years.

FIVE

Second Term

In September 2001, a few days before the attacks in New York and Washington, I spoke separately to Tony Blair and Gordon Brown. Labour had just won another landslide majority and were now trusted with power. The Conservatives had lapsed into further disarray with another leadership contest that looked likely to elect Iain Duncan Smith rather than the more popular Ken Clarke or Michael Portillo. This was therefore an extremely rare period in which the government had even more political space, at least as much as Margaret Thatcher enjoyed in 1983 when she won a second election victory.

When I saw him in the garden of Number Ten Blair outlined his priorities for the second term. He argued that they had done the heavy lifting as far as the level of public spending was concerned and now the priority was reform of public services. Already he was excited by the idea of giving users more 'choice'. He said Europe would be a priority and hinted strongly that he wanted to take Britain into the Euro during the second term. At the same time he was determined to show that he could work closely with a Republican President in the US after his strong relationship with President Clinton. President Bush had begun his term earlier in the year and members of his administration were being wooed by leading Conservatives in Britain. He made it clear that he would give the Tories no space in the special relationship and suggested that it was essential to be unequivocally pro-American in order to win the argument about Europe in a British referendum.

Brown's view of the second term was different. Concerning public services he argued that investment and reform must go together. He acknowledged there was still an issue about the level of funding for the NHS that had to be addressed. Cautiously he hinted that a tax rise might be necessary in order to pay for higher levels of investment. He suggested that improvements to the public services should be a defining theme for the second term and hinted more strongly that this meant the Euro question could not be resolved in this term. It was a mammoth issue, with too many political and economic risks attached, not least when the government would have to take some big decisions in relation to public services.

Brown was wary of the debate about 'choice' in public services. He made clear he supported the principle of 'choice' – who could be against it? he asked – and joked that the debate over choice reminded him of a poster he had seen for a candidate in an election in the US. The candidate's slogan was 'Choose Freedom', implying that his opponents were 'against freedom'. Again who could be against freedom? But Brown sought more clarity. Did choice mean that suddenly there would be a surplus of classrooms and good schools? Similarly would there be a surplus of hospitals with spare beds enabling patients to choose? He was worried about raising expectations that could not be met at a point when the government was spending less on public services than most equivalent countries in Europe and had been spending less for decades. There was a lot of catching up to do. He was also concerned that the media, while theoretically in favour of 'choice', would not in reality support empty classrooms and hospital wards, the surplus required for genuine choice.

Blair was charming, conversational, solicitous and witty. Brown delivered more of a monologue. Virtually everything that Brown described as a priority was implemented. Virtually everything that Blair had spoken of did not happen as he had envisaged. Yet Blair was Prime Minister and Brown the increasingly impatient Chancellor.

Brown revived his famous dividing lines with the Conservatives in the 2001 election. This time they were a little more politically courageous compared with 1997. They dared to focus on the importance of public spending and the threat of cuts from the Conservatives. In 1997

Labour had pledged to stick to the same spending plans as the previous Tory government. Now Brown highlighted the substantial gap between Labour's spending aspirations and those of the Conservatives. This marked quite a significant leap. In interviews during the campaign Brown repeatedly spoke of the need for 'sustained investment in public services' and contrasted this pledge with the allegation that the Conservatives would cut £20 billion, with disastrous consequences for schools and hospitals. He claimed the government could make commitments to spend more because he had laid 'the foundation of economic strength' by taking tough decisions in the first term. The message of competence was still there, but laced now with a hint of more principled conviction about the value of a government investing to improve services.

Soon Brown's dividing lines became the subject of internal derision. 'We can't win with dividing lines,' the ultra-Blairites Alan Milburn and Steve Byers argued persistently, partly because increasingly they saw no divide with the Conservatives. But the divisions were astutely posed and with a hint of daring.

The Conservatives under the leadership of the youthfully inexperienced William Hague called for tax and spending cuts, but neither had been credibly costed and both were the source of obvious tensions with the shadow chancellor, Michael Portillo. Later Hague was to admit that his campaign was based on a desperate need to firm up his party's core vote out of fear that the outcome of the election could have been even worse. The flaky policies were not based on an assumption that he would have to implement them.

The weakness of the Conservatives cleared a path for Brown. He was able to compare Labour's spending plans with their proposed cuts and make them appear to be boldly ambitious. Yet while this was a big step compared with the timidity of 1997, the publicly declared ambitions remained cautious. Compare Brown's spending aspirations with the sustained expenditure on health, education and transport in most other European countries and they would not have looked so courageous. Instead he played the trick of making comparisons with the Conservatives' misjudged and stingy spending calculations.

Brown and his team were wholly aware of this. In effect they had two different plans, the public and the private. They knew that the NHS needed a massive injection of spending if it was to become a reliable modern service. Investment had trailed demand by such a wide gap and for so long a time that every element of the service, from the availability of a GP to the chance of having an operation within civilized waiting times, was being called into question.

The way Brown and his team went about winning the case for a tax rise in order to pay for higher levels of spending on the NHS was a rare act of progressive politics bravely and tenaciously implemented. Before the election Brown had approached the former Director General of the CBI, Adair Turner, and Derek Wanless, the former Chief Executive of NatWest Bank, to see whether either of them would head a review on NHS funding. Turner equivocated. Wanless was keen, and for a time became Brown's favourite banker. Brown had a soft spot for bankers – one that was to prove disastrous as events turned out. But at the start of the century his counter-intuitive close association with the most senior bankers in the land provided him with a layer of protective clothing as he started to become a little more politically daring.

Brown, Ed Balls and Ed Miliband made clear to Wanless, as they had done to the more sceptical Turner, that they wanted the NHS to remain free at the point of use and were critical of alternative models for financing such a big project. By the time of the 2001 election Brown knew that he had run out of options for taxing stealthily and would probably have to increase national insurance contributions in order to pay for improvements in the NHS. He also knew that it would be disastrous to make such a case in the middle of an election campaign, but he was determined that Blair should not rule out such increases. That would have been a disaster too, blowing apart the major plan that he hoped would define the second term.

Brown behaved abysmally as usual during the election campaign, once more liaising only with his advisers and keeping Blair's team at arm's length. A set of desks in the open-plan office became a formal divide between the Brownites working at one end and the

Blairites at the other. Alastair Campbell's deputy Lance Price was the chief victim of the Berlin Wall divide, kept out of the loop, sent by the Brownites to negotiate with the BBC on fruitless missions. Price was convinced they sent him on the excursions to get him out of the office, like bullies excluding the weak kid from the playground game. Brown and his entourage could not deal with anyone closely identified with Blair.

The only moment of dangerous tension, as distinct from manageable tension, was when the minister, Patricia Hewitt, appeared to rule out national insurance increases in an interview. Briefly the *Sun* newspaper urged Blair to follow suit and he discussed with Brown whether or not he should do so. Brown was adamant that he should not and that the two of them had to tough it out. Blair agreed and newspapers, with no enthusiasm for the Tories and certain of the outcome, did not bother pursuing the cause for very long. Neither did the Conservatives, who for once would have been on to something if they had warned of the coming rises. But once the election was over there was another distinct division in the attitudes of Blair and Brown. We know from one of Blair's senior advisers, Peter Hyman, that the Prime Minister was far too complacent about the level of public spending once the election had been won.

In September 2001 Hyman attended a day-long meeting at Chequers in which he put the case for higher investment in public services, especially education. In another of the most revealing books about Blair's period in power, *1 Out of 10: From Downing Street Vision to Classroom Reality*, Hyman wrote of the familiar fears expressed in the meeting at Chequers: Brown wanted to focus more on tax credits in order to meet the now famous pledge to abolish child poverty.

But Hyman argued at the gathering that there was a case for investing more in public services and tackling child poverty through more generous tax credits: both were necessary. Hyman was an interesting figure, loyal to Blair, wary of Brown, and yet his politics at least at this crucial point were closer to Brown's. Blair's decency and Brown's appalling rudeness made him a Blairite.

Hyman went on to highlight the lack of investment compared with other European countries before noting: 'Tony had convinced himself that spending was broadly on the right lines and was now confronted by the fact that it wasn't.' It took a long time for Blair to accept that it was impossible to have European levels of public services while seeking to cut taxes as a rule, and Blair was not alone in his wariness. Brown was plotting his tax increase, but emotionally he was as resistant as his old friend. He knew there was no alternative route that was fair and efficient, but also feared that by making the case for a tax increase he might lose Labour the next election.

Brown's worries were most intense during the week of the Labour conference in Brighton in 2001. The event and the politics of the tax rise were overshadowed by the terrorist attacks on 11 September. Blair's messianic response to the attacks in the US had transformed him into a global superstar and had appeared to electrify a second term that had seemed to lack energy and purpose. In turn this had led to another set of parochial reports that Brown's leadership ambitions had become a victim of Osama Bin Laden – parochialism with a whiff of truth.

Brown's speech on the Monday of the Brighton conference made headlines largely because of his pledge to freeze UK-based assets that were linked to the Taliban regime in Afghanistan and promises that further tough sanctions would follow. He offered a relatively marginal slogan, arguing there would be 'No safe hiding place for terrorist funds ...' It was a step that placed him only at the peripheral of the international stage.

The rest of Brown's conference speech was much more interesting. The focus as ever was on the need for stability and prudence. Yet there was a more urgent tone in the section on public services once he had reassured the wider audience, and in particular the powerful newspapers sceptical of public spending increases, that he was dancing still with Prudence. In an almost throwaway line delivered with a muffled breathlessness Brown declared that he would 'build public support for the budget decisions now to release further resources for tackling poverty and for public services'.

Quilted by layers of reassurance, these few words gave a hint at Brown's strategy. He would seek to build a coalition of support 'to release further resources'. Tentatively it was the first public sign that he was gearing up to introduce a significant tax increase, a dramatic leap from the stifling caution that had shaped New Labour's approach to 'tax and spend'. The objective was spelt out as well. The resources would be spent on poverty and public services.

Immediately after the speech Ed Balls gave his traditional briefing to political journalists. For Balls these were always daunting sessions, knowing that one word out of place in front of the prowling pack could cause mayhem. On this occasion he was especially nervous. Surrounded by political journalists the supposedly arrogant Balls's hands shook with nerves and his face reddened as he spoke. He knew how big this was for Brown, the New Labour project and the future of the government as a whole. He and Ed Miliband were even more determined than Brown to increase funding for the NHS through a tax rise. He was also convinced, as was Brown, of the need to prepare the ground painstakingly. At the briefing therefore Balls made clear that the government did plan to reach the EU average spending levels on health and that the economic forecasts suggested there was a gap in the necessary funding. He refused to rule out an increase in national insurance to pay for it.

On the basis of the briefing the next day's newspapers predicted that Brown was preparing to increase taxes. Brown read the newspapers with even greater intensity than usual on the morning after this particular conference speech, neurotically hungry for their verdicts, seeking approbation and fearing negative verdicts. When he saw the headlines on the Tuesday morning with tax increases as the main message he panicked. At a meeting with close confidants including Balls and Miliband he claimed perversely that he had hoped the main media attention would be on his message of economic stability. He said that he did not want to be associated with tax rises for the rest of the parliament and that it could destroy his reputation as a New Labour chancellor. He exclaimed: 'Tony is wondering what is going on.' Blair and Brown were briefly reunited, the two architects of New

Labour breathing still against the backdrop of Labour's defeat in 1992. But Balls and Miliband were resolute, insisting that the strategy was in place and it was not one that they could move away from in the face of a flurry of headlines that were not in most cases especially negative.

Brown calmed down as media attention moved on to Blair's speech that was delivered on the Tuesday afternoon amidst the continuing fallout of 11 September. During the address, self-absorbed, almost apocalyptic in tone and ambition, Blair implied that Britain would intervene in any global trouble spot now that the 'kaleidoscope had been shaken'. The spell-binding oratory, conveying an impractical message given the limits of Britain's resources, wiped off any further speculation about tax for the time being. Under different circumstances the possibility of a tax rise would have been the main story to surface from the party conference, but Brown had cover as media attention was understandably diverted.

Brown's nervy response to the newspaper coverage of Blair's speech highlighted a distinctive characteristic and a weak one. Brown was strategically bold and tactically cautious. Blair was often the opposite. Every day Blair would paint pictures in big, bold colours, but sometimes the end result did not amount to very much. Brown became alarmed at any vivid definition day by day, but sometimes had radical objectives, an overt tax rise being one of them. The calmer resilience of the two Eds showed that although they were much less exposed than the Chancellor they could be steely too, and capable occasionally of challenging their intimidating boss.

The introduction of the tax rise was a near-perfect piece of political choreography. The terms of the Wanless review set up shortly before the 2005 election were defined in such a way as to hint at the outcome. Brown, Balls and Miliband asked the former banker first to examine the technological, demographic and medical trends over the next two decades that would affect the health service in the UK as a whole. Not surprisingly Wanless concluded that demand and costs were going to soar.

Next Wanless was asked to identify the key factors that would determine the financial and other resources required to ensure that the NHS could provide a publicly funded, comprehensive, high-quality service available on the basis of clinical need and not ability to pay. There were limited options for Wanless before he set about his task, but Brown had cut through the messy shapeless debate about the NHS and posed the two key questions: What would happen to demand and how did the government seek to meet it?

The sequence was as carefully thought through as the structure of the Wanless investigation. After the hints of tax rises at the party conference, Brown proceeded to unveil his pre-budget report in November. An interim report from Wanless was at the centre of the event. The joy of an interim report was that public opinion could be tested and to some extent led on this most sensitive of issues before a final decision was announced at the following budget. In fact the report had little that was 'interim' about it. The findings were definitive, but projected in the context of the need for a debate. In what Brown regarded as the most nerve-racking statement of his political career he tentatively put the case for a tax rise for the first time to pay for increased resources.

Brown spoke about the importance of reform in the NHS before announcing a further immediate increase in spending, 7 per cent in real terms. Then he hid behind the protective cloak of Wanless as he marched nervously onto the terrain of 'tax and spend' in ways that he had avoided since becoming shadow chancellor in 1992:

He (Wanless) has looked at other European and international methods of funding and finds all health systems facing rising pressures. In systems which rely on private medical insurance he concludes that compared to the NHS there is less cost control, more uneven coverage and many left out.

And in systems which rely predominantly on social insurance he has found excessive administrative overheads, insufficient incentives for cost control and for example in France large costs for employers and for employees who pay charges for every GP and hospital visit, even after their social insurance premiums.

Mr Wanless' interim report states: 'My conclusion is that there is no evidence that any alternative financing method to the UK's would deliver a given quality of healthcare at a lower cost to the economy. Indeed other systems seem likely to prove more costly. Nor do alternative balances of funding appear to offer scope to increase equity.'

So having examined whether a publicly funded NHS is itself a pressure on costs and thus whether it is sustainable, Mr Wanless' view is that the principle of the NHS publicly funded through taxation, available on the basis of clinical need and not ability to pay remains both the fairest and most efficient system for this country.

Brown/Wanless had therefore concluded that the same method of funding was the fairest and most efficient. This was an important first conclusion. Within Number Ten there were a few influential advisers advocating a switch to different forms of funding. Blair was more agnostic, but the counter-intuitive advocacy of a senior banker gave Brown important cover. It was not easy to brief that Brown was behaving like a backward-looking Old Labour figure when the former chief executive of NatWest was being quoted as a godlike source of wisdom. With an apparent innocence Brown went on to note:

Mr Wanless has also examined in detail the cost pressures facing services for the future ... Mr Wanless emphasizes in particular a problem that goes back to the foundation of the NHS – over decades – a history of under-investment over 50 years and a long-term lack of capacity. And comparing Britain to other European countries, such as France and Germany, his figures show a decisive difference in the area of finances ... I believe that as we plan to make out budget and spending decisions next year and to fulfil all our commitments to economic prosperity and social justice it will be right to devote a significantly higher share of national income to the NHS.

Finally Brown spoke of the symbolism of the decision and what it might portend for British politics:

The way we make these decisions – whether we can forge a new consensus across parties and across Britain – will determine not only the long-term future of the health service but the character of our country. I believe out of this debate an enduring national consensus can be built around the two central conclusions at the heart of Mr Wanless' first report: that a publicly funded National Health Service will need significantly greater capacity and significantly more long-term investment.

That final flourish was subtle politics and a moment of history, the only point when Labour made a case for a tax rise explicitly to improve a public service. Still it was 'Mr Wanless' putting the case and not Gordon Brown. There was the prospect of a national debate but Brown had already reached a conclusion. There was also the hope of an enduring national consensus over an issue that had marked the main divide between the parties for decades. In other words Brown was indicating discreetly a hope that the statement marked a massive leap towards a more social democratic settlement in which the value of investment in public services was widely recognized.

Brown had launched a debate, via 'Mr Wanless', pointing to its conclusion but without leaving his fingerprints over anything, so that if the public and the mighty media found it all unacceptable there was still, just, a way back from what some in the government feared would be an electoral abyss.

Immediately the tensions within New Labour erupted. As part of the 'debate' Peter Mandelson argued against a tax increase and urged that the social insurance model should be looked at. Some ultra-Blairite ministers also indicated privately that they were worried about the tax increase without offering a firmly worked-through alternative.

They were not the only ones who were worried. Brown was panicking again, fearing that the strategy could fall apart, although he was less visibly in a state than he was after his conference speech.

The other key figure was Blair. In their endless discussions since the 2001 election Brown had outlined his strategy and thought he had got

Blair's support. But by the autumn of 2001, such was the level of mutual paranoia and mistrust, Brown was not sure how Blair would respond publicly to the pre-budget report. At first Number Ten briefed evasively that it welcomed the debate. Would Blair sit on the fence publicly for months, keeping all options open? Brown could not tell.

On this occasion he had no cause for alarm. Blair realized that equivocation would not be credible. It was he who had pledged that the level of NHS spending should rise to the European average, and now was no time to prevaricate. On the Friday of the same week of the pre-budget report he gave an interview to me on a flight back from Dublin in which he declared his full support for the tax rise. In doing so he also displayed considerable political courage, as he knew he was uttering words that risked the disapproval of the newspapers he courted so fervently, and possibly the middle-England voters that he nurtured more assiduously than any other part of the New Labour coalition. In the interview Blair made the argument with forensic precision. It was the only time during his prime-ministerial career that he made the case for a tax increase openly and expansively in public:

> There are three questions we need to address. First, do we agree that health care is underfunded? If we agree that we need to invest more the second question is what is the best way of raising resources: do we pay it through general taxation, do we pay it through specific taxation, in other words social insurance which is a tax on employers and employees, or do we make people pay direct in a private health service?

He provided an unequivocal answer. 'We believe that the best way to do it is through general taxation.' Note that he also addressed the euphemism of 'social insurance' by describing it as a form of specific taxation, not as a painless alternative.

Blair also placed emphasis on reform of the NHS, one that hinted at the explosive eruptions to come with Brown, but the politics of the tax increase was one of the last occasions in which the two of them worked together reasonably smoothly.

Over the next few months in the approach to the budget Brown was even more energized than usual. This was partly due to the fact that for the first time since 1992 he had loosened the political strait-jacket. He was working on a set of policies that were more obviously social democratic than at any point since he became responsible for economic policy, an experience that was both highly charged and stimulating. His meetings with Blair during this period were less explosive than they had been because the two of them were largely in agreement and Blair's mind was on international affairs, the aftermath of the war in Afghanistan and the early build-up to the conflict in Iraq.

In the prelude to the budget Blair questioned only whether a 1 per cent rise in national insurance contributions was too transparent, the precise opposite of Brown's normal more stealthy approach. He asked Brown whether it might be possible to spread the burden in a range of smaller tax increases rather than a single clear hit on incomes of earners and businesses. But Brown was insistent that all other routes were too cumbersome or had been tried before, and Blair accepted the case. There were, though, tensions on the eve of the budget. On the night before, I bumped into a senior figure in Number Ten who told me that he thought the budget would lose Labour the next election, a sign of how nervy New Labour was even at the height of its supposed ascendancy, even when faced by a demoralized Conservative party under the leadership of the decent but hopeless Iain Duncan Smith.

They worried too much. Brown's budget was the most powerful and clearly thought through in his decade at the Treasury. His tax credits were extended generously but in the context of making work pay. There was additional child-care help for lone parents and for those who were disabled who managed to find work. The working family tax credit was expanded. He deployed his favourite theme of investing in the potential of every child irrespective of background before moving on to the NHS. Once more he insisted and meant genuinely that reform and investment must be combined. Indeed he stated emphatically that a 'precondition of new resources' was reform. He spelled out new financial incentives for hospital performance and freedoms for the high-performing hospitals.

More explicitly than before he made clear that there was 'no free way of increasing NHS resources' and that he had 'a duty to spell out what we need to pay as a nation', pledging a 43 per cent rise in health spending over five years to be paid for partly by the increase in national insurance contributions. For once a British politician was making the case for investment in public services, common in most of Europe, but a novelty in Britain.

What followed was extraordinary. The voters responded positively. A poll in the *Financial Times* prompted the headline 'Best Budget for 25 Years'. The survey found that 65 per cent thought the budget good for the country as a whole and that Brown was more popular than Blair. Another poll for the *Sunday Telegraph* suggested that 76 per cent approved, including a majority of Tory voters.

With such stunning vindication Brown and his small entourage felt a degree of satisfaction that they had never dared to feel before or since. Close allies suggested that in that budget Brown's authentic voice finally came through and it had been prepared with such intense care that voters were ready to give it their approval. Brown told Balls and Miliband that here was a chance for social democratic values to prevail with widespread support, an early expression of a progressive consensus.

The budget of 2002 marked a high point for Brown and his team. He had been responsible for Labour's economic policy for more than ten years and had finally reached a point when he could make the case openly for investment and redistribution as he had always hoped to do. The economy was booming. Tax revenues were pouring in. He had delivered a social democratic programme that appeared to be popular. This was his peak. There were to be some other highs in the coming years but they were to be more precariously based than this. There was no more creative policy making on this scale in his final traumatic years as Chancellor and in the panic-stricken prime-ministerial phase. From the 2003 budget on, too much energy was spent on his policy and leadership battles with Blair and on his desperate desire to prove that he could meet the demands of being a Prime Minister.

The government's follow-up to the budget was a disaster from which it never recovered. Brown described the sequel privately as 'a tragedy'. New Labour had reached a turning point and chose not to turn. The progressive consensus assembled in support of the budget was blown apart before it had time to form properly.

In spite of the polls Blair was uneasy about the tax rise. He had given several interviews expressing the view that taxes would fall, including the one for the *Independent* when he argued passively 'that is the way the world is going'. He regarded it as a matter of urgency that the NHS was radically reformed or seen to be reformed partly in order to justify the tax rise. The clash over reform between Blair and Brown was titanic and destructive. Both of them were making complex calculations as they established their conflicting positions.

At this stage in his leadership Blair was becoming more evangelical and crusading, a style of leadership to which he was always prone but which had been reinforced by his growing stature on the international stage. Arm in arm with President Bush he was being hailed in much of the media and the Conservative party for making bold leaps. He wanted to do the same in Britain. For Blair 'boldness' was almost becoming an end itself, another apolitical expression of intent.

He was especially evangelical about the reform of public services. As Iraq started to go disastrously wrong Blair became counter-intuitively more self-confident and determined. Once he had taken his soaring popularity as vindication for what he stood for. Now he regarded unpopularity as a form of vindication too: 'If you take the tough decisions you are bound to be unpopular,' he repeated regularly, without admitting that he had hoped the decisions would be popular.

In relation to public service reform his version of being radical and bold placed him close to the position of the Conservative party and much of the media. In so far as he had a clear and coherent programme, Blair became an evangelist for choice and diversity in public services.

He wanted a growing role for the private sector and for some local providers to be free of virtually all central control. In theory there was a strong case for such a change given the conservative complacency that infected many public service providers, the poor productivity. The devil was in the detail.

Blair was less interested in precisely how the changes would be brought about than the positioning and the well-meant objectives. He was genuinely passionate about improving public services. Conveniently the crusade placed Blair against some on the centre left of the Labour party, a dividing line he felt most at ease with. On his side of the line were many newspaper columnists and senior Tories who whispered their admiration for the Prime Minister, praise that Blair greatly valued. He was much more uneasy when hailed by his own side. Cleverly Blair argued that anyone who questioned his direction was 'anti-reform', a line again that much of the media accepted, another apolitical term.

This was absurd. There was not solely one route and no other to bring about necessary change, but the divide was tactically brilliant. The crusading Blair was 'pro-reform'. Anyone who resisted was a dinosaur.

Part of his determination to press on with a strident urgency was connected inevitably with his now wholly destructive relationship with Brown. Brown wanted his job. Blair needed reasons why he should stay on. A domestic agenda threatened by an 'anti-reform' successor was the perfect narrative.

What made the situation more complex was that Blair's impatience with the public services was understandable. They were inefficient. There was no such thing as a public ethos, a phrase that bestowed on the public sector a sense of nobility that it did not deserve. It was also the case that the government's early attempts to improve performance through targets and highly centralized initiatives had not always worked or had produced perverse outcomes. Blair demanded that his ministers come up with 'radical' proposals, partly out of an imprecise desire to be a reforming prime minister, but also because of a genuine desire to lift the quality of public services in a period when at last a government was investing huge sums of money. Alan Milburn, his Health Secretary at the time, was especially obliging. Milburn leapt from despair at the effectiveness of top-down targets to a desire to make the best-performing hospitals free of any national control. Milburn wanted them to spend, borrow and perform more or less as they wished, leaving patients to decide whether they were any good by choosing to go to them or somewhere else.

Blair was excited by this vision. It ticked so many of his boxes. Patients would have 'choice'. Hospitals would be free to innovate. The government would keep out of it. Parts of his party would be annoyed. He would show that the higher spending and in particular the tax rise was being accompanied by reform. More precisely, he was keen to introduce what would become known as foundation hospitals.

Brown was also battling for real causes and motivated by genuine conviction. He had a clearer sense of the complexities and consequences of the simplistic debate about 'choice' in public services. Ultra-Blairites argued that he was against 'choice', again an absurd and vacuous proposition.

Brown's concerns were partly those that any chancellor would have. In order for choice to be genuine there would have to be a surplus of good hospitals and schools. In giving some hospitals the right to borrow the government was taking on extra financial risks, or accepting the possibility that a hospital could go bankrupt and close, which would be politically disastrous and expensive. In one of their rows on the issue Brown pointed out to Blair that he had put his neck on the line arguing for a tax increase and now the government was going to allow some hospitals to behave more or less as they wished. He was accountable for the tax rise and yet some hospitals would be allowed to go bankrupt.

Brown was also convinced that Milburn saw foundation hospitals as only the start of a process that would end with patients being able to use vouchers in the private sector, topped up by their own income, a policy that became part of the Conservatives' 2005 manifesto.

For Brown the Blair/Milburn approach was catastrophic for several reasons. Just as the government had won a public argument for funding the NHS, Brown despaired that Blair and Milburn were following policies that would lead to the break-up of the institution. At the very least the government's message was confused when it should have been very clear. Brown's concern applied to the negotiations with the GPs as well. Milburn and then his successor, John Reid, were pressing for GPs to sign new contracts that committed them to stay within the NHS. As they were doing so Brown feared that Milburn was sending out the contradictory message that he wanted to break up the NHS.

Blair and Milburn were convinced that their ideas were the least that was necessary to lift the performance of hospitals, but Brown's concerns were justified. At a point when the government had the opportunity to focus on a well-funded modern NHS it chose instead to have a row over what might have become a two-tier service, with an expansion of the private sector partly subsidized by the taxpayer and the struggling hospitals lapsing into a disastrous decline as some of the successful ones flourished further.

Brown favoured what Ed Balls has called managed choice, still a significant reform, but billed in the surreal debate as 'anti-reform'. Instead of an anarchic free-for-all they wanted an audit on every penny spent to ensure that the new money was spent effectively. They were not opposed to the use of private providers where it could be proved that this was better value for money. They were relaxed about choice, as long as patients recognized that there were bound to be limits.

Brown was more depressed politically during this period than at any point since he realized he was not going to be leader of the Labour party in 1994. Repeatedly he said to the entourage: 'They are following Tory policies.' He was miserable too because his resistance to some of the changes was portrayed in much of the media as being 'Old Labour' and entirely to do with his ambitions to lead the Labour party. In fact he was fighting furiously in spite of his leadership ambitions. He knew he was alienating a significant section of the cabinet, the parliamentary Labour party and the media in taking a stand against the proposals. This would make a leadership contest harder to win rather than easier. He was also driven demented by the accusation that he was cautiously backward-looking when he, rather than Blair and his disciples, had taken the riskiest of rides transforming Labour's economic policy.

With Blair increasingly diverted by the build-up to war in Iraq, Brown decided to take his argument into the open, or almost to do so. Late at night and early in the morning he sat at his computer typing furiously a speech on the role of markets, where they worked and where they did not.

The speech was an important moment in Brown's career, a personal turning point. His basic strategic view was that Britain could be moved a little towards the centre left by policies, but that the public arguments that accompanied the policies should be disguised in opaque, unthreatening language, phrases that few would disagree with. Who could be against acting on behalf of the 'many and not the few' or the implementation of the 'people's priorities'? Now Brown felt so strongly that he was going to go public on the row that had split New Labour into two.

The result was the most significant speech Brown delivered either as Chancellor or as Prime Minister. In the spring of 2003 it took the form of a lecture to the Social Market Foundation, subsequently published as a pamphlet. In it he sought to address themes that had not been considered or debated within New Labour, the complex relationship between governments and markets, when markets work in the public interest and when they do not. Brown argued that there were two central questions that New Labour needed to answer as it sought to renew itself (no doubt he thought under his leadership). Where should markets have an enhanced role? Where was the market failure? Note the two-pronged question. This was largely a pro-market speech, but under the protective layer of market orthodoxy he made some points of vital importance about the limits of markets in public services. They are ones that will remain relevant in the many unresolved debates within both the Labour and Conservative parties about the future of public services.

The lecture deserves close attention because it marked the moment when an internal divide over ideology came out into the open and also because when Brown made the speech it was either ignored or dismissed wrongly as a sign that he was an Old Labour figure. The words were more significant than the reports suggested when they were delivered, although Brown was wildly optimistic in his expectations of media coverage and then angry when they were not met, as if it was somebody else's fault.

The speech was dense, repetitive and at times muddled, reflecting Brown's desire not to fall off the high wire and his own unresolved thinking over the appropriate balance between local innovation, accountability, fairness and efficiency. In the end virtually all the policy rows between Blair and Brown related to this theme, for the entirely legitimate reason that there were no clear answers. Brown's lecture did not provide them either, but his analysis was a challenge to the well-meaning but simplistic posturing of Blair, Milburn and a growing number of insecure cabinet ministers desperate to prove to Blair that they were 'radical' too.

Brown's high-wire act in the speech involved an agonizing contortion every few sentences. In virtually each paragraph he went out of his way to show that he was not putting an 'Old Labour' argument but also to challenge some of the lazy assumptions forming like blocks of cement in the minds of Blair and his most devoted followers.

Early on in his address Brown made clear that 'to hold to old discredited dogmas about what should remain in the public sector and how the public sector operates, or to confuse the public interest with producer interests makes no sense for a reforming party'. In other words he was not advancing an argument on behalf of the trade unions representing public sector employees. He was a reformer examining the most effective way of delivering the best public services.

Without pausing for breath in the same paragraph he moved on to also warn: 'We risk giving the impression that the only kind of reform that is valuable is a form of privatization and we fail to advance – as we should – the case for a renewed reformed public realm for the coming decade.'

Take the paragraph in its full sweep and the message to Blair was clear: Don't call me Old Labour, but don't put a case for the NHS which verges on a form of privatization that would not work. In a break with all his normal instincts Brown was making public the government's fuming internal debate.

Much more characteristically, in taking on Blair's more indiscriminate reverence for market solutions the Chancellor cited a range of non-partisan sources. The Archbishop of Canterbury and the Chief Rabbi were quoted as arguing that: 'Markets may be the best way of constructing exchanges and thus providing many goods and services, but are not good ways of structuring human relationships. They also argue that while markets are good at creating wealth they are less good at guaranteeing fairness and opportunity for all – and certainly not good at dealing with their social consequences.'

The Archbishop and the Chief Rabbi joined 'Mr Wanless' as respectable figures challenging market orthodoxy.

He then sought even more protection by deploying a simplistic Blairite dividing line, in order to give the impression he was navigating through the respectable centre between two positions that he characterized as those of the doctrinaire left and neo-liberal right. The left was anti-markets and the right wanted more of them. 'The result is neither left nor right has been able to give a considered view as to where markets serve the public interest.' In contrast he sought to depoliticize his own position, to make a highly political act seem like a lecture in modest common sense.

First he spelled out that he favoured extending markets where there was clear competition. He cited a speech he made as shadow chancellor two days after the abolition of Clause Four in the summer of 1995 in which he argued that competition, not its absence, was essential to a fair society. He described that early speech as a break from a hundred years of Labour history. Balls felt at the time – in 1995 – that this speech was for Labour and Brown as significant as the abolition of Clause Four, a liberating moment when competition and markets were no longer seen as a threat.

In his 2003 lecture Brown argued that competition was fair and efficient when there was fair and accurate information for the consumer, fair competition between many suppliers and capital and labour mobility. He then contrasted those conditions with the ones that apply to the provision of public services. Given his conviction that Milburn – and possibly Blair – was moving towards the Conservatives' position and in some ways beyond it in their support for vouchers and a big expansion of the private sector, Brown delivered his most provocative paragraph as a pre-emptive strike. He outlined what he regarded as sensible reform and mischievously co-opted the Health Secretary, Milburn, as an ally.

> The modern model for the British NHS – as set down by the government and the Health Secretary – embodies not just clear national clinical and access standards bur clear accountability, local delivery of services, independent inspection, patient choice and contestability to drive efficiency and reward innovation.
>
> The free market position – which would on the proposals of the Conservative health spokesman lead us to privatized hospitals and some system of vouchers and extra payments for treatments – starts by viewing healthcare as akin to a commodity to be bought and sold like any other through the price mechanism, but healthcare can never be planned by the consumer in the same way that for example weekly food consumption can.

Having established a partly provocative dividing line he explained why markets do not work in healthcare, pointing out that nobody can be sure whether and when they need medical treatment. Instead individuals and entire societies seek to insure themselves against the eventuality of being ill and in every society this leads to the pooling of risk.

Predicting the criticisms of his analysis, he stressed that he did not believe the future lay in a wholly centralized service, nor did he rule out contestability and a role for the private sector. Emphatically he did not want to devalue the importance of consumer choice, but he did want to challenge the prevailing orthodoxy that the only alternative to command and control was a market means of public service delivery.

He argued that the stark and simplistic divide had obscured the real challenge, the development of a decentralized non-market means of delivery that is not reliant on the price mechanism to balance supply and demand. His version of reform envisaged more local flexibility with the warning that autonomy might lead to increased inequity. He ended with an inconclusive reflection on the timeless debate around the appropriate balance between efficiency, diversity and equity.

Naively, Brown had hoped that his speech would be reported in nuanced detail. Sometimes his journalist's instinct enabled him to predict the rhythms of a news story – what would 'play' well in the media and what would not. But he was also an academic who forgot that newspapers and their readers did not have the time or the inclination to follow every turn of an argument.

At the very least, and with a depth not remotely matched by his critics, Brown wanted to break through the superficial thinking in relation to the public services, with the outlines of a new narrative: reforms that took account of the limits of markets. Instead, in so far as the speech was reported or commented upon, the narrative remained the same. The words were interpreted wilfully as an obstacle to reform of any sort and as proof that Brown was anti-markets. Some ultra-Blairites were reported as saying that Brown was playing to the Old Labour gallery with the leadership in mind. Blair and Milburn regarded the speech as merely the latest round in the battle over foundation hospitals, another tactical skirmish that did not signify anything more important.

The few who bothered to read the entire document were more impressed. At a social gathering in Number Eleven David Lipsey, a former adviser to Tony Crosland, described the lecture as the most important contribution to left-of-centre thinking since his former boss's *Future of Socialism*, widely regarded as one of the most influential books written by an active Labour politician. Later, when Brown was Prime Minister, Lipsey despaired of his headline-grabbing short-termism. He saw both sides of Brown.

Alan Milburn and his successor as Health Secretary, John Reid, negotiated the new contracts for the GPs. The principle behind the contracts and the ministerial premise that guided the negotiations were visionary. The final outcome was calamitous.

The context of the negotiations was important. After decades of underfunding there was a shortage of GPs. It was therefore an important move to formalize the GPs' commitment to the NHS with a new contract. What more tangible sign could there be of the government's renewal of the institution than local disillusioned doctors suddenly paying homage to the NHS? The ministerial aim was revolutionary. GPs should be paid on the basis of results and the level of their productivity. The government wanted GPs to take on more of the relatively straightforward work that was perversely undertaken by overstretched hospitals. But Milburn and Reid were not ministers to be burdened by detail. More than Milburn, Reid spent a lot of his energies proving to Blair how radical he could be with increasingly incoherent proposals for 'change' in the NHS. Number Ten loved it. A senior adviser very close to Blair told me at the time that: 'John Reid gets it. He does not let any barrier get in the way. He is a free thinker. Tony loves his discussions with John. Charles Clarke [the Education Secretary at the time] is not so radical. Tony is frustrated by Charles.'

This was an illuminating observation. Clarke occasionally dared to raise practical problems and put forward some bold policies that were immediately rejected by Blair. Clarke for example supported the replacement of A levels with more vocational exams. Blair ran a mile from a proposal that might worry middle England, but he was excited by the big, imprecise vision offered by Reid of choice, an expanding private sector adding competition to the NHS which would over time raise the standards in the public sector – all legitimate ideas but which needed much greater forensic work. When Reid's successor, Patricia Hewitt, moved into the department she discovered a hundred fragmented schemes and ideas for the NHS and no coherent overall set of objectives.

While everyone was busy wallowing in their 'radicalism', the doctors' representatives, the BMA, the most ferociously agile trade union of the lot, took the government for a ride. It negotiated a deal in which GPs were rewarded for quite a lot of the work that they were already performing. Some of them discovered that without having to do very much additional work they were hitting so many of the productivity targets that their salaries almost doubled in size. From being relatively poorly paid they leapt to being the best-rewarded in Europe. Cabinet ministers who typically had no idea what was going on started to note that friends of theirs who were GPs were suddenly taking a lot more lavish holidays and arriving at their dinner parties in newly purchased expensive cars. Quite a lot of Brown's elaborately planned tax rise financed the new GPs' contract and yet for the first few years there was no change to their opening hours and they were not available at weekends. There were considerable and important improvements in the speed at which patients could see a GP, but far too much money was spent on a massive pay increase. Brown should have been paying far more attention to this than to the admittedly important debate about structural reform.

More widely the terrible consequence of an eruption of confused reforms was the need for more bureaucrats to make sense of them, more well-paid employees a long, long way from the patients. The task of the new bureaucrats was to meet the confused array of central targets and local initiatives and to negotiate with avaricious private companies sensing a financial killing amidst the chaotic changes.

The ineffectual chaos became the overwhelming story, politically disastrous for a government seeking to justify a tax rise, but one the conflicting ministers brought on themselves. Sadly less coverage was given to the experience of many individual patients who discovered that, in spite of all the problems, the increased funding, together with the chaotic attempts to shake up the sclerotic outdated culture in parts of the NHS, did indeed bring about improvements.

Brown had little time to reflect on the battle over the NHS before moving on to the next bloody conflict, this time over the funding of universities. Once more the battle took two forms, over principle and detail. Blair wanted a system of top-up fees paid for by students and for universities to have some flexibility as to the amount they charged. With good cause, Blair was worried about the underfunding of universities in general at a time when the government was encouraging more students to go into further education. More specifically he wanted Britain's top universities to compete with their equivalents in the US and elsewhere.

Once more, for a combination of reasons – feuding spite, ambition and principle – Brown wanted to block such a move. He hinted at his concern in the speech to the Social Market Foundation:

> One of the central questions around the world is the extent to which universities should become, in effect, the seller, setting their own price for their service and the prospective graduate the buyer of higher education at the going rate whether through an upfront or deferred system of payment, and what are the consequences for equity and efficiency as well as choice of such arrangements.

Here Brown was mischievously turning the argument about choice on its head, implying that for those from poorer backgrounds choice would become much more limited if the more conventionally thriving universities charged intimidating high fees. Brown was worried that the fear of debt would deter poorer kids and their parents from applying to any university, let alone Oxbridge. He was also convinced that Oxbridge and other top universities had become lazily complacent about fund raising, turning to the government for help when they could do more themselves.

Brown loathed the Oxbridge ethos and its close links with the privileged private schools. During the first term he had made a clumsy attempt to highlight the parochial iniquity of the system by pointing to the case of Laura Spence, a girl from a state school in the North East who had not been admitted to Oxbridge in spite of spectacular exam results. As is always the case when individual cases are cited, the argument became one about whether Brown had accurately reported the aspiration of Spence and whether therefore he had made a gaffe. But Brown's instinctive dislike of inherited privilege that framed an entire life, from school to Oxbridge to the best jobs, was intense and real. He was alarmed at what he thought might be the outcome of the latest Blairite crusade: Oxbridge and a few other universities being allowed to charge uniquely high fees in a way that would entrench the opportunities available for only a privileged few.

He had cause to be wary. Blair wanted to create a marketplace for universities and to give Oxbridge the scope to charge a lot more than other institutions if they wished.

But on this he knew he could not prevail. He would never get legislation through the Commons with such a proposal (at the time the Conservatives were opposed to top-up fees, an error on their part in terms of tactics and principle that the more politically astute David Cameron would not have made if he had been leader at the time).

In the end Blair agreed a compromise, that all universities would have the right to charge up to £3000 a year in top-up fees and no more. Brown was not happy with this either. To the fury of the Education Secretary, Charles Clarke, Brown continued to indicate his opposition and the Chancellor's entourage let political journalists know about his doubts. Brown's behaviour over top-up fees was for Clarke the final straw in terms of his always stormy relationship with the Chancellor. His fury was fuelled by the fact that Brown did not offer an alternative form of funding. It was during this period that Clarke became determined to prevent Brown succeeding Blair, although Clarke was playing games too. He told his old boss, Neil Kinnock, that he opposed top-up fees, but did not have time to drop the scheme and replace it with a graduation tax. Kinnock was a passionate opponent of top-up fees on the same grounds as Brown.

Brown's reticence in coming up with an alternative to top-up fees was partly due to his ambitions over the leadership. Privately he supported a graduation tax rather than top-up fees, but only once the universities had tried harder to raise cash through business sponsorships and other initiatives – a red herring, as such schemes would never have met the shortfall in funding. But Brown told his close allies that he did not want to be associated now with another tax rise having only just implemented a big one. Already he was getting neurotically worried about being portrayed as someone who liked to put up taxes. As a result he indicated opposition to top-up fees out of principle while weakly failing to specify an alternative. Ambition was starting to determine his approach to making policy.

More robustly, Brown held out for a maximum limit to top-up fees and insisted that the repayment scheme should be fairer for less well off students. These were important details, and Brown was not being petty or vindictive in pressing for them. After a series of torrid discussions with Blair over the issue in the autumn of 2003, mingled explosively with negotiations over when Blair would leave Number Ten, Brown hinted at the nature of their negotiations and their conclusion. He told the BBC shortly before Christmas 2003: 'Tony Blair has said that the variable fee is part of the system and I can see how a variable fee can be complemented by a fair system of repayment, and that's what Charles Clarke is going to show people over the next few days.'

These carefully chosen words indicated that Blair had agreed that the only way of persuading Labour MPs to sign up to variable fees was by sweetening the repayment system. Note also that Brown carefully attached Blair's name alone to the proposal for variable fees. He did not explicitly declare his support. At this point, a few weeks before the Commons' vote on the policy, Brown accepted the proposal reluctantly and tentatively on the basis that students would not have to repay the fees until they were earning a decent annual salary and that a combination of fee remissions, maintenance grants and bursaries would help the poorest 30 per cent of students. But he had still not declared his full support. A significant number of Labour MPs, including some of his closest supporters, were still opposed.

In the build-up to the vote on top-up fees in January 2004 the Blairites were convinced that Brown was stirring the rebellion in the knowledge that defeat could fatally undermine their leader. They were particularly suspicious of the role of Nick Brown, one of the Chancellor's closest allies, who was a key figure in the potentially big rebellion, a former Chief Whip who knew all the techniques to persuade MPs to vote one way or another. They were convinced that Nick Brown was going into battle over the leadership and top-up fees were the latest ammunition deployed to remove Blair.

As ever with Brown the true situation was more complex. Partly he had convinced himself, with a degree of justification, that he was fighting a full-scale ideological battle over the direction of the government and the future of his party. Blair was a tornado of determined energy, embracing initiative after initiative that in Brown's view suffered from a tilt towards inequity and inefficiency. At one point in his increasingly embattled discussions with the two Eds he said: 'If we let them get away with this, what will they do next?' In the particular case of top-up fees Brown continued to worry genuinely that the fear of debt would deter people from going to university and that variable fees, although capped for now, could lead to a Labour government being more responsible than any other for a new era of exclusive elitism.

There was a lot of talk at the time, within the government and in the media, that there was not really a great divide between Blair and Brown, and that the tensions related solely to the leadership. This was the view of those who worked for Blair, including his press secretary, Alastair Campbell, who had been convinced since the publication of Paul Routledge's biography that there was nothing any of them could do in Number Ten to appease the fuming ambition of Brown. Such were the bizarre dynamics of the political situation that it was also in Brown's interests to play down any ideological divide, even in private. He knew there would be big dangers for him if he were seen as fighting battles that placed him a little to the left of Blair, even though that was precisely what he was doing.

In so far as his leadership ambitions played a part in the calculations, Brown was ambivalent. During this period he was working on the assumption that Blair would stand down later in the year. There was no obvious need therefore to kill him off. There again Brown was far from sure that Blair would necessarily stand down, so there was a case for weakening his position. But in the end another consideration overwhelmed Brown as it always did. He did not want to inherit a divided Labour party, with the schism at the heart of New Labour. Once the concessions had been established his instinct was therefore to make sure that Blair was not defeated on the top-up fee vote.

Nonetheless he would make Number Ten sweat in order to remind them that they could not act unilaterally in the future. They needed his support in order to get bills passed in parliament.

On the Friday afternoon before the vote I went into the Treasury to conduct a pre-recorded interview with Brown for GMTV. The wider political context was frenzied. On the Monday night Blair faced the still knife-edge vote on top-up fees. The following day the highly charged Hutton report was to be published, the inquiry into the death of Dr David Kelly, who had been the source of a controversial BBC report on the origins of the war in Iraq. In advance many in the media and in parts of the government assumed that the report would be highly embarrassing for Blair. If, as seemed possible, Blair lost the vote and was humiliated by Lord Hutton the following day, he would be seriously and perhaps fatally weakened.

On the Friday afternoon Brown strode into the room in the Treasury where we had set up for the interview. He was on an exuberant high. Often he could be brusque with the various camera people and producers, too focused on what he wanted to say to pay them much attention. On this occasion he set the room alight, kissing the women in the GMTV team and shaking hands with the two male producers. As an opening gambit, while we were preparing to record he laughed with a guttural pleasure as he declared: 'I hear the government might be in trouble next week!' I got the impression that one way or another he thought the crown was moving very close to him that weekend. At the end of the interview, in which he put the case for top-up fees in the context of all the concessions that went with them, he seemed to confirm the reason for his rare public display of joy. I asked him whether Blair would be and should be Prime Minister at the next election. His inconclusive reply made the front pages as he must have known it would:

'Should he be? Yes. Will Tony Blair be? That's a matter for him. Tony Blair has been a great prime minister for Britain and I think he has been a great leader of the Labour party as well.'

Brown made it seem as if he was paying tribute to an outgoing prime minister.

Over the weekend he continued to press for further reassurances for those on low incomes and to guarantee that the cap on variable fees would remain in place for at least two parliaments. He told Nick Brown not to concede any ground until the last moment, to ensure that the concessions were watertight. On the day itself Brown went into battle for the government, as he always tended to do, at the last moment, much more alarmed at the possibility that defeat would split the Labour party into two.

After a six-hour debate, the government won the vote by the minuscule margin of just five, with 316 voting for the bill and 311 against.

In between the battles over the two major public service reforms there was an even more epic conflict over the Euro during the early summer of 2003, soon after the formal ending of the war in Iraq. Brown had remained convinced that it would be economically and politically disastrous to hold a referendum on the Euro during the second term. He thought that a referendum was not winnable and that even if by some miracle the plebiscite was won, Britain's economy would be severely damaged if it signed up to the single currency. Once more his genuinely held views on this were spiced inevitably with his hopes to take over as Prime Minister. As one of his closest allies said to me at the height of the battle with Blair: 'Gordon doesn't want to take over with Britain in the Euro or with the government finished because it has just lost a referendum.'

Some pro-European columnists accused Brown of posturing over the issue in order to secure more support within the Labour party and the Euro-sceptic media for the moment when a vacancy in Number Ten arose. That was the wrong way to look at it. At times Brown wooed the Euro-sceptic newspapers with a reckless, destructive and clumsy determination. He did so usually when he was heading off for summits in Brussels. Newspapers would be briefed that he was opposing European initiatives in order to stand up for British interests, a cliché that reinforced the irrational hostility towards Europe in the UK rather than in any way challenging it. But over the Euro he was convinced sincerely that entry was wrong for the British economy and politically risky when the government and Blair in particular was suffering a backlash over the war in Iraq.

Blair was in a very different place. From the start of his leadership he had wanted to make a historic move in relation to Europe. Brown was convinced that Blair's motives were more or less as superficial as that, a desire to carry out a recognizably historic act. There was something in this assessment, although it underestimates the degree to which Blair wanted Britain to be a more active partner in the European Union and his recognition that this would be impossible while it was outside the single currency. Other factors now fuelled Blair's desire to make a move.

Blair's decision to support President Bush's war in Iraq was the consequence of many fevered calculations. One of them related to Europe. Blair assumed that at some point in his leadership he would fight a referendum campaign, an event that would finally place him on the opposite side to Rupert Murdoch's mighty newspapers. He knew this would be an immense and daunting challenge. In advance of the intimidating confrontation he wanted to do all he could to neuter the onslaught of his powerful Euro-sceptic opponents. One accusation he feared in a referendum was that his support for Europe reflected a return of Labour's old hostility towards the US. He could see the headlines and the articles accompanying them: There is Blair sucking up to the weak-kneed European leaders, Chirac and Schröder, while he turns his back on the world's only superpower.

One of the reasons he was so ostentatiously demonstrative in his support for President Bush in the build-up to war was in order to prove unequivocally that his support for Europe did not mean the ending of the so-called 'special relationship'.

This explains why Blair was unusually relaxed about negative headlines in the build-up to the war in Iraq that portrayed him as 'Bush's Poodle'. Normally Blair was as neurotically alert as Brown to hostile media coverage. Any headline for example that suggested Blair was a millimetre to the left of the centre ground would send him rushing to

Alastair Campbell in order to ask: 'What are we doing about this?' In contrast he was entirely relaxed about the persistent allegation in some newspapers that he was Bush's lap dog.

Blair was confident that such attacks and the praise he received in most Euro-sceptic newspapers for his alliance with the US would give him the space to fight a campaign in favour of Europe once the war in Iraq was over. He said to me over a cup of tea during the run-up to the war: 'At least they can't complain about me being anti-American or soft on defence.'

When Blair surfaced from the formal theoretical ending of the war in Iraq his thoughts turned rapidly towards Europe and to the Euro in particular. Many of his pro-European allies had despaired of the division that had arisen in relation to the war, with France and Germany on one side and Britain on the other. Although a supporter of the war, Mandelson warned him persistently over this period that Britain's relationships within the EU would need urgent attention once the conflict had ended. Others were more alarmed, warning Blair that Britain's influence was waning. France and Germany were preening themselves on being apparently right in their opposition to the war.

Blair felt there was no more vivid way of proving his commitment to the European cause than to hold a referendum on the Euro. Brown was horrified as he discovered in their conversations in the spring of 2003 that Blair was keen to go ahead. Once more their angry, suspicious exchanges were informed by the separate conversations they were having about when or if Blair would leave Number Ten. Early in 2002 Blair had told the International Development Secretary, Clare Short, that he would hand over to Brown if the Chancellor supported him in a 'Yes' campaign for the Euro. Blair knew Short was close to Brown at the time and had astutely chosen her to be the messenger. Short could hardly believe what she was hearing but nonetheless informed Brown of the possible deal. To his credit Brown dismissed it. He was not going to make a case for the Euro when he believed it would be economically wrong, even if that meant he would walk into Number Ten. But Brown told Short that Blair would renege on the deal anyway if he went along with such a scheme. Now Blair put it to Brown directly. He wanted to get Britain into the single currency. It would be his final act as Prime Minister. He would resign once the referendum had been won and entry negotiated (a possibly lengthy process).

For many years Blair had wondered about Brown's psychological flaws. Now Brown became convinced that Blair had become danger-ously delusional, on a crusade for the sake of being on crusades, believing whatever he said at any given time, even if it contradicted previous declarations or was at odds with the reality. The Prime Minister thought the Chancellor was bonkers. The Chancellor thought the Prime Minister was mad. This was the state of their rela-tionship when the Euro was added to an already combustible mix.

While Blair was almost exclusively distracted by the war in Iraq, Brown retained a grip on the issue with the Treasury's ongoing review of the five economic tests on joining the Euro. But now Blair was determined to prove that he was a pro-European as much as he was a pro-American. What made their struggle more perverse was that deep down Blair knew a referendum on the Euro could not be won. His reputation was at an all-time low as Iraq started to unravel. He was in a battle with the BBC over its reporting of the war. No weapons of mass destruction had been found in Iraq. This was hardly the most propitious backdrop to holding a referendum on an issue over which most voters were hostile and some newspapers violently so. Without the intervention of Brown, Britain might have joined at a point when its economy could not cope or the government might have called a referendum and lost, an authority-sapping defeat.

In contrast to his round-the-clock efforts to counter Blair's plans for hospitals, top-up fees and the Euro, Brown did nothing to prevent Blair going to war in Iraq. There is a straightforward reason for this. Brown supported the war.

Had he not been a supporter he would have moved to prevent Blair from going ahead. Look how he stopped Blair from getting closer to the Euro, with his tests and reviews forming a barrier as impenetrable as the Berlin Wall. There were no tests raised by Brown en route to Iraq. In the autumn of 2002 an increasingly worried Clare Short, still in the cabinet at the time, went to see Brown to discuss her concerns about the build-up to war. She had returned recently from a visit to Afghanistan and felt that the precarious security situation in Kabul was being largely ignored as the short attention spans of Blair and Bush moved on to Iraq. Brown was not responsive, telling Short that he had read the intelligence and agreed with Blair that military action might be necessary to deal with Saddam. Short, who remained supportive of Brown for a little longer, told me unequivocally after she resigned from the cabinet that 'Gordon supports the war. He agrees with Tony on this.'

A close ally of Brown confirmed to me that in the build-up to war he had no doubt that Blair was taking the right course. 'Because there was the possibility that Gordon would be Prime Minister in the second term, and there were already discussions taking place on the transition from Tony to Gordon, Gordon saw all the intelligence. He took the view that Saddam was a real threat. He might have wanted to give the weapons inspectors more time and then made another attempt to get a second UN resolution, but basically Gordon supported the war.'

Not that Blair knew for sure whether or not Brown would publicly lend his support. There were relieved cheers in Number Ten when Brown declared that he backed the war in a sound bite delivered in Downing Street shortly before the conflict began. Until then Brown had not told anyone in Number Ten what he planned to do.

Blair could have done with some heavyweight support from a Chancellor at this point, in the way that Ken Clarke would leap – a little patronizingly at times – to the side of John Major at times of trouble. But Brown felt he was leaping enough as it was. In making the public case Blair was more or less on his own, isolation he took with a restrained dignity, accepting that he could not turn to Brown for help.

Far from wishing to be helpful, Brown wanted Blair's job and he sought it on very precise terms. He wanted Blair to announce his departure voluntarily and to declare his support for Brown as his successor. Brown wanted no publicly destructive overthrow in which he would be seen as the assassin. Typically he now planned for the removal of a Prime Minister by stealth. Brown pulled it off in the end, but the extraordinarily demanding set of ruthlessly worked-through objectives took much longer to achieve than he had hoped. For Brown the long wait to take over was fatal, but he had no choice. If he had moved earlier the fragile public edifice of New Labour would have collapsed, bringing him down along with Blair. Not for the first time he was trapped, and finding an escape route was painful for all those involved.

SIX

Ambition

It is not unusual for senior politicians to be driven and preoccupied by intense ambition. In the late 1960s and early 1970s Harold Wilson was surrounded by colleagues who wanted to succeed him at the earliest possible opportunity. Indeed the sheer number of Labour frontbenchers who wanted to be leader explains both Wilson's paranoia and his long tenure in the top job. The aspirant leaders preferred Wilson to stay on rather than risk one of their rivals winning. In the 1980s Margaret Thatcher appointed several cabinet ministers who dared to wonder whether they might be leader, although in 1987 she famously observed that she had not yet met her successor. After she was removed in 1990 John Major governed nervously, wondering whether Michael Portillo or even Michael Heseltine might strike against him.

What was unusual about the New Labour era was how few senior figures contemplated leadership. Most ministers were thrilled to be in the cabinet, having worked on the assumption that they were doomed to eternal opposition after their party's defeat in 1992.

It was almost as if Brown cornered all of the ambition normally distributed amongst several cabinet ministers. The more he plotted to succeed Blair the more he wanted to be Prime Minister. As he resolved to do whatever it took to secure the leadership, the pursuit of power became partly an end in itself.

The intensity of Brown's obsessive ambition was unhealthy, a source of unnecessary turbulence in the second term and one reason why when he finally became Prime Minister he was more neurotic and insecure than either John Major or Jim Callaghan, two other premiers who followed long-serving leaders in government. In order to understand what went wrong with Brown's leadership it is necessary to understand how much he wanted it in the first place and some of the reasons, beyond ambition, why he did so.

On the Monday after the 2001 general election Brown asked Blair about when he planned to resign as Prime Minister. The tone of the exchange, the first of many on the subject in the second term, is disputed. Already sensing that he might find a new political role as a mediator between the two of them, John Prescott told close friends that tensions were high: Brown was demanding a date when Blair would leave. Close allies of Brown put it slightly differently. One told me: 'At the beginning of the second term Gordon wanted to establish that Tony would cooperate with a smooth transition over the leadership as they had agreed at Granita. Gordon knew that if the transition was not carefully coordinated the New Labour coalition could easily break up, and he wanted to avoid that.'

What no one disputes is that from the beginning of the second term Brown started to pressurize Blair about his plans for a departure. In the summer of 2001 Geoffrey Robinson met up with Brown briefly on holiday in Cape Cod. Brown had a single theme: How to get rid of Tony. Brown's aides told me he quite consciously adopted an intimidating and persistent approach, fearing that if he did not do so Blair would assume that the pressure was off and plan for a never-ending stay in Downing Street.

For Blair the intensifying of Brownite pressure was a nightmare start to a second term. The last thing on his mind was his voluntary resignation. He had told his close friend Barry Cox that he had no intention of resigning halfway through the parliament and yet he had to face the stressfully draining figure of an angry Brown demanding that he discuss arrangements about his voluntary departure within days of winning an election with a landslide majority. In these early months Blair equivocated in his tense dealings with Brown, playing for time. He did not dash Brown's hopes. He did not dare to do so, although from his point of view it would have been more cathartic to have told Brown from the beginning that he was not planning to stand down and that was the end of the matter.

Brown's behaviour towards Blair was childlike, a character trait that surfaced again when he became Prime Minister. Consumed by frustrated ambition, anger and fear that his old friend would betray him again by promoting another candidate to be his successor, he was relentless in demanding at their one-to-one meetings that Blair must address the question of leadership.

Blair's closest ministerial friends and allies started to despair of what they regarded as Brown's outrageous behaviour. With Blair's support they looked for alternative leadership candidates. Brown was right to worry that Blair was turning away from him, but his own behaviour was a cause of the prime-ministerial disenchantment. Brown's transparent impatience did him more harm than good.

The Blairites started to talk about the Home Secretary, David Blunkett, and the Health Secretary, Alan Milburn, as potential leaders. When Blunkett published a personal memoir early in the second term Peter Mandelson and Anji Hunter, the energetic charmer who had run Blair's office in opposition and continued to do so at Number Ten, attended the launch, signalling that as far as they were concerned Blunkett was the coming man. Blair's allies also went out of their way to hail Milburn as a great radical reformer and a potential leader.

There was nothing unusual about such manoeuvring. Speculation about potential leaders is an unavoidable part of politics, and there was no reason why the likes of Mandelson and Hunter should not promote cabinet ministers who they believed, or perhaps hoped, had at least some abilities and appeal that put them in the race for the top job. But life at the top of the New Labour government was not normal. Instead it verged on the deranged. Brown regarded any attempt at promoting other potential leadership candidates as a breaking of the Granita deal. He was terrified of living through another '1994' in which a vacancy arose for the leadership and he was once more in a position where he could not win, afraid that for the second time someone else might float up to become the favourite in the media and with the broader electorate.

As various potential leadership candidates fell by the wayside, Brown was widely accused of being responsible for their demise. This became another myth associated with Brown, that like a gangster he killed off anyone he saw as a threat. In fairness to some of those who spread the myth, they believed what they were propagating. The Blairite minister Steve Byers, who for a short time was seen as a possible future leader, told me he used to dream regularly that he met Brown and his entourage in an underground car park and did not survive the subsequent shoot-out.

It suited an array of former ministers that the myth of Brownite political violence was widely believed. They were placed in the rather flattering role of noble crusaders whose careers were wrecked by a manic Chancellor.

The flattery was deceptive. In each case their careers were wrecked for other reasons.

David Blunkett was twice forced to resign as a cabinet minister. In both cases he faced questions about his personal conduct. Alan Milburn resigned from the cabinet twice. In the first case he opted to spend more time with his family. In the second he left following the 2005 election after his role as party chairman had been narrowly constrained almost by public demand. Steve Byers resigned after a row about whether he lied in an interview amidst growing controversy about the way he ran the Department of Transport. Peter Mandelson's second resignation was brought about more by Alastair Campbell than Brown.

Blairites struggled to stay the course.

By the summer of 2003 when it became clear that Saddam did not have weapons of mass destruction and Iraq was becoming a bloody battlefield for terrorists – as opponents of the war and the controversial intelligence reports had predicted – Blair became even more determinedly presidential. There was no hint of public contrition.

Instead he resolved to become more crusading in relation to domestic policies in the same way as he had evangelized about Iraq.

Brown viewed Blair's messianic zeal with growing concern. Obviously this was partly for selfish reasons, with the unresolved question of personal ambition. Those who worked for Blair were and are convinced that this was the sole explanation for his conduct. Blair was such a decent, calm and good-humoured boss to work for that anyone who entered Number Ten soon felt an intense personal loyalty for the Prime Minister, not least when he was facing an onslaught from an increasingly hostile media as well as from the Brownites. As a result some of them lost their critical faculties in relation to what their boss was actually seeking to do. Campbell has since been a critic of Blairite education policies. His partner, Fiona Millar, as well as leading the opposition to the education proposals also strongly opposed the war in Iraq. The head of the policy unit in the second term, Matthew Taylor, told me on the day before he started his new job that he had profound doubts about the direction of policy. Soon he became a passionate advocate. They became ardent Blairites because they admired Blair's resilience and decency, at odds with the media portrayal in which Blair had metamorphosed from a messiah to a lying war criminal. But their unquestioning loyalty meant that they failed to see the dangers of Blair's presidential, politically rootless approach to making policy.

Brown saw the dangers partly because it was in his interest to do so, but also because he remained a sharp reader of the overall political picture.

Increasingly Brown worried that at best the rest of the Labour party had become an irrelevance. At worst there was a danger that the Labour party was seen as a drag on the great crusader. The government's successes would be associated with Blair alone almost inevitably at a time when the Prime Minister had become presidential. In this sense Brown was more tribal than Blair. He worried about the image of the Labour party once Blair had gone, whoever succeeded him.

His analysis in the summer and early autumn of 2003 was a valid one. Labour as a governing force was being lost in the focus on Blair.

The concern formed part of the labyrinthine thinking that led to Brown's most controversial party conference speech of his career, one that was so out of character in its public provocation that it still stands out and takes the breath away.

The speech in 2003 became immediately famous or notorious for the climax, the final few words which were so obviously a direct attack on his leader. Brown had been bursting with partially justified anger at Blair's theme of boldness, with its implication that anyone who questioned him lacked political courage. After an earlier Blair speech in which the word 'boldness' recurred twenty-four times, Brown told his court that boldness was not an end in itself. Sometimes Brown recited the number of occasions when Blair tried to block *his* radical policies, from the scrapping of museum admission fees to so-called stealth taxes, out of timid fear that some of his vast coalition of support would be alienated. Brown wanted to claim boldness for the entire party, and to be more precise about the practical manifestations of political bravery.

After much discussion with his courtiers Brown ended his 2003 speech with a flourish:

> Have confidence in our principles. Have confidence that these principles can be advanced in Labour policies for our time. Have confidence that Labour values are the values of the British people. This Labour party – best when we are boldest, best when we are united, best when we are Labour.

Brown had even dropped the adjective 'new', to make his point that party and leadership – or at least this leadership – marched as one.

Within seconds of Brown's standing ovation drawing to a close, politicians and journalists were in a frenzy. Brownites felt a cathartic barrier had been leapt over. All of them looked ten years younger. Blairites regarded the speech as an act of treachery, although Blair, who had been absent at a funeral, came back with a characteristically dignified and gracious sense of perspective. With his leader's speech to prepare, Blair returned to his hotel suite and made the frenzy-puncturing declaration that he saw nothing inherently wrong with others wanting to lead the Labour party.

By ending the speech in the way he did, Brown had turned the media focus solely on his eternal feud with Blair. Normally he was more restrained, but this was an example of the clunking fist rather than a shrewd political operator. The rest of the speech was much more effective, an important and powerful attempt to link Labour and its values to the government's successes. In highlighting full employment, the minimum wage and tax credits he argued that the government had taken 'the Labour road' and had followed 'Labour values'. Reforms such as Bank of England independence and the new deal were 'Labour reforms'. The changes did not happen because of some sort of coincidence. They happened because 'we are Labour'.

Although Brown worked at his speeches obsessively, or perhaps precisely because he did so, the result was often repetitive and static. Blair's speeches had far more tonal variety, including self-deprecating wit. They had a recognizable beginning, middle and end. His speeches nearly always had an argument, conveying a sense of clear purpose. In this case Brown's speech had the familiar failings. The same point was made repeatedly. Nonetheless it was a vitally significant one at a stage where Blair alone appeared to rule and when because of Blair's tendency to look rightwards for policy inspiration, Brown was reclaiming the terrain for the party that both were supposed to represent.

The speech was not 'Old Labour', as some Blairites argued at the time. Prudence got as much of a look-in as the minimum wage. Fiscal rules were highlighted as much as spending increases. But it was a defiant scream against apolitical, managerial, presidential leadership. He also openly challenged Blair's basic foreign policy, that Britain was the bridgehead between the US and Europe. Brown claimed greater international ambition: 'Britain can be more than a bridge between Europe and America. Our British values – what we say and do, marrying enterprise and fairness – can make Britain a model, a beacon for Europe, America and the rest of the world.'

The defiant statement followed a classic definition of what Brown had been seeking to do as Chancellor, bringing together the innovative entrepreneurialism of the US and the high standards of public services in Europe. It sounds hubristic from the perspective of what happened after 2008, when the British economy suffered a severe recession, but at the time Brown was speaking with justifiable confidence. Equivalent countries had been suffering from a downturn for several years. In 2003 the British economy seemed to be on a safe trajectory, growing against some global trends. But Brown was not instinctively boastful. He was deploying all the ammunition available in the increasingly fraught internal battles. His assertion about Labour's distinctive qualities reads well in the light of the collapse of the financial markets later in the decade. At the time some Blairites saw the following passage as cloyingly outdated:

> It is because we the Labour party understand what the Tories do not
> – that the town square is more than a marketplace, the city centre more
> than where people buy and sell, community more than a collection of
> individuals. And it is because we owe obligations that go beyond
> contract and exchange that we are proud of this Labour party's unique
> and special contribution – the NHS – healthcare determined not by
> your individual ability to pay in the marketplace but by your shared
> citizenship and your need.

Shortly after the party conference Brown discovered that Blair had removed his seat from the party's National Executive Committee. Brown had taken the seat as chair of Labour's election campaign. Amongst several other symbolic points, Blair was indicating that if he had anything to do with it Brown would not chair the next election. Brown did not take the snub in brooding silence, as Blair had assumed he would. Instead, following his public revolt at the Labour conference Brown took to the airwaves in a deliberate attempt to rattle the bars of the cage. Blair was taken aback. This was a different Brown. Blair had expected hostile off-the-record briefings from various Brownites. He could handle that. Hostile briefings had become a constant motif. But Brown's decision to take it out in the open generated disastrous headlines.

On the morning of 6 November Brown appeared on GMTV to declare: 'The reason that it came up is that I ran the Labour party's general election campaign in 1997 and I was a member of the NEC at the time. I also ran it in 2001 and wasn't, and I felt it would be better running the next election campaign from being a member of the NEC.' Asked whether he would be running the next campaign Brown stated: 'I have to say it's a decision not for me. It's a decision for the Prime Minister.' Brown was on one of his highs in terms of public opinion at the time, while Blair was starting to suffer low ratings as a result of the ongoing calamities in Iraq and the still raging controversies over how Britain went to war. He was more vulnerable than at any time since he became leader, and was not in a strong enough position to win a public row with his Chancellor. Brown knew this. It was why he went public.

The deputy Prime Minister, John Prescott, claimed at the time and subsequently a pivotal mediating role. On this occasion, the evening after Brown's GMTV interview, he hosted a dinner with Blair and Brown in an attempt to mend fences. It was a tense event from the beginning. Blair sat on a chair that was slightly lower than the other two. Prescott suggested that he should switch chairs. Blair responded with characteristic good humour: 'That's alright John. Gordon has always looked down on me.' Gordon did not laugh, but rearranged his knife and fork. What followed was more serious. Most immediately they agreed to resolve their differences over the spat about Brown's membership of the NEC. Both Blair and Brown could unite within seconds whenever the Conservative party appeared to be getting its act together. As the Conservatives showed few signs of getting their act together they had little cause for iron discipline.

But shortly before Prescott's dinner the Conservatives had dumped their leader, Iain Duncan Smith, and replaced him with Michael Howard. The Conservatives were heading for annihilation under Duncan Smith's increasingly mocked leadership. But Howard was a more skilful politician and briefly appeared to seek out the centre ground, New Labour's own comfort zone. The fact that Tory MPs had acted so ruthlessly was also a sign that they were finally regaining a hunger for power, or at least a desire to oppose effectively.

So used to losing elections, Blair and Brown were alert to any signs of a Tory revival. Sometimes they were virtually alone in the country in detecting them. This time they were neurotic enough about Howard's leadership to pull together. Subsequently they issued a joint statement in which Blair made it clear that Brown could attend NEC meetings whenever he wished. It was bizarre that the two most senior figures in the government, arguably the only two senior figures, were involved in such public negotiations, but by then their relationship demanded constant eccentric solutions.

Prescott's role in keeping them together was overestimated and widely misunderstood. The fear of a Tory recovery was the key binding force. In their different ways both Blair and Brown were irritated by Prescott's increasingly overblown attempts to be the equivalent of a RELATE counsellor. Brown had decided to go on the warpath because he wanted Blair's job and disagreed with the direction of policy. Blair was ready to take Brown on over policy direction and was keeping options open in relation to his job. There was not much space for a peace-keeping intermediary, but both of them thought they needed Prescott on side in order to buttress their positions. In this sense the deputy Prime Minister wielded immense power. If Prescott had come out for Brown, Blair would have been finished. Conversely Brown wanted Prescott's support in a future leadership contest and in what he still hoped would be a smooth transition. Therefore both Blair and Brown took part in the lengthy mediating sessions largely to please Prescott rather than to reach a new working relationship with each other.

On this occasion there was a dramatic development. Blair told Brown that he wanted to implement his Prime Ministerial programme of public service reforms. If Brown supported him in getting the proposals on to the statute book he indicated he would stand down within a year, regarding his job as completed. He specified the reforms as those relating to university finance and the NHS. He also wanted the briefings to stop and insisted that he did not want the events of this particular evening to surface in the media. Like Brown, Prescott formed the impression that Blair was in effect saying he would go within twelve months and would cooperate with Brown in a transfer of leadership.

Brown returned from the dinner in a state of considerable excitement. He briefed the two Eds and a small number of other advisers about what Blair had said and insisted that no one should tell the media. They kept to their word. The only message of substance that surfaced in the next few days was that the dinner had been 'constructive'. For the next few months Brown worked on the assumption that he would be leader by the following autumn, a little more than ten years after the Granita dinner.

What was Blair thinking? Almost certainly he was playing for time. He did want to push through the reforms and knew that he could only do so with Brown's cooperation. He was under intense pressure because of Iraq and therefore contemplated genuinely the possibility of standing down before the next election. Brown and Balls came to conclude that Blair was one of those types who mean what they say at any given time even if they said something completely different at another point. Certainly Blair had a convenient capacity to develop strong convictions once he had decided on an expedient route. Perhaps he felt strongly over dinner that his mission would be accomplished once some of the so-called reforms were in place.

Such evenings with their fleeting calculations and expedient positioning always did no more than paper over the cracks. Blair and Brown continued to have blazing rows over the comprehensive spending review that the Chancellor was scheduled to announce in the spring. Working on the assumption that he would be Prime Minister when the spending plans were implemented, Brown wanted even more autonomy than usual. Determined to cement his reforms in place and set the course for the subsequent decade, Blair was more active than he had been in previous spending rounds and in the build-up to the annual budgets.

For the period between Prescott's dinner and the early summer Blair was torn about whether or not to stand down. Part of him was ready to quit. He suffered some terrible blows over this period, ones that would have tested any individual. The first came with the publication of the Hutton report in January 2004 on the death of David Kelly, the scientist caught in the middle of the row between the government and the BBC who had committed suicide the previous summer. Hutton condemned the BBC's reporting on the origins of the war and cleared Blair and Alastair Campbell of deliberately seeking to mislead. Fleetingly Blair hoped that the unequivocal verdict might lead to a less hysterical form of reporting. Since the war in Iraq parts of the media had condemned virtually everything he said or did as 'spin' or lies. Now he hoped for some space in which to conduct a more mature debate about where he was taking the government. Even BBC-haters in the media backed the Corporation on the grounds that they hated Blair more. The *Independent*'s front page, with the single word 'Whitewash', summed up the media's reaction. Blair was subjected to a renewed assault when he had hoped for a fresh hearing. I saw him a week after the publication. He told me that 'while other prime ministers have faced world wars or major economic crises I have faced the modern media. It is like living with a demented tenant. I never know whether to soothe it or bash it over the head.'

Meanwhile Iraq was descending into a nightmare of bloody chaos, made worse by the surfacing evidence that prisoners in Iraq were being abused by American and British soldiers. Some photos published in the *Mirror*, suggesting that prisoners were being tortured, proved to be fakes. But the picture they conveyed proved to be more or less true, sapping any moral justification for a war that was going horrendously wrong. Blair had miscalculated. He had thought it likely that by now the conflict would have enhanced his authority. Instead he was aware that he was a potential vote loser for his party, a reversal of the previous position in which his soaring popularity had helped to get his party elected.

He was also facing family problems during this period and was feeling more isolated politically. Alastair Campbell had gone. Others were leaving Number Ten. Some cabinet ministers were switching allegiance subtly, moving towards Brown. Almost, he was getting ready to go, and he went through some of the formalities of preparing for departure, asking the Cabinet Secretary, Sir Andrew Turnbull, to prepare a document setting out the method by which he would announce his resignation and hand over power.

During this period the cabinet minister Tessa Jowell, a close friend of Blair's, pleaded with him that he should stay and urged three other colleagues who she knew felt as strongly as she did to do the same. John Reid and Charles Clarke went to see Blair and told him he must stay. Patricia Hewitt wrote him a letter.

Their interventions were not decisive. What made him resolve to stay on was a conversation with the party's focus-group guru, Philip Gould, on the weekend after the June European and local elections. On the surface the results were bad for Labour: the party suffered some significant losses, largely because of Iraq. But the Conservatives did not make much headway under Howard. Gould told Blair that on the basis of these results he was on course to win a third landslide at a general election. Gould was normally a pessimist. In the build-up to the 1997 election he was always writing memos warning of a Tory recovery that never came. Now he was forecasting a third landslide win. His wider analysis was even more flattering. It was Blair who was responsible personally for the failure of the Tories to climb back. Labour might have lost some support to the Liberal Democrats, but Blair's leadership kept potential Tory voters from returning to the fold. He thought that Labour would become more vulnerable under Brown, a counter-intuitive insight at the time, but obviously one that Blair liked to hear.

Gould's message reinforced that part of Blair which had always wanted to stay on. As well as some cabinet ministers, Cherie was adamant that he should stay on rather than concede to Brown. Her contribution at this point was significant. If she had told him to pack it in because of all the family pressures and the media abuse he might well have done so. Far from it, she urged him to stay on. In April he announced suddenly that there would be a referendum on the European constitution, a massive U-turn. The announcement followed a long discussion with Irwin Stelzer, a close colleague of Rupert Murdoch's. Murdoch had indicated to Blair that the *Sun* would be unable to back Labour at the election unless it promised a referendum. If it made that pledge he guaranteed support. Blair and Stelzer had an exchange that sources described to me at the time as something closer to a negotiation. I saw Blair on the day he made the formal announcement on the referendum. He seemed genuinely up for a future campaign. Why would he be so bothered about the *Sun*'s endorsement and contemplating a defining battle over Europe if he planned to resign as Prime Minister in the summer? I suspect that Blair was keeping his options open all along and that Gould's prediction of a third landslide was decisive. He had so much he wanted to do and he was walking away with a historic third victory in sight.

None of this altered Brown's belief that he would succeed Blair in the autumn. He had immersed himself in foreign-policy issues and had for some time received the reports from the intelligence agencies that would never normally arrive on a chancellor's desk. He had asked for the reports on the basis that he would soon be in charge of foreign policy. Brown and Balls started cooperating closely on Robert Peston's biography of Brown, provocatively titled 'Brown's Britain' on the assumption that by the time the book was published Brown would be Prime Minister. Brown told his close advisers to cancel any plans for a summer holiday in 2004. Either they would be in Downing Street or be preparing to move there in the summer. There would be no time for a break. Senior Brownites claim that at one point in the spring Blair offered to announce that he would step down at the party conference, but Brown talked him out of it fearing a protracted and divisive leadership contest. Brown had a fear of leadership contests, a running theme of his career from 1992 onwards. There were other more public manifestations, the most spectacular being John Prescott's claim in a *Times* interview on 15 May that 'when the plates appear to be moving everyone positions themselves for it'. Separately Prescott told Blair's biographer Anthony Seldon at this time to work on the assumption that there would be a new prime minister by the end of the year.

Only in the summer did Brown sense that Blair had changed his mind. On the first Saturday in July Brown and his inner court met in the Treasury to prepare for the unveiling of the comprehensive spending review, plans that had been much fought over. The event was almost as big as the budget and the Brownites followed the budget routine, gathering over the weekend to go over the final details and prepare a media strategy. They met in a state of stunned bewilderment. On the *Today* programme that morning the BBC's political editor, Andrew Marr, had reported that four cabinet ministers had urged Blair to stay on as PM, fearing he was about to quit. Marr revealed that the PM had been 'seriously reviewing his position' and that he had gone through 'a long night of the soul' about whether to carry on. Marr claimed that the intervention by the four ministers was 'well timed and had quite an effect'. Crucially Marr added: 'Mr Blair has decided to stay on and he is now in steely mood.'

Marr's report marked a classic New Labour moment. Not surprisingly the initial impact was made by the vivid phrase that Blair had gone through a long night of the soul and the revelation that he had contemplated resignation. Accurately Marr conveyed the degree of Blair's tortured introspection, and his well-informed insights generated acres of coverage about the turbulence at the top of the government. Yet the more sensational revelation as far as Brown was concerned was the confirmatory news that Blair had decided to stay on and was now in a steely frame of mind. This was the news that Blair's cabinet supporters wanted to convey. His friend Tessa Jowell made that very clear by giving a series of media interviews on the day of Marr's report, in which she stated emphatically that Blair would not resign. 'These have been difficult times and during difficult times the important thing is that everybody pulls together,' she told Sky News. Asked whether she had spoken to the Prime Minister about his future she replied: 'Of course, I talk to him on a regular basis.'

Downing Street sources were quoted throughout the day echoing Jowell's public comments, insisting that 'Mr Blair is not a man who is about to give up.'

Gathered in the Treasury on the Saturday, the Brown camp had got the message and was devastated. By then Brown had started to have doubts about whether Blair was going to stick to what he regarded as a firm pledge to stand down. The combination of the Marr report, the

Jowell interview and the Downing Street source was brutal confirmation. Significantly, Marr also reported that Brown felt ready to be Prime Minister and that this month would be the last chance for Brown to make his move. After that he felt that Blair would be 'home and dry' as the next election moved into view.

This was the strongly held view of Ed Balls as well. Balls had always had doubts about whether Blair would go of his own accord and felt that Brown should make his move in some form of overt challenge if there was no possibility of the so-called smooth transition. Normally when Brown suffered a setback – and there was no bigger setback for Brown than realizing for sure that his dream of being Prime Minister was being dashed again – he worked with even greater intensity. Hard work was a comfort, a form of therapy. But even Brown found it hard to focus that Saturday on the finer points of the comprehensive spending review. Instead he and his inner circle were plunged into yet another intense exchange about how they dealt with Blair's determination to stay on, a resolve that was confirmed again in the *Sun* newspaper on 12 July when it reported on the front page that Blair had vowed to remain in office for another five years. The story was based on a discussion between Blair and the paper's editor Rebekah Wade.

As Blair had correctly calculated, Brown resisted calls from Balls and others to launch a challenge over the summer of 2004. Once more he concluded that an act of regicide would not be forgiven by a large section of the party and parts of the media. He would possibly become Prime Minister, but with too much blood on his hands. Conceivably he would be closer to Michael Heseltine, the assassin who does not inherit the crown. Brown was haunted by the Heseltine experience in particular. Angry, dismayed, and demoralized, Brown accepted that Blair would be Prime Minister up to the election and there was nothing he could do about it.

The Marr report confirmed what Brown already knew deep down. To his suspicious fury he had witnessed Blair becoming remarkably re-energized. After his bleak spring he displayed in the summer a messianic verve that had not been witnessed since the build-up to the war in Iraq. Over the summer he launched a series of five-year plans for health, crime and education with a presentational flair that combined salesmanship, cunning and increasingly personal commitment to 'reform'. Now that Campbell had left, Blair was by far the most accomplished journalist in Number Ten. When he read for example the final version of David Blunkett's five-year plan on crime he was worried that there was no obvious 'top line' for the newspapers so he asked his media team to brief the *Daily Mail* that the proposals signalled the 'end of the 1960s consensus' on law and order. Even Blunkett, no advocate of 1960s-style permissiveness, was taken aback when he awoke to hear that his plans were being projected in such a light.

Only in the early autumn did Brown realize the degree to which Blair had decided to reassert his leadership and at the same time to marginalize Brown. Blair returned from his summer break looking ten years younger and planned right away a cabinet reshuffle in advance of the party conference, yet another set of changes aimed at putting Brown in his place. The key appointment was the return of Alan Milburn, replacing Brown to take charge of the next election campaign. For Brown the move could not have been more provocative. He and Milburn loathed each other.

Milburn was the mirror opposite to Brown. He was not driven by ambition, had seemed genuinely relaxed out of the cabinet and took a huge amount of persuading to return. On the Monday of the reshuffle Tessa Jowell and John Reid went together to plead with him. In the evening he was with Blair for more than two hours. At one point their exchanges had become so drawn out and tortuous that Blair deployed the ultimate argument of desperation, telling Milburn that he must say 'Yes' now because to do otherwise would greatly weaken his position as Prime Minister. By then the entire world knew that Blair was trying to get Milburn to return.

The reason for Milburn's hesitation and the theme of his negotiation with Blair was straightforward and yet complex: Gordon Brown. Milburn needed assurances from Blair that this time he would get full prime-ministerial support when the inevitable Brownite onslaught

began. He wanted it to be made clear publicly from the very beginning that Milburn was in charge of the election and that the themes
of the campaign would go beyond the familiar Brownite dividing
lines. Most obviously he needed to know that Blair intended to stay
on, fight the election and lead through the next term.

Blair sought to reassure him on all the Brown-related concerns. He
pointed out that in the last dispute involving the trio over foundation
hospitals Blair had to find a way through policy differences not just
with Brown but a significant section of the party. This was different.
Milburn was being placed in charge of the campaign and of drawing
up the next manifesto. Once it was announced, there would be nothing Brown could do about it. On the contrary, here was a chance for
the two of them to shape the course of the next few years by seizing
control of the manifesto and the subsequent campaign. Without
going into all the details, Blair also told Milburn that he planned to
make a statement about his intentions to fight the election and remain
as Prime Minister if Labour won.

Finally, and still far from sure he was making the right move,
Milburn agreed to the new role. The election scheduled for the following May would have a new supremo, Brown's biggest political enemy
after Peter Mandelson.

The Labour conference in Brighton was dominated as always by
the Blair/Brown relationship. The newspapers erupted with briefings
that implied Brown would return the party to an Old Labour past
and counter-briefings suggesting that Blair and Milburn were
becoming divisive figures at a point when Labour needed to unite in
the build-up to the election. On the surface Brown's speech was more
loyal than the one he had delivered the year before in Bournemouth.
In fact it was virtually the same speech, but this time more subtly
argued. Brown spent a large section of it warning about the dangers
of disunity, but in doing so he was seeking to highlight what he
regarded as the divisive approach of Milburn. This was another New
Labour moment: a warning about disunity was a deliberate act
aimed at destabilizing the Blairite wing. The call for unity was
divisive.

He revisited the great dispute with Blair and Milburn about the relationship between markets and state in the provision of public services: 'The commitment of doctors, nurses and home helps demonstrates values above contracts, markets and exchange and that public services can be a calling and not just a career ... I have seen this ethic of public service at work in times of great joy and sorrow ... I have seen doctors and nurses who show not only exceptional skill and professionalism but extraordinary care and friendship.' Explicitly he endorsed the theme of his speech the year before: 'Ours is a vision that works for Britain not in spite of our Labour values but as I said last year because of our Labour values.' Every word had been crafted, as the year before, with the battle for the future of Labour and his own future in mind.

Much of Blair's speech the following day was dominated by a silly debate about whether he would 'apologize' for the war in Iraq, an issue that he skirted around with a 'sorry' inserted that did not, understandably, address the substance of the issue. He could not say 'sorry' for sending soldiers to their deaths on a false premise without following up with a two-word sentence: 'I resign.' Far from resigning, Blair had other plans. In another bizarre contortion, all aimed at seeing off the threat from Brown, Blair called in the cameras to Downing Street for a series of interviews the day after the conference had ended. Conveniently Brown was out of the country, flying to Washington for a meeting of the IMF. Blair made his dramatic statement that he planned to serve a full third term but would not serve a fourth, and that he was going into hospital the following day for a minor heart operation.

The next day most of the newspapers interpreted the statement as an act of desperate weakness, pointing out that the clock would start ticking now that Blair had laid out the limit of his prime-ministerial ambition. In fact the opposite was closer to the truth. The whole performance was an astonishing act of determined assertiveness. Blair was now planning to stay in office for what could be another four or five years, longer than some prime ministers' entire period in power. In addition, if he was planning to serve most of a third term he would inevitably be at the helm when plans were being laid for a fourth. In a statement that was viewed as an act of weakness, Blair was seeking to shape the course of politics for another decade at least.

Once more the contortion was a consequence solely of the Blair/Brown relationship. Blair wanted to send the clearest possible signal that as far as he was concerned their endless discussions about when he would leave were over. He had laid out a timetable in public that stretched well ahead, although again in classic New Labour style the apparently clear statement was blurred at the edges. What did he mean by a full third term? Obviously he would have to give his successor time to prepare for an election. Blair was vague about the precise timetable, but in his own mind he was clear that he had every intention of handing over to a like-minded leader shortly before the election. At this point he was working on the assumption or hope that it would be someone other than Brown. If it was Brown he was determined to shape his prime-ministerial agenda.

Brown had no idea that Blair was to make his dramatic statement – not surprisingly, as it was aimed at him. Blair was hardly likely to consult in advance with the main victim of his declaration. Balls, who by then had left the Treasury and was a parliamentary candidate, watched the news bulletin at his home in London with disbelief. In effect this was the Granita deal in reverse, Blair opting to stay on in power without consulting Brown. It marked the total breakdown of their relationship. Brown was shocked and depressed when he heard the news soon after landing in Washington, but was in the crazy position of having to give sound bites wishing Blair well as he recovered from his heart operation.

For Brown this was a massive setback. Would there be new leadership candidates emerging? Would he be sacked as Chancellor? If he stayed on would the economy be as strong as it was now when the elusive vacancy arose? What would happen to his plans for entering Number Ten that he had started to formulate on the assumption he would be Prime Minister soon? What would happen to Labour as Blair became even more presidential and in Brown's view antagonistic to the party he led?

When Brown returned to London the following week he was more isolated than at any point in his political career. Blair was striding on, determined to implement more 'radical reforms'. Milburn was in the Cabinet Office planning the election assisted by Blair's other close ally, David Miliband. The most vivid example of Brown's isolation came just before Christmas in 2004. Blair and Milburn chaired a political cabinet to discuss the forthcoming general election. The meeting was scheduled for a day when Brown was out of the country. For the previous two elections Brown had been chair of election planning. Now he was so peripheral that his attendance at a special pre-election cabinet was not required.

But Brown and his inner court never gave up. Their resilience and determination to prevail broke all normal boundaries. Ed Balls pointed out to the Chancellor on his return from Washington after the Blair statement that the clock would be ticking after the election. There was no way he would be in a position to serve a full term. Brown agreed that the party would not accept it, especially if he continued to move in a rightward direction.

Brown responded to his setback, as usual, by working even harder. During this period he read more, focused more on global poverty, began work on his pre-election budget, the one lever that was in his hands rather than Blair's.

The lowest point of all in the Blair/Brown relationship, came in the opening days of 2005, an election year. The ingredients were familiar, involving the publication of a book, a battle for pre-eminence between the two warriors and a breakdown in discipline that would have horrified the antagonists only a few years earlier. One of the ironies from this period is that in the early years Blair and Brown were neurotically concerned about party discipline, worrying constantly that other colleagues might go off-message, fearing that MPs or activists would give them all an unruly reputation. By January 2005 their party was a model of cowed discipline. The problem was Blair, Brown and their rival courtiers.

On Thursday 6 January the new year – an election year – began with a bizarre clash. At ten o'clock in the morning Brown addressed journalists in Edinburgh on his long-planned aid-for-Africa programme. Brown's event had been scheduled for some time and was known about in Number Ten. Yet at precisely the same moment Blair gave his monthly press conference in Downing Street. Blair's aides were quoted as saying that the clash was a coincidence, but of course it was not. Blair had by now lost all patience with Brown and was irritated that he was taking all the flak for Iraq while the Chancellor was highlighting global poverty, an important but politically less challenging theme. Blair had knocked Brown out of the pre-election team. This was a calculated attempt to knock him off the bulletins.

It was also a disaster. News 24 split the screen mischievously to show both press conferences at the same time. The first question to Blair was whether if re-elected he would retain Brown as Chancellor. Another asked: 'What an earth is going on with the clashing press conferences?' Later the main bulletins also deployed the split-screen technique. Not a word of Blair or Brown would have registered with the wider electorate. The sole impression conveyed was one of divisive disarray.

A few days later the *Sunday Telegraph* began its serialization of Robert Peston's Brown biography, *Brown's Britain*. It included quotes from Brown telling Blair that he would never trust him again. I am told, though not by the author, that Brown himself was the source. Once more a book had become explosive. Like the Routledge book it was obvious it had been written with the cooperation of the Brownite court. This time the objective had been to outline Brown's thinking on the assumption that he would be Prime Minister, hence the title. Instead the publication led to another intensification of the Blair/Brown battle.

As ever, Blair surfaced from the latest bout of infighting with a stylish dignity. Later in January I travelled with him for a two-day trip to Manchester. At each point – a visit for questions at the *Manchester Evening News*, a speech at a new housing development, an appearance on GMTV on a council estate, a walk on the set of *Coronation Street* – he was engaged and capable of adapting to every contrasting situation. Most of the national media was attacking him relentlessly. It was the new fashion, the attack on Blair on the front pages and by columnists from the left and to the right. But it was clear that away from the national media mindset he still had a popular appeal and it was also clear to me that he cared still about how he was perceived. On the second day after his GMTV interview I was in the car behind his with his press secretary, David Hill. At one point Hill's phone rang. It was Blair phoning from the car in front. He wanted to know how Hill thought the GMTV interview had gone and what Hill had thought of the photos in the local papers where Blair was captured being enthusiastically embraced by a large female voter. Hill sought to reassure him. 'The photo is really good. It shows that not everyone hates you!' Blair was delighted at this verdict.

It was during this trip that Blair told me privately he knew that the *Sun* would endorse Labour at the election. This was January, months before a campaign. Rupert Murdoch had given the guarantee after Blair had offered a referendum on the constitution.

But although Blair could still perform like an ageless rock star, questions were being asked about Labour's build-up to the election campaign. Under Milburn's direction Blair had been pursuing what had become known as the 'masochism strategy'. During the weeks preceding the war in Iraq Blair had taken part in TV discussions with angry voters. Milburn was pursuing the same strategy again. Every now and again Blair appeared to be bashed around by furious voters. He handled these situations with an appealing good humour, but some cabinet ministers began to worry that the message being conveyed was that voters hated the government. There were also concerns about the tone of the preliminary campaigning. The influential *Guardian* columnist Polly Toynbee argued that under Milburn there was an alienating and vacuous machismo at the heart of the campaign. Polls suggested that Labour's lead was narrowing.

Brown was keeping his head down. He indicated that in the campaign he would travel around the country. In the meantime he prepared for his budget amidst rumours that Blair would move him from the Treasury after the election. They were rumours that Brown took seriously, and with good cause. He told Balls that if Blair ever tried to move him he would not accept another job in the government. But the budget as ever took up most of his attention and that of his closest allies, including Balls, even though he was no longer formally working in the Treasury.

The budget was a typical pre-election mix of reassurance and tasty policies aimed at addressing possible thorny policy areas, cuts in stamp duty, help for pensioners, petrol duty frozen, higher child tax credits. Pre-election budgets are always viewed with particular urgency and yet are in some ways the least interesting, framed with short-term considerations in mind. But this one had a single important political consequence. Immediately afterwards Labour's poll ratings started to rise. Helped by the reassuring ritualistic choreography of budget day, Brown appeared the master of all he surveyed. The economy was growing. He had the scope for some modest giveaways without putting up taxes. Homeowners were helped. So were motorists. But there was space for moves aimed at addressing child poverty, his and his party's passion. Blair and Milburn had not wanted to make the economy the centrepiece of the election. They felt that in order to win a third term they needed to change the pitch, and anyway wanted to secure a mandate for further reforms of the public services. Yet the positive reaction to the budget seemed to vindicate Brown's view that the economy would be the key to another victory.

This was a period when Brown's personal ratings were soaring. Shortly after the budget YouGov suggested that 61 per cent of voters approved of Brown's stewardship of the economy. The following month the figure was even higher. Other polling organizations published similar findings. These were extraordinary figures for a Labour chancellor who had been responsible for the party's economic policies since 1992. Brown's internal critics complained that it was easy for him to get high ratings because all he had to worry about was the economy. He disappeared when other difficult issues arose. But the economy was central. In 1992 it was Labour's economic policies that were responsible for another election defeat.

Philip Gould's focus groups confirmed the findings of the polls. Brown was a popular asset for Labour. Gould told Blair that Brown must be given a publicly prominent role in the campaign. Observing closely from outside Downing Street and preparing to play a discreetly active role in the campaign, this was also the view of Alastair Campbell. Blair's former press secretary had despaired of Brown's behaviour and that of the courtiers, but his burning desire for Labour to win big overwhelmed all other considerations. With Campbell it always did. Shortly after the budget Campbell contacted Balls and suggested that Brown must be brought back to the heart of the campaign and it would be crazy to give the Tories ammunition by having the Chancellor in effect running a separate, disconnected campaign.

Campbell's concern about the benefits for the Tories chimed with the ambitions of Balls and indeed with Brown. There was speculation in the media and among some Labour MPs that Brown was being uncooperative because he wanted Labour to win by only a small majority so that Blair would be under pressure to resign soon afterwards. Nothing could have been further from the truth. Brown ached for the biggest possible majority partly because his chances of winning a fourth term if he became Prime Minister would be all the greater. Suddenly it looked as if he might be the key to achieving a more substantial majority. For all the tensions and mutual antipathies, bordering on despair and hatred, the Blair and Brown courts could unite when they faced the challenge of defeating the Conservative party.

Once more Brown and his inner court sought a deal with Blair. They were always on the lookout for deals, from Granita onwards, as if they were not all on the same side, part of the same team – and of course in some ways they were not. In this case Brown had suffered so many setbacks it is not surprising that he sought to make the most of his latest stronger hand. Over Easter, 2005, Ed Balls attended a meeting with Alastair Campbell and Philip Gould to discuss how Brown could be brought back to the centre of the campaign. Campbell and Gould were receptive to a series of possibilities. According to some Brownites they even raised the possibility of Blair clarifying publicly when he would step down after the election. In the end the agreement represented another remarkable comeback for Brown. The Chancellor and his team would move in to run the campaign. There would be joint press conferences with Blair and Brown. Blair would confirm that Brown would remain as Chancellor after the election and that the two of them would work together on a smooth leadership transition after the election.

With Balls and Campbell mediating, Brown was brought back to the heart of the election campaign. The move was almost as significant as Blair's earlier attempt to place him on the margins. As so often in their joint dance the footwork required a set of counter-steps. This time it was Brown who was in a position to dictate terms. He told Blair he wanted his team to move into the party's headquarters in London and that the economy should be placed at the centre of the campaign. Blair agreed, although the concession was not a total retreat. He had the manifesto, already written largely by Milburn and Miliband, as his protective shield. But as a result of this latest deal the choreography of the looming third term changed dramatically in Brown's favour. Milburn was humiliated for the second time in his cabinet career, once more sidelined by Blair's need to keep Brown on board. He took the changed situation with typical good grace and humour, but his public role in the election was much diminished. Blair's hopes that Milburn might be a possible successor were dashed. The dreams of his senior allies that Brown could be moved from the Treasury were also ended. Irrespective of the behind-the-scenes agreement Blair knew that he would be asked at the start of the campaign about whether he would reappoint Brown as Chancellor. He could not equivocate given that the suddenly refocused strategy was to project the two of them as the solid alliance at the heart of the campaign. Sure enough, Blair told GMTV when both of them were sitting together on the sofa that while he would not appoint the rest of his cabinet in advance of the election he would confirm that Brown, who had been a 'brilliant Chancellor', would keep his job.

What followed was an extraordinary campaign that was conducted on two entirely different levels. On the surface Blair and Brown were projected as the closest of friends. They appeared together at many of the press conferences and on several TV programmes. A soft-focus party election broadcast featured the two of them reflecting on their friendship and mutual admiration. Out on the campaign trail Tony bought Gordon an ice cream. Gordon insisted he would have taken the same steps as Tony in the build-up to the war in Iraq. Both were committed to public service reform.

Yet behind the scenes the two of them were involved in another high-stakes game of poker. Brown was at the height of his powers and popularity with the electorate. He knew that such popularity would not last for ever. All chancellors are doomed to a period of unpopularity at some point and he feared his trough might come soon, making it difficult for him to succeed Blair. He was also alarmed that the issue of 'trust' was dominating the election campaign in a way that would begin to tarnish the entire government. In the campaign it was Blair personally who was being subjected to intense questioning once more about whether he had lied over Iraq. But there was growing evidence that the issue was starting to make an impact on Labour's support and not just on Blair's personal ratings. Therefore even as the two of them were holding hands during the election campaign Brown was calculating and discussing with his allies how he could start putting pressure on Blair to go fairly soon after the election rather than stick to his publicly stated intention of serving a full term.

I got a call from one member of Brown's extensive entourage half-way through the election campaign. He suggested we met some way from Labour's HQ in Westminster, so we walked along the River Thames on the South Bank. The Brown supporter said that it was essential Blair outlined the route map for his departure at the party conference in September. He predicted there would be pressure for him to do so immediately after the election in the media and from Labour MPs. The prediction sounds treacherous at a time when Blair was campaigning to serve a full third term, but actually the apparent treachery was perceptive. This is precisely what happened, and in a way that had not been organised by Brown's aides.

But separately Blair was making an entirely different set of calculations. He was determined to make use of the time available to him to press on with reforms of the public services. In a long interview with me for the *Independent* during the campaign he said that he knew now how to implement reforms, to get things done. He admitted that when he first became Prime Minister with no experience of government he had not known which levers to press.

Blair was hoping that an election victory would help him to move on from Iraq. He had an agenda and he was going to see it through. Once Brown had delivered by returning to the election campaign and it was clear that Labour was heading for victory, Blair became more assertive. From the perspective of the Brown camp Blair reneged on the new arrangements three days before the end of the election campaign. According to one Brown ally: 'It all reverted back to what it was like before the election campaign. Tony couldn't accept emotionally or politically that Gordon Brown had turned the campaign around, so he had to assert himself. There was silence about the reshuffle following the election. There was no consultation. And after the election Tony made clear he was not consulting Gordon on policy either. Suddenly all contact was broken off.'

Labour won the election with a smaller but still substantial majority. Once more a campaign was dominated by two individuals, Blair and Brown. But this time they were planning for battles to come, the climax that would finally bring some kind of resolution.

SEVEN

Coup

The two years following the 2005 election were the most bizarre in New Labour's history, almost insane in their intensity and ambiguous outcome. They were dominated by more scheming and manoeuvring between Blair and Brown, a more and more frenzied dance to the death. On one level the struggle brought about a near-total victory for Brown, as Blair left office earlier than he might have done and without too much of a publicly bruising battle. But at a more subterranean level the internal conflict landed Brown with an impossible legacy when he finally acquired the crown, several years too late at a time when voters had tired of him and he was exhausted.

Blair was determined to define the future long after he had left office, committing Brown to a range of long-term plans for education, health, law and order and security. In this respect it was Blair who came out on top. Brown was terrified of saying or doing anything that appeared to be a fraction to the left of Blair during the period between the 2005 general election and his accession to the leadership, and so in his public declarations he narrowed the scope for a marked shift of direction when he became Prime Minister, even though the voters did yearn for some sort of 'change'.

As a result the seeds of Brown's calamitous first year as Prime Minister were sown after the 2005 election and long before he entered Number Ten. By the time he came to office he was already on a doomed mission marked by contradictions. He had made a series of statements that were more Blairite than Blair. Yet he was supposed to mark a change from Blair. Who was he?

His closest supporters thought they knew. To them he was the great strategic thinker with a conscience, a leader who would make capitalism work for the poor if he was given a freer hand without having to worry all the time about what Blair was up to as Prime Minister. But during this final fraught climb to the summit Brown continued to evade clear definition as a deliberate act, hoping to acquire as broad a range of support as possible.

His apparent victory in 2007, when he acquired the crown unchallenged and without a bloody insurrection, was a triumph of will and yet was the outcome of fatal endeavours carried out in an impossible context.

The mood of Labour MPs in the immediate aftermath of the 2005 election was anxious and febrile, a vivid sign that the New Labour coalition which depended on an extreme form of discipline was breaking down. Blair had led his party to a third successive election victory, and yet during the weekend that followed polling day several MPs gave interviews in which they called on him to stand down, or at least make clear when he was going to do so, an unprecedented sequence and a signal that New Labour was becoming dysfunctional as a coherent political force.

On one level the outburst was extraordinary. When Margaret Thatcher won a third successive victory in 1987 she was at first even more revered by her grateful, awestruck party. Now a range of Labour MPs cited the fall in the government's majority from 161 to 67 and the continuing fallout from the war in Iraq as reasons why Blair had to go.

On another level the angry response to an electoral triumph was also understandable. Iraq had sapped Labour of moral purpose, blurred its identity even further than Blair had already done, and cost it support at the 2005 election. To make matters more tantalizing for Blair's opponents, he had declared that he would not serve a fourth term, so they knew he would be going at some point before the next election. They thought he should go soon, not least because the Conservatives were breathing down their necks in England. In spite of running an amateurish and desperately strident campaign the Conservatives secured the most votes in England, largely because some Labour supporters stayed at home or voted for the anti-war Liberal Democrats.

But that was not the full story of the 2005 campaign. Blair had kept part of his contradictory coalition of support intact precisely because of Iraq. Obedient to Rupert Murdoch, the still highly influential *Sun* newspaper advised its readers to vote Labour solely on the grounds of Blair's foreign policy, another token of Labour's contorted appeal. An assiduous reader of newspapers, Brown noted that Murdoch's support for Labour was hanging by a thread, totally dependent on a robust approach to Iraq and the threat posed by terrorism. Brown shared Blair's view that a Labour government could only survive with the backing or at least fair reporting of some key newspapers. For Brown a trap was set already, before he made his moves: Labour performed badly in 2005 because of Iraq and what it had come to represent. Labour won because of Iraq and what it had come to represent.

In the immediate aftermath of the 2005 election the political situation had already become impossibly contorted. Labour's internal dissenters wanted an end to the Blairite version of Big Tent politics. Brown was determined to rebuild an equally spacious canvas crammed full of contradictory supporters. On the Sunday after the election the former cabinet minister Robin Cook told the BBC: 'The question Tony Blair should be reflecting on this weekend is whether now might be a better time to let a new leader in who could then achieve the unity we need if we are going to go forward.' Another ex-cabinet minister, Frank Dobson, appeared on GMTV to observe that Blair had been an enormous liability in the election: 'I don't think we can go into important local elections next year with Tony Blair as leader and expect to keep many of the councillors we've got now.' One Labour MP told a Sunday newspaper: 'It would be nice to see Brown crowned as early as the next party conference.' This was Labour's mood music forty-eight hours after its third election victory.

The former cabinet ministers and restive Labour backbenchers were expressing their own views separately and of their own accord.

The fact that they were exerting precisely the kind of pressure that Brown wanted to place on Blair is not proof that the weekend activity was an overt Brownite conspiracy. The various weekend political programmes sought out the rebellious interviewees rather than the other way around. Nonetheless their views chimed with Brown's ruthless strategy. Brown wanted Labour MPs and influential newspaper columnists to put intense pressure on Blair to declare his departure date. He knew his fingerprints could not be visible on any of the acts of destabilization, but he hoped that journalists and MPs would shout in a chorus so loud that Blair would have to yield. First he wanted Blair to announce at least a route map that would lead to his departure at the forthcoming party conference. Then he wanted him to announce a date and go, preferably within the next year or eighteen months.

Brown wooed some of the rebels with a shameless transparency. Any internal enemy of Blair's quickly became an ally of Brown's. His pragmatic attitude to political friendship was demonstrated in his rapprochement with Cook, a dress rehearsal for his later even more sensational reconciliation with Peter Mandelson. Brown recognized that Cook, who had courageously resigned over the Iraq war, could become a highly significant ally, an opponent of the war backing a New Labour leader and possibly bringing with his endorsement many disillusioned voters.

Brown and Cook had a famously bad relationship until Cook resigned from the cabinet. Many explanations have been offered for the origins of their mutual hostility, from their early rivalry at the top of Scottish Labour politics to various imagined or actual slights. The most convincing explanation is simpler, and provided by one close Brown ally: 'Gordon found Robin irritating and his politics unreliable. Robin was one of those attacking Gordon for being too pro-Euro and then when he switched positions he attacked Gordon for being anti-Euro. Gordon never rated Robin as a strategic thinker who understood what it was like making tough decisions which might mean short-term unpopularity.' One of Brown's less publicly conspicuous flaws was a gargantuan capacity for irritation to the point of extreme anger.

Cook was almost as dismissive in his attitude towards Brown. In the mid-1990s he was more impressed by Blair and feared that Brown was taking Labour's economic policies too far to the right. When he was Foreign Secretary and keen for Britain to sign up to the Euro he suggested as a joke to Blair that he should pretend to be an opponent on the ground that his opposition might help to make Brown more of an enthusiast.

But after Cook's resignation from the cabinet, and following his increasingly public criticisms of Blair's leadership, Brown started to make contact. Following his departure from the cabinet as Leader of the House on the eve of war in 2003, accompanied by a speech in the Commons of intelligent and prophetic insight, Cook moved into a big office in the parliamentary building as a backbench MP only a stone's throw away from the Treasury. Brown became a regular visitor. 'Gordon came in for a cup of tea every couple of weeks,' one of Cook's former aides told me at the time with a mischievous look. Cook became expansive in private about their newly cordial relationship, explaining how they had started to speak and meet regularly not just in Westminster but in Scotland too.

In particular the two of them spoke at length about the need to restore trust in politics. Brown told Cook he wanted constitutional reform to play a defining role in the early years of his leadership in order to restore political trust, in the way that Bank of England independence ensured a Labour government was trusted to run the economy. Brown urged Cook to give him some thoughts on the issue. On several occasions he told Cook that he wanted to bring him back into government.

Brown's wooing of Cook had nothing to do with a new, less irritable approach to working relationships. A former senior cabinet minister who had known Brown and Cook for decades, and who shared Brown's original doubts about Cook, says Brown had never been won over. 'Robin was deluded about the degree to which he would have played a significant role under Gordon. The rapprochement was nowhere near as real as Robin thought or made out. In the end Gordon still thought he was flaky.' Brown was capable of real friendship outside politics. Inside politics, relations were formed on the basis of a thousand calculations.

Cook died suddenly of a heart attack in the early summer recess of 2005, a terrible loss to British politics, a distinctive, radical voice and the most articulate critic of Blairite and Brownite expediency. Outside the inner circle Cook was closer to the publicly declared spirit of early New Labour than either Blair or Brown. He was a pluralist who believed in electoral reform, a pro-European and internationalist. He was also an unapologetic advocate of Keynesian economics when it was unfashionable to be so, seeing through some of the market ortho-doxies willingly accepted by Blair and pragmatically celebrated by Brown. Cook could have claimed further vindication if he had lived, when it became the new fashion to challenge market orthodoxy.

At a memorial service for Cook in Westminster in the autumn of 2005, Brown spoke movingly about their belated friendship and also how he regretted the long period in which they had fallen out. In the context of Cook's tragically early death, the words were sincere, but what is also clear is that to begin with Brown seized on Cook's disil-lusionment with Blair for partly expedient reasons. As another of Brown's allies told me: 'Robin was fantastically useful for us. He could bring the anti-war wing of the party to Gordon and help us reunite.' These words sound thoughtlessly ruthless, but Cook was capable of making crude calculations too. Although he was enjoying his exile from cabinet, thriving in particular as a journalist, he wanted to have another high-profile ministerial post. He knew that could only come about by making up with the old enemy who looked certain to be the next Prime Minister.

While Brown had a unique capacity to fall out with colleagues, he could apply a more emollient approach. Whenever he sensed that an influential MP or newspaper political columnist was revising a previ-ous high opinion of Blair, he would pounce, offering them access that Blair had appeared to deny. He was also quick to express sympathy with ministers who had lost their jobs in reshuffles. After one of these he wrote to each of the victims, an unsubtle and time-consuming act of self-interested solicitousness.

In the immediate aftermath of the election Brown and his court were consumed by the importance of getting a date out of Blair for his departure. By contrast, as Blair saw it he had the most important set of policies to implement since becoming Prime Minister. He was not animated by policies that had pleased his party in the past. Privately he described policies such as the minimum wage and support for the social chapter as 'low-lying fruit', easy to pick and digest. His agenda after the 2005 election stimulated him much more: new anti-crime initiatives known as the 'respect' agenda; the introduction of ID cards; choice for parents in what he regarded as a 'schools revolution'; a major reform of pensions; new security measures aimed at tackling the threat posed by terrorism.

Blair was excited not only by the substance of this agenda but by the position it brought him in the political spectrum. Quite a lot of it placed him at odds with the Labour party. Instinctively he regarded such a distance as healthy, as he was always fearful that Labour would head towards what he called its 'comfort zone'. At the same time his policies had the support of much of the media, not least Rupert Murdoch's influential newspapers, so he was not being quite as tough as he seemed or felt he was being. Once more he was in his own comfort zone, taking on his party with the backing of mighty voices in the media and being praised for his perceived boldness.

At times Blair's resilience and empathic energy were still in full force. His post-election summer was lifted by personal involvement in the successful bid to secure the 2012 Olympic Games in London. A day after the announcement London was attacked by terrorists as Blair was hosting the G8 summit at Gleneagles. He rose instinctively to the extreme range of differing emotional tests. The quality of his public performances made projection an even more important skill. The media and the voters came to expect a performance even though they tended to dismiss Blair towards the end of his leadership as an unprincipled thespian. When they got Brown they missed the actor.

The shocks came one after another, the euphoria of the Olympics bid followed the day after on 7 July by a series of coordinated suicide attacks on London's public transport system during the morning rush hour. The bombings were carried out by four British Muslim men.

At first Blair was resilient and tonally restrained, but as his final act before the summer break in 2005 he announced out of the blue that 'the rules of the game' had changed as he outlined a ten-point plan for tackling terrorism. The so-called new rules had been compiled with such speed to please some newspapers that even the Home Secretary, Charles Clarke, on holiday in the US, knew little about the headline-grabbing initiative. Not a single point in the ten-point plan was ever implemented.

The media mood, positive towards Blair in the late summer, changed once more by the time the political year started up again in September. The events of the summer, celebratory and then tragic, were not usual. The fundamentals had not changed.

Brown wanted to get into Number Ten partly because policy differences were erupting again. He thought that the introduction of ID cards was a waste of money (although he changed his mind as Prime Minister when at first it appeared that ID cards were popular). He feared that the Olympics would cost a fortune and benefit London disproportionately (he never understood London and the infrastructure needs of a major capital city, but he was right about the soaring costs of the Olympics). He thought that the 'respect' agenda was too negative and punitive. He feared that Blair's plans to give the police powers to hold suspects for ninety days was based on too crude a form of populism (although weakly he was to play similar games as an even more insecure Prime Minister), and he worried that Blair's plans for schools would lead to benefits for a few privileged children without lifting standards across the board. The worries were convenient and never fully addressed when he became Prime Minister, but sincerely held at the time.

In acrimonious discussions with the Number Ten policy unit, Ed Balls and Ed Miliband voiced their frustrations aloud. Balls had always done so. Miliband had been more conciliatory but, against character, was also adopting a more confrontational approach. 'This is so right-wing,' they declared as they faced another policy that seemed to bypass the state in a theoretical attempt to 'empower people' and give them quite often only an illusion of 'choice'.

In the meantime Brown's close allies sniffed the air and wondered whether they were finally riding a tide in their favour. On the eve of the 2005 Labour conference Ed Balls, now a Labour MP, told me in an interview for the *Independent*: 'The next few years will be critical. They will be about the renewal of the country in the face of new economic and social challenges. They will also be about the renewal of New Labour.'

The implication was clear. Renewal would come about only once a new leader was in place. The term 'renewal', its innocent vivacity, became Brownite code for a change of leader. Balls went on to argue: 'We need to show once more the discipline and rigour it took to create New Labour in the first place. We must analyse our weaknesses and strengths in the way that we did in the 1990s. If we do that we can renew Labour in this parliament and then go on to renew the country.'

This was a very different analysis from the one offered by Tony Blair and his allies, who were working still on the assumption that Blair would serve a full term. Balls was seeking to frame the public debate in a way that would make it impossible for that to happen.

In the same interview he outlined what he and Brown regarded as the policy agenda for the third term. It was different from Blair's. Balls made no reference to 'choice' in schools, ID cards or the 'respect' policies. Instead he outlined a set of priorities that implicitly pointed to a subtly different relationship between state and the individual compared with Blair's vision:

We have not made enough progress in developing adult skills. More widely the inherited problem of the country's infrastructure was huge when we came to power. There is still a long way to go to establish a world-class infrastructure. No one can be satisfied with the number of kids from state schools going to university. China and India place great emphasis on schools and science. We must meet that challenge, which is partly a challenge to our cohesion as a society. On the environment

we are meeting our international commitments but nobody can feel
we are making the necessary progress. We must decide what we are
going to do with pensions. We must do more in order to meet our
pledge to abolish child poverty. This is a big agenda.

Here is a rare public glimpse of the policy differences between
Brownites and Blairites. Blair was moving rightwards, increasingly
looking at ways to bypass the state in order to bring about change. In
a limited but more expansive way, Brown, Balls and Ed Miliband still
saw that the state had the potential in certain circumstances to be a
benevolent force. They sought to empower people by exploring ways
of getting more of them to university. They still recognized that issues
relating to the levels of public spending had not been resolved, in spite
of some improvements to Britain's creaking infrastructure. They
sought more levers to pull in order to address child poverty. Blair had
lost patience or interest in the state as an effective instrument.

Education was to some extent an emblematic policy. Blair wanted
to allow more or less anyone to set up schools who felt inclined to do
so, a policy subsequently adopted by the Conservatives. Brownites
tended to ask questions about accountability and responsibility in
relation to schools. If a private company set up a school, would it have
any wider responsibilities to the local community? They were also
more emphatic in their support for an admission code that barred
selection of pupils, a code over which Blair and his Schools minister,
Andrew Adonis, had more mixed feelings.

The pivotal political battle during this period related to the future
of schools and went well beyond the familiar Blair/Brown internal
tensions. It added significantly to the decline of New Labour as a
distinct and formidable force. With quite a fanfare, in October 2005
Blair published a White Paper on schools which aimed to create 'independent state schools with the freedom to innovate and succeed,
backed by not-for-profit trusts'. According to the White Paper the
objective was to create a system that was increasingly driven by paren-
tal demand and choice. Local authorities would become commission-
ers rather than providers of school places.

The document, subsequently described by the Commons Education Select Committee as the worst-written White Paper it had ever scrutinized, raised many questions. Would the schools be free to select pupils? With a hint of reluctance Blair addressed the question belatedly by proposing a strict admissions code. It was not entirely clear to whom the independent schools would answer. Blair argued that they would be accountable to parents, but he could not fully address the practical question: if parents were unhappy, how could they move their pupils if others schools were full?

There were other related questions. How could the successful schools expand? Would they remain successful if they became bigger? What would happen to the schools which some parents were leaving? Presumably over time they would close. But that would not happen immediately, with the implication that for a time there would be many more schools and teachers. Where would the additional teachers come from and would they be any good?

Gordon Brown, Ed Balls and Ed Miliband asked the questions in their discussions with each other and were deeply uneasy when they could not come up with clear answers. Others in the Labour party were in turmoil. The normally ultra-loyal Alastair Campbell joined his partner Fiona Miller and the former Labour leader Neil Kinnock in rallies against the proposals. One close ally of Brown's told me to speak to the Labour MP Jon Trickett. The ally advised me that Trickett had the most intelligent insights on the flaws of the White Paper. Fortunately Trickett's views were recorded in an article for the *New Statesman* in November 2005. They were close to those of the Brownite court.

Trickett noted that the White Paper bore a close resemblance to the policies outlined in the Conservatives' manifesto. He suggested that at least Blair might have concealed it better. 'The White Paper lifts Tory policies wholesale and even plagiarizes their words.' At the suggestion of Ed Miliband, Trickett became Brown's Parliamentary Private Secretary in the autumn of 2008.

Trickett was not the only one who recognized that Blair was adopting Tory policies with his characteristic messianic fervour. The new

Conservative leader, David Cameron, noted it too. Astutely he recognized that the most effective way of undermining Blair was to support him.

As his first brilliant move as leader, Cameron changed the dynamics entirely. During his game-changing debut at Prime Minister's Question Time he told Blair that his party would work with him to get his policies on schools through in spite of the opposition from Labour MPs. This was a radical change from Cameron's predecessors, each of whom had fallen into the trap of moving further to the right of Blair in order to oppose him. Normally Blair was able to argue that the Labour party might not like what he was doing, but the alternative position being put forward by the Conservatives was much more right-wing.

What made the situation more complex was that the coming together was not just a question of expediency. Cameron and Blair were genuinely close in policy terms. Cameron had described himself as the heir to Blair, and to a limited extent the description was accurate. Partly this was a big compliment to Blair. In the 1980s Labour looked on helplessly as the Tories won general elections with ease. Now in 2005 the Conservatives had elected a leader who paid homage to a vote-winning Labour Prime Minister. In December 2005 I asked Blair what he thought of Cameron. 'He's playing me', Blair observed. He added 'Cameron wants to decouple me from the Labour party. The test is therefore whether Labour will allow that to happen or will support what I am trying to do.' But the test was slightly more complicated than that.

Politics was fracturing and the new groupings were reflected in the different approaches to the White Paper. Cameron and Blair looked towards a form of individual empowerment that bypassed the state. To the right of Cameron were some MPs and columnists who thought that any policy of Blair's should be opposed almost as a matter of principle and were worried in particular that Cameron seemed to support the rigid admissions code. On the centre left there was continuing support for local authorities, with the likes of Neil Kinnock and Alastair Campbell arguing that councils needed strengthening rather than weakening and that schools would benefit if more middle-class parents became engaged with the state system. Brown's view remained consistent: while nobody would oppose 'choice' as a matter of principle, he was concerned that given limited resources there was a danger that choice was not attainable, in which case voters would feel disillusioned, or that it would be attainable for a few, reducing the rest to sink services. He felt the whole agenda had not been properly thought through.

Cameron's support for Blair was a decisive moment. It removed Blair's raison d'être, a Labour leader who offered an alternative to policies that were even further to the right. The evening in March 2006 when Blair needed the support of Conservative MPs to proceed with his flagship proposals on schools hastened his demise as Labour's Prime Minister. But it also proved to be another trap for Brown. While supporting Blair, Cameron portrayed Brown as 'the roadblock to reform', the Old Labour Chancellor who would take Labour back to its vote-losing ways. Brown became more and more touchy about the portrayal, fearing in particular that newspapers who had supported Blair would switch to Cameron, accepting the stereotype that his own leadership would be a move to the vote-losing left.

In response to the onslaught Brown resolved not to fall into the trap being set by the Conservatives. He would show he was as much on the centre ground as Blair. The resolution, while arguably the right one to make in the circumstances, led Brown into another series of convoluted strategic decisions that would cause him fatal problems when he became Prime Minister.

In this final phase the government worked on two levels, with supporters of Blair and Brown each seeking to undermine the other camp and yet at the same time working at a limited form of mediation, another bizarre and characteristic third way, in which the mediators and those acting treacherously were often the same people.

In the autumn of 2005, worried that the Conservatives were on the verge of electing a more effective leader, Alastair Campbell and Philip Gould became even stronger converts to the idea of a smooth transition. Both had intense doubts about Brown and knew at first hand how difficult he could be. Neither could ever forgive him for the way he had treated Blair at times. But unlike some ultra-Blairites they recognized that he would almost certainly be the next leader and they wanted him to beat the Conservatives.

In November and December Campbell, Gould and Balls mediated several meetings between Blair and Brown in an attempt to discuss how they could work together and then transfer power from one to the other. The meetings were fruitless. Blair was not interested in engaging in any discussion that touched upon his departure. Uncharacteristically, he conveyed his irritation and annoyance with what he regarded as another wretched Brown-related diversion. He arrived late for one meeting and tried to get another cancelled, citing other engagements. He was totally focused on delivering a range of reforms and on setting out the agenda for the next decade. Brown and his senior allies feared they were dealing with an increasingly delusional Prime Minister who was in denial about the time limit on his leadership and the damage this was causing – as they saw it – to the government and the Labour party.

Tensions between the two sides reached even greater extremes. Even the most placid figure in the Brownite court, Ed Miliband, conveyed frustrated anger. At one point he stormed into Sally Morgan's office in Number Ten and yelled: 'When are you all going to go?' Morgan, who had taken over from Angie Hunter as Blair's gatekeeper and close adviser, was not especially surprised.

There was, however, one serious consequence from the fraught Blair/Brown discussions. Blair did not say very much at the meetings, but he did at one point say, perhaps to justify his continued occupancy of Number Ten, that Rupert Murdoch had noted to him that Brown lacked experience in dealing with the threat posed by terrorism. Brown took the observation to mean that he should be seen in public addressing the theme, and that if he failed to do so Blair would cite his own distinct experience in this area as justification for staying on.

Over Christmas and the New Year, while David Cameron appeared to settle with ease into the role of Tory leader and established a lead in the polls, Brown decided that he would make it much clearer that he rather than Cameron was the heir to Blair. It was the start of his doomed contradictory enterprise: He would out-Blair Blair while personifying change from the whole Blair era.

In February Brown made his first move in outlining a set of cautiously defensive policies that would come to define his early period as Prime Minister. He made a speech on how he would face up to the threat posed by terrorists in the post-11 September era. Usually Brown's speeches were the product of intense teamwork, although he nearly always wrote the final drafts. This one he wrote mainly on his own. He knew the two Eds in particular had doubts about what he was trying to do. In effect he was triangulating over the issue of terrorism, navigating a third way between Blair's failed attempt to give the police the right to detain suspects for ninety days and those who opposed any move to extend the period suspects could be held.

The speech was a typically self-conscious act of contortion, but had also some political cunning within it as he attempted a unifying theme: 'There is a British way of seeking and building a unified national consensus around a framework that is tough in ensuring security but also by being tough in ensuring proper accountability as we sustain public support for the action that must be taken.'

Here was a first take of his pitch when he became Prime Minister. He sought to highlight a range of issues over which he could build a national consensus. So he was not only going to adopt tougher security measures, but also to increase the level of accountability in which security decisions were taken. He described the combination of the two as an example of 'Britishness', his other big apolitical theme much highlighted over this period.

Brown's less subtle critics assumed that he chose to highlight 'Britishness' because he was worried as a Scot about his appeal in England. In fact Brown was fairly relaxed about being Scottish, arguably too relaxed. The fact that he sought to be a Scottish Prime Minister in a devolved United Kingdom raised more questions than he seemed to recognize. But in raising 'Britishness' Brown was seeking to do something far more ambitious than change perceptions about his own national identity. He wanted to transform the debate about what it meant to be British, seizing the patriotic flag for more progressive values that included fairness and a sense of duty. It was an early attempt to build a progressive consensus which he hoped would include the flag-waving *Daily Mail* and defiant left-of-centre *Guardian* readers.

Although he made promises about more robust accountability, he had taken the calamitous first step towards a big prime-ministerial initiative that got nowhere.

A few months after the speech on security Brown moved into another policy area with no direct connection to his Treasury brief. He did so with the same range of fevered calculations. In the early summer he became wary again that Blair was seizing on a whole range of security issues as a reason why he must stay in office. According to one of Brown's aides he sensed that Blair had resolved to renew the Trident nuclear deterrent and was telling his inner court that he doubted whether 'Gordon would be willing to take the party on over this'.

As a result Brown decided to get there before Blair, behaving as if he was facing a trial in which Blair set the terms. In June he inserted a passage in to his annual Mansion House speech: 'The government would demonstrate a sense of strong national purpose in protecting our security in this parliament and in the long term – strong in defence, in fighting terrorism, upholding NATO, supporting our armed forces and retaining our independent nuclear deterrent.' In a frantic briefing session in advance of the speech, Brown's press secretary, Damien McBride, told political journalists that the Chancellor was giving the go-ahead for a replacement to Trident. The cost was imprecise and certainly not outlined by Brown, who did not even refer specifically to Trident in his speech. Defence experts estimated that the replacement would cost up to £25 billion.

As so often happened with Brown, he overreached to prove a point. He had no need to be associated with such a commitment at that point and was following orthodoxy rather than daring to challenge it. Soon even senior Tories such as Michael Portillo and Michael Ancram were arguing against replacing Trident, as were mainstream Labour figures, including the former Home Secretary, Charles Clarke. But Brown was happy to be associated with orthodoxy: the more orthodox the better, he felt.

In the meantime Brown was stepping up the pressure on Blair to name the date of his departure. The local elections in May 2006 were a key staging post. Predictably the results were terrible for Labour. It lost control of councils that the party had run for years. At the time I presented GMTV's political programme on Sunday mornings. On Thursday Damian McBride phoned me to offer Brown for a pre-record on Friday morning. He knew the interview would be broadcast on Sunday and reported in the press on Monday, a sequence that applied almost whatever an interviewee said. Brown planned to say quite a lot, or hint at quite a lot. He also offered himself for the main ten past eight slot on the *Today* programme on Friday morning. The Brownites were planning a media blitz that would last from Friday to Monday.

In the interviews Brown followed the formula deployed by Ed Balls in the interview with me in the *Independent* the previous September. On the BBC *Today* programme he argued that the government and the party needed 'renewal', his code for a change of leadership. In the interview he used the term 'renewal' eighteen times in a twelve minutes.

On Sunday TV bulletins some reports edited all the references to 'renewal' together, highlighting the lack of subtlety in Brown's rigidly formulaic approach to raising the temperature. Brown sought to indicate he was ready to take charge, but wanted no public words that could be seen as openly disloyal to Blair. This was another challenging balancing act, but once more he lugged a mallet on to the high wire.

Balls and Miliband were losing patience by now. This had been going on twelve years. They wanted Brown to make a more overt strike against Blair. Specifically they urged him to state in public that Blair must name a date. Their impatience was heightened when Blair told Brown on the Sunday after the local elections of his very different take on the results. Blair thought they were encouraging given that the government was taking some tough decisions and that Cameron was on a honeymoon. Brown could not believe the analysis and phoned Balls: 'He thinks the results were good for Labour.'

For such a sharp observer of the political scene – he often spoke as a columnist rather than the main participant of the ongoing drama – Blair's analyses of election results were erratic and subjective. When Labour was soaring under his leadership from 1997 arguably until 2003, he tended to be a pessimist when judging elections, refusing to get carried away when he had cause to do so. In some ways this was an admirable exertion of self-discipline, but the misguided pessimism also fuelled a paralysing caution in government and indeed in opposition. In perverse contrast, when Labour had become genuinely vulnerable in 2006 Blair became optimistic about the party's chances. He had strayed recklessly out of touch, whereas before he was cautiously out of touch.

The defeated Labour leader of Camden council, Raj Chadha, was closest to the truth when he told a party post-mortem at Westminster a few days later that for the first time since the 1980s he detected an anti-Labour coalition forming. He felt the voters' main priority was to keep Labour out. He saw clearly that the anti-Tory coalition, so potent in the 1997 and 2001 elections, was crumbling.

In spite of pressure from the two Eds, Brown had grown used to making strategic decisions about the leadership, and he was right not to make any overt moves. There was still a marked divide within Labour and in the media about whether Blair should name a date for his departure. The usual range of voices spoke up after the local elections as they had done in the immediate aftermath of the general election. They were not enough for Brown to claim – as he was determined to do – that he was acting on behalf of the whole party. He had no choice but to wait, not out of cowardice but self-interest.

But the waiting was doing him lethal harm. His high poll ratings up until the 2005 election were falling fast. Voters were tiring of Labour, becoming more interested in Cameron's leadership. In particular they were expressing doubts about Brown. Voters tire of long-serving governments. They tire of long-serving chancellors too.

In turn Brown's confidence started to flag. After a series of stilted and charmless media performances he decided after much hesitation to get some advice on how better to handle television interviews. The two Eds had been urging him to do so for some time. As one adviser said, 'It was very difficult for Gordon. He had been a public figure for decades and thought he knew more about the media than just about anyone else.' Seeing that his public performances were as wooden nowadays as a *Thunderbirds* puppet, his assumption of media awareness was flimsily based.

To his credit, Brown was receptive to constructive criticism and was at this point willing to do whatever it took to get the top job. He asked the broadcaster Scarlett Maguire to advise him in a few secret sessions on how to come across more effectively in a studio. But the sessions petered out. He lost interest. Brown had other crises to face and he carved out no further time for media advice. Indeed, one of the developing themes in Brown's later period was his relative indifference to the practical handling of media matters. He was still intensely bothered about the media, but the obsession did not extend to analysing more forensically how to get more positive coverage. When he became Prime Minister the operation was embarrassingly amateurish.

In spite of the unavoidable reference about making a strike, the Brownites had been very successful by the summer of 2006 in framing the internal and media debate over Blair's departure. By then it was almost as if Blair had never declared that he would serve a full third term. Cleverly the Brownites had brushed aside the Blairite formula for prime-ministerial longevity and replaced it with another question: how to achieve a necessary change of leadership (renewal, renewal) without harming the governing party? They refused to accept any narrative about Blair serving a full third term, but nowhere did Brown or his closest allies make a public statement that was openly disloyal.

In the end it was Blair who did more than Brown to create the circumstances where his departure became inevitable. Already he was pushing at the boundaries of what a leader could do, in the teeth of his party's worries: Iraq, schools reform that placed him closer to the leader of the Conservatives, poor local elections. In July he pushed the boundary further by supporting Israel's bombing of the Lebanon, or rather he backed President Bush in his support of the Israeli onslaught. Even the normally supine cabinet started to twitch. His ally and admirer David Miliband dared to raise the issue at a cabinet meeting, the last before the summer recess. Privately Miliband had concluded that the war in Iraq had been a calamitous misjudgement. Now it appeared as if Blair was becoming thoughtlessly messianic over Israel. The Leader of the House, Jack Straw, still bewildered and angry about being moved from the Foreign Office (where towards the end of his period as Foreign Secretary he was proving to be a highly effective operator, not least in seeking a diplomatic solution to the threat posed by Iran), wrote an article for his local newspaper in which he was far more outspoken in criticizing the Israeli attacks.

As ever with Blair, not everything was quite what it seemed. He calculated that public appeasement of Israel was necessary in order to exert pressure privately. He also knew that the US was the key to any prospect of the route map towards a peace process being followed. He therefore saw no purpose in breaking with the US.

Nonetheless the fact that he felt able to make these calculations in isolation, acting once more like a president, showed just how detached he had become from the growing rumblings inside his party. He had become so focused on making the utmost use of every minute of power available to him that he forgot that power could be easily removed. Or rather he calculated, in their eternal contestation, that Brown would never commit an act of regicide, and hence he had room for manoeuvre, whatever the party thought of him.

In the end that was Blair's miscalculation. Important barometer figures such as Neil and Glenys Kinnock, already tested by Blair's approach to schools, wondered how much more they could tolerate after his attitude to Israel raised the level of dissent over the summer.

The trigger for the shapeless insurrection known as the 'September coup' was an interview Tony Blair gave to *The Times* on 1 September: 'I have said that I will leave ample time for my successor. Now at some point I think people have got to accept that as a reasonable proposition and let me get on with the job.'

Brown and Balls had spoken several times on the phone since their return from holidays about how they could force Blair to name a date for his departure before or at the party conference. They felt at last that their self-interest coincided with the passionate desire from most of the rest of the party as well. On the August bank holiday Monday one of Brown's allies told me that one way or another Blair would be persuaded to name a date for his departure.

The choreography of the 'September coup' shows the total involvement of Brown and his inner court, this time in league with disillusioned Labour MPs, including some who were identified previously as ardent Blairites. The Blairite MP Siôn Simon was a pivotal figure, organizing a letter from some of the 2001 intake calling on Blair to stand down. As news of the letter started to spread Balls wrote an article for the *Observer* repeating the knowingly mischievous call for a 'stable and orderly transition'. Similar letters were in circulation amongst the 1997 and 2005 intakes. One of those who had signed the 2001 letter was a minister, Tom Watson, who had strong ties with Brown. Another Blairite, Chris Bryant, signed the letter too.

The trigger had been squeezed, but remarkably Brown's fingerprints could not be identified. Of course he was involved. The choreography was a form of evidence, but of a classically intangible kind. Watson had visited Brown at his home in Edinburgh the day before the letters became public. Both have denied discussing the insurrection, but it is impossible to imagine that there was no exchange at a pivotal moment when power might at last be changing hands.

The Blairites hit back by circulating their own letter to MPs, although they now only sought some breathing space, more or less suggesting in the letter that Blair would be gone within a year. But both sides knew that resolution could only be reached by a conversation between Blair and Brown. There were two on the Wednesday morning. If Brown was disconnected from the revolt, why was he sitting in Number Ten bargaining over what should follow next? After years of expedient restraint he had made his move, but he could not have done so if Labour MPs beyond the Brownite tribe had not been in a restive mood.

Even so the move was limited, and did not go entirely according to plan. At one point in those feverish September days Brown and his court had hoped that a bigger name would go public and call on Blair to name his departure date – possibly Jack Straw or Neil Kinnock. Neither did so, although Straw had been candid privately with Blair about the need to clarify his departure plans. There was also something of a mood swing by Wednesday, with many cabinet ministers and quite a few Labour MPs livid with Brown for what had happened. This was the mirror image of the coups that followed against Brown. No big name would speak out. The pliant politicians in the cabinet preferred to sit tight and wait on events.

Unusually, Blair lost his temper with Brown in the first of their two meetings on Wednesday. Until then Blair had been incredibly and admirably calm, his most appealing quality. On Monday he had delivered a speech in York and stayed on to answer questions from the audience while his aides took calls about the growing insurrection. On Tuesday afternoon he had a long conversation with the journalist Will Hutton about markets and the role of the state, in the Downing Street garden. Hutton could not believe it. Blair was facing a coup d'état and yet could find time to focus on an exchange about economic policy. Blair had a gift for being able to compartmentalize. But when he met Brown he lost it, not because of the attempt to force his departure but at the nature of the negotiations, which Blair described as a form of blackmail. Brown knew that more junior ministerial resignations were in the pipeline as he demanded that Blair should go, preferably by the end of the year.

Blair's close allies say that Brown made demands that no leader could meet – that Brown would in effect become co-leader, that Blair would ensure there was no significant challenger. The stormy meeting was an echo of the exchanges at the Granita restaurant in the summer of 1994 and reflected Brown's intense neurosis about what happened then. Still he worried that the crown might be snatched from his head at the last moment by another Blairite coup, and still he feared that a turbulent leadership contest would undermine him and the Labour party perhaps fatally. After their second meeting Blair famously agreed to make a public declaration that he would leave within twelve months and the forthcoming Labour conference would be his last.

After that meeting Brown was photographed leaving by car with what appeared to be a self-satisfied smirk on his normally sober face. For Brown the photo looked awful, not only suggesting he was at the centre of the coup but also that he was already gleefully celebrating the outcome. In fact the truth was more complicated. Brown was fairly pleased at the outcome of the sequence, but nowhere near as ecstatic as the photo suggested. He had hoped to force Blair out sooner, and possibly right away. There were still loose ends. How would Blair approach his final phase in power? Would Brown be challenged? When precisely would Blair leave? Once more Brown faced unanswered questions even when it appeared as if his ambition was being fulfilled.

Yet in spite of the lack of clarity, Brown had cause to feel more satisfied than he had been at any point since the 2005 general election. At last he had the public declaration from Blair. There was no escape clause for the long-serving Prime Minister.

Brown was heavily criticized for the 'September coup'. Some cabinet ministers fumed with anger. One famously told the BBC's political editor, Nick Robinson, that he would do anything to stop Brown from becoming leader. The source was John Hutton, who remained a prominent cabinet minister when Brown became leader and declared his support for Brown at the start of the leadership contest. Another cabinet minister, Peter Hain, who had moved deftly from being an occasionally candid confidant of Blair's to playing the same role for Brown, warned the Chancellor in a lengthy phone call that the insurrection was going down badly with activists. Quite a few non-Blairite MPs went on to the airwaves to declare that enough was enough and the whole affair was alienating voters. The former cabinet minister Charles Clarke was especially vitriolic, giving an interview in which he argued that recent events proved that Brown was unfit to be leader.

On the whole newspapers were critical of Brown, even though some of them had been attacking Blair for years and calling on him to go. Some wondered whether the sequence would cost Brown the leadership.

The angry reaction to the 'September coup' vindicated Brown's cautious approach to moving against Blair. If this was the reaction when Blair was still in Number Ten, imagine the furore if Brown had challenged him overtly, as Michael Heseltine had done in his bid to topple and replace Margaret Thatcher. Even though Blair was testing the patience of his party, he still commanded the passionate support of an influential section of the media and the affectionate loyalty of a group that went well beyond his devoted disciples. Ever since the summer of 1994 Brown had planned for a smooth handover. He did not want a bloody regicide that would lead to an ongoing civil war. Brown had achieved another classic New Labour solution. Blair was being forced out at a time of his choosing.

The strange sequence played out in a way that on the surface at least was the smoothest transition Brown could have dreamed of. There were also many more examples of New Labour surrealism. Tony Blair gave a dazzling farewell speech to the Labour conference in Manchester, good-humoured and inspiring. There was hardly a dry eye in the house by the end of the performance. Yet once the tearful conference had reached its conclusion Blair returned to his desk at Number Ten and declared he had a massive agenda to address. Blair had resigned and then continued with his prime-ministerial duties, another third way.

His main duty as he saw it was to bind his successor to his policies. This was the other slightly surreal element to Blair's departure. After his farewell he continued to be PM. Even out of office, he aimed to be PM in spirit. Cohorts of ministers and officials set to work on various long-term projects that Blair planned to unveil before he left office.

Brown and his aides viewed the continuing animation in Number Ten with alarm. One said to me in the autumn of 2006: 'I don't think they care whether we win the next election. Tony will be gone by then, but what about the rest of us who will have an election to fight?' Blair's continuing messianic approach prompted some columnists to wonder whether his attitude had become '*Après moi le déluge …*'

They wondered misguidedly, since Blair was as tribally committed to Labour as ever. Out of self-interest alone he knew that an election defeat would probably undermine his legacy. He had noted that Margaret Thatcher's reputation declined when the Conservatives lost their election appeal after she had left. She got the blame even though the Conservatives had won elections under her leadership. Blair did not want to be blamed for the deluge, but he had a different notion of what was necessary to win in what he had described in a speech to Rupert Murdoch's annual conference of news executives in the United States in July 2006 as an era of 'political cross-dressing'. Brown told close aides he considered it to be the most disconnected and rootless speech ever made by a Labour leader.

Brown's task on the final leg of his marathon to become Prime Minister was daunting. He had to remain publicly loyal to Blair's agenda, partly because Blair was still Prime Minister, but also because he had calculated that expediency compelled it. In alliance with some Blairites, the increasingly confident Conservatives were portraying him ever more relentlessly as the 'roadblock to reform'. In order to stave off the onslaught Brown resolved to make no move that enabled his coalition of critics to shout even louder. As he had done in advance of becoming Chancellor, he chose to tie himself in knots and limit what he could say and do.

Brown had a strategy in place already. In the summer of 2004, when he mistakenly assumed that Blair was about to resign, he and the two Eds had talked extensively about tactics. They agreed that up until a general election Brown would 'out-Blair Blair', giving no ammunition to Blairites, to the Tories, and importantly to some newspapers that were keen on Blair's approach to security and public services. In particular Brown kept a wary eye on the *Times* newspaper. He was always bothered when *The Times* appeared to be moving away from him. In that summer of 2004 Brown had planned to present himself as a consensual figure, moving on subtly from parts of the Blairite agenda only when he sensed he had some space to do so. He followed the same plan now that Blair was finally stepping down, or stepping down at some point soonish.

Brown's attempt to project himself as a figure that defied caricature was in some ways accomplished with delicate skill. Once more books played their part in his political journey, but unlike the ill-advised biographies the latest publications were subtle, even if the objective was the same: the projection of a heroic national and international leader.

The first book was an anthology of Brown's speeches under the innocuous title *Moving Britain Forward*. The speeches were compiled by his close friend Wilf Stevenson, who outlined in the introduction the considered and yet promiscuous thinking that united the range of speeches selected for the book:

> His vision is that of a Britain founded on liberty, responsibility and fairness: hence his interest in Britishness and British values, and the ideals and policies that flow from them. He starts from a dauntingly wide view of the individual in the changing global economy: men and women whose potential needs both encouragement and opportunity; men and women who are not alone, selfish or isolated, but living together in villages, towns and cities; living in communities within which we have responsibilities towards each other.

The figures chosen to endorse the speeches convey the purpose. They included Nelson Mandela, Alan Greenspan (who Brown took on a visit to Kirkcaldy in 2003, the birthplace of Adam Smith and Brown), Sir Jonathan Sacks, J.K. Rowling, Sir Derek Wanless and Kofi Annan. Only the Pope appeared to be unavailable. None of them had a reputation for being active Labour figures, which was of course the point. With David Cameron and Blairites seeking to portray him as a tribally backward-looking Labourite, here was a cast list of his dreams. What is more, the list was not a contrived one. Brown's critics were not accurate in their caricature. Although he was a Labour politician to his fingertips, he was also a thinker who ranged widely, but always with a political purpose. He was not simply an academic who was also a politician. He was seeking by implication to recruit his cast of non-partisan superstars to his political cause. At this point his main cause was to show that he was a national and international leader who could dance as happily with Alan Greenspan and Sir Derek Wanless as with leading members of Labour's National Executive Committee.

Brown's second book followed soon afterwards, just as he was being crowned Prime Minister. Once more it was deliberately non-partisan. The book was entitled *Courage*, and in it he wrote about eight of his heroes. They included Edith Cavell, who was a nurse in Belgium during the First World War, and Dame Cicely Saunders, the founder of the hospice movement. All those included had displayed heroic devotion to a cause, but the causes were not rooted overtly to the left of centre. Most embryonic prime ministers write books about their hopes for government. Brown had done the same, but in a subtly different way. He was planning to be the consensual Prime Minister, admiring and encouraging the display of human qualities, ones that could be admired by the *Daily Mail* as much as the *Daily Mirror*. Who could be against courage?

And yet at the same time he was injecting into the speeches some values more associated with the centre left, most specifically by advocating discreetly a role for government in securing fair outcomes. The balance was delicate and he never travelled far on the journey. At least he ventured to attempt it.

Brown managed to convey similar broader and non-partisan messages in some of the TV profiles that were broadcast as it became clearer that he was on course to become the next Prime Minister. One broadcast by the BBC's Nick Robinson was a perfectly compressed evocation of Brown, or one side of him.

The profile began in the church where Brown's father had preached in Kirkcaldy. Brown and Robinson leafed through a book of the Reverend John Brown's sermons. The titles included 'Use Your Time Wisely' and 'Towards Better Objectives'. Robinson noted that the themes could have come from a self-help manual. Brown spoke passionately in the profile about his father's desire to help people reach their full potential, confirming that in his Calvinistic desire to help others help themselves, his father was his first and overwhelming inspiration. He mentioned too how people, including the very poor, were always invited to their home and given help, advice and sometimes money. The profile showed a photo of Brown as a teenager leading a group of kids as they raised money for refugees in Africa. Brown then talked about the rugby accident in which he lost the sight in one eye at sixteen. 'I was kicked in the middle of a scrum … I knew after that I wouldn't play football or rugby again … it made me focus more on what I could do.'

The profiles that were based in Kirkcaldy managed to capture Brown's authentic voice. He became publicly more at ease, slightly less awkwardly shy and self-conscious, in an intellectual setting or one rooted in Kirkcaldy and the student politics of Edinburgh.

Ominously, he was less successful when seeking to project himself as an ordinary connected human being. In the months before he became Prime Minister in 2007 he comically gave interviews that gave the impression he listened to the Arctic Monkeys at breakfast. The impact on his credibility was so serious that he had to give interviews about what he had really meant to say. He told the *Observer* in September 2006: 'You've got to laugh because actually I was asked did I prefer Arctic Monkeys to James Blunt and I think I said I'd prefer Coldplay. But I made a joke that Arctic Monkeys would certainly wake you up in the morning. So, I mean, I've heard Arctic Monkeys and they're very loud.' This explanation bordered on the deranged.

Perversely, Brown managed to sound inauthentic even when he was talking about football, one of his genuine passions. Sport should have been a way in which Brown made connections with a sport-obsessed nation. Sometimes he managed to pull it off, giving relaxed and informed interviews on BBC Five Live. Brown followed football obsessively. In March 2009 he went as far as watching a tape of the Carling Cup final between Manchester United and Spurs. It was an unspectacular goalless draw that was decided after two hours on penalties. Brown started to watch at half past eleven on the Sunday evening. He was gripped to the very end. And yet he managed to get into difficulties in the media over whether he supported England or

Scotland. He spent wasted hours agonizing over how to deal with such questions, and the more laborious the preparation the more contorted the answer: 'My ideal scenario is that Scotland play England in the final and Scotland win ... but if we don't qualify or we go out in an earlier round, then I would transfer my allegiance to England.' In order to compensate England fans further he added that one of his favourite goals was one scored by Paul Gascoigne against Scotland. This did not ring entirely true either.

The attempt to please his critics led to the biggest catastrophe in the build-up to the moment when he became Prime Minister, one that illustrated the degree to which he felt cornered by the more self-confident and appealing Tory leadership, the Blairites and newspapers watching him more warily than they did Blair.

His budget in March 2007 was the last set-piece event in which he could offer a clearer definition of his priorities as Prime Minister in Waiting. For Brown the context was intimidating. David Cameron's claim that Brown's leadership would mark a shift to the vote-losing left appeared to be resonating. Once more making the most of his informal alliance with Blair, Cameron argued that the current Labour Prime Minister was instinctively someone who did not approve of high taxes, whereas his future successor liked nothing more than putting up taxes on hard-working middle-England voters. To Brown's torment polls suggested in the early months of 2007 that the government would fall further behind the Conservatives under his leadership compared with Blair as leader. His senior aides were worried and to some extent baffled. Shortly before the budget one asked me with a hint of despair: 'Gordon was really popular in the general election campaign. What has changed since then? He is still the same as he was then.' It was a valid question and the answers were ominous.

Even the question reflected Brown's fragile hold on the respect and affection of voters. At times they respected him, but that respect could quickly dissolve, as had happened during other low phases in 1994, 2001 and 2004. Now he was being subjected to a range of assaults that were bound to have an impact on his reputation. A combination of Cameron's attacks and Blair's patronizing attempts to commit Brown to a programme sent out negative signals. There was much media speculation in the spring about whether the Blairites would field an alternative candidate to Brown, scheming that again conveyed a less than flattering impression of the ambitious Chancellor. Brown's attempts at projection had been clumsy and his recent cautious policy agenda – Trident, detaining suspects without charge – had not been inspiring. There were signs also that the economy was stuttering badly. In the budget Brown had to admit – and not for the first time – that the public finances were worse than he had predicted they would be. The economy was no longer growing quite as fast (although it was still performing relatively well in comparison with other similarly sized countries) and yet public spending continued to climb, a trend supported by the Conservatives, who were pledged at this point to match Labour's spending levels if they won the next election.

As a result of the more precarious economic situation Brown had no room for manoeuvre in his final budget. His plans had to be fiscally neutral. If he cut taxes he would have to find increases elsewhere. Yet he was determined to prove his critics wrong, to show that he was capable of being a tax cutter as much as anyone else. What is more he was determined to make a cut that everyone would understand immediately, which meant, as far as he was concerned, a cut in income tax, the great emotive tax of the New Labour years, the one Brown had never dared to increase but occasionally had cut.

In the autumn of 2006 Brown told his advisers and senior Treasury officials that in the budget he wanted to complete a range of tax reforms that included more targeted help for the low-paid. As the budget moved into view he saw that the scrapping of the 10p starting rate would pay for a cut in the basic rate of income tax. In fairness to Brown he had wanted to abolish the rate for some time, preferring more targeted allowances where possible. But this was also an act of desperate expediency.

Both the Eds and his most long-serving and senior adviser, Spencer Livermore, warned him that those earning less than £17,000 would lose out from the abolition of the 10p rate. In Livermore's view he acted for a single reason: to please the Murdoch newspapers.

In March 2007, with Blair's leadership finally moving towards a close, the most political of chancellors delivered his most political budget. Brown had been criticized for not being interested in environmental matters. The budget increased car duty on the most gas-guzzling cars. He had been accused of neglecting people who had lost their pensions when their employers went bust. He announced new help for those pensioners who had lost out. He was determined to make much in an indirect way of the Etonian backgrounds of Cameron and his wealthy entourage. He announced more cash for schools, which he said would narrow the gap in funding between pupils in state and private schools. In the autumn he had declared that he 'aspired' to close the gap altogether – neat politics, as aspirations symbolize where you stand, but with plenty of get-out clauses in advance of implementation. But it was the end of the budget speech that captured the headlines, the unexpected announcement of the 2p cut in the basic rate of tax delivered with a mischievous flourish:

> And I have one further announcement. With the other decisions made today we are able to hold to our pledge made at the election not to raise the basic rate of income tax. Indeed to reward work, to ensure working families are better off and to make the tax system fairer I will from next April cut the basic rate of income tax from 22p down to 20p. The lowest basic rate for 75 years.

Labour MPs cheered ecstatically and Cameron looked briefly thrown, two fleeting joyful moments for Brown as a prelude to a self-induced nightmare. Note the timing. Brown was not cutting income tax immediately, but in April 2008. Here is an indication of his medium-term thinking. If the polls permitted, Brown was hoping to hold an election in May or June 2008. The campaign would have begun with a cut in income tax. Instead, in the midst of other calamities the spring and early summer of 2008 became the darkest phase of his career so far. The measures announced in his budget proved to be the main source of the darkness.

The immediate impact was more ambiguous. One of Blair's aides told me that the outgoing Prime Minister returned to Number Ten after the budget and declared perceptively: 'Gordon has not learnt. You can't keep on pulling the same tricks.' The newspapers were questioning rather than negative. The *Independent* headline was fairly typical of the tone: '2p Or Not 2p? That Is The Question'. Brown had stated at the beginning of the budget that it would be fiscally neutral, so there was no attempt to hide the fact that the tax cut was being paid for by other measures. But there was no doubt that Brown had hoped naively that the main headlines would hail uncritically the cut in income tax.

Most commentators argued that at least the budget was politically clever. Some thought it much better than that. Only the *Guardian* columnist Polly Toynbee predicted perceptively that the tax cut would be a 'one-day wonder', but she did not foresee the dire impact, arguing that: 'At least this cut benefits only the lowest and middle earners, giving nothing to the top 10%.'

After the budget Brown knew the end was almost in sight. The Blairites' clumsy attempt to field a candidate against him highlighted why they were not very good at politics.

Most of them were out of the cabinet and without many strings to pull within their party. They pinned their hopes on David Miliband, but he had a clearer sense of political reality, recognizing quickly that he would stand and lose. Brown promised him a top job in his government, and wisely Miliband took that rather than fight a fruitless campaign against the Chancellor. Brown got his way against the Blairites as he usually did in the end. He was to face no candidate in the leadership contest.

This was another classic New Labour episode: a leadership contest in which there was no contest. Brown had dreaded a public debate within embryonic New Labour in 1994 and did not stand against Blair. Twelve years later he still feared a rigorous scrutiny of the precarious, shapeless New Labour coalition that a contest would have brought about.

EIGHT

Prime Minister

Gordon Brown became Prime Minister with a deceptive ease. He faced no opponent in a leadership contest, unlike Jim Callaghan and John Major, the last two prime ministers who had entered Number Ten between general elections. Both Callaghan and Major had been challenged by heavyweights, although they won their respective contests with relative ease. Brown had no challengers, heavyweight or otherwise. In addition Tony Blair had departed in relatively calm circumstances, not a claim that could be made about the fall of Margaret Thatcher in advance of Major's rise to the very top.

Callaghan and Major came to power in the midst of economic crises. Brown became Prime Minister at a point where the British economy had been growing for more than a decade under his stewardship at the Treasury.

Like so much about the New Labour era, what appeared to be happening was almost the precise opposite of what was actually taking place. Brown and a small entourage of devoted allies had sweated blood to secure the leadership and to do so in a superficially calm context. Partly as a result of that transparent struggle, Brown became Prime Minister unchallenged and yet surrounded by enemies. The context was also much more fraught than it seemed – a frail economy, a fragile, confused Labour party, a sceptical media and a new leader of the Conservative party showing some signs of talent. In the summer of 2007 Brown took control of all the levers, and yet he was on trial and had to please or reassure an army of doubters, more so than Callaghan and Major when they first became prime ministers.

This was another oddity about his rise to the top. Callaghan and Major had been erratic or untested in their various cabinet roles and yet both arrived in Number Ten without many questions being asked of their prime-ministerial abilities, at least at first. Major enjoyed a honeymoon that lasted more or less until his election victory in 1992. Yet he had been Chancellor only long enough to deliver a single budget. As Foreign Secretary he was barely in post long enough to leave Britain. His lack of sustained experience did not seem to matter. At first within the Conservative party and beyond, Major came to personify calm competence after the final wild months of Thatcher's regime.

Callaghan had been at the top of British politics for more than a decade when he became Prime Minister, but he had rarely stayed in the same role for very long, moving from the Treasury to the Home Office and finally the Foreign Office after an interlude in opposition. Although he went on to rule during a period of unrelenting economic crises, his personal ratings as Prime Minister remained constantly high, and there was never a hint of a conspiracy against his leadership.

In contrast Brown had been a record-breaking long-serving Chancellor when he moved in to Number Ten. At the time he was perceived widely to have been a successful one. And yet there were squadrons of critics in place watching with extreme wariness or loathing, some of them willing him to fail. There was a tangible sense that he had much to prove in the summer of 2007, but the tests being set varied depending on who was carrying out the critical examination of his abilities.

Tony Blair had gone. The media paid fleeting homage. The cabinet was fearfully subservient. Yet Brown even at the beginning was nowhere near as authoritative as he seemed to be. On the contrary, he had little power to do as he pleased. Instead he felt the need to please virtually everyone, from disillusioned traditional Labour supporters to ultra-Blairites and on to his friend Paul Dacre, the editor of the *Daily Mail*. The events leading up to his apparent elevation explain why.

* * *

On Thursday 10 May 2007 Brown had his usual crowded timetable of meetings at the Treasury, the recently modernized building over which he had presided as Chancellor for ten years. That morning he was due to meet amongst others the Chief Rabbi and the Director General of the CBI.

Halfway through this particular morning Brown broke off between meetings to emerge from his office in order to watch the rolling news coverage on Sky television. Brown's relationship with the rolling television news was a complex and unpredictable one. Sometimes he dropped everything to watch the latest developments even if they were relatively trivial. On other occasions the events on the flickering screen seemed to pass him by. Specifically he tended to avoid watching Blair's monthly prime-ministerial press conferences because they infuriated him.

His senior advisers and officials in the Treasury never knew for sure what his mood would be, but on this occasion they were not at all surprised when he appeared to watch the event being reported with an undisguised excitement. There was a big-screen TV in the open-plan office where senior civil servants and advisers worked or gathered frequently to watch the latest news stories. This morning Sky was reporting an event that Brown had dreamed about for more than a decade. Tony Blair was announcing the date of his resignation as leader of the Labour party and Prime Minister.

Blair was conducting the longest farewell tour in prime-ministerial history. Already there had been several tearful valedictory addresses, after which Blair had returned to Number Ten to continue as Prime Minister. His Third Way in resignations, announcing his departure several times and then returning to continue as Prime Minister, had several outings.

This morning, several months after his farewell conference speech, Sky was broadcasting Blair live from his Sedgefield constituency where he had been the MP since 1983. Again there were tears from the local constituency party members as Blair said his latest round of goodbyes. Once more Blair returned to work as Prime Minister after he had delivered yet another farewell speech. He was not actually leaving until 27 June.

His speech in Sedgefield was even more introverted than usual and revealed inadvertently the degree to which Blair had come to regard government as a personal fiefdom: 'I ask you to accept one thing. Hand on heart, I did what I thought was right. I may have been wrong. That is your call. But believe one thing if nothing else. I did what I thought was right for our country.' He was referring mostly to Iraq, but the first-person pronoun was revealing. What about the cabinet, parliament, his party? They had been largely irrelevant. Although Blair had not been anywhere near as dominant as his speech implied. Many of the key domestic policies had originated with Brown, or had been inherited from John Smith and Neil Kinnock.

Brown watched the Sedgefield Farewell almost glowing with anticipation. Whether depressed or upbeat, he could never hide how he felt even when he tried to do so. On this occasion he did not even try. As he watched Blair deliver the definitive words about his departure date Brown became less slumped in demeanour. Of Blair's many farewells this one named the date. His other farewells had omitted the vital piece of information. One of those watching the TV in the Treasury with Brown suggested that it was like seeing someone putting down a heavy load he had been carrying for years. Brown looked ten years younger. There were no get-out clauses this time. Blair was going within weeks. Brown was free of Blair.

Blair's farewell tour took many forms. He had begun with an announcement that had been forced out of him in September 2006 when he declared that the next Labour conference would be his last as leader and Prime Minister – another classic New Labour moment, an enforced voluntary departure date. He then delivered his emotional conference speech, but gave no indication precisely when he would be gone. Brown had hoped Blair would leave by Christmas 2006. There was no chance of such a speedy departure. On the contrary, Blair had been determined in his final few months in power to secure a legacy that made it impossible for Brown to be a free agent as Prime Minister. In between his farewell speeches, Blair spent much of his time

246

coordinating ten-year-plans for the future, an extraordinary act of wilful leadership in which he sought to be more assertive over Brown in his prime-ministerial afterlife than he had been as Prime Minister.

Brown's sense of triumphant release as he watched the Sedgefield speech lasted no more than a few days. Soon the broader context became a new intimidating challenge. According to his close allies he saw new trials within minutes, refusing to celebrate.

The weekend after Blair had announced his departure date, Brown and his closest aides met at his home in Edinburgh to discuss the strategy for the forthcoming leadership campaign, the contest with a single candidate. They had always hoped to be preparing for a contest without a contest, and yet the mood was far from celebratory. All of them, not just Brown, saw more obstacles to overcome. They always did. Brown had taught them never to rest in politics, but to anticipate instead what would follow apparent triumph or setback.

Gradually over the three days of a sunny bank holiday weekend Ed Balls, Ed Miliband, Spencer Livermore, Damian McBride, Bob Shrum and Douglas Alexander arrived at Brown's home in Edinburgh. This was the entourage that had in various permutations met many times before, sometimes sensing victory, often meeting in a mood of despondency. Balls and Miliband were now ministers, having been loyal advisers to Brown at the Treasury and in opposition. Livermore was an influential aide in the same building. McBride was Brown's press secretary, a former Treasury official who in this supposedly impartial role could not hide his passionate admiration of Brown, his fascination with the media and his love of football, three qualities that the putative leader rated highly. Alexander had risen up the Scottish Labour party, a protégé of Brown and now a cabinet minister. Shrum was a senior Democrat from the US who had become extremely close to the Brownites, so involved that he had been a central player in the preparation for every budget Brown had delivered as Chancellor since 1997.

The group had one distinctive trait. They never stopped working to advance their cause. When they suffered setbacks their solution was to work even harder. Brown was capable of phoning them at any time of the day or night. They had become used to responding. Plotting, planning, policy making had become their lives. Some of them, Brown included, had children, wives, partners. It made no difference to the relentlessness of their drive. Over the years their various opponents had assumed fleetingly that they had delivered a knockout blow. The Brownites never recognized such a concept. They were the equivalent of boxers who always bounced back, sometimes to the amazement of foes who were never so committed to staying in the ring.

Once more they prepared for another bout. Brown set the tone of the weekend gathering by outlining his thoughts on the leadership, ones they had all heard before, because at various points he had worked on the assumption since 2004 that he was about to be leader. This time, knowing for certain he was about to acquire the crown, he told his confidants that the campaign must be about establishing him in the country as a national leader. He had already won the contest in the Labour party, although there were worries in the party that he wanted to address. More specifically he revisited the themes of similar discussions in the early summer of 2004 when the same group had all worked mistakenly on the basis that Blair was about to resign.

Over the bank holiday weekend Brown and his allies agreed that since their earlier discussions in 2004 the necessity for Brown to be more Blairite than Blair had become far more complex. The contortion now required the agility of a world-class gymnast. By the early summer of 2007 on several fronts Brown still felt the need to show that he was Blair-like, and yet Blair was retiring as a deeply unpopular Prime Minister, his integrity questioned persistently over Iraq and his domestic policies the source of sceptical controversy.

On the bank holiday Monday the newspapers reflected Brown's dilemma. Both *The Times* and the *Sun* ran leaders arguing that the big test for Brown was whether or not he would endorse and build on Blair's programme of public service reforms. 'What do they mean by "reform"?' Ed Miliband asked at one point as they pored over the newspapers. The term 'reform' had become comically imprecise. Some newspapers hailed Blair as a great pioneer, although the nature of the pioneering stayed fluid. Other newspapers continued to rail against him for Iraq and his style of leadership, particularly the Labour-supporting *Guardian*. Brown ached for the approval of both sets of newspapers, those that admired Blair and those that did not.

That weekend the entourage was in agreement. Brown needed to find a way of personifying both continuity with Blair and overdue change – an impossible task, and doomed to failure in the longer term, but one that might be achievable for a year or so.

Brown and his inner circle had reached a peak. At long last they had won their seemingly eternal struggle with Blair and his allies. Blair was going and Brown would be Prime Minister. Yet they were downbeat, the default position of a group used to disappointment. Their discussions that weekend were solely tactical. In recent years tactics had come to override more principled discussions, although this group was capable of rooting its exchanges in more recognizably ideological terrain. Brown could do so, but usually only in private. The two Eds were young politicians with strong beliefs that were recognizably left of centre. Ed Miliband's father had been a famous Marxist academic. Ed had said openly that his father was the biggest inspiration in his politics. Balls was a youthful economist who had reframed Labour's economic policy. All of them were at least as excited by ideas and policy making as they were by the political game, the machinations required to succeed. Yet it was the machinations that had come to dominate in recent years. How does Gordon get the leadership? How does Gordon win an election when he gets the leadership? These questions mattered more for the time being than policy or ideology. Plotting had become more important than policy making partly because the plot had lasted for so long.

They received one piece of good news over the bank holiday weekend, or at least it seemed like good news at the time. On the Sunday the Home Secretary, John Reid, one of Brown's severest critics, announced that he was stepping down. Brown wanted to promote some of the younger generation to his first cabinet and did not want too many Scots occupying top posts, not least because he was getting the most senior post of them all. Fleetingly Reid had considered standing for the leadership, but like other potential candidates he recognized that he did not stand a chance. He blamed Brown for this without reflecting for too long as to whether his own shortcomings might have been a factor. Brown was delighted to hear that Reid was stepping down, although within fifteen months he was pleading for him to return.

His conflicted attitudes towards Reid, and on a bigger scale towards Peter Mandelson, serve as a barometer of his wild experiences as leader. Before he was Prime Minister Brown felt strong enough to do without the likes of articulate advocates such as Reid. From the supposedly lofty context of being Prime Minister, he needed Reid for the first time in his career.

In spite of Reid lending his old foe a helping hand in creating vacancies, Brown worried about the formation of his first cabinet. He was agonizing already when he and his aides met for the bank holiday weekend, an ominous display of indecision given the amount of time he had had to prepare for his first round of ministerial appointments – around ten years at least.

To be precise he agonized over one specific post. He could not make up his mind whom he wanted to be Chancellor of the Exchequer. Long before his official campaign for the leadership began, Brown had told his old friend Alistair Darling, a calm Edinburgh Scot in comparison with the more excitable Glaswegian Reid, that he would be his Chancellor. For several months Darling had been preparing for the new challenge, never doubting that the post would be his.

But Brown did have his doubts. As his close allies dispersed after the meeting over the bank holiday weekend Brown had a separate conversation with Balls. He told his former adviser and then the respected City minister in the Treasury that he had been giving the post of Chancellor a lot of thought. He had decided that Balls should get the post immediately rather than 'earn' his elevation in another department. Brown had always wanted Balls to be Chancellor at some point once he had become Prime Minister. The issue had always been about timing. Would it damage Balls, and therefore Brown, to promote him right away? Would it be a waste of Balls's talent as an economist and policy maker to place him in another department?

The conversations between Brown and Balls were suddenly multi-layered. They had moved on from the relative simplicity of the two of them working as a team in the Treasury. Now they took into account Brown's soon-to-be-acquired powers of prime-ministerial patronage. Balls reiterated his constant position, telling Brown that he would be happy to run a big department outside the Treasury before becoming Chancellor. Brown was adamant. He wanted Balls as Chancellor right away.

Brown also saw the case for Darling. There was a strong argument for the older, less controversial figure to be his first Chancellor. He allowed Darling to continue working on the assumption that he would be moving to the Treasury. Brown was being sincere with both of them in that he genuinely could not make up his mind.

For the next few weeks, as Labour staged its leadership contest with only one candidate, Balls and Darling both thought they were about to be Chancellor, an early example of Brown's brutish, thoughtlessly amateurish people-management skills. In particular Balls spent a nerve-racking time preparing for the hostile reception he knew he would receive in parts of the media and the government if appointed.

Fortunately for Brown the launch of his leadership campaign and the subsequent trail around the country tested no political skills of any kind. After a long, arduous climb he floated to the top. His opening message in the party's non-contest was well crafted, the beginning of his formal bid to appeal to the wider electorate. At his launch in central London he declared that he wanted to form a government 'of all the talents', an unsubtle hint that Brown was going to go out of his way to prove that he was not a tribal Labour figure. Once more there was an awkward contortion: Brown was seeking to show that he could work with others outside his party in order to advance Labour's cause, and of course his own. Political leadership is partly about casting spells, but this act of magic had an obviously limited shelf life: a national leader seeking consensus and a victory for the Labour party at the earliest opportunity.

At his so-called launch Brown also declared that the NHS and education were his priorities and that he was a supporter of 'reform'. This could have meant anything at all, but the language of politics had grown so debased that such declarations came to signify something important, that he would not be tribal and would not undo Blairite reforms, although privately he remained sceptical about most of them. His delivery was wooden, but he had accepted the need for an expensive haircut and therefore looked more sharply defined than usual, like an old car that had been given a good clean.

Few TV viewers would have failed to notice the physical message as Brown accidentally stood behind an autocue device that covered his face. No member of his team had noticed in advance that he would be partially blocked from the cameras. Like his indecision over who should be Chancellor, this was an ominous sign. New Labour had been associated with slick choreography, not always with justification. But now Brown had no journalist to advise him. His press secretary Damian McBride's previous job had been in the VAT department at the Treasury. Briefly Brown had been a journalist at the BBC and he thought his own expertise in the media, along with the raw instincts of McBride, would suffice when he got to Number Ten. They did not even get him through his leadership launch.

The limited media knowledge of Brown and McBride was not an issue during the campaign, although it would be one soon after. For the next few weeks Brown did not utter a memorable phrase and was delighted not to have done so. He was content for the campaign to be boring. Haunted still by the 1970s and 1980s, when Labour's internal politics were never dull and nearly always conducted in opposition, Brown believed as a matter of principle that party matters should be resolved without attracting much attention, a rule he applied even when his party changed leaders.

Such wariness of public internal debate showed that Brown still regarded New Labour as a fragile creature, even after ten years of power, one that might not recover from a few weeks of intense public scrutiny. His reticence was also fuelled by his determination not to be perceived as being to the left of Blair, as he would have been had he faced a challenge from an ultra-Blairite.

During the campaign that followed Brown spoke at one surreal rally, the only event in which he stood on a stage with potential challengers. Two left-wing Labour MPs, Michael Meacher and John McDonnell, were desperate to stand as candidates in the contest, still dreaming of the previous era when noisy debate played its part when Labour selected its leaders. Before nominations closed Brown debated with them on the first Sunday evening of the campaign. The event was absurdly false and therefore Brown fully approved. He would not have taken part if the rally had mattered. As the three of them stood on the stage of a conference hall in central London it was already obvious that neither Meacher nor McDonnell would receive enough nominations from Labour MPs to stand. Brown therefore had agreed to participate in order to be seen taking on the left, as a counter to those who argued that he was left-wing. Balls sat in the front row and told Brown immediately afterwards: 'That worked brilliantly. It is a shame the other two did not attack you more, but at least you attacked them.' By the end of the following week Meacher and McDonnell had announced they did not have enough support to stand. This was another illusory episode in the history of New Labour, a leadership debate between three candidates when only one was standing.

Apart from the one attempt at internal debate, Brown spoke at literary festivals, increasingly his favourite forum, and was interviewed gently by sympathetic journalists at Labour party meetings around the country. For someone who had been through hell in his attempts to become leader, the final few weeks could not have been easier.

In retrospect the lack of a challenge came to damage Brown, who was quickly condemned as an unelected prime minister, a leader who did not even take part in a proper election. But that is a hindsight judgement, shaped by what came after. If Brown had been more successful as Prime Minister, or won a general election, the ruthless ascent to the top would have been seen as a strength, an example of disciplined political application that preserved the pubic unity of a party no longer united about very much at all and gave Brown a platform to woo the electorate.

At the Manchester conference nobody knew what would follow. For the moment, the fact that Brown had become leader in ways he had envisaged for more than a decade was at least testimony to his intimidating resilience and political guile. Brown had always wanted to succeed Blair without a public confrontation and there were good grounds for wanting to avoid one. He had pulled it off. For someone who was supposedly a poorly attuned politician, this was a triumph.

In the previous autumn Blair had described him indirectly as a 'great clunking fist', and Brown was not displeased by this macho vision. But dogged assertiveness alone does not explain the level of the achievement – a Labour Chancellor for ten years, and a leader in waiting for at least as long, finally getting to the top. Such endurance in an exposed position requires dexterity as well as a knockout punch. Brown's rise suggests that he was not as poorly attuned as his critics suggested then and since, and there were several factors that partly explain his dramatic fall.

One of these factors was the restless state of the Labour party in the summer of 2007. After ten years in power led by a highly unusual Prime Minister, one defined by his gaping distance from his own party, Labour had managed to lose its grasp of how it had survived in power for so long and why it had done so. Was it a centre-left party any more? What did it mean to be on the centre left? Was Blair such an extraordinary election winner because he was never perceived as a tribal Labour figure? Could Labour win if they were led by a figure more clearly rooted on the centre left? Was Brown such a figure? Was England essentially conservative and Conservative-supporting, a country that had switched in 1997 because the Tories were in disarray and Blair posed no threat? Had England changed after ten years of a Labour government so that it would be more responsive to a more overtly left-of-centre message? The unresolved questions swirled around a party that had lost a clear sense of identity and arguably had never had much of one for decades, including during the years of New Labour, always a slippery project, deliberately elusive.

In the summer of 2007 a party suffering from an identity crisis was about to be led by a figure who kept his own identity vague in order to maximize his appeal and in the hope that he would not offend any voter. New Labour had always highlighted dividing lines with the Conservatives. In reality it had risen through the use of blurred lines in which clarity and definition were assiduously avoided. Such pragmatic evasiveness helped leadership and party when all was going relatively well for them and when the voters willed them to succeed.

The external context in the summer of 2007 was also shapeless, suggesting that the country, and not just the Labour party, had lost a sense of coherence and identity. Surveys showed that a majority of the electorate wanted Britain to pull out of Iraq, that the Conservatives were now more trusted to run the NHS, that most voters wanted more investment rather than less, and that Blair's recent policy agenda had been deeply unpopular. Yet Blair had his ardent followers and Brown wanted them to follow him too. As he waited to take over the leadership in Manchester several observers remarked that Brown was finally a liberated political figure. In reality he was trapped by a context of daunting complexity.

Before Brown made his victory speech, one in which he sought to address his many conundrums, the conference in Manchester staged a genuinely unpredictable event: the contest to be deputy leader. Six candidates had taken part in an election for a post that had no clearly defined powers. That was part of the attraction. Even though five of the six candidates were ministers, all were fearful of power, as they had never wielded any. Blair and Brown had decided more or less everything. As it turned out the election produced a surprise. Harriet Harman was elected, a triumph of dignified persistence.

Harman had been sacked as Social Security Secretary in Blair's first reshuffle during the first term. Most former cabinet ministers simmer with self-pity and never return to government. During her long exile Harman focused constructively on a few issues as a backbench MP, came back as a junior minister and was now the party's deputy leader. Brown had supported her candidacy, or at least almost did. He began to have doubts about it towards the end of the campaign and wondered whether Alan Johnson might have more electoral appeal – another early instance of indecision as he assembled his team.

After the deputy leadership had been announced Blair made a brief appearance on the stage to welcome Brown as the new leader of the Labour party. Blair made no attempt to upstage his successor. As ever he played the moment with perfect pitch. This was not his event and he knew it. After a speech lasting under a minute he left the stage to Brown, although he had his farewell Prime Minister's Question Time still to come.

Brown's own personal views as he stepped up to make his first speech as leader of the Labour party were almost irrelevant. His overriding task as he saw it was to bind together once more the contradictory views and aspirations that had once formed the New Labour coalition. Quite as much as character, context determines the way a leader behaves. Blair became leader in 1994, a perfect moment in which his party, desperate to win an election, and much of the media, disdainful of John Major's government, were willing to dance to his tunes. By 2007 circumstances had changed inexorably. Brown needed to show the guile of a Harold Wilson, a leader who regarded party unity and election victories almost as ends in themselves, rather than means towards ends. This was not a context for the seemingly freshfaced evangelism of Blair in 1994.

To a limited extent the complex background played to Brown's strengths. He resembled Wilson in many ways, both men manoeuvring and scheming, sometimes more openly than they realized. Wilson became famous for his deviousness – a contradiction in terms: truly devious leaders apply their arts invisibly. Similarly, Brown had become famous as Chancellor for his 'stealth' taxes. Why call them stealthy if they came to define public perceptions of his tenure at the Treasury?

The confused mood of party and country explain partly why Brown's leadership was doomed to be troubled. From the beginning his critics argued that there was one explanation that overwhelmed all others. With a dismissive wave of the hand, they claimed that Brown had no strategy for what he wanted to do when he became Prime

Minister. This was a view held by most cabinet ministers and passionately espoused by more persistent dissenters. According to this theory, Brown spent so much energy plotting to get the top job that he did not have a clue once he got it.

If true, this widely shared assessment condemns Brown as a megalomaniac who wanted power for its own sake, for the glory of winning and nothing more. As an argument it does not hold water. Brown was wilfully competitive and determined to be Prime Minister, there is no doubt about that. But as a politician he had usually had a plan as to what he wanted to do. A close reading of Brown's victory speech in Manchester proves, contrary to legend, that he did have a programme for government, only it was one that was never properly implemented. Or to be more precise, the strategy was too successful too quickly, but fatally, nowhere near successful enough. It hinged on the timing of an election that Brown felt the need to call at some point soon after he became Prime Minister in order to acquire the authority that only a victory could bring. An election victory would indeed have liberated Brown in a way that a mid-term leadership could never have done.

Provisionally Brown hoped to call an election in the spring of 2008, possibly on the same date as the local elections. The electoral strategy was not carved in stone. No electoral timetable can be when prime ministers have a choice of options as to when they go to the country, a freedom they find nightmarish but have never given away until David Cameron proposed fixed term parliaments when he became Prime Minister. Brown had calculated he would need close to a year to prove that he was up to the job and to reassure voters that he was moving on from parts of the Blair era of which they disapproved, while echoing Blair on some fronts to reassure the former leader's influential admirers. In addition he wanted to call an election within a year or so in order to make the most of any honeymoon that greeted him and before voters tired of the novelty of a new PM. After winning an election Brown could perhaps be bolder, although he was vague even with close allies about the form that his post-election boldness would take.

His victory speech showed the way he planned to make his moves, the degree to which he had thought through precisely how he wanted to solve his overwhelming riddle, that urgent need to personify change and continuity.

First he claimed that the party had always been an agent of change:

> We the Labour party must renew ourselves as the party of change. Our mission has always been to be the party of progressive change. Our party was born because of a demand for change. We became a governing party because we championed the need for economic and social change.

Brown had no gift for understatement. The word 'change' occurred in every sentence of the opening paragraph, although its application remained imprecise.

Next he echoed Margaret Thatcher by declaring: 'I am a conviction politician.' Polls in the summer of 2007 suggested that voters were unsure what David Cameron stood for. Unlike Blair and Brown in 1994, Cameron had no personal history in which he had sought to reform the Conservative party. Now suddenly he was claiming to be a great crusading modernizer. One of the ways Brown planned to expose Cameron's superficial pragmatism in opposition was to seize the mantle of conviction, another vague term but one that since the Thatcher era had attracted positive notices.

Conviction was accompanied by his favourite theme, that people must have the chance to realize their potential. He followed it through with a passionate defence of the NHS, made urgent by polls suggesting that the Conservatives were more popular on the issue. With a carefully weighed ambiguity he declared: 'We will build on what has gone right and we will continue our successful reforms.'

In political terms this was an artful promise. What about the unsuccessful reforms and the ones that had gone wrong? After more than a decade at the top of politics Brown had almost ceased to have clear personal views. His ideas had become subsumed by the overwhelming political project to acquire the leadership. But he was clear and distinct about the future of public services, regarding Blair's support for the private sector as indiscriminate and the much-hyped notion of 'choice' for users as simplistic. In his carefully constructed sentence Brown had stressed his commitment to 'reform' but did not offer detail as to which of Blair's changes he counted as successful. Instead he pledged that more schools would become directly linked to businesses and universities, spending on state pupils would rise, and everyone would have the right to education or training up to the age of eighteen. He wanted more teenagers on low incomes to go to university.

Brown repeated his pledge that the NHS was his 'immediate priority', a phrase that conveyed a sense of urgency without indicating what action would be taken. He promised a 'new settlement' in which patients would have more powers, but he would work with the providers too. Brown did not use the term 'choice', the term that had led Blair down several false trails.

With the *Daily Mail* in mind, Brown cited his interest in Britishness, but he did so by offering a more progressive definition along with a traditional one, a third way in patriotism:

> We will apply the shared British values of liberty, civic duty and fairness to all. Let us affirm that in return for opportunity for all that we expect and demand responsibility from all: to learn English, contribute to and respect the culture we build together – and not just the hardworking majority but everyone must play by the rules.
>
> But let us affirm that no matter your class, colour or creed every individual citizen has the right to rise as far as your talents take you. That is why our way of life is to reject the prejudice and discrimination practised by those who preach xenophobia and racism.

At this high point in his career Brown had hopes of making Britishness a progressive cause, or at least a means towards progressive ends. Soon he would be too weak to make much of this aspiration, or would do so in ways that were clumsy and self-defeating. But as he became Prime Minister the ambition was fairly high, to link a progressive consensus around orthodox themes such as Britishness and create political mood music where it might become more possible to address issues such as the level of poverty in Britain. This was a preoccupation of the Brownites, and a noble one. In their dreams they wanted to create a situation where newspapers and voters were pleading with them to put up taxes in order to make Britain fairer. They dreamed on.

On Iraq a single evasive sentence in the speech gave him the scope to make change without appearing to renege on recent events: 'We will learn lessons that need to be learnt' – a vague way of indicating a change of direction without specifying what the new approach might be.

He dealt with his doubts about the election of Harriet Harman as deputy leader by being utterly ruthless, announcing in the speech that Harman would be party chair, excluding her at once from one of the senior posts in the cabinet.

In the same section he announced mischievously and yet with an inadvertent transparency that his ministerial ally Douglas Alexander would be election coordinator, 'so that we are ready not just to fight but to win a general election'. On the very first day Brown became leader he raised the prospect of a general election. He wanted to scare the Tories by suggesting that he would be ready to call one at any time. Every word of speculation harmed Brown and revived the Conservatives, by leading him towards a trap in which he was forced either to call an election or to look weak if he did not. It was his only error in an otherwise perfectly pitched speech that provided a sustainable prime-ministerial route map for around a year.

Brown was going to make some changes in public services, while preaching the continuing need for 'reform'. There would be some adjustments in Iraq, but not an immediate withdrawal of troops. He would act in ways that showed he was the agent of 'change'.

He also made clear in his victory speech that he planned to 'reach out beyond party'. As often with Brown, the aspiration combined significant insights and parochial self-interested cunning. In private he was intrigued and excited by the success of non-party campaigns such as Make Poverty History. He had given much thought to how politics must adapt to the decline of parties and the rise of single-issue pressure groups that enthused a range of voters, especially younger ones.

He wanted to prove the point in order to benefit his tribe at the earliest possible opportunity by calling a general election. This was another conundrum at the start of Brown's leadership. Echoing his speech at the start of the contest, he sought to be the consensual leader of the nation while desperate to win a general election as leader of the Labour party. Inadvertently he was paving the way for Cameron and Clegg and the culture of coalition politics.

The defection of the Conservative MP Quentin Davies was the most vivid early manifestation of Brown's prime-ministerial strategy. Davies was a grand, self-important Tory, the least likely defector. He switched sides the day before Brown became Prime Minister. Defectors are always unlikely figures. Notorious mavericks, rebels who raise constant conjectures about their fickle intentions, never defect, almost as if the guesswork purges them of their frustrations with the party they belong to. There had been no speculation about Davies. He had been a pro-European Tory and therefore part of an endangered minority in his party, but his support for Europe was based on the premise that the Euro and the strict public spending limits that accompanied it were a Thatcherite project rather than a threat to the Conservatives. He did not have a left-of-centre bone in his body, which was part of his appeal to Brown, who wanted to prove that he could reach as many parts of the wider political world as Blair.

For Brown the symbolism was potent. Newspaper columnists, Blairites and Conservatives had been arguing for years that he would not appeal to potential Conservative voters in the same way that Blair had managed to do. Yet here was Davies, a quintessential Tory MP, announcing his dramatic defection two days after Brown became leader and on the eve of him becoming Prime Minister.

Davies's statement also built on Brown's objective of portraying Cameron as a lightweight. In it he wrote of Cameron: 'Although you have many positive qualities you have three, superficiality, unreliability and an apparent lack of any clear convictions which in my view ought to exclude you from the position of national leadership.' In contrast he stated that Brown was 'a leader I have always greatly admired who I believe is entirely straightforward and who had a towering record and a clear vision for the future of our country which I fully share'.

Aware of the significance, Brown had been on the lookout for any defectors while he was still Chancellor. He had some hope that the Conservative MP John Bercow might switch sides. Bercow had several conversations with Ed Miliband, but proved resistant to making the move even though he expressed more disillusionment privately with the Tories than Davies had done. To Miliband's bewilderment Bercow declared an interest in being the Speaker. The highly political Brownites could not understand anyone wishing for a neutered future as Speaker. Bercow kept his options open and never ruled out switching sides until he did indeed become Speaker in dramatic circumstances during the summer of 2009.

In contrast to Bercow, Davies was willing to make the leap at a moment that was perfectly timed for a new prime minister. Brown had bumped into him a few times after votes in the Commons and in the corridors of Westminster. Alert to any scope for partisan advance, he noted Davies's discontent. In April, Davies spoke to him at greater length. They had two more meetings at the Treasury and in the third Davies broached the possibility of defection. These highly charged and sensitive arrangements are never finalized until close to the point of announcement. Brown met Davies twice on the Monday, the day after he was elected leader. Early on Tuesday afternoon Davies issued a statement announcing his defection.

The switch marked a neat and compelling interlude between Brown's victory speech at the Manchester Labour conference and his first statement as Prime Minister outside Number Ten early on the Wednesday afternoon following the departure of the Blairs. Davies was part of a carefully planned sequence, political choreography aimed at conveying a new sense of unity, both within New Labour and beyond. But his defection also heightened the sense of unresolved ambiguity as Brown prepared to become Prime Minister. Was Brown a replica of Blair, a political cross-dresser who was as close to the Tories as Labour? At first Brown was delighted that such questions were being posed. His delight soon turned to bewildered despair when his lack of definition became an acute problem rather than an advantage.

The defection also highlighted again the degree to which the game of politics had become so time-consuming for the Brownites. From 1994 to 2004 their intense scheming was nearly always directly connected to the implementation of clearly thought-through policies. More recently the manoeuvring had been free from policy considerations or had resulted in calamitous policies. In policy terms the Davies defection had no significance whatsoever.

On the Wednesday after his final Prime Minister's Question Time, MPs had stood and clapped Blair as he left the chamber, a reminder of the outgoing Prime Minister's unique capacity to engage with almost any audience and claim its respectful attention. The half an hour in the Commons was Blair's last prime-ministerial engagement. The Third Way in farewells had run its course. There was no returning to be Prime Minister, although he popped up on TV the following day in Sedgefield to explain how odd it was to be functioning without prime-ministerial resources.

Soon after Blair's bow in the Commons Brown was standing outside Number Ten as Prime Minister, the moment he had contended for with a tortured, neurotic anxiety for more than ten years. In all the ups and downs he had never lost the focus, the desire and the over-blown sense of entitlement. In terms of the long road travelled, Brown's arrival outside Number Ten as Prime Minister was one of the greatest achievements in postwar British politics.

The statement he delivered on the doorstep, which he had played in his head many times over recent months, was a compression of his speech in Manchester:

This will be a new government with new priorities and I have been privileged to have been granted the great opportunity to serve my country …

I have heard the need for change: change in our NHS, change in our schools, change with affordable housing; change to build trust in government and extend the British way of life.

And this need for change cannot be met by the old politics, so I will reach out beyond narrow party interest; I will build a government that uses all the talents …

Now let the work of change begin.

Brown had begun his walk on a high wire. He had been at the centre of the government for ten years. How could he stand for change? He had some answers ready, most of them politically very astute.

Before he revealed them he formed his first cabinet. This was a key prelude to the unveiling of his new strategy. Broadly he knew he must signal with his ministerial changes that he could work with Blairites and as a unifying figure with those outside the Labour party as well. The specifics were more problematic. Although he wanted to show a willingness to make peace with some Blairites, he was also keen that his key aides should play central roles, not as a reward but because he rated their judgement and needed them for advice.

Such considerations are a reminder again of the constraints Brown was about to work under as a new leader. In the mid-1990s Peter Mandelson used to mock Harold Wilson for having to appoint balanced cabinets in order to keep the left and the right of his party on board. 'Tony will appoint ministers on merit alone,' Mandelson used to claim. This was not wholly true. Blair had Brown breathing down his neck during reshuffles, an exercise that became increasingly highly charged as their relationship corroded. But Mandelson was right to point out that Blair in his dominance had more freedom to select ministers than most of his predecessors. Perhaps he was too free. Blair made a mess of all his reshuffles. Brown was much less free to do as he pleased, even in the immediate aftermath of his unchallenged coronation.

One of his key decisions was over what to do with Ed Balls. Most of those who had worked closely with Balls were in awe of his youthful capacity to make the elusive connection between policy making, principled conviction and expedient scheming. According to one of Brown's senior allies: 'The intention went way beyond making Ed chancellor. Gordon always saw him as his successor as leader. He was easily the most talented of the next generation. It was talked about quite openly with other advisers in the Treasury.'

But not all of Balls's colleagues shared that view. Working behind the scenes, devoted to Brown, disdainful of Blair, he had acquired enemies who viewed him with deep suspicion and in some cases, loathing, detecting his fingerprints on every story that was harmful to Blair and his ministerial allies. When he was Brown's special adviser Balls used to joke that if he became an MP Blair would get his revenge by making him junior minister for Agriculture, as far away from the centre of economic activity as possible.

Aware of his reputation amongst Blairites as a malevolent trouble-maker, Balls had also been torn about his immediate ministerial ambitions, especially during the weeks since Brown had told him that he would be Chancellor. Balls's medium-term ambition was to be Chancellor, and he knew he was better qualified for the post than any other candidate, at least in terms of mastery of the brief and of the potentially intimidating Treasury. At the same time he felt the need to prove himself as a departmental cabinet minister away from economic policy and distant from the immediate Number Ten entourage.

Brown had been equally torn since telling Balls that he would appoint him as his first Chancellor. He too recognized that Balls would benefit from a widening of his repertoire. Partly because of this he had told Alistair Darling to prepare for the task of being Chancellor. Brown admired Darling's genius for keeping out of the news pages. He had a knack of taking over from a poor, wrecked minister and calming things down in the media. The Department of Transport was rarely off the front pages until Darling moved in, at which point rows about trains, leaks to the media, the fate of Railtrack quietly disappeared from the media agenda. The performance of trains was no better and in some cases much worse, but the media lost interest. When Darling switched to the Department for Work and Pensions revolts over benefit reform and headline-making internal splits seemed to quietly subside. In what retrospectively seems a comical vision, Brown imagined Darling quietly presiding over the economy as the two of them guided Britain towards a general election in an atmosphere of reassuring calm, two experienced hands at the tiller compared with David Cameron and George Osborne, who had no ministerial experience at all.

Yet Brown's restless mind was not entirely settled on this crucial appointment. He also knew that Balls had a natural ability to grasp big economic themes.

In the end Brown told Balls during the weekend he was elected leader that he had opted for Darling. Brown and Balls were close enough to have discussions without any of them being framed in terms of 'deals'. The two of them were in agreement: Balls knew Brown wanted him to be Chancellor before very long. In their discussions he reassured Balls that he could choose his department. The two of them discussed various options, including the Home Office. Balls opted to be Schools Secretary in an expanded department, which acquired extended responsibilities for children and families, a remit that reflected his genuine interest in the linkage between economic and social outcomes.

Again contrary to the mythology that soon grew up about Brown's inadequate planning, his cabinet was cleverly constructed, aimed at giving the impression of generosity towards internal opponents while actually placing his trusted allies in the areas he regarded as pivotal. He moved Douglas Alexander to International Development along with another of his devoted advisers, Shriti Vadera, much valued as a committed around-the-clock Brownite who had actually worked in the City. He promoted Ed Miliband to the cabinet and placed him next door in charge of the Cabinet Office, a non-job that kept him on tap for advice at any time. Crucially he placed another old reliable ally, Nick Brown, back into the Whips' Office as deputy Chief Whip. The promotions of David Miliband, John Hutton, James Purnell, Hazel

Blears and Alan Johnson made most of the waves. None of them was part of his close entourage and some had been sworn enemies. But the so-called stealthy Chancellor showed early signs of being equally devious as a PM. Behind the unifying gestures Brown had his allies where he wanted them, or where he thought he wanted them.

But desperate to keep internal critics on board, he also made some foolish promises. The former Home Secretary, Charles Clarke, was one of Brown's biggest public critics. During the week he became Prime Minister Brown phoned him to explain that he could not bring him back into the cabinet straight away, but wanted to give him one of the top jobs in a year's time. Meanwhile Brown said he would be in touch within days to give Clarke another important assignment outside the government. Clarke heard nothing. With good cause he also had doubts about the longer-term promise. After all, Brown had only just made David Miliband Foreign Secretary and appointed Darling as Chancellor. He would not be in a position in a year's time to create a vacancy for Clarke to fill.

As for the short-term pledge, Clarke heard nothing until finally in November he did get an offer of comical insensitivity. Brown offered Clarke the chance to be a special envoy in Basra with responsibility for supervising the renovation of parts of the town. Not surprisingly Clarke turned down this attempt not only to remove him from British politics, but to place him in a war zone. Clarke joked that if he had not been assassinated en route to Basra someone would have got him as he presided over the building projects in the town. This was no way to appease a critic, and yet Brown gave the offer little thought before it was made, or subsequently.

For someone who had been so dominant in the government, Brown had no previous experience of reaching out to colleagues, deploying patronage in ways that kept them happy. Only prime ministers had the power to appoint ministers, although unusually Brown had assumed the right to do so as Chancellor – a right that was not always granted. His handling of Clarke and the appointment of Chancellor were early signs that people management – so important a part of leadership – would become a significant issue. A leader can only get away with being clumsy at handling colleagues when he or she is soaring in the polls and being seen widely as a success. Colleagues are less tolerant of thoughtless treatment when a leader is unpopular. At the height of his authority Brown had told two close colleagues that they would be Chancellor and offered an internal foe a role in a dangerous place three thousand miles from home.

His most audacious move in relation to his first cabinet was to invite the former Liberal Democrat leader Paddy Ashdown to be Northern Ireland Secretary, a proposal vetoed wisely by the party's leader at the time, Ming Campbell. But other outsiders accepted. A former CBI Director General, Digby Jones, became a trade minister, another figure without a left-of-centre bone in his body and one who refused to join the Labour party, rather to Brown's disappointment. Lord West, vice admiral and chief of defence intelligence, was made a security minister and Lord Malloch Brown left his post at the UN to move into the Foreign Office. They came to represent the so-called government of all the talents, or GOATS. None of them was particularly successful and some were not surprisingly politically inept. In an era of anti-politics their failure was an inadvertent tribute to the professional democratically elected politician, a species that had come to be despised.

At first Brown got the short-term boost. This was the narrow justification. The GOATs formed an important part of the early narrative, the experienced one-nation Prime Minister taking on a new lightweight Conservative leader. But as Brown almost knew from the beginning, there was a strict time limit to the political benefits of enlisting outsiders. The limit was around a year. After that even those outsiders with a degree of political agility were the cause of unavoidable problems in a party-based democracy. But Brown hoped to hold an election by May 2008. If any of them looked as if they might cause trouble he could have discarded them in the aftermath of a victory that their appointments would have helped to bring about.

The buzz of activity that followed the formation of the government was equally calculated, with the potential to be either meaningless or the start of a revolution. It was Brown's distinct version of Harold

Wilson's self-declared pragmatic ambition to keep all his options open. In the build-up to his coronation he had meticulously analysed ways in which he could show he was a 'change' from Blair without alienating Blairites in the Labour party and in the media. As far as he was concerned there were changes he could make that would win praise across the political spectrum. Those were the ones he focused on at once.

Blair had been criticized, even by his admirers, for an excessive dependence on spin. In particular the media had become obsessed with spin and with Blair's alleged mendacity. This preoccupation had begun even before Labour secured power. The BBC went hard at the theme, presumably because it could not take sides on policy matters but could seek to expose spin without facing accusations of bias. Spin was not a left or right issue, nor was it obviously partisan, although the BBC's obsession with it did Labour immense harm.

Somewhat comically, Brown, as obsessed with presentation as Blair, chose to pretend to move on from spin as Prime Minister. The new spin was that there would be no spin, a claim that highlighted the circuitous absurdity of the entire issue. Brown declared that ministers would not make announcements in advance on the BBC's *Today* programme or in the press. Parliament would hear policies first. He did not appoint a high-profile journalist to become his press secretary, seeking to convey that he would do without the aggressive guile of an Alastair Campbell figure. The entire Number Ten media operation was downgraded to the extent that quite a few junior press officers had no idea what was happening or what they were supposed to do.

Still, in the honeymoon the media gave Brown the thumbs up for downgrading spin, although it soon started to miss the slick presentation. The media disapproved of spin until the government stopped spinning.

Next, Brown sought to show that he took cabinet meetings seriously. Blair had been criticized famously for his sofa government. Brown, who had shown no interest in cabinet discussion while he was Chancellor, started to preside over lengthy ministerial discussions. His

first cabinet on the Friday afternoon lasted for two hours and ministers emerged, blinking in the new daylight, to hail the high-quality
political exchanges that had taken place.

The policy initiatives were ambiguous. There were lots of them
in the summer of 2007, their number in themselves further
evidence of prior planning. Within weeks Brown announced his
plans for constitutional reform, a package aimed at rebuilding 'trust'
with the electorate. Polls suggested that voters had ceased to trust
the government, largely because of Iraq and also because of spin.
The debate was conducted with a simplistic intensity, but Brown
was desperate to deliver the equivalent of his economic coup when
he made the Bank of England independent as his first act as
Chancellor in 1997. He had made that move almost entirely for
political reasons. Labour had not been trusted to run the economy
so he gave away power to set interest rates in order to restore trust.
In July as Prime Minister he proposed to give away some powers in
his constitutional reforms in the hope that Labour would be trusted
once more.

The package was illuminating, containing the characteristic
Brownite touches, but applied with less coherent verve than when he
was at his peak as a politician. Brown could not resist resorting to
blatant political guile as he sought to secure the voters' trust. With a
flourish he announced that the prime-ministerial prerogative to
declare war without a vote in the Commons would end. The proposal
was typical of the package as a whole. It seemed more significant than
it was. In reality no Prime Minister could go to war without the
consent of the Commons. Blair faced a vote before the war in Iraq and
won it easily, in spite of the biggest Labour rebellion since 1997. In a
statement to the Commons Brown claimed that he wanted to 'surren-
der or limit these powers to make for a more open twenty-first-
century British democracy'. In this very limited sense the twenty-first
century was already open.

The rest of the package gave away some theoretical powers, but
none of them significant. The omissions were more pointed. Brown
showed no interest in electoral reform for the Commons, nor did he

give any indication that he had a clear idea what he wanted to do with the Lords. The package was a ragbag of policies, its spirit summed up by the promise of a summer statement on the autumnal legislative programme 'to reinforce the accountability of the executive to parliament and the public'.

What nonsense. This was a move to give Brown a new agenda-setting event in the summer, the equivalent of his pre-budget report when he was Chancellor. Now he would have a pre-Queen's speech report. This had nothing to do with constitutional reform. Virtually every item in the package had been included for short-term political reasons. Under Blair there had been complaints that protests had been restricted outside parliament, so Brown proposed to change the laws that restricted rights to demonstrate in Parliament Square, a well-meaning initiative, but one that would not have attracted his attention if the original restrictive policy had not become so associated with Blair.

The package shows that by the summer of 2007, after fifteen years at the top of British politics either as shadow chancellor or Chancellor and now Prime Minister, Brown was thinking as politically as ever, but in contrast with his first creative phase that began in 1992, had lost the ability to match the thinking with joined-up policy making. Brown lost interest in this package once his pre-election strategy had been blown apart in the early autumn. Some of the policies became law several years later, but few noticed. Nevertheless, though briefly, in the heady summer of 2007 the political guile worked, attracting headlines about Brown's 'constitutional revolution'.

In his Commons statement the familiar themes were highlighted once more: 'All the people of this country have a shared interest in building trust in our democracy.' Here he is speaking as a leader not just for most voters, but for every single one of them, the biggest of big tents. In case there was any doubt he added: 'It is my hope that by working together for change in a spirit that takes us beyond parties and beyond partisanship, we can agree a new constitutional settlement.' The sentence includes a call for change, but of an unthreatening kind in which there is consensus. So he called for a debate on a written constitution but added it should happen only 'when there is a settled consensus'.

The statement highlights another frustrating political law. Prime ministers are never more powerful than in the early months when they nearly always enjoy an authority-enhancing honeymoon, and yet their inexperience makes them instinctively cautious. Having waited so long to get to the top, Brown was in no mood to take risks, and yet he was never going to get a better chance to do so.

The balancing act between change and continuity was applied more deftly in relation to the NHS. Brown commissioned the senior surgeon, Lord Darzi, to conduct a review of the NHS for the following summer, the fiftieth anniversary of the health service. The peg was spurious, but conveniently vague. Brown wanted to quietly dump some of Blair's reforms and win back the support of the NHS employees, many of whom seemed to be switching to the Conservatives. Shortly before Brown became Prime Minister David Cameron addressed a meeting of health workers and won a lengthy ovation, for outlining in broad terms his support for devolving power to those who serve the patients. It was after that meeting that Cameron confided to his closest aides that he thought for the first time he had a chance of winning a general election. The response to Cameron had been in marked contrast to the jeers that greeted Blair's Health Secretary, Patricia Hewitt, whenever she spoke at similar conferences. By appointing a surgeon Brown hoped to signal a willingness to work with NHS employees rather than against them, but also a desire for 'reform'. There would be no point in holding a review to announce that there was no need for any change.

The timing of the review was significant, with an interim report scheduled for early the following year. Brown wanted the NHS to be a Labour issue again in time for a 2008 spring election. The new Health Secretary, Alan Johnson, summed up the mission: 'This is a once-in-a-generation opportunity to ensure that a properly resourced NHS is clinically led, patient centred and locally accountable.' Such aspirations sounded sweeping and yet were more flexible than Blair's relentless focus on 'choice' and the use of the private sector.

In between the announcements on these supposedly big projects, Brown moved quickly in his second Prime Minister's Questions to scrap the planned super casino in Manchester. The super casino was evidence that Blair regarded politics as an entirely secular activity, one in which any moral or spiritual dimension in his life played little part. To the bewilderment of some of those that had worked with him, Blair had no moral qualms about super casinos, attracted by the entrepreneurial endeavour that would bring them about. In contrast Brown declared at PMQs: 'I hope that during these summer months we can look at whether regeneration in the areas for the super casinos might be a better way of meeting their economic and social needs than the creation of super casinos.' Although the era of spin was supposed to have ended, McBride briefed journalists that these words meant there would be no super casinos. But there were also limits to Brown's moral purpose. He announced in an ominously weak act of triangulation that the sixteen smaller casinos also being planned would still go ahead.

Brown's hectic summer ended with a summit with President Bush, another event that demanded a balancing act, which he pulled off with a dexterity that was almost universally admired by the political journalists who accompanied him. With a determined ruthlessness Brown conveyed a distance from Bush in their joint press conference, even though he said nothing that could be discerned as overtly disloyal. Here is the interpretation of the *Washington Post*:

> Brown announced that Afghanistan is in the front line against terror-ism ... contradicting Bush's claim that Iraq is the central front in that battle. Bush spoke passionately of terrorists as evil, Brown spoke of terrorism as a crime ... Brown praised the US as a country rather than Bush personally.

And yet here is the assessment of the pro-war, largely pro-Bush editor of the *Spectator*, Matthew d'Ancona, who had been invited to accompany Brown on the trip – an invitation that reflected Brown's determination to woo admirers of Blair:

> In the motorcade speeding down Second Avenue towards the airport, one could only reflect that this Prime Minister's greatest triumph to date has been to persuade the world that he is not an exhausted traveller, limping and grey after ten years in office, but a man at the start of the journey ...

The midsummer policy initiatives and diplomatic manoeuvring had common characteristics. They had echoes of Brown's approach as Chancellor. He had used the model many times before, hinting at a radical departure in policy but keeping all options open, including not doing very much at all. As Chancellor he began by increasing public spending by a few pennies here and there. Within a few years he had almost doubled the NHS budget. His constitutional reforms might have ended in a radical place, with a written constitution and possibly a fully elected second chamber, but in keeping his options open Brown could just as easily turn away from constitutional reform. Similarly, in his approach to Iraq and relations with President Bush he did not utter a word that openly talked of a new relationship or fresh thinking in relation to Iraq, but left room for a change of direction.

The strategic calculations were also based on Brown's period at the Treasury: make a general argument; back it up with cautious policies with the chance of going further later; keep all options open including not doing very much at all if public opinion is not receptive; always look for the quick opportunistic hit in the media; present the moves in ways that are awkward for the Conservatives; project every move as one in the interests of the country as a whole and not for one partisan group. When Brown was Chancellor his slogan was 'for the many and not the few'. Now he sought 'a settled consensus' for his moderate incremental changes, seeds that could grow into more spectacular plants, or equally that might fail to bloom at all.

There was, though, a big difference between Brown's earlier phase at the Treasury and when he was shadow chancellor. Between 1992 and 2003 (his final years in the Treasury were far more erratic) the link between the political scheming and the policy making was robust. In every sense of the phrase Brown was at the height of his powers as shadow chancellor and Chancellor.

The policies and positioning adopted in July showed signs of being thrown together more haphazardly. The narrative was less clear as the new, insecure Prime Minister tried to keep everyone on board. Some of the policies did not lead very far when scrutinized. A pre-Queen's Speech report in the summer was a PR stunt for the government and not a way of holding the executive to account. A super casino would not go ahead, but sixteen smaller ones would. The summer policy announcements, the only ones he made with the authority of an opinion-poll lead and that had been on the whole carefully thought through, were the equivalent of a promising rock band's second album. Quite simply they were not as good as the first, when he was rocking with more energy and his antennae were still sharp.

In his defence, he had understandable reasons for not wanting to take risks in his first phase as PM. Brown could not afford to have any move go wrong as he strove to prove that he could be an effective Prime Minister.

Immediate judgements from the media and voters in the summer of 2007 had less to do with his policy announcements. Instead Brown was tested by four challenges that no prime minister could have prepared for in advance. In retrospect two of them were trivial, but that was not how any of them were regarded at the time, and with good cause. It is a cliché to quote Harold Macmillan's observation that 'events' determine the fate of prime ministers and governments, but a terrorist attack, an outbreak of foot-and-mouth, flooding on an epic scale and the collapse of a bank would have tested the nerves of a more experienced leader. Already on edge as a new Prime Minister with a lot to prove, Brown faced the eruption of all four nerve-racking events in the space of his first few months in power.

He was awoken in the early hours of Friday morning, his second night as Prime Minister, to be told of an attempted terrorist attack in Piccadilly, in London. Two car bombs had been discovered, and disabled before they could be detonated. On the Saturday afternoon there was an attack on Glasgow Airport, when a car loaded with explosives was driven into the doors of the terminal and set alight. It was the first terrorist attack ever to target Scotland.

Days later, parts of Britain were under water after an episode of intense and protracted flooding. June was one of the wettest months on record in Britain, as if the gods were sending Brown a warning about the political storms that were to follow. Parts of the country were flooded and TV news bulletins were dominated by vivid images of houses, pubs and hotels half covered by water.

On the day Brown left Number Ten for a short holiday there was an outbreak of foot-and-mouth, centred on a farm in Surrey. The previous epidemic in 2001 had caused a major crisis in British agriculture and tourism, and also amidst much drama had delayed the timing of the general election held in that year.

In his public appearances Brown struck the right tone, reassuring without being messianic. In his interviews after the foiled terrorist attacks he was calm and avoided Blairite proclamations about being at war with the insurgents. He and the new Home Secretary, Jacqui Smith, were widely praised for their steady demeanour. When the rain started to fall Brown recognized immediately the importance of being seen to take action. Once more he was hailed for his reaction compared with David Cameron, who left the country – and his own flooded constituency in Witney – in order to travel to Rwanda. When foot-and-mouth broke out the opinion polls suggested that voters appreciated Brown's conscientious sense of duty, scrapping his holiday within hours of arriving at his chosen English seaside resort to take command in Whitehall.

In the event none of the unexpected crises were as dramatic as they might have been, but Brown did not know that when they broke. Each one was a test for a new Prime Minister daunted by his elevation, suddenly aware of the intensity of the demands from a thousand different directions.

Until the middle of June all the opinion polls had put Labour behind the Tories. After Brown took over Labour had secured a lead of six to nine points, not dramatic, but a switch of some significance. The new lead was partly a reaction to Blair's departure, but also a testimony to Brown's prime-ministerial strategy, applied with some guile and subtlety, along with his determined sense of duty in the face of the unexpected.

Brown's relatively authoritative public appearances were not the whole story of this early phase. From the beginning there were also ominous signs of his explosive temperament. He also continued to display a distinct inability to manage a team and his own time.

One of those who worked closely with him in the Treasury and then in Number Ten observes: 'The first point is that Gordon was only human and anyone becoming Prime Minister is bound to be awestruck at first. The second point is that Gordon had spent so much physical and mental energy getting the job that he had not spent enough time preparing the logistics once he got it.' By the summer holiday Brown's wife Sarah was admitting to friends: 'Gordon is finding it much harder than he thought it would be. The truth is that it is a big step up, bigger than he realized.' This was at a point when he was well ahead in the polls.

Brown had spent so much of his energy despairing of Blair's approach as Prime Minister that he never stopped to reflect on the huge pressures a prime minister was under at all times. While he had sought to prove in recent months that he was up to the job, he had not learnt what that might mean when he got there. Behind the scenes there was chaos from the start in Brown's Number Ten. Beyond a short-term hit on the back of the 'anti-Blair, anti-spin' frenzy, his media strategy was absurd and inept.

At least as serious in the longer term, the close allies on whom Brown had grown dependent both while shadow chancellor and at the Treasury were scattered around government. Balls was at his new department. The former banker who had become another close ally at the Treasury, Shriti Vadera, was a minister at the Department for International Development, joining another Brownite, Douglas

Alexander. Only Ed Miliband was nearby as Cabinet Office minister, but even he was not in the immediate vicinity, as he was in the Treasury. Sue Nye, who had run his office since the opposition days, moved across to Number Ten along with special advisers who he had worked with at the Treasury, but none of them were close confidants to compare with Balls, or to a lesser extent the other ministers no longer available around the clock to address his needs and concerns. He had no equivalent of Alastair Campbell, Jonathan Powell and David Miliband, all of whom Blair had worked with in opposition and who moved with him into Number Ten. At the very peak of his career, Brown was suddenly quite isolated.

He had been sheltered as Chancellor by the much bigger Treasury, with its huge resources and more limited range of responsibilities. He had not absorbed the implications of working in a much smaller and less well-resourced Number Ten. Although he had carried the immense responsibilities of being shadow chancellor and then Chancellor, he had never been in charge of running an organization of any sort and had never shown any interest in doing so. At the Treasury he dealt mainly with those few he trusted. It was the same in opposition.

Shortly before his resignation Blair met Brown for one of their routine meetings. Blair suggested he talk through the logistics of working in Number Ten, combining the practical demands of being Prime Minister and the need to work also towards a general election victory. Brown told him he was not interested in what he had to say and had his own plans. Blair emerged from the meeting in despair, saying to a close aide: 'He won't listen to me even when all I am trying to do is help him.'

Most immediately, Brown had given virtually no attention to the choreography of Number Ten, even such everyday routines as where his team would be based. One of those who worked with Blair and stayed on for the early months of the Brown regime described the Brownites arriving at Number Ten like a revolutionary army within minutes of Blair's departure, as if they could not wait to break through the barrier that had tormented them for eleven years. But comically, once they had broken through some of them did not know where to go, which office to occupy. Brown's large number of advisers moving from the Treasury wandered around the new premises awkwardly looking for an office to occupy. They had not organized who would sit where. Such matters cut no ice with Brown.

As a result there was chaos and alarm from Day One, an atmosphere fuelled by Brown's almost manic desire to prove to everyone that he was up to the job. All the neurotic energy that went into acquiring the prime-ministerial perch was now erupting shapelessly in his determination to show that he should stay there. But there was no effective structure to cope with his informal, unfocused way of dealing with each day's agenda.

There were no regular meetings within Number Ten. Press officers who were civil servants were never entirely sure where McBride was or what he was up to. Suddenly and without warning officials and advisers found that in September 2007 Brown's old American friend and ally Bob Shrum had arrived in Number Ten. Shrum spent most of September there, but few knew quite what he was doing. He dealt with Brown alone, away from any structured meetings, and the new Prime Minister did not feel obliged to explain his presence. It probably did not cross his mind to do so.

Characteristically, Brown had thought through the political symbolism of his move to Number Ten. He did not work often in the room where Blair had spent most of his time, an office famous for its sofa, which characterized what became known as 'sofa government'. Brown chose to work in the more rigidly formal room used by Margaret Thatcher. But he had not worked out how he was going to arrange his days and make the most of the staff around him. The key strategic meetings remained the conference calls held most mornings on the telephone, involving his old allies Balls, Miliband and Alexander. Sometimes there would be meetings in Number Ten but they were on an ad hoc basis, and again no one else in the building seemed to know when they were taking place or what they proposed to discuss.

By the end of the summer there was much talk amongst senior civil servants and journalists about the new chaotic arrangements. On a trip to Afghanistan in August, Douglas Alexander became acutely aware of this too. Britain's ambassador in Kabul told Alexander he found it almost impossible to make contact with anyone in Number Ten even when there was a degree of urgency. Messages were not replied to, calls not returned. This was during Brown's honeymoon period.

Some of those who had worked with Blair were astounded by what they were witnessing. Even those advisers and officials who sometimes disagreed with what Blair was doing had liked working with him. Blair never lost his temper with them. As far as they could be, the prime-ministerial days were fairly well organized. In spectacular contrast, one official described the experience of working with Brown in Number Ten as the equivalent of being on a hallucinogenic drug. He could scarcely believe what he was seeing as Brown raged around the corridors, shouting at the telephonists on the switchboard and demanding at times that 'heads should roll'.

During the foot-and-mouth drama some officials noted that Brown would call meetings of COBRA, the body of officials and ministers that met in emergencies, when there was no obvious need to do so. They were convinced that the meetings were held solely for Brown to appear on SKY news afterwards to give a comment. One described the mood in Number Ten as one of 'chaos and self-pity'. Another says that Brown was in 'a permanent rage, acting as if the media were in a conspiracy against him'. COBRA meetings and some of those in Number Ten would be punctuated by Brown saying of the media, or an apparently incompetent official: 'Why have they done this to me?' One suggests: 'There was no thought beyond the next bulletin whether he was dealing with foot-and-mouth or the introduction of a supposedly new policy. He was obsessed only with the next bulletin.'

Brown's behaviour, his temper, rudeness, accompanied by allegations of his fragile mental state, was to become a much-talked-about theme when his leadership imploded in the autumn of 2007. But in the anti-Brown hysteria that was to overwhelm the final phase of Labour's third term a degree of context is required.

Brown was under immense pressure in these early months. Already feeling on trial after the intense and ridiculously long build-up to becoming Prime Minister, he was understandably shaken to be told of a terrorist attack in his first full week in charge. It could have been the start of another eruption of bloody carnage. He was not to know that the threat would quickly peter out. Foot-and-mouth would also become a relatively minor outbreak, but it might have spread across the country. Always self-conscious, he felt the need not only to act, but to be seen to do so. When he detected any signs of failure he sought distance and blamed others. Having wanted to be Prime Minister for so long, he feared with some justification any association with a botched job would take the most elevated post in British politics away from him. He dreaded headlines that suggested he was not up to the job. Ironically, in his fevered attempts to prevent highly critical front pages from appearing he made sure that they did.

Brown faced one more test during this early 'honeymoon' period, incomparably the most significant and daunting for the new Prime Minister, even if it was the first of the crises that brought him back to the familiar terrain of economic policy making.

On Thursday 13 September 2007 Northern Rock was on the verge of bankruptcy and asking for emergency financial support from the Bank of England. The summer reports of the seemingly obscure sub-prime mortgage crisis in the US had suddenly been placed in a more immediate and dramatic domestic context. Following the calamitous losses made by investors in loans to US homebuyers with poor credit history, investors became terrified of buying all mortgage debt, including Northern Rock's. The bank had focused overwhelmingly on providing mortgages. Soon it became clear that it had done so with exorbitant recklessness and that it was by no means the only bank to have been intoxicated by a culture that had blossomed in the lightly regulated financial markets.

The following day Northern Rock's shares fell by 30 per cent and anxious depositors queued outside their local branches to withdraw their cash. The images on the television screens of never-ending lines of alarmed depositors heightened the sense of crisis. Shares fell further and the bank's survival became precarious.

The political response to the opening act of a much bigger drama was revealing. In effect there was a divide between politicians who were economists or who had experience in economic policy making and the rest. Brown was horrified and fearful. This was only his third month in the job, and having confronted terrorism, foot-and-mouth and floods, he now faced the prospect of being a prime minister when there was a run on the banks. Alistair Darling was at this early point in his chancellorship out of his depth, although his Buddhist calm was an asset in what was truly a frightening situation, much more intimidating than the bigger collapse the following year, because at least then financial institutions around the world were falling as well. In September 2007 Northern Rock stood out. Isolated in Number Ten without his old allies, Brown was alone in the world as Britain's banking system tottered.

Economists in other parties were alert to the implications of the drama. The Northern Rock crisis erupted during the Liberal Democrats' annual conference in Brighton. Chris Huhne and Vince Cable gave interviews outlining why in their view the financial system was on the verge of collapse, more or less the only message their conference conveyed. It was something of an annual ritual that crises broke during the Liberal Democrats' yearly gathering, but nothing like this had happened since the government was forced to withdraw from the Exchange Rate Mechanism in 1992, a drama that erupted when the Lib Dems were gathering in Harrogate.

Non-specialists – who included most of the cabinet – had no grasp of the scale of the crisis, let alone of what to do about it. One senior cabinet minister told me that he had just received a call from the economist and journalist Will Hutton. The minister added: 'Will thinks it's the end of the Western world as we've known it, but I haven't been following it too closely.' Although the dominant Brown had left the Treasury, economic policy was off limits for the rest of the new cabinet.

Brown constantly sought the advice of the two economists who were his confidants, but who were now shaping political careers of their own. When he realized that Northern Rock was on the verge of bankruptcy he put no faith in the inexperienced Darling. Instead he wanted to hear from Ed Balls and Shriti Vadera. At the height of the emergency Brown instructed the Downing Street switchboard to track down Balls, but he was not immediately available as he was visiting a school in Bristol in his new role as Schools Secretary. As a minister in the Department for International Development, Vadera was abroad. Here was an early warning sign of Brown's isolation in his new job. Some of those he trusted most, and whose judgement he valued, were not available when he needed them.

But in the midst of the crisis over Northern Rock something quite unexpected happened. Labour's ratings went up in the polls and Brown's personal popularity soared. Voters were not angry with Brown and the government but pleased that they were there to address the crisis. In contrast David Cameron and his young shadow chancellor, George Osborne, appeared out of their depth, as to some extent they were. In the week before Labour's annual party conference in Bournemouth, polls gave Labour a lead of at least ten points. The party won a council by-election in a solid Tory seat in mid-Worcester, a gain that commanded the front page of the *Daily Mail*.

Northern Rock had looked like a hideous trap and then it became a release for Brown, confirming that voters trusted him to lead in a crisis. The release soon morphed into another trap, this time a fatal one. It was the polls taken in the aftermath of the Northern Rock drama that prompted him for the first time to think seriously about calling an early general election in the autumn of 2007. There had been a lot of media speculation during August and early September about an election. On the whole Brown was wary. He did not kill off the speculation, but refused to engage with the issue and veered towards dismissing the idea when aides raised the prospect.

But suddenly he appeared to have crossed a threshold. Voters were backing him in an economic crisis, not just in fleeting emergencies such as the floods and foot-and-mouth. He was also on a good run.

Shortly before Northern Rock collapsed he had mischievously invited Margaret Thatcher to tea in Number Ten at a time when parts of the Conservative party were expressing disillusionment with Cameron. Some of his closest aides thought this a contortion too far. Ed Miliband could not bear to look at the television pictures of Brown and Thatcher outside Number Ten. But the stunt worked for Brown, partly because when a leader is performing well in the polls the tricks seem clever. (When the same leader is suffering from low ratings, the very same devices are dismissed as shallow and desperate.) Brown again proclaimed that like Thatcher he was a 'conviction' politician, although typically he did not go into any detail as to what form his convictions took. But that did not matter. Most of the newspapers approved of his association with Thatcher and the choreography was awkward for Cameron.

Brown's early prime-ministerial strategy had not failed. It had gone too well. His government was relatively united, with Blairites and Brownites working well together. Outsiders had been recruited to challenge the idea that Brown was a tribal Labour figure. Brown stated repeatedly that on virtually every issue he was seeking a national consensus. He had instituted a review of the NHS under the authoritative leadership of the surgeon Lord Darzi, an initiative that had purged the internal divisions over public-service reforms. Just before the summer recess he had signalled a slight distancing from President Bush, at least compared with the love-ins with Tony Blair. He had unveiled some modest constitutional reforms aimed at restoring trust in politics and they had been reasonably well received. Brown's pre-election strategy had been shaped on the assumption and in the hope that after around nine months or so he would have proved himself to be a competent and consensual Prime Minister, at which point he would call an election. He had other vague but more ambitious ideas if Labour should win office under his leadership.

Instead his thoughts turned to calling an even earlier election, one that would be held within weeks of the party conference season. The temptation was understandable. Any new prime minister desperate for greater legitimacy would have considered the option. The error was to contemplate the option in the full media glare. The three weeks of election fever, followed by an announcement that there would be no election, destroyed Brown's premiership.

NINE

Election Fever

When he became Prime Minister Gordon Brown wanted to call an early election. He had in mind the late spring or early summer of the following year, 2008, more or less the limit for a non-elected prime minister to govern with authority. Brown's calculations on timing had been clearly thought through, in so far as these matters can be prepared for in advance, and to some extent address the criticism that when he finally made it into Number Ten he did not seem to know what to do. He knew, but he chose not to do it.

When some of his close advisers started to press harder for a much earlier election, one to be held in the autumn of 2007, Brown was at first extremely reticent. Characteristically he told them that they had not prepared for such a big move over the summer holidays: if they wanted an election they should have all scrapped their holidays to prepare for the campaign. Brown equated success with hard work, the ultimate triumphs coming about when holidays were cancelled.

Brown never thought twice about ditching summer holidays. He had asked his allies to do so when he thought he was going to take over from Tony Blair in the early autumn of 2004. They all happily obliged. They would give up virtually everything for their master.

On one level Brown's every utterance and act was made with the electorate in mind as he sought to prove he could be a successful prime minister. Yet he gave no consistent thought to an autumn election during the summer. In some ways he was too busy to do so, what with the terrorist attacks, the floods and foot-and-mouth. For Brown an election campaign was an event that demanded almost total attention for a few months. He did not feel ready and did not allocate the time to plot and plan. There was no time available. Being Prime Minister was proving to be even more exacting than he had assumed. He was a workaholic without the time to meet all the demands of his new work. Suddenly planning ahead beyond a few hours seemed like an elusive luxury.

At the end of August Labour's former deputy leader, Roy Hattersley, met Brown briefly in Edinburgh and asked him about the election speculation that was breaking out in the media. Brown conveyed no zeal for such a prospect. He told Hattersley that it would be hard to justify an early poll and that he wanted more time to show he could do the job. Hattersley left Edinburgh convinced that Brown would not call an election and did not want to do so. He regarded Brown's caution as justified and right, as did most veteran Labour figures, who could remember previous campaigns that had been conducted largely in autumnal darkness.

Brown's prime-ministerial schedule since taking over from Blair was an underestimated cause of the chaos to follow. The demands, while always absurdly intense, had been even greater than normal and would have drained the energies of a more experienced prime minister. Having had virtually no time to think about an election, he was unready to call one.

The problem was that Brown became too successful in his defiant centrist leadership. He enjoyed such a heady first few weeks in September 2007, with his apparently assured response to Northern Rock, foot-and-mouth, biblical floods and terrorist attacks, that he inadvertently fuelled the speculative talk in the media about an election. For the newspapers and the broadcasters it became more or less the only topic worth talking about. The polls were good. The economy was bound to get worse before very long. The Conservatives were confused and demoralized. A lot of commentators and pollsters argued that the case for an early election was overwhelming as far as Brown was concerned. There would never be a better time.

Towards the end of July Brown hosted a cabinet meeting at Chequers. Afterwards Spencer Livermore, the two Eds and Douglas

Alexander had a separate discussion with Brown in the drawing room. Livermore told Brown: 'You know, given how things are we should consider an early election.' Brown asked: 'You mean next April?' Livermore had already concluded that the following spring was out of the question because he was acutely aware that the abolition of the 10p tax would come into effect then. He replied: 'No, when I say early I mean properly early.' Livermore got the firm impression that Brown was dismissive of the idea.

Livermore returned from holiday towards the end of August. Polls continued to show Labour's lead growing. He thought that this was too big an opportunity to casually dismiss. The idea of an election needed more serious consideration. He wrote a memo to Brown outlining the points in favour and those against. Reflecting in the summer of 2010 Livermore told me: 'Initially he continued to be of the view, I think, that it was still too early, but regrettably I think he saw it as an opportunity to bait the Conservatives rather than a strategic decision to take.' Brown did not respond directly to the memo. According to Livermore: 'He let it lie on his desk for a week or two and only then came back to it. And when he came back he was much more convinced.' Later Brown regarded the lost two weeks in late August and early September, in which he paid no attention to the memo, as costly.

On the Friday before the Labour conference Brown met his close aides over lunch at Chequers. The occasion should have been celebratory. It was the first time all of them had met in the Prime Minister's official rural retreat for a smaller more intimate gathering since Brown had taken over from Blair. As usual with the entourage, there was not a hint of celebration in the air. They had too much to do. They always did.

The original aim of their meeting had been to discuss Brown's conference speech. The regular group attended once more, the basic cast: Douglas Alexander, Spencer Livermore, Ed Balls, Ed Miliband, Damian McBride and Bob Shrum.

Oddly, for quite a lot of the Chequers lunch there was no talk of an early election. Instead Brown went doggedly through the themes

289

of his speech as if planning for an ordinary conference, albeit his first as Prime Minister and party leader. Sometimes Brown could behave with an indiscriminate wilfulness, focusing on what he had decided was important rather than what those around him knew was the key concern. Only towards the end did Livermore and Shrum raise the possibility of an early election. Livermore pressed him on an issue he had first raised in July: 'Look at the polls. We have got to address the issue of an early election. There is a case for holding one.'

Brown was still highly cautious, which is probably why he had not raised it earlier. He responded to Livermore by pointing out with good cause, and one underrated by observers calling casually for an early poll: 'If that's the case we should be much better prepared.'

He was right. Elections are like military campaigns. They involve preparation on a colossal scale, from the writing of the manifesto to timetabling the schedules of leading politicians. They are also expensive. Labour had just spent its dwindling resources on the non-leadership contest in the summer. It was then that Brown suggested that if an election was in prospect they should have spent the summer holidays making plans. Livermore replied candidly: 'We needed a holiday. We were all knackered. But we are where we are. We need to look at the current situation. Cameron's doing badly. We have a big poll lead.'

After a brief discussion Brown took a first step towards his nightmare. He declared: 'We need to get the work done to see precisely where we stand with the country.' This was the first time he authorized any form of preparation for an election. He agreed to commission a poll of marginal constituencies in order to make a more informed assessment of Labour's chances.

The seemingly innocent and obvious move changed everything. Brown moved from being the consensual 'father of the nation' leader to one contemplating an election. There is no more partisan act than seeking to destroy your opponents. From that moment onwards Brown was in a trap, caught in a sequence from which he never escaped. The media was bound to get hold of the news that Labour had commissioned a poll in marginal seats. The news would confirm that Brown was eyeing an early election.

At the Friday lunch Livermore, Alexander and Shrum were fairly robust advocates of an early election, although with qualifications. The two Eds were more cautious, not least because they had been with Brown from the beginning of the arduous journey and were aware that having arrived they risked ending it all in the space of a few months. But all of them spoke as if they were discussing a journey across thin ice. They knew they could sink, but there was a big prize if they could make it to the other side.

It was at this point in their lunch that they made a crude miscalculation. Although Brown showed no enthusiasm for an early election he agreed with the others that discussion of an early campaign would be destabilizing for the Tories who would be found to reveal not-yet fully formed policies. This was the fatal error. No one at the Chequers lunch suggested that the threat of an election might unify the Conservative party around Cameron's fragile leadership, which is what happened, and not unpredictably. No one asked what the consequences would be if they talked up the possibility and then did not call an election. They agreed therefore in interviews and with journalists privately to talk up the possibility of an election in order to frighten Cameron, even though they had by no means agreed to hold one. It was a calamitous strategic judgement. Brown and his entourage were trying to be too clever by half.

The Brownites, capable from the mid-1990s to around 2004 of making sharp strategic decisions, had entered a phase that was so highly charged they lost control.

The Chequers gathering was the last time this group came together in a mood of relative harmony. They were on the edge of disaster.

The degree to which the election was at most a tentative possibility as late as the build-up to Labour's conference was reflected in Brown's more immediate strategy, which was to focus on a few particular policy issues in the pre-conference weekend interviews and to use the speculation to highlight famous dividing lines with the Tories. Brown and the Brownites still had faith in dividing lines as a way of winning elections, which in itself was a divide with the Blairites, who did not.

During their wider discussion at Chequers about the messages they should convey in the avalanche of pre-conference publicity, Balls and Miliband stressed that they should make the issue not the election but the choice between Labour and the Tories. The two of them were worried that Brown had sought to become too much the father of the nation, so consensual that few had a clue what the difference was with Cameron's party.

But inevitably, with the news of the specially commissioned poll in marginal seats being briefed in an attempt to unnerve the Conservatives, any talk of dividing lines was reported in the context of election fever. In his pre-conference interview in the *Sunday Telegraph* Balls stated that the election, whenever it came, would be about the dividing lines, but 'what we've got to do in the coming months is spell out the choices'. Balls referred to the 'coming months' in order to keep open the option of an election in 2008. In his capacity as election coordinator Alexander gave a *Guardian* interview in which he said that while nothing had been decided, the party was on an election footing. He could hardly deny that this was now formally the case, but the robust provocative talk, conveyed with the machismo of a group that had turned around Labour's position in the polls, meant that the fever became even more intense at precisely the moment when cabinet ministers and journalists were gathering in Bournemouth for the annual conference.

Party conferences are now a kind of annual jamboree of politicians and journalists, a school trip for them all away from Westminster. Ordinary party members do not get much of a look-in. As a result even relatively small stories are magnified during the few days of high-octane political gossip. In Bournemouth the only topic was whether or not Brown should call an election. If election fever had broken out at any other point in the year it would not have been reported with quite the level of intensity it inevitably was during the week of the annual conference.

When the court met in Brown's hotel suite late on the Saturday afternoon Damian McBride advised strongly: 'We don't want to shut

292

this one down. I'm going to brief that you're not ruling an election out.' Still the entourage was convinced that the speculation was in itself helpful, even though Brown and indeed the rest of them were not sure whether they should actually call an election.

The next three or four days were extraordinary, and, although no one knew it at the time, the death knell for Brown's leadership. Senior cabinet ministers and journalists were asking each other whether they thought Brown would and should call an election. Ministers asked journalists for advice. 'What do you think we should do?' was a common question. Most journalists told them to go for it.

Brown's speech on the Tuesday afternoon was rewritten in the light of the election fever. He had still not decided for sure what to do, but he needed to keep the option of an election open. As a result his speech was not about a new Prime Minister with a clear agenda for the coming years. Instead it was deliberately thin, more an election-eering address aimed at pleasing or not offending as many voters and newspapers as possible. This was another disaster. After Brown failed to call an election commentators looked back at the speech and cited it as evidence that Brown had no route map as a Prime Minister. Yet his only route map at the time he delivered the speech was one that gave him the chance to get his own almost immediate electoral mandate. The speech was a vague celebration of Britishness, fairness and public service reforms. Later it became famous for one clumsy sentence promising British jobs for British workers, a slogan that had been deployed by the British National Party. At the time, or at least the following day, newspapers were generous. Only subsequently was the speech dismissed as vacuous. The media reaction was in itself reveal-ing. Brown could do little wrong at this point, always a dangerous situation for a leader, as it can breed complacency and lead to casual misjudgements. If Brown had delivered the same speech a year later, when he was deeply unpopular, he would have been slaughtered.

During the conference week Balls moved decisively in favour of an early election. He noted that Brown's speech had gone down well and the media was focused on an election with an intensity that would make it difficult to pull back. He also made another important observation. In his discussions with journalists he sensed that the newspapers were moving rightwards, particularly *The Times*, which had become the base for some influential and dedicated followers of David Cameron and George Osborne. Every lunchtime and evening the dining room of the main conference hotel was a scene of never-ending election gossip. Balls would be a guest of the *Sun* one evening and of the *Independent* the next. On a nearby table Douglas Alexander had similar conversations with *The Times*. Not so far away Ed Miliband was a guest of the *Guardian*. They rotated at each meal. Balls calculated that if they were to win an authority-enhancing election the march to the right of the still influential newspapers might be halted or their capacity to sway would be diminished. He told Brown that most of them would endorse Labour in a few weeks' time but possibly not in a year's time. This piece of intelligence from the world of newspapers had a major impact on the media-obsessed Brown, who also began to move for the first time in favour of an early election.

Sometimes the frenzy behind the scenes surfaced in public. Caught up in the conference heat, Balls told the *Today* programme that the decision on the election depended on 'where you thought the balance of risk lies', going early or later. He was revealing the innermost calculations of the Brownite court to millions of listeners, fanning the speculation. Each of them was agonizing over whether an early election was conceivably the least risky option,even though it was fraught with risks.

During much of the conference week Brown was still cautious, saying repeatedly in his hotel suite to various courtiers, with a naive futility: 'We are going to have to think this one through.' For Brown the stakes were unbearably high. If he held the election and won he would be a liberated leader. His authority would be hugely enhanced. If he called an election and was defeated he would have lost everything after only a few months.

The calculation was also multi-layered in its complexity. It was far from clear whether his authority would be enhanced if he won, but with a smaller majority. What would have been the point of replacing a parliament with a big majority for one with a smaller one? Or would

the media claim such an outcome as a triumph for a new leader w.
had won an election on his own terms? These questions were whirling
around Brown's mind, but he was also enjoying the apparent turmoil
of the Tories as Labour's conference came to an end. Brown was at his
most politically fulfilled when he sensed he was outmanoeuvring the
Tories. Much of the media hailed Labour's conference as one that
displayed an awesome discipline and unity. Political commentators
doubted whether the Conservatives would be so united as they gathered for what many expected would be a fractious conference in
Blackpool the following week. Throughout the week Balls had been
telling journalists that Cameron was a 'transitory figure' as he acted
on the assumption that the election speculation would cause mayhem
for Cameron at the party's conference.

On the Sunday after the Labour conference Brown and his entourage gathered again at Chequers. The mood was still tentative, but
more resolved than it had been a week earlier. Brown agreed to accept
an offer from the Unite union to pay for a 5-million direct mail shot
of voters in marginal seats. Key operational decisions were taken
about employing more staff at Labour headquarters. Ed Miliband was
instructed to prepare a draft manifesto as a matter of urgency.
Labour's General Secretary, Peter Watt, revealed later that the party
spent £1.2 million preparing for an autumn election. From the weekend of the Labour conference onwards Watt was convinced an election would be called and that he was in effect already running a
campaign. Labour MPs and candidates headed for their constituencies in order to have campaign photographs taken. Watt held a series
of meetings to discuss the logistics of the campaign.

Over the Sunday lunch Brown and the entourage discussed the
policy areas that would dominate an election and looked for potential
trouble spots. Brown said they needed to say more of substance on
Iraq before an election, the issue that had cost Tony Blair support in
2005. Quite a lot of Labour voters had stayed at home or switched to
the Lib Dems largely because of Iraq. Brown wanted to win them
back. According to senior aides, Brown himself took the decision to
visit Iraq the following week, during the Conservative party

conference. He wanted to appear prime-ministerial, addressing the troops while Cameron struggled to stay afloat at his conference in Blackpool. At the same time he was desperate to convey a sense that Britain's role in Iraq was coming to an end. This was another step towards Brown's nightmare, and a colossal misjudgement on his part, a sign that his ability to make sound political calls was fading fast under the intense pressure of being a Prime Minister who felt he was on trial every moment of the day.

He had nothing new to say on Iraq. Traditionally leaders did not seek to upstage other parties during their conference week. When Brown flew out to Iraq on Tuesday, pretending to have new announcements about reductions in troops, the political mood turned against him in a way that could be discerned almost physically. Here was a supposedly statesmanlike Prime Minister using even Iraq to prepare for an election. Brown was still viewing events through the wrong prism. Anticipating feuding chaos at the Conservatives' conference he assumed the image of a Prime Minister in Iraq would highlight the contrast between a struggling Cameron and a leader at ease with power.

But the Conservatives were not struggling. Even before Brown had set out for his disastrous trip they had regained a sense of momentum. In his pre-conference interviews on the Sunday Cameron was calm and good-humoured, getting away with the pretence that he would welcome an election, when he dreaded such a prospect. More significantly there was an air of determined harmony in Blackpool. The threat of an election had unified the Conservatives, precisely the opposite of what Brown and his close advisers had thought would happen.

On Monday morning the shadow chancellor, George Osborne, electrified the gathering with his pledge to abolish inheritance tax, a move to be paid for, at least in theory, by a tax on wealthy non-domiciles, an ingenious proposition. Brown's allies admitted later that Osborne's announcement was 'destabilizing'. What did they expect? In all their naive and misjudged calculations some of them had not bargained for a popular and credible tax cut aimed particularly at the

South East of England where the value of properties had soared and where there were several key marginal seats. Only Livermore and his pollster, Deborah Mattinson had strongly urged him to cut inheritance tax in his final budget as Chancellor. Brown ignored them.

By the following day, as Brown flew out to Iraq, it was clear that Osborne had given the Conservatives some momentum. When Brown returned to London on Wednesday he faced a media backlash against his visit, intensified by a rare intervention from the former Prime Minister, John Major, who condemned the supposed father of the nation for acting with cynical opportunism in exploiting Iraq for electioneering purposes. Brown's entire strategy for his opening phase as Prime Minister was being exposed as a sham. From being the consensual leader he was perceived suddenly and accurately as making every move with an election in mind.

By now Brown was losing control of the agenda. There was nothing he could do about Iraq. The mistake had been made. But he was in more of a panic about Osborne's inheritance tax pledge. His Chancellor, Alistair Darling, was due to deliver his pre-budget report the following week, after Brown had made his decision as to whether or not to call the election. Brown wanted the economic statement to act as an enticing prelude to the campaign, if he decided to call one. After a series of frantic calls with Balls, he contrived a response. The government would pledge to cut inheritance tax too, but at a lower threshold. Once more Brown and Balls thought they were being cunning. They had hit upon a new dividing line. The Tories would cut inheritance tax for millionaires. Labour would do so for the many and not just the few, leaving some spare cash to spend on schools and hospitals. Brown told Ed Miliband to incorporate the new policy into the manifesto and instructed the still meekly inexperienced Darling to change his pre-budget report.

Darling got the shock of his ministerial life. He had painstakingly prepared his first big statement as Chancellor in order to project a message of calm prudence. Now he had to find the cash to pay for a tax cut. He had no idea how this would be done convincingly, so stole the proposal put forward by Osborne and targeted the non-domiciles.

Senior Treasury officials were taken aback. With days to go before the statement they were suddenly preparing an emergency budget. All because of Brown's need to win an election. But after Osborne had played his ace, Livermore concluded that it would be too risky to call an early election.

On Thursday Brown spent much of the time in intense discussion with advisers. By late afternoon they received details of two opinion polls showing a significant narrowing of the Labour lead. This led them to focus even more intensely on a discussion about whether Brown's authority would be diminished if he won but with a smaller majority. They were aware that the Conservatives required a lead of around 10 per cent to win an overall majority. For sure that was not going to happen. Late on Thursday evening Ed Miliband phoned sympathetic journalists seeking advice as to how the media would interpret an outcome in which Labour won, but with a small majority. Miliband got conflicting advice. One or two told him that if Brown should call an election on such a basis, a victory would be a victory. At least one warned him that the momentum was moving fast against the government and in favour of the Conservatives and that Brown would be daft to call an election in such circumstances. If he won with a small majority Miliband was warned that the media and some Blairites would easily turn against Brown.

On Thursday afternoon Cameron added to Brown's anguish. He delivered his leader's speech in Blackpool with a theatrical flourish, speaking without notes and conveying a steely, good-humoured calm in the face of a genuinely testing storm. Cameron spoke while aware of the possibility of imminent election defeat and perhaps the end of his short-lived leadership.

The calm delivery of his speech reflected Cameron's wider outlook at this most testing phase in his still early leadership. At no point during the entire sequence did Cameron lose his cool, and he was privately more confident than any of his aides that if an election were called he could at least deprive Brown of an overall majority. He had noted that over August the Labour lead had wobbled a little when Cameron adopted a higher profile, and he thought it would wobble still more in a campaign. But obviously his preference was for no campaign in the near future since the Conservatives were not remotely ready. During their conference Cameron's most influential adviser, Steve Hilton, exclaimed several times to colleagues: 'We are on to something exciting here, but we need more time to do the work.' The substance of Cameron's speech was forgettable, but the delivery was mesmerizing and started a trend for speaking without notes. No one else did it so well, although Blair could have done. Of more immediate significance, most of the newspapers gave the speech the thumbs up, confirming Balls's sense that the media was moving rightwards.

On Friday at 6 a.m. Brown phoned Balls, who was in his constituency in West Yorkshire. Tantalizingly the first results from the marginal polls showed a tiny lead for the Conservatives. By then Balls was absolutely convinced that Brown had to call an election. He was not especially disturbed by the poll, arguing that it was too late to go back on an election and that the Tories had got a bounce from their conference and in particular the inheritance tax cut proposal, a policy that could be dealt with. Brown agreed, or appeared to do so. By the end of the early morning phone call between Balls and Brown the early election was on.

A few hours later Miliband, Livermore, Alexander, Shrum, his fellow American analyst Stan Greenberg and Deborah Mattinson attended a meeting in Number Ten. The final details of the marginal polling confirmed that the Tories were ahead but that Labour would still win an overall majority. In a chaotic meeting, which Brown left and returned to several times, the mood swayed dramatically against an election. All of them argued that Brown would be taking too big a risk at a point when the polls were turning against him. There was no guarantee, they argued, that he would reverse the momentum now that it was clearly moving against him in the seats that needed to be won. Their advice played to Brown's cautious instincts. From the beginning of the deranged sequence he had been most wary of an early election, and he almost felt a sense of relief in deciding against. More senior members of the cabinet had been urging him consistently against it on the grounds that a wet, dark autumn was the wrong season for a highly charged election that did not need to be called. The former leader Neil Kinnock was also firmly opposed. He had urged Brown against the move in several discussions. But the key was Brown. He had never wanted an early election and only succumbed to the prospect late in the day.

By 5 in the afternoon Brown phoned Balls to say that the election was off and urged him to join the rest of them on Saturday to discuss how they should handle the anticlimactic announcement. Balls could not believe what he was hearing and urged Brown to think again. Brown told Balls it was too late. He had taken the decision and was convinced that with the polls suggesting that the Conservatives might actually win there was no case for going early.

The handling of the decision was more inept than the sequence that had preceded it, reflecting the entourage's naive and limited understanding of the media. There was no journalist amongst them as they gathered in Number Ten on Saturday, none of them quite realizing that they were all moving from one relatively stable political context to a new more tempestuous one. Dangerously, a few of them, including Brown, thought they understood how to manage the media. They agreed that Brown should give an interview to the BBC's Andrew Marr, whose programme was broadcast on the following day. With a mad logic the entourage became focused on this interview. Brown had to be in Chequers for a breakfast meeting with Rupert Murdoch the following day, so Marr would have to make do with a pre-record on Saturday afternoon. They therefore thought they would cleverly invite Marr into Number Ten that afternoon to pre-record an interview and would offer a clip to all outlets in advance of the broadcast. Brown was insistent that he did not want to give a press conference in which every angle of the last few weeks would be subjected to scrutiny. He wanted to convey a single positive message, that he needed more time to outline his vision for the country before calling an election.

Predictably he was forced to hold a news conference anyway after the outcry at the exclusivity handed to Marr. The other broadcasters were especially angry at their lack of access at such a pivotal moment, placing almost as much focus on their slight as on the dramatic news that there would be no election. Sky's political editor, Adam Boulton, broadcast and blogged in a state of undisguised fury. The BBC's political editor, Nick Robinson, could not hide his angry dismay as his predecessor in the post, Andrew Marr, strolled into Number Ten in order to get an exclusive. Bizarrely, Marr emerged from the interview to give details on BBC News 24 as to what Brown had told him, as if he had briefly become Brown's spokesman.

The rage in the media meant that Brown had no choice but to call a news conference on Monday. His confidence shaken, his image as the consensual one-nation Prime Minister in tatters, he handled the aggressive questions with the agility of an elephant in quicksand. The dynamic of the news conference was itself testimony to the transformed political situation. When Brown held a press conference in September he was in command and popular. The questions were polite and journalists laughed at his familiar jokes. Now there was no laughter, but the same question asked in a hundred different ways. Why did he not call the election?

At one point towards the end Brown was asked specifically whether the opinion polls had been decisive. He ineptly denied that they had been and insisted once more that he had not called an election because he wanted to show 'his vision for the country'. Even on the basis of Number Ten's own narrative this was self-evidently false. At Labour's party conference only a fortnight earlier McBride had briefed openly that they had commissioned a poll of marginal seats. The week before Brown's press conference McBride had briefed persistently that they would consider its findings on Friday, still naively confident that such a prospect would unnerve the increasingly self-assured Conservatives. That was the day Brown decided not to go ahead with the election. The polls had not been good enough.

There were a thousand ways Brown could have acknowledged the truth, that the polls had weighed strongly in the decision. In these situations humour can be a valuable weapon. He could have joked about the irrelevance of polls in a way that showed he took them with a deadly seriousness. Virtually any response would have been better than the one he gave. Once more none of his advisers offered an alternative to the formula, mechanically repeated, of Brown's desire to outline a vision. The pretext was universally derided on the solid ground that it could not be true.

The ordeal continued. On Wednesday Brown faced his first Prime Minister's Question Time since the summer, a season that seemed so distant that it might as well have been decades away. Brown arrived in the Commons looking drawn and pale. Once more the calculating, evasive politician was physically transparent. In this case he communicated fear with his ghostly appearance. To make matters worse, Cameron delivered one of his wittiest sound bites, mocking Brown's pretence that the polls played no part in his decision. He accused Brown of being the only prime minister to call off an election because he was frightened he would win it. In the space of two weeks Brown had become a figure of fun.

In between the press conference and Prime Minister's Question Time Darling delivered his pre-budget report in outlandish circumstances. When Darling heard on the Friday night that the election was called off he was briefly euphoric, assuming he could return to his original plans for a prudent statement without a sudden cut in inheritance tax paid for vaguely from the same source as the one targeted by George Osborne, the elusive non-domiciles. Darling contacted a senior official at the Treasury and suggested they returned to their original prudent plans. The official told Darling that such an option was impossible because the pre-budget report was at the printers. As a result a deflated Darling had no choice but to deliver his pre-election pre-budget report without an election. It looked pathetic, aping a Tory proposal that itself had been plucked out of the air in desperation. At the ghostly, ghastly Prime Minister's Question Time Cameron asked Brown whether he would have announced a cut in inheritance tax if the Conservatives had not proposed it. Brown insisted the Treasury was reviewing the tax, which was true, but it is also the case that Darling had no intention of making his debut with a tax cut that had not been properly costed.

The consequences of the entire sequence were devastating. Brown's pre-election strategy of being a consensual prime minister was blown apart. His carefully cultivated reputation for statesmanlike integrity was destroyed, replaced by a perception of Brown as a leader of self-interested deviousness.

More significantly, having generated election fever in the autumn of 2007 Brown could not do so again the following year. Indeed he as good as ruled out an election in 2008 at his grim press conference. This was the biggest calamity of them all, the end of the pre-election strategy in which he would play the father of the nation and subtly address the conundrum about standing for both change and continuity. He was now doomed to stumble on without a personal mandate and without a strategy for dealing with the long and precarious journey that lay ahead before an election could be called. Brown had been determined to avoid the humiliation of what Roy Jenkins had called 'tail-end Charlie' prime ministers, those leaders who take over from a long-serving predecessor and then lose an election. He had aimed to avoid that fate by calling an election at a time of his choosing, in a context of controlled, consensual leadership. By succumbing to the lure of an even earlier election he was doomed to the fate of tail-end Charlies, taking the flak until the bitter end.

There were two other profound consequences. Brown's close entourage fell apart in a dismal round of recriminations and an eruption of mutual doubts about the strategic intelligence and trustworthiness of previously close colleagues, or at least colleagues united in a common cause. Brown blamed his election coordinator, Douglas Alexander, and his senior adviser, Spencer Livermore, who soon departed. Others in Number Ten behaved more erratically. The previously reliable Sue Nye was less visible. Brown communicated less with Alexander after the debacle. Balls and Miliband, two rising stars, instructed their advisers to make sure that the media knew they had behaved responsibly throughout. McBride felt particularly protective towards Balls. The media got to know that Balls was in favour of an early campaign. Sensing that McBride was briefing on behalf of Balls, Miliband's advisers stressed that he had always had an open mind on the issue. They were fighting for their individual reputations, seeking distance from the wreckage. In doing so they ensured that the scope for reconstruction was limited. If they were no longer working together as a team, then who was? Brown no longer had a team of wholly reliable allies working together. Although as individuals they still felt loyalty towards him, very soon Alexander would grow deeply disillusioned. The paranoia over briefings, rather than the decision about the election itself, fractured the Brownite court. In the summer of 2010 Alexander told me, in an interview for the BBC Radio 4 series on the Brown premiership, that he and Ed Miliband had joked nervously on the Saturday that they would be blamed for the sequence in briefings to the media 'within twenty minutes of the news breaking that there would be no election'. In his interview for the series Livermore said this is precisely what happened. 'I only know what I am told, and at that point on the Saturday afternoon Damian McBride told me that he had been instructed to blame certain individuals.' I asked Livermore who McBride was briefing on behalf of. There was a pause. 'Ed Balls.'

I put the allegation directly to Balls, who denied it unequivocally – he gave no such instruction, there were no such briefings on his behalf.

As far as I could tell there was a level of unjustified paranoia in relation to Balls, but the paranoia unquestionably existed and intensified in the months to come. The consequences were long-term. In Labour's leadership contest in 2010 Brown's court split three ways instead of uniting around a single candidate. Alexander ran David Miliband's campaign while both Eds stood as candidates.

Amidst briefings and counter-briefings Brown needed all the loyalty he could muster. The final consequence of the non-election was the impact on his self-confidence. He always knew he was walking a high wire as Prime Minister, with an army of enemies willing him to fall off. Now he was clinging on with his well-bitten fingernails. When visitors came to see him in Number Ten he was often slumped on a chair, unable to disguise his depression at what had happened. Sometimes he would note to startled visitors that all he had done was call off an election. No one had been hurt and the decision did not damage the economy. But he knew the seriousness of what had happened. 'We will never seem new and fresh again,' he exclaimed often in the autumn of 2007 as he wondered how to get through the next two or three years.

How did it happen that Brown and his entourage lost all momentum, popularity and credibility in the space of two weeks? One answer, eagerly promoted by some of his Blairite enemies, is that they were always clumsy and inept strategists protected in the past by the subtler, more sophisticated Blair. In their first solo outing they blew it. This assertion does not stand up to scrutiny. No one who manages to be Chancellor for a decade and then becomes Prime Minister on terms he has always sought lacks strategic skills.

The simple explanation is that much of the nightmare was unavoidable. When Labour started to gain a significant lead in the polls the question of an early election was bound to arise, in the media and within the Labour party. The Brownites were slow to appreciate quite how intense the speculation would become, but they were doomed to face it. There was only one way in which Brown could have killed it off, and that would have been to announce in early September that there would be no early election. He would have been crazy to rule out the possibility. Labour's poll lead widened during September. If it continued to move in the same direction an autumn election would have been irresistible, not least because Brown was desperate to show he could win one as Prime Minister.

Some ministers and senior Conservatives suggested subsequently that Brown should have called the election in early September, immediately after the summer holidays. The suggestion ignores the awkward fact that Brown and his party were at that point wholly unprepared for a campaign.

So Brown took the only sensible course available to him, which was to keep all options open and make an assessment at the end of the party conference season. The one fundamental mistake he and his aides committed was to assume that the speculation in itself would help them and destabilize the Conservatives. As a result they

were guilty of fuelling the speculation during the Labour conference, but the dynamics of conferences are such that the possibility
of an election would have been the overwhelming theme even if they
had all behaved like Trappist monks. The media handling of the
decision to call off the election was clumsy, and Brown's subsequent
press conference was even worse. But by then they were in an impossible position. A media strategist with flair would have struggled to
make a positive case for calling off an election that was very nearly
called.

There was a much deeper reason why the decision over the election
traumatized Brown, one that goes to the heart of his dilemma when
he became leader and to the wider and ultimately insoluble tensions
within the New Labour project. Brown could not decide whether to
make a distinct public break with his Blairite legacy. To be more
precise, he could not decide whether he had the space to make a move
in a fresh direction without splitting his party and losing support in
the media. For his own part he wanted to make a break, but as a leader
of a divided party he did not feel strong enough to do so.

The dilemma arose specifically in relation to an early election.
Labour had a mandate to govern for a full term if it chose to do so. It
had won an election under Blair's leadership with a big majority in
2005. In theory Brown had no need to call an election until 2010. His
only justification for doing so would be if he wished to follow a
programme that was distinct and different from the one on which the
party won in 2005. Brown agonized here. What wording would he use
to indicate a fresh direction? What policies would be included in a
manifesto that could not have been introduced under the mandate
secured by Blair? He was especially troubled by a column written by
Martin Kettle, a *Guardian* journalist and a close friend of Blair's.
Kettle argued that there was no need for an early election unless
Brown wanted to move on from the New Labour settlement. Kettle
bumped into Brown during the Labour conference and made the
point again. Why did Brown need to call an election unless he was
proposing to act differently, in which case he would need to spell out
clearly the new direction? Brown became deeply aware that the act of

calling an early election could, by what it implied, blow apart his efforts to unite the party.

Here was another reason why Brown was relieved when he decided to call off the election: he was not entirely sure what he would say during the campaign and wanted more time to move away subtly from his Blairite legacy, as he had originally planned.

There is a twist to the whole affair. Although the sequence was catastrophic, the decision to call off the election was the correct one, even though Brown was to tell aides within weeks how much he regretted it. If Labour had won in the autumn of 2007 it would almost certainly have been with a smaller majority and possibly with no majority at all. The polls suggested they would not win and the tide was moving towards Cameron. Both outcomes would have been disastrous for Brown, who would have faced accusations of unnecessarily making the government far more precarious than it needed to be. Imagine a Brown-led government facing all the external crises that were to follow without a majority or with only a tiny one. The irony of the non-election trauma was that in the end Brown called it right and then spent the next two years depressed that he had called it wrong.

A series of events followed that could not have been more damaging to Brown and the wider reputation of the government. They had very little to do directly with his leadership and yet they helped to destroy it, as if scripted to perfection by a shrewdly malevolent outside force.

Before he became leader Brown was ruthlessly obsessed with proving two points: that the so-called era of Blairite sleaze was over and that he could govern 'for the many' with an authoritative competence.

The immediate context for his anxieties about sleaze had been the 'cash for honours' police investigation that haunted Blair and his close allies during the final year. Police officers questioned Blair twice and arrested two close advisers, although neither was charged. Predictably the investigation went nowhere, but for several months towards the end of Blair's leadership the newspapers and the BBC lionized the main investigator, John Yates, as a heroic figure bravely challenging the mighty and devious figures who wield power. The opposite was closer to the truth. Downing Street was virtually powerless as Yates and his team went about their work, much of which leaked somehow to the press or the BBC. Later Yates denied briefing any lobby journalists at Westminster, but then had to qualify his comments by saying that he did not realize that the likes of the BBC's political editor were in the lobby.

The so-called investigation was the scandal, a vivid example of a growing trend in which non-elected figures undermined democracy by sniping from privileged cover against those who were elected. After his fruitless investigation, Yates should have been demoted to a junior post in a rural police station where crime meant stealing turnips. Instead he was promoted, and acquired responsibility for dealing with the threat posed by terrorism in London, a challenge that demanded a degree of sensitivity that he had not shown in the past.

None of this bothered Brown very much. By the final phase of Blair's premiership and arguably well before the last year, Brown viewed any event that damaged Blair as an opportunity for him to acquire the leadership. In so far as he did reflect more widely on Blair's problems with Yates, it was only to worry that the episode was damaging Labour as a whole. He also saw an opportunity. This was one area where he could make a break with the Blair era and be universally cheered: there would not be a hint of sleaze under his leadership. On the contrary, Brown could claim genuinely to be largely uninterested in material gain. He had not been remotely bothered about living in the glamorous Dorneywood, traditionally the Chancellor's residence at weekends. He never spent much money on clothes or holidays. He did not drive a car. He could make much of his Calvinistic austerity.

So neurotically fearful was he of being associated with any hint of sleaze that he exploded several times when he sensed in the spring of 2007 that stories might damage him. The blogger Guido Fawkes, at that point barely known outside the Westminster village, was making a few waves with his inquiries into the funding of the Smith Institute, a think tank led by several allies of Brown, including his close friend

Wilf Stevenson. Brown had planned to make Stevenson the head of his policy unit in Number Ten. But from January 2007 Guido Fawkes claimed on his blog one or twice a week that the Smith Institute had abused its charitable status. Starting to pay homage to Guido, newspapers made inquiries too.

In the spring of 2007 Brown panicked. 'This is going to destroy me. This will bring me down,' he wailed to close allies. He was so determined not to be tainted with any alleged wrongdoing, even by an anonymous blogger, that he told Stevenson he could not appoint him to Number Ten.

As events turned out, Brown would have been delighted to deal with a minor matter of a think tank and its charitable status. In the autumn of 2007 the police investigation, the symbol of the Blair era, suddenly took a wider form under Brown's leadership. A few minutes before he was about to host his monthly Downing Street press conference in November, the follow-up to the one that had gone so wrong after he had called off the election, Brown heard that Harriet Harman had received money during her deputy leadership campaign from a woman who had acted as an apparently unlawful conduit for a wealthy property developer from the North East, David Abrahams. Brown had hoped to use the press conference to refocus the agenda on public services. Instead it was dominated by questions about Harman.

Brown had not had time to speak to Harman before the press conference got under way. He faced another nightmare, the leader who sought to personify political purity after the 'cash for honours' inquiry being questioned about the alleged impurity of his deputy leader. Awkwardly, and only after persistent questioning from journalists, Brown expressed his personal confidence in Harman.

Earlier in the week Brown had ruthlessly sacked Labour's General Secretary, Peter Watt, who was also now being investigated by the police. Later in the year it emerged that another cabinet minister, Peter Hain, had broken the rules over donations during his deputy leadership campaign. Hain was also investigated by the police. Unlike Harman, Hain was forced to resign from the cabinet over his alleged misdemeanours, although he was later cleared by yet another independent inquiry and returned to the cabinet.

The impact on Brown, the government and Labour was devastating. On one level the situation was darkly comical. Brown had arrived in Number Ten determined to be purer than pure and was now responding to three police investigations. At least Blair had to face only one. Parts of the media had a field day. Many commentators were disappointed that the 'cash for honours' investigation had not led to series of charges against Blair. Now they had a chance to make hay once more.

Even the relatively restrained *Guardian* went over the top, printing in its edition the day after Brown's tormented press conference what it regarded as the Key Questions, a device to convey an overwrought sense of unresolved drama:

> Is it possible that Watt as party general secretary was the only Labour official to know Abrahams was using conduits to send money to Labour for four years?

> Lady Jay told Hilary Benn (another candidate for the deputy leadership) not to accept a donation from Kidd. What alerted Jay to the problem?

> Should Harman have made more effort to check out the bona fides of Kidd or was the gift sent unsolicited?

The key questions and the frenzied headlines that accompanied them gave the impression of a long-serving government that had become corrupt. Far from being a break from what were seen as the worst aspects of Blair's regime, Brown's leadership appeared to have tolerated fiddling on a grander and wider scale. Brown's main pre-election objective of restoring a sense of trust between Labour and the electorate had been blown apart.

Almost as damaging was the impact on the morale within the government. Senior figures were appalled at the way Brown appeared to be willing to dump on anyone facing allegations of any sort. Harman watched his press conference angry and saddened at his reluctance to endorse her fully. She felt a deep sense of betrayal during a period in which she had been loyal to him in spite of having some cause for resentment at her relative lack of influence, not least during the discussions about an early election. Peter Watt had greater cause for grievance, having lost his job and being the subject of a police investigation. Later he declared publicly: 'I was resolute then and now in my belief of my innocence and that I had acted in good faith. I wish the same good faith and loyalty had been shown to me.' The early election had driven a wedge through the relatively close Brownite entourage. The allegations over donations led to a much wider range of tensions, and from several cabinet ministers a sense of despair at Brown's apparently self-interested and yet inept response to the affair.

Later the Crown Prosecution Service announced there would be no charges against senior officials in the Labour party on the grounds of insufficient evidence. The anticlimactic denouement was barely reported. Harman paid back some of the donations out of her own money. Few suggested at the time that perhaps the reason why the situation had arisen with Harman was a cock-up. Even journalists who were critical of her as a politician did not believe she was corrupt.

So why was there such a fuss? As with 'cash for honours', stories of alleged wrongdoing are more dramatic and easier to report, not least for the BBC, an institution that is not allowed to be partisan, but can get as excited as newspapers about non-partisan issues such as over-hyped claims about corruption.

On the substance of the issue, Labour was neurotically obsessed about raising money to fight elections, including the non-election. They raised more than they needed. Cash does not win elections. Blair was proud of the fact that business leaders made big donations, proving that Labour was no longer dependent solely on the generosity of trade unions. Before the 'cash for honours' inquiry he used to boast about the generosity of business leaders. Brown just wanted the money in order to fund an election campaign. This was partly a story about the decline of political parties and a group at the centre seeking cash to help them stay there.

It was also a story about the rarity of leadership contests in the Labour party. After 1997 the Conservatives seemed to enjoy their regular competitions. Labour had a contest in 1994 and then there was nothing until 2007. The half-formed politicians who fought for the deputy leadership in the summer of 2007 probably had only a limited grasp of what such campaigns involved. Quite often the more trivial reasons explain what happens in British politics.

Brown was flailing around by November 2007, his self-confidence shattered and his pre-election strategy in tatters. But his culpability was limited. A leader in a stronger position might have defended his colleagues more robustly, but Brown was so grievously weakened that he did not have the authority to back the likes of Watt during another police investigation even if he had been inclined to do so. Not even at the height of the frenzy was Brown personally accused of corruption, although voters might have formed that impression from another frenzy of headlines about Labour Party funding. This was a sequence of events over which he had no control and, as a new leader, it inevitably damaged him more than anyone else in the end.

Brown's other pre-election objective had been to convey a strong sense of prime-ministerial competence. This hope was smashed to bits at around the same time the police began their new investigations.

Early in November it emerged that two discs had gone missing containing the private information of all those who received child benefit. The lost data was thought to concern around 25 million people, nearly half the population. All hell broke loose. Could this government get nothing right? That seemed to be the only question worth asking.

By the end of November, two months after the election that wasn't, Brown and his government were floundering. Quite a lot of the government blamed Brown. The depressed, bewildered Prime

Minister blamed quite a lot of his government. The reversal of fortunes was without precedent. Some commentators compared the sudden decline with the drop in support for John Major after Britain left the ERM in September 1992, but in scale and significance the comparison did not stack up. The withdrawal from the ERM was an event of momentous economic importance and followed a day of extraordinary drama in which interest rates fleetingly soared as Major tried to keep the besieged currency at a level that was proving unsustainable. The withdrawal was especially humiliating for Major, who as Chancellor had persuaded Margaret Thatcher to join the ERM. Brown's sequence was incomparably more trivial.

None of it signified very much. He called off an election because Labour was falling behind – not too surprising for a government in mid-term. The police were investigating ministers fruitlessly. An official had lost a couple of discs. None of these issues bristle with ramifications, and yet they were deadly.

Ministers started to question whether Brown even had a strategy for power. The answer was that he did not have one any longer. He did not have a clue how he was going to keep going for two or three years without a mandate of his own. Yet he could no longer call an early election. In the meantime external events robbed him of his desire to exude integrity and competence. The chaotic new context was captured vividly when Brown failed to turn up in Lisbon to sign the Lisbon Treaty in December 2007 with the other EU leaders. He signed alone later in the day. Some commentators assumed this had been a cunning plan to please the Euro-sceptics. Number Ten was incapable of cunning plans by then. It was another cock-up.

Sometimes ministers phoned his office to discover that Brown himself would answer. What was Sue Nye doing? Where were the senior officials? On the day of the Treaty signing Brown had been booked in for a meeting with the Liaison Committee of MPs. He did not want to miss the event, having made much of the need to boost parliamentary accountability. He was even more nervous about missing it in order to turn up for the signing of a treaty viewed by some in the media as undermining parliament. The scheduling was a mess.

But the appalling choreography, the crescendo of external crises, the growing despair of some ministers, had little to do with the fundamental policies. Brown had once been seen as too strong. Now he was attacked for being a weak ditherer. The onslaught was stylistic, not substantive. Its impact suggested that Labour's lead in the summer was soft. Conversely Labour's capacity to stride into the lead suggested also that the Conservatives' recovery was equally precarious. Politics was more fluid than it seemed, but Brown's mood was constant. He was desperately low, caught in the trough that he had been destined to slip into ever since that brief flash of fatal success in the summer.

TEN

A Vacuum

When a political leader has lost a strategy and failed to find a new one the vacuum is rapidly filled. Disparate events become the defining narrative because there is no other story to tell.

The furore over the autumn election that never was meant that his carefully planned strategy for an early election, probably in 2008, had to be dumped and he was left with no alternative plan. That is partly because there was none available. In order to move on from Blairism he needed to win an election. Now he could not hold one for a long time to come. He was trapped.

In the mayhem that followed Brown could think of no new script, so he reverted to being the apolitical, managerial figure 'getting on with the job', aloof and humourless. The inauthentic public voice was matched by increasingly desperate behaviour behind the scenes. And yet in the end the sheer epic nature of the events that swept over him in the autumn of 2008 was a form of salvation. Responding to them gave him a new raison d'être and therefore a degree of political hope. His cabinet colleagues and some Labour MPs saw little cause for optimism and reflected more on the chaos of Brown's thoughtless style of leadership. Some of them began to contemplate removing him.

Brown had begun his leadership knowing that one wrong move before he had acquired the authority of winning an election would fuel insurrectionary thoughts amongst his many enemies. He started to make wrong moves from hour to hour, although given the astonishing array of daunting events that erupted around him it is not easy to see what the right ones would have been.

In the depths of gloom Brown clung to his single strength. Although he had lost a strategy he had a vision, albeit ill defined, about what he wanted to do with power. His noisy rebels, while exalted in the media, were a lot less clear about their policy direction once they had done the easy bit, which was to articulate the failings of a vulnerable Prime Minister. They lost even more conviction when economic policy assumed greater importance, as it did just as some Labour MPs were preparing to mount a coup against him in the autumn of 2008. Apart from Brown and Balls no one in the Labour party had given sustained thought to economic policy making. The lack of thought, let alone experience in matters relating to the economy, was the most important factor in Brown's survival. His opponents huffed and puffed, but did little else besides. In the 1970s the leaders of both Labour and the Conservatives were surrounded by heavyweight colleagues who gave much thought to economic policy. Brown was under pressure because he did not seem to know what he was doing. But almost drowning, he had a clearer idea of how to keep afloat than any of his rivals.

One of the great myths about leaders in trouble is that they are sustained by arrogant self-belief. The opposite is closer to the truth. Drained of self-confidence they make more mistakes. Leaders are human beings who would rather be liked than loathed. They read the focus groups, the newspaper columnists and opinion polls. When they are in trouble they know it, and in most cases the way they are perceived troubles them deeply.

Brown was aware of his plight, and the knowledge made things worse. He told one friend: 'Every time I walk into a room people think, there is the guy who has a made a mess of everything.' Political leaders cannot avoid being self-aware. An avid reader on a variety of fronts, he devoured the many words in which his leadership and personality were under fire.

As so often in the past during bleak political periods, he lapsed into angry gloom and behaved appallingly, while never remotely aware that his treatment of others was becoming an issue. Yet at the same time he was determined to find a way back, all his intense competitive instincts compelling him onward.

The self-absorbed moodiness was never hidden. He shouted at cabinet ministers and senior officials. After one outburst in the autumn of 2007 the Home Secretary, Jacqui Smith, was so upset she contemplated resignation. When Brown shouted at Tessa Jowell she told him that his behaviour was unacceptable and that they should resume the discussion about the funding for the Olympics at another time when he was calmer.

What became clear to close observers, ministers, advisers and officials during this period was that Brown's flaws had grown rather than diminished since he had moved into Number Ten. His leadership is partly a lesson in the importance of good manners and civil behaviour. He alienated old friends and enemies needlessly. A leader can get away with such behaviour when he or she is ahead in the polls or has recently won an election. When leaders are trailing they are much more dependent on good will from colleagues – always an elusive quality in politics. In the autumn of 2007 there was virtually no good will towards Brown anywhere. In contrast Blair aroused a deep sense of loyalty amongst close colleagues, even if as a politician he was less rooted and principled than Brown.

A few torrid months later in December, Brown instigated a panic-stricken overhaul of the Number Ten operation. Shortly before Christmas he wanted to remove Tom Scholar, the senior official who he had brought back from the UN in New York a few months earlier to run Number Ten. Scholar was on his wedding night when Brown sought to convey the news that he was no longer required in Number Ten. In a fractious meeting involving a few officials he demanded that they contact Scholar straight away. Only the brave resistance of other officials stopped him from making the call himself. Brown's motives were not malevolent. The wrecking of Scholar's wedding night was not part of his thought process. He was submerged in a nightmare and was focused solely on desperate moves to escape from it. Wanting a new team in place in Number Ten for the New Year, he needed to get some of the old ones out in time, vaguely hoping that a purge would

317

revive his fortunes, unwilling to contemplate the possibility that his own management of Number Ten and the rest of the government was the main cause of the internal chaos.

This is not altogether surprising or unusual. No prime minister surveys the wreckage and concludes that his or her departure might help to put things back together again. In recent times only Harold Wilson has resigned voluntarily and even he did not do so on the basis that his leadership was the cause of the government's difficulties. Brown did what all prime ministers tend to do and rearranged those who worked for him.

First he responded by doing what he did so often in times of crisis and turned to Ed Balls, the only figure for whom he had unqualified respect in terms of judgement and ideological outlook. Two weekends before Christmas, Brown contacted Balls and asked him to come over to Chequers for an urgent meeting. Balls had agreed to appear on the BBC's Andrew Marr show on the Sunday morning to promote his new plans for schools and told Brown politely that he could not cancel the appearance or cut short the preparations. An impatiently restless Brown said he would come over to Balls's department, where he was preparing for the interview. On a cold wet Saturday night, a miserable but still epically determined Prime Minister appeared at the department and told Balls he wanted him to become a senior minister working in Number Ten in charge of policy and strategy. Balls was the only one he trusted to address the dysfunctional operation and ensure a more strategic approach.

Brown had taken advice from old allies such as the former Treasury minister, Geoffrey Robinson, another ardent Balls admirer. Robinson told Brown over a drink in November that he needed people around him he could trust. 'You've got to bring back Ed to Number Ten,' Robinson told him.

But Balls did not want to go to Number Ten. He was unhesitating in his response to Brown's offer, adamant that he could not make such a move. Seeking fresh definition as a departmental cabinet minister, he did not want to return to his old role in which he would be regarded once more as a scheming henchman. Brown did not give up. He said the move would be good for Balls and portrayed as a promotion. Balls did not concede any ground. He had been a cabinet minister in charge of a department for six months and wanted more time. Brown pressed him again, insisting that the government's unpopularity was on such a scale that it needed the old Treasury team to regroup in order to find a way out. Balls refused again. Around this time there were reports that Balls had actively turned against Brown. He had not done so. He acted for other reasons. With good cause he recognized that such a career move would have been a disaster for him and probably for Brown too, an ill-defined role in Number Ten being a well-known graveyard for previously highly regarded politicians.

Nonetheless Balls's rejection meant that Brown felt even more lost in the storm and started to flail around in a search for calm. No longer acting rationally, he made a spectacular error. He appointed someone to run Number Ten whom he had never met.

The day before Christmas Eve, Stephen Carter was travelling back to London on a train from a business trip, contemplating a relatively peaceful break. He was reading Alastair Campbell's diaries, gripped by their evocation of power New Labour style: intense, concentrated at the very top and fearful. Suddenly his phone rang. It was a telephonist from Number Ten, the main location of the events erupting in Campbell's diaries. The operator announced politely that the Prime Minister wanted to speak to him. Carter was working for the consultancy firm Brunswick at the time, and had previously headed the media regulator OFCOM. He was recommended to Brown by Alan Parker, an ebullient friend of the Prime Minister's who had founded Brunswick.

In private meetings Brown was going through a phase of uncharacteristic, endearing and slightly alarming candour. To those he trusted, even if he did not know them especially well, he was admitting to personal failings. Brown had been quite open in discussions with Parker about needing a figure who had experience of running a large organization and could frame messages in a way that was accessible and politically astute. He admitted that he lacked these experiences and had also lost the language to put across his message. Parker suggested Carter, a tough leader of complex institutions, and with experience of the media as its chief regulator.

Brown leapt at the suggestion, regarding Carter's lack of political experience as an advantage. Carter was not a Labour party member and had not been actively engaged in politics for years. As far as Brown was concerned the appointment would prove that he could attract authoritative outsiders to work for him, and not just those acting out of a sense of tribal loyalty. For an isolated, friendless Prime Minister, Carter was a trophy, as well as someone who could make a practical impact: 'Look, respectable business types want to work with me, the unpopular Labour leader.'

It was a sign of Brown's steep decline that such an instinctive tribalist, happiest working with only a clan of chosen allies, was choosing to hand over his working life to someone he did not know.

During his opening call to an astonished Carter, Brown suggested that the two of them should meet during the holidays. The two strangers had several meetings between Christmas and New Year, but Brown's mind had been made up before their first exchange. He wanted Carter. The meetings were acts of persuasion, not exploration.

Sensing correctly that he was in a strong negotiating position, Carter was flattered and assertive. If he was to make the move, he told Brown, he wanted complete control of the operation in Number Ten and everyone to be made aware that he was in charge, including those he was close to such as Ed Balls and his press secretary, Damian McBride. He would attend cabinet. He would analyse what had gone wrong and take action. Brown told him at length what he was trying to do, but repeatedly said he had not found the pertinent words to convey his objectives. Carter agreed to the move on the basis that he was being invited into the heart of power. There was no obvious affinity with Brown, although Carter was struck by Brown's intense intelligence. Politically he had always felt more empathy towards Blair, although he had not known Blair either. Brown had handed over Number Ten to an outsider and was delighted at the prospect of a fresh start.

Carter arrived as a special adviser, a non-civil servant who could extend his range to matters relating to the Labour party. To balance the inexperienced newcomer, Brown also brought back Jeremy Heywood, a senior civil servant who had managed to work at different times for both Blair as PM and Brown as Chancellor – a test of any official's diplomatic skills. Heywood was another figure in Number Ten who thought he understood the rhythms of the media and would quite often preside over the chaotic Downing Street grid for the following week naively assuming that various trivial prime-ministerial announcements would excite the press and the broadcasters.

Brown had not thought through how the new arrangement would work in Number Ten. What would be the impact on those who had been close to Brown previously? How would Carter work with Heywood? Where did this leave the likes of Balls? Brown did not ask the questions, let alone come up with constructive answers.

Within days of his arrival Carter identified the key problems with a forensic ruthlessness. At the end of his first week he had a list that included the mismanagement of Brown's time, a related failure to prioritize key policy areas, terrible relations with the media, Brown's inability to communicate a clear message to the wider electorate and a poor relationship between Number Ten and the rest of the government. This was quite a list for a newcomer to address, making Carter the equivalent of the hotel inspector in *Fawlty Towers*. When the inspector reads out a long list of nightmare problems with his hotel, Basil pauses and then asks: 'Apart from that is everything else alright?' Brown did not have the chance to respond. Carter kept his early observations to himself and to a few trusted confidants.

But while Carter had intelligently recognized what was wrong, he had no clear solutions. Instead some of his tentative ideas revealed a degree of naivety. Within a fortnight of his arrival he suggested to Brown that Number Ten should scrap the daily lobby briefings to political journalists. Such a move would have only enraged political editors and further damaged Brown's media coverage.

Carter was fortunate that his ideas were not tested immediately. Typically a familiar pattern reasserted itself. A major event soon swept away all other considerations, at least for a few days. Since the near-collapse of Northern Rock, Brown and his Chancellor had desperately sought a buyer, but without success.

The search was Brown's obsession, shared by no one else in the cabinet including Darling, who was still a Chancellor carrying out prime-ministerial instructions. The relentless quest, so obviously fruitless, showed that while he was trapped by his Blairite inheritance, he shared Blair's fear of being associated with Labour's past. In some ways he felt it more acutely because of the jibes in the media and from the opposition that, unlike Blair, he was really an Old Labour figure. Given that fear, Northern Rock was as great a threat for Brown as the non-election and the missing discs, the episodes that had blown his reputation for solid competence, and the police investigations, which had meant he was no longer trusted. He had made strenuous efforts to prove that he was not an Old Labour figure, and now he was suddenly under pressure to nationalize a bank. Not even Old Labour had nationalized a bank.

Brown could not bear to contemplate such a move, and in his alarm became blind to an extraordinary coalition of support, including the *Economist* and the *Financial Times*, forming in favour of state ownership. The Liberal Democrats' Treasury Spokesman and acting leader, Vince Cable, was attracting rave reviews as a supporter of state ownership, but Brown could not see it. All he could see were headlines about taking Britain back to the 1970s. As a curiously hyperactive journalist, Brown was always seeing imaginary headlines. They were his version of nightmares. At around this time the BBC's *Today* programme would end its interviews with Brown by asking him whether he was enjoying being Prime Minister. The question was mischievous because he was so obviously wretched. Yet it was not exactly the toughest example of the interrogator's art. It threw Brown completely. His usual answer verged on the deranged: 'I get up in the morning and ask myself what I can do to serve ...'

The stilted words are explained because he saw the imaginary headlines if he had responded casually: 'Brown enjoys himself as

Britain sinks.' Brown's entire public career can be partly explained by his fear of anticipated headlines.

In this case even Brown recognized that he had no choice but to face the media response. There was no credible buyer for Northern Rock. Darling had reached this conclusion by the late autumn of the previous year. In the end Darling announced the state takeover on a Sunday afternoon in February, a rushed statement in time for the opening of the markets the following day.

Brown's anxious fingerprints were all over Darling's statement. The government would 'hold on to Northern Rock for a temporary period'. Still Brown could not sanction the dread word 'nationalize', and made sure the qualification accompanied the various euphemisms. The move was only temporary. On the Monday his close ally and Deputy Chief Whip Nick Brown phoned him during a trip to Cuba. Nervously the Prime Minister told his namesake that the government had taken over Northern Rock. Nick Brown replied jokily that he would let Fidel Castro know. There was no laughter at the London end of the phone call. Gordon Brown paused and explained: 'It's only in temporary public ownership.'

He could not cope with the idea. Brown had ambitions for redistribution and the provision of public services, but he was a deeply cautious conservative in terms of ownership, largely accepting Thatcherite orthodoxy and in some respects building on it.

Revealingly, David Cameron and George Osborne were also trapped by their pasts, in some ways more so than Brown had been. At least in the end Brown had made the right call. On the Monday afternoon Cameron and Osborne held a rare joint press conference proclaiming the death of New Labour and arguing that the decision to nationalize the bank was a terrible, backward-looking mistake. They could barely contain their excitement, having been brought up politically in the 1980s when nationalization was regarded as the ultimate sin. Their own plans for Northern Rock were vague and unconvincing, but they were as slow as Brown to recognize that the public and parts of the media had moved on. This was to be a common theme as economic events became more tumultuous. Quite often political leaders shaped by the 1970s and 1980s were not as far ahead as the voters.

The past was not the only cause of Brown's anxieties. The sums involved were colossal, almost comically so. UK taxpayers were now subsidizing the bank in loans and guarantees to other lenders to the tune of about £55 billion. A year earlier Brown would have had sleepless nights explaining away additional expenditure of any kind. Now he was buying a bank for £55 billion. For a cautious politician, Brown was behaving recklessly, acting this way on the assumption that audacity was far the safest option.

As Brown purchased his bank, Carter was failing in his mission to quell the storms. At first Brown treated Carter like a saviour. What Carter said Brown followed. In a rather pathetic way he saw Carter's arrival as affirmation of his prime-ministerial status at a point when derision was almost universal. Briefly the old entourage did not get much of a look-in, except for Ed Miliband. Carter liked and trusted Miliband. Typically Miliband did not share or convey the suspicious animosity to Carter felt by other Brownites.

In the early weeks of 2008 Carter held sway. On arrival he occupied the office previously used by Spencer Livermore, Brown's senior adviser.

Livermore had been more and more disconsolate since the non-election in the autumn and left Number Ten soon after Carter arrived, his departure symbolizing the collapse of Brown's carefully laid plans for his first prime-ministerial phase. Livermore had planned to leave before Carter's arrival, after serving Brown for eleven years. Brown felt betrayed by the departure. At Livermore's farewell party Brown attended for five minutes and did not speak to his old ally.

McBride continued to function as a solo operator, but Carter had Brown's ear and started to brief senior political journalists. Across government he set about working on a major policy agenda linked by the theme of fairness. Within the Labour party he also exerted control, holding a special one-day meeting for senior party officials and special advisers in which speakers were invited by Carter to highlight the flaws as well as the positive elements of the government.

Not surprisingly, Carter failed to improve Brown's standing and in some ways made matters worse. The two of them had no rapport, personal or political. On one occasion Carter wrote a draft speech for Brown in which he referred several times to choice in public services. Brown was furious, explaining to Carter why he felt uncomfortable about using the term. Carter pointed out that Brown had made speeches in which he used 'choice'. Brown responded dismissively by saying: 'Hardly ever.' After a television interview Brown and Carter were driven from the studio back to Number Ten. Brown said to Carter: 'How did that go?' Carter responded diplomatically and evasively: 'How do you think it went?' Brown erupted. 'It's your job to tell me how it went. Do you understand television or not?' More widely, Carter was not entirely politically attuned. Knowing few Labour MPs, he was in no position to warn Brown about the growing revolt over tax rises for those on low incomes. Brown's old allies started to complain to him that they were being marginalized.

At the same time Carter was increasingly dismayed by Brown's working arrangements, the determined micro-management of every government department, the factionalism in Number Ten, the dependence on a few trusted courtiers and the flailing around for defining themes. When there was speculation in the summer of 2008 that Carter would be sacked he joked to friends: 'I know enough to be dangerous.'

By Easter Brown had dropped Carter in the way children discard Christmas presents that once excited them. He remained in post, but of no great significance. Sympathetic onlookers in Number Ten were horrified but not surprised at Carter's humiliation. In April he delivered to a cabinet meeting what was supposed to be his tour de force, the outcome of his proposals that were supposed to be the government's unifying theme: fairness. Using charts and deploying the language of the marketing world from which he had come, he spoke at length. Brown kept his head down, appearing distracted, conveying his lack of enthusiasm. One or two favoured correspondents were told that Brown had given Carter's efforts the thumbs down. Carter assumed that McBride was briefing against him with the active support of Ed Balls. This was supposed to have been a more functional Number Ten.

By the spring of 2008 senior cabinet ministers despaired of Brown's leadership and had good cause to do so. No prime minister in modern times had functioned in such noisy chaos and fallen so far behind in the polls so quickly. John Major's personal ratings declined more gradually and never reached the depths of Brown's, in spite of the more obviously humiliating withdrawal from the ERM, the event that triggered Major's descent into political hell.

Privately ministers were articulate about Brown's failings, the inability to communicate with voters and the shambles in Number Ten. They started talking openly to journalists. The critics were not only those who had been wary of Brown at the start, but some who had been his supporters. The long-serving veterans, including Jack Straw and Geoff Hoon, were joining those ministers associated more with Blair in expressing deep concern about Brown's leadership.

But crucially, none of them allied sweeping, heartfelt condemnation with a clear vision of their own. Given the total dominance of the Blair/Brown duopoly, perhaps they were incapable of doing so. They had become managerial and technocratic politicians waiting for Blair and Brown in their very different ways to spell out what they were in power to achieve. Shortly there were to be several attempted coups against Brown, all of them confused and badly organized. There was a deeper reason for their failure. The insurrections were policy-free. The growing band knew they did not want Brown, but were far from sure what, or who, they wanted instead.

This was Brown's one sustaining and underrated strength, hidden from view in the crises that marked the first half of 2008. He had a capacity to think more deeply and politically about the role of a centre-left party in the UK, a country that more often than not elected Conservative governments, how to match expedient policies with progressive or social democratic aspirations. Contrary to the myth – believed by many in the cabinet – that he clung to power for its own sake, Brown still had a fairly well-developed sense of how he wanted to move forward as Prime Minister.

Amidst the manic gloom he tried to outline his thinking in an article for the *Observer* in February 2008. It displayed a distinct clarity of vision, a clear view of what was happening to the global economy and of Britain's place in the world. The article pointed to some big ideas from a leader who was shrinking on all other fronts:

> Once, we worried about a global arms race. The challenge this century is a global skills race and that is why we need to push ahead faster with our reforms to extend education opportunities for all.

Brown linked the global economy, the rise of Asia, to his education policies, ones that were projected as beneficial for the entire country. He gave his reasons why:

> Some argue that in this next stage, the mature economies of Europe and America can only lose and that all the benefits will flow only eastwards. I disagree. We are about to see a doubling of skilled jobs in the global economy. This heralds a worldwide opportunity revolution, bringing new chances of upward mobility for millions. And Britain, with its centuries-old record of innovation, enterprise and international reach, can be one of its greatest winners.

Brown was linking economic growth in Britain with left-of-centre policies aimed at giving more hope to poorer families. He hints at this, but only by hiding behind poetry:

> British literature is full of laments for talent wasted, potential unfulfilled and opportunities forgone. Just think of Thomas Gray in his 'Elegy Written in a Country Churchyard' reflecting sadly on the unfulfilled, unnoticed fate of a 'mute inglorious Milton'.
>
> Yet now we can be the first generation to commit ourselves to offer all our young people the fullest possible chance to make the most of all their talents. To achieve this – and to guarantee a better economic future – we must make long-term strategic choices.

The article was a tentative argument in favour of active government as well as the more fashionable private and voluntary sectors. Brown could not use the term 'state' or even 'government', fearing, probably rightly, that they would evoke negative reactions in Britain. He chose 'public realm'as an alternative. But lurking in the conceptual undergrowth was a more developed sense of how to connect global issues not only with British interests, but also with the political issues raging in the country: delivery of public services, the role of government and its relationship with the private sector. The phrase 'opportunity revolution' was almost meaningless, but not quite. If Brown had been in a stronger position he would have used the phrase to build up support for measures that helped those especially from poorer backgrounds under the guise of a revolution that few would oppose – for who was against 'opportunity'?

The article hinted at Brown's strengths as a politician, qualities that had been so much more evident in the past, a capacity to connect economic policy with values and political expediency.

His much weaker qualities and the cruel tide of events swept away the big ideas. Few read the article, let alone had the energy or inclination to seek its inner meanings. There was a single public narrative in place and nothing could disturb it: Brown's leadership was falling apart. More than ever Brown was trapped by the past, unable to escape from Blair's legacy and his own as Chancellor, which in its final phase was partly a crude attempt to convince unconvinceable critics that he was more Blairite than Blair.

At around the time that Brown was composing his article for the *Observer*, Labour MPs were beginning to stir over the abolition of the 10p tax band, the policy that Brown had announced the previous year in his final budget as Chancellor. Brown had abolished the band partly to pay for a cut in income tax, which he had wanted to make in order to show that he was not an Old Labour 'tax and spend' leader. He had also calculated that the income-tax cut would come into effect in the spring of 2008, the period when he had hoped to call an election. Instead of conducting a triumphant election campaign, Brown faced a waking nightmare where every carefully planned device blew up in his face.

Now that spring 2008 had arrived there was no chance of an election, nobody paid attention to the cut in income tax, and virtually everybody noted the end of the 10p tax band.

Led by Frank Field, an MP who loathed Brown, backbenchers across the party started to express their concerns in public about the changes that appeared to make their poorer constituents worse off. The dynamics of the row were painful for Brown. As a result of the Iraq war Labour had alienated a significant section of so-called middle-class liberal support. Now Brown was on the wrong side of a debate about penalizing traditional voters in poorer areas.

His initial response to the protestations made matters worse. Brown refused to believe what backbenchers were telling him. At one ill-tempered meeting with Field in Number Ten he shouted that he had written the bloody budget and knew the figures. Field was wrong. Later Field was to complain that Brown flared up in 'tempers of an indescribable nature …'. Labour MPs present at the Parliamentary Labour Party meeting held in March, on the eve of the changes coming into effect, emerged to declare despairingly that Brown insisted no one would lose out. Ann Black, a member of Labour's National Executive Committee, was even more illuminating on Brown's true feelings. Referring to a meeting of the NEC on March 20, she noted: 'Brown said that no one would be worse off because of the 10p changes – I sat there shaking my head. Then he invited people to send him in their pay slips to prove him wrong. It was quite clear that he was being specific.'

Part of the problem was that Brown had convinced himself that he was right and everyone else was wrong. As its main architect he knew the nearly incomprehensible tax credit system better than anyone else, or thought he did. He pointed out to Labour protesters that if a low earner had dependent children, was sick or disabled, was caring for someone, was over sixty, recently bereaved, pregnant or had recently given birth, then there were tax credits and allowances they could claim that made up for other changes. Even when reciting the long list to bemused MPs, Brown ignored one significant group of obvious losers. People who did not fit into any of those categories were most notably under-twenty-fives ineligible for tax credits, those who had retired early, and part-timers working too few hours to get tax credits. They comprised a lot of low-paid workers.

But Brown did not pause to reflect. Instead his anger grew, and for reasons that were slightly more justified than anyone acknowledged at the time or since. His last budget as Chancellor had given an extra £3 billion in pension allowances, an increase in the working tax credit, and an increase in the child tax credit. These substantial increases were followed by another £1 billion of support for rises in the child tax credit. Although he had wanted to make a splash with his income-tax cut, he had gone out of his way to redistribute as well, the familiar Brownite balancing act of giving something back ostentatiously to middle England in the hope they would support redistributive measures. He clung to these proposals like an obstinate child.

There was also the characteristic political calculation: stick to a public narrative even if the evidence points in another direction. Brown could be perversely stubborn in the face of the evidence. Privately he used to argue that Blair was not a liar, but had a capacity to convince himself that what he was saying was truthful even when it was not. Brown was the same. One of his former Treasury ministers recalls sitting next to him in the Commons during Labour's first term when a row had erupted because Blair had admitted the tax burden had risen under Labour. Brown was furious, fearing that such a public acknowledgement would scupper his entire 'tax and spend' strategy. When Brown was next standing at the Despatch Box in the Commons for Treasury questions, the minister says he saw Brown's copious notes. They included a vividly clear chart that showed the rise in the tax burden since Labour had come to power. In Brown's exchanges with his opponents he refused persistently to acknowledge the increase, in spite of the chart next to him contradicting his proclamations. He was determined not to change the public narrative.

Similarly, in the case of the 10p tax losers Brown had not gone mad, although some Labour MPs thought he had done so. His resistance was based partly on a fear of the new embryonic narrative: 'Brown hits the poor'. He thought it would be disastrous to accept any element of the opposing case because the arguments as a whole had been exaggerated. In particular he feared a media onslaught if he conceded ground. Based on past experience, when he was much stronger, his instinct was to battle on even if the evidence was against him. He followed this characteristic instinct only because he was genuinely convinced that the tax credits compensated most if not all of the losers and that his enemies were stirring the pot for their own reasons, far removed from the politics of poverty.

Unusually, Ed Balls gave him bad advice, urging him to fight it out rather than give in. Both took this view partly because remaking a year-old budget was almost impossible and costly.

Above all Brown held firm at first because he believed he was right to scrap the 10p rate in favour of more targeted help for low earners. He had introduced the rate earlier as a crude and expensive mechanism for ensuring that all those on low incomes received more pay, but in its sweep the rate helped those on relatively high incomes too. Brown felt that with the panoply of tax credits there was no longer a need for a catch-all rate. The change in his final budget had been aimed at reforming the tax system into one that focused more help on the lowest-paid.

More immediately, Brown had also convinced himself that he needed to stand firm in the current row and compensate some low earners in due course when it was clearer who had lost out – a more financially prudent and politically less humiliating course. In terms of timing he had in mind the autumn pre-budget report as the more suitable vehicle for addressing the problem, rather than presenting what would amount to an emergency budget and borrowing a significant additional sum of money in a panic to pay for an indiscriminate compensation package, or what seemed a significant sum in those innocent days before the collapse of Lehman Brothers the following autumn. Brown was already in a state about what the government had borrowed to bail out Northern Rock. He did not want to spend more.

There was method in the apparent madness, but Brown's reasoning applied to calmer times when he was a mighty Chancellor and not a weak and increasingly loathed Prime Minister. Labour rebels were growing every day. Privately despairing cabinet ministers compared Brown's position to Margaret Thatcher's in relation to the poll tax, a stubborn attachment to a fatally unpopular policy.

Within days of taking a defiant stand it was clear that Brown lacked the support to be obstinate any longer. He faced a catastrophic Commons defeat on the wrong side of a debate about helping the poor, a contortion that was utterly perverse given his lifelong passion for the subject. His stubbornness up to the point where he faced humiliation is partly explained because no one in Number Ten was strong or astute enough to warn him that he was heading for another disaster. Balls would have done so, but he agreed with Brown's line. So did Carter, out of his depth and struggling to be listened to. Alistair Darling had warned Brown in their discussions about his first budget, but at that point Darling had no authoritative pitch as a Chancellor. He bowed to Brown's demands. Blair would have had Alastair Campbell to alert him that a growing mutiny was impossible to contain and looked terrible in the media. In contrast Brown had McBride, who saw his task as feeding stories to selected journalists who sought to damage the rebels.

Brown had no choice but to give in, but he did so only because he faced a Commons defeat, not because he ever accepted that there was a need. Having denied that there were any losers, he announced an expensive compensation package, one designed in semi-darkness, as it was still not clear how many losers there would be once the tax credits had been taken into account. Deliberately Brown had devised a tax system so intricate that it was almost incomprehensible to all but a few mathematical geniuses. The opacity was a deliberate ploy that had enabled him to redistribute without the media and middle-England voters making a fuss. If they had understood what was happening they almost certainly would have revolted noisily. But they did not. The downside had been apparent to small businesses and accountants for years. The complexity was surreal. Now it baffled

Brown and Darling. How to compensate losers when they were not sure who they were, or how many, or how much they required to bring them back in credit?

In the end the government opted for a fairly substantial package. Towards the end of April Darling announced a series of payments aimed at low-paid workers without children and pensioners under sixty-five, two groups who had clearly not been adequately helped by tax credits. In a desperate commitment he had no choice but to make, Darling added: 'Whatever conclusions we come to, all the changes will be backdated to the start of this financial year.' He had rewritten his budget within weeks of delivering it, in the same way he had rewritten his earlier pre-budget report within days of its delivery because of the urgent chance of an early election. Darling was the calmest minister in the cabinet, and yet his behaviour had been wild, a symptom of the extreme instability that marked Brown's premiership. As Chancellor, Brown had prepared all his budgets in meticulous detail and announced them according to plan. Darling was rewriting his policies almost from day to day and in ways that involved borrowing additional billions.

In response to the latest oscillating announcements, a triumphant Frank Field announced the withdrawal of his rebel amendment to Darling's Finance Bill, declaring: 'The Chancellor's statement is to be welcomed. The Government has listened, and more important has agreed to all our demands.'

In a subsequent BBC interview an exhausted-looking Brown replied formulaically and listlessly, sounding like a bank manager: 'I don't think I've been pushed about at all. What I've done is look and make the right long-term decisions … My whole mission in politics is to do what I can to help people … It means we have got to judge things right at every point.'

As the storms gathered he surfaced every now and again in the spring and summer of 2008 to declare with the tedium of a time-serving technocrat: 'I'm taking the right long-term decisions.' His public appearances were as inspiring as listening to a speak-your-weight machine played at slow speed.

The machine was not being very candid. Brown asserted that the cost of the compensation package would be substantially lower than £1 billion. This was not true. The actual figure was closer to £3 billion, as he must have known or feared.

Soon after his U-turn Brown embarked on another doomed policy, the plan to allow terror suspects to be detained without charge for forty-two days. He had dreamed up this policy when he was still Chancellor, as he plotted his pre-election, father-of-the-nation, apolitical phase. Blair had failed to extend the period suspects could be detained to ninety days. He suffered his first Commons defeat over the issue. But the ever-watchful Brown noted that polls suggested Blair's stance was popular with voters and with key newspapers such as the *Sun* and *The Times*. Tory-supporting columnists such as the much-wooed d'Ancona were also keen. There was little evidence to suggest that Brown cared very much about the policy either way. He was not excited by law-and-order issues. But the politics of this issue excited him hugely. If he could succeed where Blair had failed he would be feted by those voters and newspapers that had enthused about the original policy. In addition Cameron would be on the wrong side of the argument, as his party was opposed to an extension. Brown therefore proposed a shorter time period than Blair, confident that he could convince some of the Labour rebels (many of whom were his close supporters) to back his policy.

The calculations were similar to those Blair made in relation to Iraq, and with the same consequences. Blair assumed that at least he would get backing for the war from much of the media and the Conservatives. In the end he got the backing of virtually no one. Brown found himself introducing his policy at a point where he had no credibility and when there was no general election imminent. There was not a hope of him getting the proposal through the Commons, let alone the Lords. When the Home Secretary, Jacqui Smith, introduced the proposal in the Commons Ed Miliband was asked to appear on BBC's *Question Time*. He turned down the invitation. Miliband told friends he could not defend 'forty-two days' and therefore would prefer to keep his head down. Balls was also opposed.

He assumed that Brown had come under pressure from Blair to show he was tough on terrorism and was now stuck with a policy that had little support. Balls was being too generous. Brown had made a series of clever political calculations that might have paid off in different circumstances, but not at a point when his authority and scope for cunning had evaporated.

Brown dropped the proposal in the midst of the economic crisis the following autumn. Under different circumstances another humiliating climbdown might have destroyed his leadership. As the global economy moved to the precipice, no one noticed, one of the many ways in which Brown's leadership was saved by the collapse of the financial markets.

Brown's speedy downfall was brought about by misjudgement, political context and misfortune. It is a false cliché that political leaders make their own good or bad luck. Sometimes events erupt that have no connection whatever to the struggling leader, and yet they contribute to the decline. Part of Brown's rotten luck in this phase of his leadership took the form of by-elections intervening as if to torment him personally. Blair was lucky with by-elections. There were few of them during his leadership, a reflection of the relatively youthful House of Commons that was elected in 1997. Those contests that did take place were not especially significant. The by-election that arose in Crewe and Nantwich in the immediate aftermath of the 10p tax storm could have been especially designed to expose Brown's unique unpopularity. It had been a Labour seat since its formation in 1983, the general election in which Labour was slaughtered. Amidst the wreckage Crewe elected a Labour MP in 1983, the formidable Gwyneth Dunwoody, whose sudden death in 2008 was a characteristically challenging political act.

The by-election was significant for one reason beyond the result. The local Labour party sought to torment the wealthy Conservative candidate and his leadership in Westminster by running an 'anti-toff' campaign. It did so with the subtlety of a bunch of students after a long night out. Activists took to the streets dressed in toffs' uniform

– top hats and dinner jackets. It was all fairly harmless, but totally useless at a point when the party they represented was falling apart in London. As a result of the campaign's failure an army of columnists who had gone to public school or sent their children to such schools declared that the Etonian background of Cameron and his team was off-limits: all such attacks were counterproductive. The issue of class, still so pervasive in Britain, was more or less censored as a theme as the media declared it out of order.

Seeking to kill off any further onslaughts against his and his team's background, David Cameron proclaimed 'the end of New Labour' the day after the Conservatives won the by-election victory with an impressive 17.6 per cent swing. It was the first time for thirty years that the Conservatives had taken a seat from Labour in a by-election, a triumph for Cameron's underestimated agility as an opposition leader. The end of New Labour became a common theme in the post-mortems as 'class warfare' was deemed to have been a return to Labour's past failures. In reality the loss had nothing to do with battles over class. Labour lost because of the 10p tax row, general fears about the economy and the unpopularity of Brown.

The defeat, which was far heavier than many Labour MPs expected, intensified the pressure on Brown. For the first time one former minister openly called for him to be replaced as party leader. reflecting the private views of several ministers and Blairite MPs. Graham Stringer urged Brown's cabinet colleagues to force him out, warning that Labour faced 'electoral disaster' at the next general election if he were to remain as Prime Minister. Stringer declared:

> The real debate that goes on within the Labour party among MPs and amongst party members is: 'Is it more damaging for the party to change leader, or to hope that things will get better in the next two years?'
>
> If the party is to renew itself and gets its policies in line with what the people we represent want, then it is the responsibility of senior members of the cabinet to say we're going in the wrong direction, it's

impossible to change the situation that we are in at the moment and to say to Gordon that they intend to stand for election.

Without that, we are heading for electoral disaster at the next general election.

He was right to point to the 'real debate', although at this stage it was one that on the whole reflected the old divide, with Brown-hating Blairite MPs foremost in asking whether there should be a change of leader. Stringer was not precise as to what policies should change in order for an election to be won. Had he been precise, a substantial section of his party would have disagreed and offered an alternative agenda. Labour was more divided than it seemed. Part of Brown's role was to hold it together, always an unglamorous task, and one that invites derision from the conflicting sides and from external observers in the media.

In his response to the Crewe result, Brown told reporters that the lesson of the by-election was 'clear and unequivocal. The message we are getting is: people are concerned. They are concerned about food prices, concerned about petrol prices and concerned about what is happening to the economy. My task is to steer the British economy through difficult times and that is what I intend to do.'

He was largely correct, although he could have mentioned his own leadership as a major cause of the government's unpopularity. The manner of his response illustrated part of the problem. He was wooden in the face of a spectacular defeat. As one of his closest allies observed at the time to another close Brown admirer: 'He just doesn't connect with voters. We always knew it might be a problem, but not as bad as this.' Suddenly even the most intensely loyal Brownites were starting to recognize Blair's strengths in terms of his easy communication skills and ability to respond deftly in the thick of colliding, unexpected events.

In the days following the by-election few cabinet ministers felt able to appear on the airwaves to put the case for Brown and the government. On the whole his old allies were the only ones available, with Ed Miliband especially ubiquitous. Privately Miliband's assessment was almost comically erudite and yet insightful: 'I don't believe the by-election was a vote against collectivism. It was almost the opposite. Why is the government not doing more to help the low-paid? Why can't it intervene to prevent petrol prices from rising? What's it doing about the rise in unemployment? Voters are calling for more government, not less. But in doing so they want to punish this particular government.' Miliband was on to something big, speaking on the eve of the credit crisis. Voters were demanding more active government, not less, and yet in Crewe and elsewhere they were voting for Cameron, who argued that the state should be smaller and that government should do less.

The distance between voters' demands and the underlying philosophy of the increasingly popular Conservative party yawned wide in the year that was to follow. Few voters seemed disturbed by the gap, supposing that they noticed it. Nor was this especially surprising, given that Labour was commanding nearly all national attention, as it had done since the 2005 election. The attention was wholly deserved as Brown entered, after the contest in Crewe, his first phase of maximum danger. Some cabinet ministers wondered whether he would and should suffer the same fate as Margaret Thatcher after the October 1990 by-election in Eastbourne, a solid Tory seat that fell to the Liberal Democrats on a swing of 20.05 per cent. Within six weeks she had been overthrown.

ELEVEN

Summer Holidays

'They say it is close, but we are going to lose.' With a single sentence Stephen Carter confirmed there would be no escape from the darkness that had swallowed Brown's leadership. It was mid-morning on the final Thursday of July 2008. Carter was informing the Prime Minister about the latest information on the by-election taking place that day in Glasgow East. Brown had been Prime Minister for just over a year.

Earlier in the week the local Labour party in Glasgow had been more optimistic about clinging on to the safe seat, but not any longer. Labour was heading for defeat, with disillusioned supporters staying at home or switching in anger to the SNP.

Carter had come to loathe delivering bad news. Previously he had held several senior jobs in the private sector, where he applied a brusque ruthlessness as a matter of routine. Although by then their professional relationship was brittle at best, Carter felt for Brown as he delivered news such as the prospect of a potentially fatal by-election defeat. They had no rapport and Carter was powerless to sugar the pill.

One of his gloomier duties had been to inform Brown about the latest opinion polls. In truth it had become one of his only roles as their relationship quickly decayed. Playing the equivalent of the messenger in a Shakespeare history play, he was reduced to being the bearer of bad tidings and not much else.

Sometimes Carter sensed that Brown did blame him personally for the messages he had to deliver. In recent months each new poll had suggested that Labour's support was collapsing and that Brown's low personal ratings were breaking all records. Prime-ministerial initiatives that had been sweated over into the small hours seemed to make no difference to the government's popularity. Instead the policy announcements, the speeches and the rest of the frantic commotion were followed by the thin, austere presence of Carter passing on the latest catastrophic poll.

Slumped in his chair, pale with exhaustion, Brown sometimes asked Carter if there were any positives in the latest national surveys. 'The Conservative lead is soft,' Carter replied fairly often. He noted a flicker of hope as he did so, like watching a veteran boxer cling to the ropes in the hope that one good punch could still save him. On the day of the by-election there was no such flicker. The loss of Glasgow East had been widely billed as a knockout blow for Brown. For weeks some Labour MPs and several influential newspaper columnists had predicted that a by-election defeat would trigger an unstoppable insurrection against a Prime Minister who had served for little more than a year – the ultimate snub. This was the summer of 2008. He had only won the job he had longed for in 2007. This was meant to be the honeymoon phase. It was becoming a fiasco.

As Carter had warned him, the SNP won Glasgow East with a swing of 24 per cent. Reversals on such a scale against the governing party had not taken place since John Major's administration was heading for a landslide defeat in 1997. At the general election Labour had won the seat with a majority of 13,507 and the support of more than 60 per cent of the voters. Now the SNP had won with a majority of 365, a tiny but pivotal victory.

Brown was besieged on all fronts. A few months earlier the Conservatives had won the by-election in Crewe. Now the SNP was rampant in Scotland. In both England and Scotland the voters' simple calculation appeared to be 'anyone but Labour'. So much for a summer holiday on the back of a triumphant election win.

The grisly rituals of a heavy by-election defeat were played out over the airwaves on the Friday morning. A few cabinet ministers put the case for Brown. Indeed more did so than after the Crewe defeat, when virtually none of them could be persuaded to mount a defence. At this point still a close and loyal friend, although an exasperated one, the Chancellor, Alistair Darling, declared on the BBC: 'I believe Gordon Brown is the best Prime Minister. He is the best leader of our party.'

Inevitably the defence exposed what it intended to protect. Brown's own precariousness was the issue, and the ritual answers were not going to cancel out the fear of electoral oblivion under his leadership. In some ways they prompted the sense of panic.

Brown heightened it further with a speech to his party's policy forum on the Friday lunchtime. Coincidentally the forum was meeting at Warwick University as the voters in Glasgow East were hammering six-inch nails into the party's coffin. Cabinet ministers, senior MPs and trade union leaders were supposedly on the campus to agree a range of proposals that would form Labour's programme in the build-up to the next election and beyond.

The audience could not have been more testing. Cabinet ministers were wondering fearfully about the party's future and in some cases reflecting on their own still incipient ambitions. Senior Labour MPs were worried about losing their seats. Trade union leaders dreaded the return of a Conservative government. They were gathered at the university scheming tentatively and hoping with mixed expectations that Brown might rise to the occasion, that he would send them off on their holidays with some sense that there was a way out of this, an alternative to the prospect of a decade at least in opposition.

The night before his speech in Warwick Brown had been to see *Hamlet* in nearby Stratford with his friend Paul Dacre, the editor of the *Daily Mail*. The unlikely friendship was formed out of a mutual regard for the Calvinist work ethic and calculated expediency. Dacre had a genius for recognizing authenticity, voices that could not deceive even if they tried. He liked Brown's tormented integrity. Brown was frightened and fascinated by the *Mail* and its hold on middle England. For a time he thought there was common ground and that under his leadership the *Mail* would support Labour. Now he clung to their friendship in the hope that the mighty paper would not turn all its guns on his already war-torn body. As they sat there with their wives the claustrophobic court of Elsinore must have seemed to Brown like a model of open transparency compared with the suppressed unease in Warwick as ministers and others speculated about his future.

In politics context determines how a speech is heard and how it is more widely perceived. The broader background also shapes how we view a leader. Tony Blair delivered some vacuous speeches in the mid-1990s, but he was walking on water at the time and his addresses were hailed widely as masterpieces. In contrast when the unpopular William Hague was photographed wearing a baseball cap in his early weeks as a Conservative leader in 1997, he and the cap were targets of derision.

The problem with Brown's final public words before the summer break was the immediate backdrop of the by-election defeat combined with inept political choreography and, with a predictable irony, an *absence* of spin, almost a perverse indifference to the art of projection. The backdrop of the stage where Brown spoke was defiantly red. Plastered over that single colour were the artless words 'National Policy Forum 2008' – about as enticing as the party's slogans in the early 1980s.

Brown arrived on the stage looking drained and yet resolute, as if deep within he was giving it his all. Most of the cabinet sat in the front row of the campus lecture theatre, smiling and applauding with a defiantly artificial enthusiasm. Brown spoke without notes, a device that had become fashionable after David Cameron had dispensed with the autocue and opted for the conversational approach at his party conference in Blackpool the previous autumn.

For Brown the impact of the stylistic change was less intimate and created more of a sense of distance, as if he were an old-fashioned preacher.

Brown urged the assembled cabinet ministers and senior party officials to have confidence as he took them on a tour of his passions: tackling global poverty, better public services, the need for fairness to be the key consideration in making policy. There was in the vote-losing context and misjudged style of delivery an echo of Michael Foot speaking with genuine oratorical passion as he led Labour towards its landslide defeat in 1983.

If Labour had won a by-election the day before, Brown's words would probably have been seen as an inspirational sermon, a defence of politics and the values that drove him and the government forward. He had prepared arduously in advance, consulting widely about the speech's themes, range and purpose, knowing its importance. But in the light of Glasgow East the response of the audience in the hall varied from polite detachment to alarm.

Several cabinet ministers were in the alarmed camp. It suited them to be so, but their reaction was spontaneous rather than calculated. The Foreign Secretary, David Miliband, sitting in the front row, told colleagues that he thought the speech had been 'disastrous'. The Justice Secretary, Jack Straw, who a year ago had been Brown's campaign manager in the leadership contest, reached a similar conclusion. Straw left the Policy Forum refusing all requests for interviews and headed for a holiday in the United States, wondering what would happen next to him and his government.

For months some ministers and a few Labour MPs had been urging Straw to tell Brown that he had to stand down. He had not at this point resolved to do the deed, had not even decided whether it would be the right move to make, but he knew there were mutinous possibilities or perhaps obligations in the months ahead.

Like lots of eager predictions about Brown's possible demise over the years, the speculation that the by-election defeat would force him out proved, partly for purely logistical reasons, to be totally mistaken. There were stirrings, but most of the plotters were scattered around the beaches of Europe or in the United States. Jack Straw was not alone in making a quick exit. The summer holidays had begun. Brown was safe until his colleagues returned.

Brown had one more engagement in Downing Street before his holiday, a two-hour meeting with Barack Obama the aspirant US president, completing a European tour of rock-star impact. With newspapers reporting the possibility of meltdown for Labour and speculating about whether Brown could be removed within months, the two of them were photographed in the Downing Street garden, but only Obama held a mini-press conference for twenty minutes outside Number Ten. Protocol demanded prime-ministerial neutrality in the race for the US presidency. Brown had to keep out of the way. He did not mind especially, knowing that he would have been forced to address further questions about his possible electoral demise. One aide observed later that this summer weekend, the one after the by-election, was the worst so far in Brown's political career. There would be no stardust by association with Obama, only the playing up of the contrast, the self-assured international superstar on the verge of power and an unpopular, exhausted Prime Minister.

Immediately after his meeting with Obama he and his family left for a holiday in Southwold.

Before the holiday had even begun there was a last political skirmish: the contest over the holiday photos. Downing Street advisers had arranged for a photo opportunity with Gordon and his wife Sarah at the start of their holiday. The model for the arrangements had been the Blairs, who reluctantly made available a photo of the family at the beginning of their more sun-kissed vacations. For the Browns the location of their holiday photos for the media was Whittingham Country Park in Norfolk, not exactly Tuscany in its manicured celebration of unhurried leisure.

The English backdrop was supposed to be the point. Brown was playing at not being Blair, a driving theme of his early months as Prime Minister and one he was no longer entirely sure about as he struggled to find a distinctive identity. Brown wore a light cotton jacket, a blue shirt and chinos for the photocall while Sarah had arrived in a blue dress and a pink cardigan that suggested she had an idea about the way the dubious summer weather was going to turn.

The media reaction to the photos showed which way the political weather had already turned. On the same day David Cameron and his wife Samantha were photographed walking hand in hand on Harlyn Bay in Cornwall, a vast sandy beach which looks as good as any on the Mediterranean when the sun is shining. Unusually for Cornwall that

summer, the sun peeped through while the Camerons were performing. It rained for the rest of the time they were in the South West, but
not when the cameras clicked. Samantha in a light black top and floral
skirt looked like an elegant film star, effortlessly cool. Cameron looked
fashionably at ease too in a blue T-shirt and shorts. The couple
appeared to embody a modern, progressive country as the Blairs had
done, and they too were in England, like the Browns. In fact they were
not there for very long. Soon the Camerons were heading for Turkey,
while the Browns stayed put.

The contrivance of the Camerons' few days in Cornwall did not
stop the newspapers juxtaposing the youthful Tory leader and his wife
with the more staid-looking middle-aged Browns. The photos of
Brown came to be seen as symbolizing an awkward out-of-touch
dowdiness in the same way that photos of Hague in his baseball cap
were proof of his unsuitability for leadership.

The reaction was further evidence that political context determines
what we choose to see. If the same photos had been published a year
previously, when Brown was on a high and doubts were rife about
Cameron's leadership, the verdicts would have been very different.
Almost certainly Brown would have been praised for his casual but
businesslike appearance and Cameron criticized for being a lightweight playboy. But that was twelve months earlier, before the season
of chaos in Brown's premiership. Now he was seen as ill at ease, his
supposedly misjudged clothes emblematic of a leader out of tune with
the times.

In the same forty-eight hours that followed the by-election, tentatively and self-consciously the Foreign Secretary, David Miliband,
dared to wonder whether he might be a leader more in tune with the
times. He had not gone on holiday yet, but had one week to go before
a break in Majorca with his wife and their two young children. He was
renting a villa near Will Hutton and David Goodhart and their families. Hutton and Goodhart were two of several senior journalists with
whom Miliband was close. Over the weekend the holiday was far from
his thoughts. Instead he was contemplating a significant and explosive

move in relation to the leadership, an explosion that would break the summer calm.

Miliband's rise to the position of potential leader had been fast and effortless. At no point had he schemed zealously to get close to the very top. Most ambitious politicians strive upwards with long-haul persistence. Miliband had potential leadership thrust upon him. He had learnt to be ambitious.

In the summer of 2008 he was still learning. Miliband had been head of Tony Blair's policy unit in opposition from 1994 and then moved into Downing Street after the first election victory. But although bursting with intellectual energy and commitment, he had been sheltered from most of the political storms that had battered Blair, Alastair Campbell and Peter Mandelson. He had rarely attended the bruising meetings in Number Ten, gatherings where participants required layers of steely political resolve to survive for more than a few moments. Instead he was mostly elsewhere in Number Ten, promoting summits about the Third Way in Rio de Janeiro, working on the next manifesto, devouring books, ideas and articles from around the world.

Miliband was decent, modest and rooted politically, unlike some in Blair's Number Ten. While working behind the scenes for Blair he maintained close contacts with a few columnists, proving that amidst all the contentions raging inside New Labour, politics could be a civilizing force. He was never a pure Blairite, daring to reflect in private on some lost progressive opportunities of landslide Labour governments.

He became an MP in the 2001 election for the safe seat of South Shields and rose fast up the ranks, staying in posts too briefly to work out his ideas or test his ministerial grasp. Briefly as Schools Minister he formed a constructive relationship with his boss in the department, Charles Clarke. Together they sought to convince Blair that they should scrap A levels in favour of more vocational qualifications. Miliband was certain subsequently that given a bit longer he could have persuaded Blair to make the radical change, but he never got the chance. He was off again to other departments where he floated vaguely defined radical ideas. Most of them continued to float as he moved on to the next department. When he was Environment Secretary he made some of the most boldly visionary speeches of any minister since Labour came to office. In private he was more candid. He reflected, with good-natured regret, that he was relatively powerless to implement his ideas. Blair and Brown took the decisions on climate change as they did on most matters.

It was while he was Environment Secretary that Miliband became an embryonic leadership candidate without really striving to be one. In the spring of 2007 a small army of Brown-haters – a few former cabinet ministers, aides who worked for Blair, and some in the media – became convinced that Miliband was the candidate who could stop Brown from becoming leader. Even Blair got caught up in the excitement when bizarrely but characteristically he took part in a football World Cup phone-in on the BBC in 2006 and described Miliband as his Wayne Rooney. By the following spring the former cabinet ministers Alan Milburn and Charles Clarke were pleading with Miliband to stand against Brown and insisting that he could win. Others including Peter Mandelson spoke to him about the possibility. Some friendly and influential newspapers, especially the *Guardian* and the *Observer*, were bubbling with excitement at the prospect.

Wisely Miliband resisted the temptation to stand against Brown when Blair stood down in the summer of 2007. As he told some of his wooers privately and with wary resignation: 'We need to have this phase with Gordon in charge. There is no way of avoiding it. Gordon and his people must have their chance. We need to get through it. The party won't accept another course.' He regarded Brown's elevation as a tidal force that could not be challenged, even if he feared its consequences.

At the same time Miliband was starting to enjoy the limelight. He would not have been human if he had not done so, waking up to newspaper headlines suggesting that he could be Prime Minister within weeks and the saviour of his party. In contrast, Brown had viewed the headlines with horror, promising him one of the top jobs as a reward for his support in the 2007 contest. Miliband became a youthful Foreign Secretary, almost as young as the more patently

347

ambitious David Owen, who secured the post after the death of Tony Crosland in 1976.

In the early summer of 2008 Miliband started to make a tentative move. Some of his closest allies urged influential left-of-centre columnists to write that Miliband should take over from Brown as a way of saving Labour and taking the government forward. They argued that in writing such articles the columnists could open the door, encouraging more Labour MPs to call for a Miliband leadership. Quite a few political journalists obliged. In the *Guardian*, columnists who had previously enthused about Brown switched to arguing that Miliband could be the 'change' candidate for Labour as Obama was proving to be for the Democrats in the US. Once more the small army of Brownophobes was urging him to stir the pot and to assert his credentials with a greater sense of boldness.

What those credentials were had never been altogether clear. Miliband had written articles with gestural phrases about the need 'not for Old Labour but bold Labour', and advocating a vague 'social democratic liberalism'. He had been close to Blair and sought to follow the master in reducing complexities to simple concepts. But Miliband sometimes reduced them to banalities, or elevated concepts to a point past understanding. Even so he was fresh-faced and principled at a point when Brown seemed old and reduced to a politics driven by desperate but timid expediency.

Over the weekend after Labour's by-election defeat in Glasgow, Miliband decided to write an article about Labour's future. He had spent the weekend speaking to demoralized activists in his constituency and some influential Labour-supporting journalists. Most of his ministerial allies were on holiday and were not involved in his decision to write the article. He acted more or less on his own, a conspiracy of one.

His words were published in the *Guardian* on Wednesday 30 July. Miliband was like a naive political terrorist playing with explosives for the first time. With no way of knowing quite how big the explosion would be, he set off a political bomb. Under the provocative headline 'We Can Still Win On A Platform Of Change' he mapped out Labour's future without mentioning Brown's name, beginning with a distinctively mischievous pitch: 'When people hear exaggerated claims, either about failure or success, they switch off. That is why politicians across all parties fail to connect. To get our message across we must be more humble about our shortcomings but more compelling about our achievements.'

This was no cryptic opening. There had been much talk in the previous few days about Brown's failure to connect with voters. In fairness to Miliband he was also convinced of the need for ministers to apologize for past errors. He had discussed the theme with his younger brother Ed many times. Also a cabinet minister, Ed had his doubts about the wisdom of such public humility.

In his article David cited the delays in NHS reform as a suitable case for apology. More precisely and obviously he said that planning for winning the peace in Iraq could have been better. With a hint of genuine but indefinite radicalism he argued that the government should have devolved more power away from Westminster. He also stressed the need for a more explicit drive towards a low-carbon economy. The rest of the piece was largely an attack on the Conservatives, a good one that exposed the paucity of David Cameron's alternative at the time.

He concluded with a flourish, one that appeared to set the seal on a torrid summer and to pave the way for an autumn that would make the storms of June and July seem puny: 'New Labour won three elections by offering real change, not just in policy but the way we do politics. We must do so again. So let's stop feeling sorry for ourselves, enjoy a break and then find the confidence to make the case afresh.'

When the article was published all hell broke loose, far more than the still instinctively modest Miliband had anticipated. He knew the article would make waves, but he had not foreseen the late summer hysteria that followed. The media took it as a dramatic sign that at last, after previous hedging, Miliband was making his bid. On beaches around the world ministerial mobile phones throbbed with speculative excitement. Now Miliband could pack for a holiday in the sun.

*   *   *

Miliband's manoeuvre brought Number Ten back to life. On Tuesday in the first week of the summer holiday the place was virtually empty. Whatever the time of year there is always a sense of quiet calm in Number Ten, a deceptive tranquillity. That stillness had been especially illusory over the last year, the least calm and stable period at the top of the government for decades. But today had been different. The tranquillity had been genuine, with Brown and much of his entourage away.

Carter almost felt relaxed. He had delivered the bad news on the by-election the previous Thursday. Surely there would be no more bad news this summer. His holiday was also almost in sight, and he knew that after the long summer break the tenor of life in Number Ten would not continue in the way it had since his arrival in January – a stranger in the midst of a traumatized family. Something would have to give, and very soon.

But Carter was feeling relatively upbeat for the time being. The word from Southwold was that Brown was starting to relax a little. As Carter saw it, this was a huge achievement.

By late Tuesday afternoon the moment of calm had passed. Brown's new media adviser, the former journalist Paul Sinclair, was in charge of press relations for the first week of the holiday. By now Brown's press secretary, Damian McBride, was also away on vacation.

Sinclair, a political journalist from Scotland whom Brown had known and trusted for many years, had been brought in to the media operation the previous spring. He was the only person in the building with a background in journalism, who understood from the inside the way journalists worked. Carter trusted him.

It was Sinclair who brought news of the Miliband bomb that would explode in next day's *Guardian*. As Sinclair read out the opening paragraphs Carter lost all sense of early summer tranquillity.

With great reluctance he and Sinclair decided they had no choice but to alert Brown. Sinclair made the call. Sounding relaxed, Brown told his press adviser that he had just returned from an hour's session with a personal trainer in the grounds of his holiday home. Sinclair told him about the Miliband article. Later he emailed the words to

Brown and then they talked at length on the phone. Brown asked: 'What's your take on the article?' Sinclair suggested that it was not quite as explosive as it seemed. He pointed out that in the Sunday papers a lot of the focus had been on what Alan Johnson, Jack Straw and Harriet Harman were up to. Probably this was Miliband raising his profile: 'This was Miliband saying "Don't forget me." But it isn't a leadership bid.' Sinclair advised that the official reaction should be calm, that he should brief journalists that Number Ten was relaxed about the article. Brown agreed, and even pointed out to Sinclair that a lot of the attacks on the Tories in the article were precisely what cabinet ministers should be doing. Both of them knew that the article could herald trouble in the autumn, but sensed that in itself it did not launch a fatal insurrection.

Sinclair's view was confirmed in his mind the following day when he and Carter watched Miliband give a frenzied pre-scheduled joint press conference with a bewildered Italian foreign minister. Miliband was asked solely about his article, but he said nothing new. As he had agreed with Brown, Sinclair spent the day telling political journalists that Number Ten was at ease with the article, one that he portrayed as being largely an excellent attack on the Tories.

Some of Brown's closest and most protective allies saw things very differently. As Miliband's waves started to roll on Wednesday morning, Gordon Brown's closest political ally, Ed Balls, was driving to Southwold, a visit planned before the two of them knew they would be meeting in the middle of another political crisis.

The trip to Southwold was an attempt to reconnect away from the whirlwind and also at a distance from Carter and the rest of Downing Street. As Balls drove up he listened to the BBC *Today* programme broadcast several items on Miliband's article, all suggesting this was in effect a leadership bid. The news bulletins were leading on the piece, reporting it as a dramatic intervention that threatened Brown's future. Balls and Miliband were near-contemporaries, and had moved into the different camps at around the same time, Balls as an adviser to Brown and Miliband to Blair. In terms of policy development Balls had been the more influential, but on the public stage Miliband had leapt ahead, a senior cabinet minister seen by some in the party and in the media as a possible Prime Minister within months. Balls was ambitious too, but now he was driving to help out a Prime Minister rather than plotting to become one.

In times of crisis, which was most of the time, the close Brownite circle, those who had been together in the Treasury during other dramas, spoke to each other as a matter of instinct. The exchanges could happen at any time of day or night. They had learnt from Brown that politics never stops. Often they were attacked for their close-knit macho tactics, but what their critics failed to acknowledge was that quite often they did prevail in those vital political clashes, and that in the end Brown did make it to Number Ten. Sometimes they could be subtle as well as brutal. Always they were resilient.

As he was driving to Southwold, and without even thinking about whether their holidays had started or boundaries were being crossed, Balls phoned McBride, and his predecessor, Ian Austin, who was now a Labour MP and parliamentary aide to Brown.

McBride and Austin were on tenterhooks. They were expecting an attempt to remove Brown in the early autumn. The Miliband article had not been anticipated and had shocked them. The three of them took a different view from the Number Ten line. They agreed that Miliband's act was destabilizing and had to be dealt with at once. Miliband must learn that actions had consequences.

By early Wednesday afternoon the *Evening Standard* was quoting a source close to Brown stating that Miliband was 'disloyal, self-serving and lacking judgement and maturity'. Number Ten was now sending opposite messages. They were relaxed and they were furious. That is what can happen when allies work from two separate camps. Even in a crisis they made their conflicting moves, heightening a sense of chaos.

In this case there were arguments for both strategies, but no argument to deploy both at the same time. Within weeks Sinclair had left Number Ten of his own volition. Carter was gone soon afterwards. Both despaired of McBride, but also of Brown's failure to get a grip.

By mid-morning on Wednesday Balls arrived at Brown's holiday home, Shadingfield Hall, a nineteenth-century listed building set in five acres of wooded grounds. He noticed that Brown already looked slightly more relaxed and less haunted. Brown told Balls the personal trainer was making a difference, the running through the acres and at the end of the hour some Pilates too.

The two of them discussed briefly the Miliband situation. Balls argued that with most people on holiday, the Foreign Secretary had shown misjudgement in timing and execution. Why show his hand, without a plan of action? The move seemed pointless. They had been at the top of politics for so long that they were smart readers of other acts of attempted mutiny. Their analysis of Miliband's initiative was the equivalent of two veteran footballers on a TV panel explaining why a mid-table team was aiming high but not playing too well.

In preparing a response they did not discuss one option being mooted in the media, that Brown should make Miliband his Chancellor, binding him to his leadership while exploiting his apparent popularity in the key job in the government. Such a move would have been impossible without destroying Brown's relationship with Balls, who ached to be Chancellor at some point.

Brown was in listening mode, as he could be at times when he felt vulnerable or intensely curious. Balls spoke from an unusual perspective. Unlike many cabinet ministers and much of the media, he remained convinced that Labour could win the next election under Brown. His confidence had something to do with those previous comebacks. He knew the degree of guile and dogged resilience that Brown could display under fire. But this time the stakes were even higher than usual and Balls felt he had no choice but to be more expansively candid than in their previous recent and more fleeting conversations.

He began with the operation in Number Ten, saying that Brown had to remove Carter and bring in people who understood him and possessed more of a feel for politics. He stressed also that there was a need to reconnect with the Labour party as well as with the wider electorate, and that the current group running Number Ten had no background in the party. The crazed juxtaposition was not unusual: Carter working in Number Ten to save Brown, while Brown engaged in a conversation about dumping Carter.

Brown and Balls moved on to the related issue of a cabinet reshuffle, one of the few weapons remaining in the Prime Minister's depleted locker. The two of them agreed that he needed a new Chief Whip whom he could trust without reserve. The current occupant of the post, Geoff Hoon, was no longer wholly on-side. He had to be moved, and the unswervingly loyal Nick Brown put in place. Balls urged strongly that Brown bring back Margaret Beckett as a strong voice on the media, a figure who could put the government's case with confidence and vigour. On this proposal Brown was less keen. He had sacked Beckett when he became Prime Minister and was unsure about bringing her back, but he took the notes.

To some extent the two of them were extemporizing in a Suffolk garden. They had no idea whether the political context would permit a reshuffle of any kind in the autumn. Brown might be too weak to make his moves. They spoke as if the reshuffle was an opportunity, but knew that it could stir up problems too. If Brown could not make big changes the media would see the reshuffle as a symbol of his political impotence.

The figure that most excited Brown in Southwold was Alastair Campbell, Tony Blair's former press secretary. Earlier in the summer, during one of their regular conversations, the editor of the *Daily Mail*, Paul Dacre, had suggested to him that he needed a Campbell-type figure to advise on media strategy. Brown had seized on this friendly observation. If the editor of the *Daily Mail* saw the case for a more sophisticated media operation he surely would not be attacked for reneging on his previous foolish declaration that there would be no spin under his leadership. Brown told Balls of his plan to make Campbell a peer and a minister in the cabinet office. He pointed out to Balls that the return of Campbell would prove he was not running a purely Brownite operation, that he could work with those closely associated with Tony Blair. They agreed that the return of Campbell would be dramatic and have a galvanizing impact. There would be attacks about the return of spin, but Brown thought they could deal with those, given the state of his media coverage after a year in which he affected to do without it.

They spoke briefly about Peter Mandelson. Brown had begun to speak to him again. Mandelson talked with Brown several times on the phone while he was on holiday, a sign that the rapprochement was more than tentative. But Brown did not raise with Balls the possibility of bringing Mandelson back to the cabinet. The focus of their discussion at this stage was Campbell.

As the clouds gathered over Southwold in the darkest, wettest British summer for years, Brown and Balls moved on to discuss policy. Balls stressed the need for a narrative about the economy, the importance of claiming ownership for the more upbeat indicators, the danger of talking the country gloomily into an avoidable recession. The two of them were speaking on the edge of history, weeks before the economic situation darkened considerably. In August their focus was on housing, fuel and food prices, jobs. Soon such themes would rate lesser attention, or none at all, but then they seemed really to matter. Brown was preoccupied by the need to show he could have an impact on petrol prices and looked with some optimism to an autumn summit in London with representatives from some of the biggest oil-producing countries.

Balls was more focused on overall strategy. He told Brown that he needed to return after the holidays looking in control of events and not the other way around, stressing that he was willing to take whatever actions were necessary to guide Britain through, as he had done as Chancellor, and to tackle the concerns of ordinary people. Balls warned that there could be no more mistakes like the early election fiasco and the abolition of the 10p tax band. By being associated with those two errors Brown had pushed the limits of prime-ministerial survival as far as they would go. But they both agreed that while the autumn would be tough the party as a whole was not up for getting rid of him. Brown could pull through.

There were times over the years when Brown and Balls had taken part in more elevated discussions, exchanges in which convictions, policy objectives, outcomes and expediency all played their part. Only twelve months ago Brown had clung to nobler if vaguely defined ambitions to make Britain a fairer place, to escape from some of the policy traps set by Tony Blair. Now survival was an end in itself. His role as Prime Minister was to save himself, a raucous reminder of how much had gone wrong.

Brown was not the only member of the government planning his political survival during the summer break. For the busiest ministers the holidays were a time of intense activity in a different setting.

The Chancellor, Alistair Darling, had resolved to acquire a higher public profile, an important resolution for a politician who had relished his unique capacity for maintaining a low public presence in each of his previous ministerial posts. Events and suddenly changed contexts were transforming his personality.

While Balls was discussing strategy with Brown in Southwold, Darling's special adviser, the former journalist Catherine MacLeod, flew to the Isle of Lewis in order to take part in an exercise aimed at boosting the Chancellor's image in the media. Darling wanted to become interesting.

A week after Balls left Southwold to prepare for an extended family holiday in Spain, the journalist Decca Aitkenhead arrived to spend a couple of days with Darling and his wife Maggie during their vacation at their family croft on the Isle of Lewis. Periodically over the previous torrid year the couple had invited political journalists to their flat in Downing Street for an elegant dinner cooked by Maggie and relaxed conversation with both of them over wine. The dinners had been a great success, an informal way of conveying to journalists the Chancellor's humour and decency. The interview with Aitkenhead took this form of intimacy several steps further. A former journalist herself, with a natural exuberance, Maggie had told Aitkenhead that she could stay with them in their home. For the fascinated and slightly bewildered Aitkenhead this invitation was a leap too far. She had never met the Darlings and now she was to join them for their summer holiday. She opted to stay nearby.

MacLeod had hoped that the end result of the sequence would be a lengthy and glossy portrait in the *Guardian*'s Saturday Weekend Magazine, one that would humanize a political figure normally heard explaining away bad news on the *Today* programme. Darling talked to Aitkenhead for hours. In so far as he sensed there would be any news story from their conversation, he thought that his comments on the state of the Labour party might be reported and followed up by the rest of the media. In the interview he was stronger than usual on his party's prospects: 'We've got our work cut out. This coming 12 months will be the most difficult the Labour party has had in a generation. We've got to rediscover that zeal which won three elections, and that is a huge problem for us at the moment. People are pissed off with us.

'We really have to make our minds up; are we ready to try and persuade this country to support us for another term?'

Darling could see a headline or two out of that gloomy political assessment. For the rest he looked forward to the profile, accompanied by photos of him relaxing on a boat and posing on land against the backdrop of spectacular scenery and grey skies, the same grey skies that had cast a shadow over Southwold, although Darling half joked to Aitkenhead that they were always grey on Lewis.

The publication of the interview was perfectly timed for the August bank holiday weekend, the end of the summer holidays and the start of a new political year. It was a weekend when political figures can make their mark as politicians and journalists return with a refreshed appetite for the fray.

On the Friday before the publication in the *Guardian* Brown was preparing for a trip to Brussels and beginning to map out more clearly in his mind the narrative for the autumn, and in particular his determination to offer hope and not just be associated with gloom. As discussed with Balls in Southwold, he wanted to show he could make a difference on housing and petrol prices in particular. He had plans for both. At the end of August the economy was on a cusp. There were plenty of ominous statistics and the banking crisis lingered, but the scale of the coming collapse was not apparent. Brown still sensed or clung to the hope that by talking up the prospects for the economy a recession could be avoided. Catherine MacLeod had been told, to her alarm, by one political editor that Brown was making optimism his central post-holiday theme. On the flight home from his short visit to the Beijing Olympics he briefed Philip Webster of *The Times* that the economy would be looking up within six weeks. It was not clear how Brown had reached such a sunny conclusion, but evidently he was determined to convey an upbeat message.

Quickly the message was countered. Late on the Friday afternoon Brown's press secretary, Damian McBride, phoned him with the news that the *Guardian* was running a story quoting Darling as saying that the economic situation was the worst in sixty years and with worse to come.

At first Brown could not believe it. 'What are they basing it on? Alistair would not say that.' McBride explained that it was an on-the-record interview and that the report was based on direct quotes. Brown was livid. 'This destroys our whole strategy,' he exclaimed. He was taken aback partly because it seemed so out of character for Darling to behave in such a fashion. The two men were old friends and allies, a relationship that had been inevitably tested now that one was Prime Minister and the other Chancellor. On the whole, though, the working relationship had been functional up until this point. From the beginning Darling accepted that he could never be a dominant Chancellor as Brown had been. For his part, Brown almost adjusted to the fact that Darling at times was better briefed on the latest economic data. Those close to the Chancellor noted that Brown was quickly out of touch with the finer details of economic policy when he moved to Number Ten.

But what baffled Brown on that Friday afternoon was that Darling had acted with uncharacteristic recklessness. He had always assumed that, whatever else, Darling would be a safe pair of hands.

McBride too was furious. He flared up when he phoned MacLeod. 'What was he doing giving an interview with Decca Aitkenhead? She's dangerous.' MacLeod phoned Darling to warn him that the *Guardian* was leading with his comments on the economy and that, mysteriously, the *Daily Telegraph* had got hold of the story too and was running it big. At first Darling could not recall what he had said about the economy. He could not remember saying anything outlandish. Then MacLeod read out the headline and the story. Darling had not said anything out of the ordinary. He had told the truth. The truth was sensational.

The *Guardian* front-page headline was stark:

Economy At 60-Year Low, Says Darling. And It Will Get Worse

Brown phoned Darling directly instructing him to give interviews on the Saturday explaining that he was not referring to the British economy, but the global context. Brown told him to be upbeat about Britain, that it was still well placed to weather the storm. A shocked Chancellor agreed to clear the day for a retreat.

Normally Darling was capable of displaying an eerie public calm, a stillness at odds with the gales that blew around him. On that Saturday afternoon as he gave a series of television interviews justifying his comments he was visibly shaken and even shaking a little as he delivered his unconvincing sound bite: 'Economies across the world are facing tough challenges, but I have always believed and still do that Britain is well placed to weather the storm.' His remarks in the *Guardian*, followed by the defensive explanation in which he looked like a startled burglar caught in the act, were the lead item on all the news bulletins.

Almost immediately stories started to appear in newspapers that Darling was doomed. There were also anonymous criticisms of MacLeod. Darling and MacLeod were convinced that McBride was briefing against them, a theme that was to develop in the early autumn.

A Miliband article began the summer break. A Darling article ended it. The latter sequence, with its echoes of the chaos of scheming paranoia that preceded the holidays, was the prelude to Brown's formal return on the Monday, the start of the first full week in September, a re-entry that seemed to continue where he had left off.

Brown made a series of announcements supposedly aimed at first-time buyers and those threatened with repossession, but the proposals had not been fully thought through or costed. There was a sense that he was seeking headline-grabbing initiatives in an attempt to save his political skin, another pre-holiday echo. The announcements also seemed flimsy because, for some reason or another, the media had been expecting the unveiling of a major new economic plan. The Downing Street adviser who described the weekend after the Glasgow East by-election as the lowest moment in Brown's career pointed to the early days of September as the second worst.

On the Tuesday after the bank holiday Monday Brown made a big claim for his relatively minor initiatives, saying that voters should be reassured that the government would 'keep the housing market moving forward'. In contrast, an aide to the near-invisible Chancellor was quoted as saying that these measures were not aimed at propping up the housing market, but focused specifically on helping two specific groups, first-time buyers and those in trouble repaying mortgages. On the BBC *Today* programme a relatively junior cabinet minister, Hazel Blears, was the interviewee put up to hail the measures. For obvious reasons Darling had to keep clear.

The whole unofficial relaunch was a mess, as even those inside Number Ten who were close to Brown and wanted him to do well were bound to recognize. Some of his closest allies, who had worked with him in the Treasury and had been in awe of his strategic discipline as Chancellor, noted with alarm the compulsion to rush out half-baked initiatives with a confused message. As one of his close allies put it to another, 'Gordon the Chancellor would have disapproved of the way Gordon the Prime Minister is operating.'

The summer break of hyperactivity in Southwold and on the Isle of Lewis had appeared to redouble the chaos of the previous twelve months rather than address the causes of the various crises.

For a few days his usually crammed-past-bursting diary was a little emptier. Brown went back to basics and instead of demanding a diet of hourly initiatives discussed with some of his entourage how he

360

should communicate in a context made suddenly more thorny by the candour of his Chancellor. The Cabinet Office minister, Ed Miliband, was back from his holidays, emotionally torn by his close relationship with his brother David and his loyalty to Gordon. The devotion to Brown was prevailing, but Ed had witnessed the hasty housing launch with despair. He wondered whether Brown still had it in him.

On the Friday Brown had to deliver a speech to the CBI in Scotland, an annual event that demanded an overview of the economic situation. Ed urged him to inject some of his own political values into it, not to make his comments purely managerial. His comments were not dissimilar to those made by Ed Balls in Southwold. But now Brown had a speech to write, a challenge that always focused his mind in an unfocused sort of way. There would be drafts and redrafts, but as one of those involved puts it, 'the intense process produced clarity of thinking even if the speeches themselves were poor'.

In this case Brown delivered a more robust address than he had managed to do in recent months, one that ranged widely and confidently. As Ed Miliband had advised, he also included a few paragraphs that went beyond the familiar and hinted tentatively at the ideological:

> We will do whatever it takes to bring security to families on modest and middle incomes. And we will ensure that no one who is prepared to work hard and adapt to change will lose out as a result of global forces. We will act responsibly to prepare people for the inescapable challenges ahead – in the short, medium and long term.

Brown was very wary about revealing his social democratic instincts, his belief that government can be a benevolent force. He always looked for cover, some banker to pin his case on. But he noted that the headlines next day were a little more friendly. Several newspapers and Channel Four News preceded their reports with the headline 'Brown pledges to do whatever it takes'. The words had a positive ring. That is how the speech had been briefed in advance by Number Ten – 'The Prime Minister is going to say he will do whatever it takes to help hard-working families.' For once the sequence of briefing, delivery and media reports had worked.

Brown had told close allies for months that he could not find the words to convey what he had been trying to do since taking office, and certainly since the fiasco of the non-election the previous autumn. He was making an admission of failure that was greater than he realized. If a leader could not communicate, could not make contact, then he should not be in politics, let alone at the top office. The ability to convey and engage is a prerequisite for leadership and not a useful extra if you happen to have the skill. But Brown was struck by the phrase 'Whatever it takes'. The three words placed him on the side of worried voters and hinted at his belief that government could be a benevolent force. He resolved to use the phrase again.

He had cause to do so sooner than expected and in supremely more dramatic circumstances. The following week the Republican administration in the US was forced to intervene to save the housing giants Fannie Mae and Freddie Mac, respectively the Federal National Mortgage Associaion and the Federal Home Loan Mortgage Corporation, from going bust. In effect a right-wing US government was nationalizing two of the biggest and most revered private financial institutions. This sensational development made waves around the world. On the morning after the nationalization the BBC's *Today* programme hosted a discussion between two senior bankers pleading with the US government to do much more to prop up the ailing banks. Ed Miliband awoke to the discussion and assumed that the contributors must be members of the left-wing Compass pressure group, such was the focus on the need for massive state intervention. He could not quite believe it when he heard at the end that the speakers belonged to Goldman Sachs.

Something big was happening in the United States, bigger than anyone seemed to have allowed for or foreseen. There was talk of world-famous banks and financial companies going bust within days, with calamitous repercussions for the entire global economy, not least for the UK, with its reliance on vibrant financial markets. Suddenly

Brown's worries about petrol prices seemed marginal, and Darling's comments on the state of the economy models of exemplary restraint.

In Britain the sense of an impending economic storm led to an extraordinary conjunction. Throughout September there continued to be feverish speculation about whether Brown could survive as Prime Minister. David Miliband invited *The Times* into his home for a glossy pre-party conference profile. Cabinet ministers speculated with journalists about what might happen next. Some Labour MPs called publicly on Brown to stand down. Meanwhile the world's economy was an avalanche ready to happen.

The reaction of the US administration to the collapse of Fannie Mae and Freddie Mac was to do whatever it took to save these national institutions. Brown was seized by the significance of the event, sensing that economic assumptions were being turned on their heads. He should have recognized this a year earlier when Northern Rock collapsed in Britain, but he had been intimidated then, as any Prime Minister would have been. Of the many crises he might ever have feared, the collapse of a bank and its subsequent nationalization was not among them. Now and unexpectedly in the early autumn of 2008 he was not alone in facing such emergencies, and other countries – countries with right-wing governments, doctrinaire free-marketeers – were responding with state intervention on an unprecedented scale. Brown was always more confident when he had cover to act. As the crisis grew ever more vividly global, he became more willing to follow his personal instincts, rather than his cautious political ones, and to take the lead on behalf of active government. If a Republican president was doing whatever it took, then so could he, and with far more conviction.

The many internal doubters were not silenced. Indeed three cabinet ministers, Jack Straw, Geoff Hoon and James Purnell, were meeting regularly to review whether they needed to make a move against Brown in order to save the government and the Labour party. But they were making their tentative moves against a Prime Minister who had acquired a renewed confidence. Perversely an apocalyptic economic crisis came to his rescue.

TWELVE

Revolts and Recovery

Gordon Brown was fortunate in his dire misfortune. From flailing pointlessly in the vacuum that followed the non-election in 2007 he faced a titanic dual challenge in the autumn of 2008, almost exactly a year after he had lost his way.

Both were potential disasters, and dangerously unpredictable. One could have finished him off, the other could have ruined millions. Yet for Brown they were fruitful ordeals, since they gave meaning to his lost leadership.

They took the form of political insurrections against his leadership, unprecedented for a prime minister who had been in power for so brief a time, and an economic crisis that might at one point have led to the collapse of the global banking system. From drifting neurotically and pointlessly towards humiliating oblivion, Brown faced a mammoth task, the kind that he was made for. He was saved by calamity. The economic crisis in particular became almost a source of comfort. Part of his long agony was salved. He knew now that whatever happened his leadership would not be an empty coda to the rest of his career. The concluding chapter would have some verve to it. History would record the key part that he played in a sequence of events that changed the world. Brown used to fume that Blair was obsessed by his place in history. A year in office changed his perspective.

Even the first attempted coup played to his strengths. He was a machine politician so experienced at manoeuvring in order to stay at the top of British politics that the rebels were the equivalent of a non-league team taking on Manchester United. The economic crisis allowed him to articulate more clearly his belief that governments have a role in regulating the economy as well as markets, a view so unfashionable previously that he had not dared to speak so plainly in the mid-1990s when he reshaped Labour's policies to appeal to the market, the media and middle England. Brown also used the crisis to seize control of economic policy once more by setting up a new economic council that he himself chaired rather than the Chancellor, Alistair Darling. The move was an extraordinary display of energy weeks after facing down a rebellion.

All at once the party dynamics had changed. David Cameron and George Osborne, agile till then on the trapeze, were thrown and never fully recovered in opposition. This was not because the acrobats had lost their skills, but because the world was in a state of flux. They were facing a new situation that called into question their fundamental beliefs about the role of markets and the state. The Thatcherite ethos that had been endorsed and in some ways sealed by Blair's victory in 1997 was at last being challenged by events. Cameron and Osborne, while more socially liberal than their predecessors, had formed their free-market, small-state economic outlook in the 1980s and 1990s. With governments intruding into the markets on an unprecedented scale, where did events leave their passionate belief in a smaller state? At first they did not appear to know.

But the way was not clear for Brown. It never was. A recession could hardly be an entirely liberating experience. In the same way that Brown had been trapped by 'Blairism' when he first became Prime Minister, now he was awkwardly defined by his own past, the long-serving Chancellor, the hands-off regulator, close friend of Alan Greenspan and senior bankers. His early accommodations with the Thatcherite spirit of the times became a painful handicap as he finally had the room to say a little more clearly what he really believed. He had affected a passion for banks and bankers in order to make Labour electable. After such affectation, his true voice sounded false.

* * *

There were three attempted coups against Brown in the period between his elevation to Number Ten and the election, an average of more than one a year. No prime minister in British history was subjected to so many persistent attempts aimed at removing him.

Yet each coup fizzled out. Like so many of the dramas associated with New Labour, the apparently confident posturing of the rebels disguised a lack of clarity about aims and objectives. There was also a policy vacuum. In the case of all three attempted coups the rebels wanted to get rid of Brown because they thought he was weak, irascible, unpopular, incompetent, or had not offered them jobs. That is a long and compelling list, but not a clinching one. When the Conservatives dumped Margaret Thatcher in 1990 they were focused on more elevated and clearly defined policy areas such as the need to scrap the poll tax and a change of approach towards Europe. The objectives gave the act of regicide shape and purpose in advance of the revolt and after it. In 2008 and 2009 rebels and potential rebels popped up from time to time and huffed and puffed. Cabinet ministers unused to acting outside the Blair/Brown duopoly plotted tentatively and without resolve.

During the first embryonic coup in the early autumn of 2008, the former cabinet minister Charles Clarke led the charge. Unlike most of his fellow rebels involved in coup number one, Clarke was a thoughtful politician and had been an innovative cabinet minister, especially during his brief reign as Education Secretary in Labour's second term. Like them he was a clumsy operator, his moods too transparently angry, not knowing what to do after the cathartic screams. He had some radical policy ideas, although some of them would have been deeply unpopular if he had espoused them as a besieged prime minister. Clarke was a genuine constitutional reformer, recognized the urgency of environmental issues, and advocated taxes earmarked for specific public services. He also dared to argue for additional charges for public services as a way of raising resources, although he never explained why voters would be enthused by such a development.

Clarke's best chance of implementing parts of his agenda would have been to rejoin the cabinet, or to put the case for his ideas without slinging mud at Brown. All that came across in Clarke's public appearances was his baleful disdain. He wrote an article for the *New Statesman* in September 2008 in which he claimed that Brown was leading Labour to 'utter destruction'. He urged party members to act in order to prevent 'disaster'. Shortly after the publication of the article several Labour MPs called for a leadership contest. None of them raised any policy issues or outlined what they would do in the light of the unfolding economic drama. They wanted Brown out and hoped that once they started trouble others would join in.

Tenuous substance was matched by inept timing. They made their move weeks before the Labour conference in 2008, an event in which rallying behind the leader had become as ritualistic as knifing the leader used to be in the late 1970s and 1980s. The disparate rebels tossed pebbles into the sea and hoped for a wave that would wash Brown out of Number Ten.

Foolishly they also placed their hope in the cabinet. The cabinet placed theirs in the rebels. In so far as they gave their actions any deep thought, the rebels calculated they would be a destabilizing force, enabling cabinet ministers to look as if they were dutifully responding to a mood in the party. But there was no discernible overall party mood and the cabinet, unused to the public spotlight, had no focus.

Jack Straw came back from holiday still keeping his options open. A few MPs were begging him to strike against Brown, but the veteran wanted a chance to be leader if he did the deed, and that was never a likely outcome. More nobly he also worried what impact the act of regicide would have on his party, in which there was still a fair amount of support for Brown's leadership. Throughout September and early October Straw kept in touch with his long-serving colleague Geoff Hoon, another minister who had campaigned enthusiastically for Brown but was now disillusioned. The two of them formed an unofficial alliance with the younger James Purnell, a minister who had decided long ago that Brown was a disaster, but possessed no clear alternative agenda of his own beyond support for vaguely defined concepts such as 'empowerment'. Purnell kept in regular touch with David Miliband, who was giving interviews and accumulating magazine profiles in which he tried too hard to look like Tony Blair, a laid-back family man with the casual touch. Miliband had also decided that Brown was a disaster and had started to believe the exhortations that he could be Labour's saviour, always a potential hazard in a political career.

One of Brown's biggest critics and Blair's closest friends, Tessa Jowell, had spent the summer at the Olympics in China despairing of Brown in conversations with the army of BBC journalists reporting the event. But Jowell had not joined those wondering whether to take part in a coup. Sensibly she asked her fellow Blairites what would follow such a move, pointing out there was no certainty that their favoured candidate, David Miliband, would win. The soon-to-be Defence Secretary John Hutton had for years been one of Brown's most strident ministerial critics, but he was thinking of a career outside politics. Brown had hinted to him that he would be made Defence Secretary in the autumn, Hutton's dream job. Having no relish for a fight, nor any faith in the chances of a coup, he made no attempt to join one.

Meanwhile Brown's small number of ministerial supporters was rallying yet again. Ed Miliband insisted that his elder brother supported the Prime Minister, which was not the case but not a falsehood either, in the sense that David had no idea what form an insurrection would take and was determined not to lead it.

Ministers could have forced Brown out in the autumn of 2008 if they had wanted to do so. There were enough of them who were disillusioned. But they were unused to organizing for political causes of any kind, let alone one as testing as the removal of a prime minister. They had left all the politics to Blair and Brown. When the time came they did not orchestrate a ruthless campaign and were not even sure they wanted to do so.

The party conference in the autumn of 2008 was a bizarre event. Ministers and journalists spent their time speculating whether Brown would survive, while most of the activists declared their support for his leadership and expressed their anger at the behaviour of the rebels.

But Straw, Hoon and Purnell had still not made their minds up what to do. They had become self-appointed grandees without knowing how to act grandly. They met immediately after Brown's speech on the Tuesday afternoon to assess their leader's position, agreeing that Brown was stronger than he had been, but the key gathering would be that of the Parliamentary Labour Party when MPs returned to Westminster after the long summer recess. They thought it possible still that enough MPs would call on him to go to make a leadership contest likely or at least possible.

Brown had other ideas. His cabinet reshuffle, carried out immediately after the conference season and before MPs returned to Westminster, was both a work of art and an act of desperation, a display of his conjuror's skills and a symbol also of his weakness.

The main act of magic was the invitation that brought Peter Mandelson back into the cabinet. No one saw this coming, the move that saved Brown's career and left the baffled rebels running for cover. Suddenly the Blairites' hero was working with Brown and not with them, not seeking to remove him.

Mandelson told me at the time that he and Brown had been holding conversations of 'brutal candour' over the previous summer. During one conversation in July a depressed Brown had told Mandelson he wanted to change the way he was perceived, alike by voters, colleagues and the media. Mandelson suggested to him that he needed to change from within and not to adopt a superficial makeover. He urged Brown to seek ways of relaxing, even suggesting that yoga might help. He added that Brown needed to view others with less anger and suspicion. Unschooled in self-awareness, Brown was taken aback at a character assessment shared by all of his colleagues.

During one exchange Mandelson also demanded an apology. Brown asked if he was referring to recent tensions about his future as a European Commissioner. Mandelson answered: 'No. I want an apology for the last fourteen years.' This was the period since 1994 when Brown had been aggressively hostile. Brown offered an apology 'in his own way' and the two of them moved on to discussing how Labour could recover from its low ebb.

But Brown did not decide finally to offer Mandelson a place in the cabinet until early September. He floated the notion with Balls when they met at Brown's house in Scotland. They had not discussed the proposition when the two of them met in Southwold during the frantic August. It was only when Alastair Campbell turned down a peerage and a ministerial role that Brown's thoughts turned to Mandelson. At first Balls was alarmed and suggested to Brown he needed to consider the risks of such a move. Mandelson had been the ultimate hate figure for the Brown circle. They had spat out his name in anger virtually every day at the Treasury, regarding him as a malevolent right-wing schemer, often blaming him when he was entirely innocent.

Balls's bewilderment captured Brown's fate as Prime Minister. Brown had yearned to be PM and yet was more powerful when he was a frustrated Chancellor. In the Treasury he prevailed in nearly all the key policy decisions. If he disagreed with ministers such as Mandelson he was able to barge them aside. Now he was Prime Minister he was about to resurrect the career of Mandelson and was in solicitous discussions with other enemies such as Alan Milburn. He needed them now, and in his dependence he could not dismiss their ideas.

The wooing of Mandelson was slightly more subtle than an act of pure self-preservation. Both men had moved. Mandelson's role as a European Commissioner had led him to revise some of his ultra-Blairite assumptions as he witnessed governments around the world intervening more energetically to boost their industries. Brown read a lecture that Mandelson had delivered in Cambridge earlier in 2008 and exclaimed to the surprise of his inner circle: 'Mandelson gets it' (it was still not 'Peter'). What Mandelson got was the changing politics in a global economy, Brown's obsession.

Conversely Mandelson knew from working with Brown in the 1980s and early 1990s that he was one of the few politicians who, at his best, could link policy with strategic positioning. There were sustaining elements of mutual respect and affection in a pact of such special expediency that Brown would not ever have contemplated this particular scenario in all the years he had planned to replace Blair.

Astonishingly Brown achieved all his objectives in the reshuffle even with his back to the wall. He removed Stephen Carter from Number Ten, placing him in the Lords and giving him a ministerial role. A potential leadership candidate, Alan Johnson, was promoted to the Home Office. Having accepted the post, he could hardly turn against Brown and showed no inclination to do so. Ed Miliband was promoted to a big job addressing climate change. Mandelson was made Business Secretary and was effectively Deputy Prime Minister. In terms of buttressing his position the reshuffle was further proof that Brown could read the play effectively at times, not least when his own survival was at stake.

Cameron and Osborne were bewildered. Their limited and superficial reading of New Labour made no sense of such a development. They admired Mandelson as much as they did Blair. Cameron told friends in the immediate aftermath that he assumed Mandelson had taken the job in order to put the knife into Brown. The opposite was true. He was there to save him.

The ruthless assertion of power did not stop with the reshuffle. Brown also set up an Economic Council, partly an attempt to wrest control of economic policy from the Treasury. Having little faith in Darling, or in some of the officials who advised the Chancellor, he created an alternative institution. The Council was attended by a range of ministers, including Balls and Mandelson. Brown was in the chair. Balls noted at the time that a strong Chancellor would never have accepted such a sweeping takeover. He spoke too soon. Darling would become strong too, discovering assertiveness later in his ministerial career as he had already found a new interest in self-projection in the media. Darling would raise his game, but not right now.

The Council met frequently at first, although as with many of Brown's internal arrangements, his interest faded. His motives were a naive faith that a grand gesture would look impressive, a desire to keep his allies close at a time of economic crisis, as well as the wish to stage his personal coup against the Treasury. The Council comprised seventeen ministers, including some brought in from the business world under Brown's latest reshuffle.

The seemingly mighty Council was part of a new and vital sense of economic purpose. On 15 September, as a handful of Labour MPs and cabinet ministers were still deciding whether to remove Brown, Lehman Brothers went bankrupt. The juxtaposition was comic, a bunch of amateurs scheming in the dark as the world transformed.

As Darling reflected later, the sudden closure of Lehmans 'changed everything'. For a few weeks the global banking system was on the verge of collapse. In Britain Bradford and Bingley, Halifax and the Royal Bank of Scotland were the most immediately vulnerable in the wake of Northern Rock the year before. No one was sure what would have happened if they had collapsed – the lost deposits and social unrest. No one dared to think that far ahead. It was safer to take one short step at a time.

The collapse of Lehmans was a repeat of Northern Rock, but now it was the already hard-pressed US financial market that was thrown into panic. Lehman Brothers, while it was a large and complex business trading in a web of assets, also underwrote 100 per cent mortgage loans offered by specialist lenders to people with few visible means of support. When interest rates jumped, borrowers could no longer afford their monthly payments. Like Northern Rock, it mattered less that 80 per cent of its assets were solid if 20 per cent were toxic. In the dying days of the Bush presidency the US Treasury concluded that it had reached the limit of taxpayer funds it was willing to gamble on propping up investment banks. It had already intervened in a way that pained the ideological instincts of the laissez-faire free marketeers at the top of the Republican administration.

Henry Paulson, the Treasury Secretary, had committed $3 trillion to saving Fannie Mae and Freddie Mac earlier in September. If they had failed, the mortgage market in the US would have collapsed and hundreds of banks around the world that invested in US property would have suffered huge losses. Paulson had also bailed out Bear Stearns earlier in the year, but he had reached the limit of his sudden belief in government effectiveness, concluding that a trading house like Lehmans, which had little direct connection with retail markets and ordinary homeowners, could be allowed to go bust without causing the kind of systemic risk posed by Fannie and Freddie. He soon discovered he was wrong.

Share prices around the world collapsed as investors took flight from a sector that appeared to be run by a group of bankers who were in denial about the extent of their mistakes and the problems their firms now faced.

The subsequent sale of Merrill Lynch to Bank of America was a more startling development in the year-long credit crunch than the collapse of Lehmans. Once it was clear that Lehmans was going under, Merrill realized it too was vulnerable. There was a dramatic reversal of roles. Earlier in the year Merrill was approached by Bank of America, but rebuffed takeover talks. Suddenly it was Merrill that went cap in hand to the US's largest retail bank for a rescue deal.

Darling described the sequence as sending 'shockwaves around the world … whatever happens to one institution affects all others … no one knew the level of bad loans were so high'.

The economic crisis marked a phase of heightened ambiguity in Brown's mercurial career. Apocalyptic events endorsed his deepest instincts. For years he had been making speeches about the need to adapt to the new global economy, to develop institutions at an international level, to invest in Britain in order to ensure that a relatively small country could compete in the global economy. He was also a believer in government as a benevolent force, the big difference from the Blairites and the Conservatives' leadership. While Cameron, Osborne and the ultra-Blairites were bewildered at first by the tide of events, Brown and his closest allies were on a new political high, perhaps in the way that some mourners feel oddly euphoric at a funeral. At last events were in alignment with their deeply held and long-suppressed beliefs.

Towards the end of the year Ed Miliband accepted a parliamentary award at a swish London hotel from the right-wing *Spectator* magazine. In front of his throng of small-state, free-market hot-gospellers, Ed claimed that the collapse of the financial markets had shown his father, a famous Marxist academic, had been right all along. Later I asked if him he had been joking. He told me he had been deadly serious.

At the Labour conference in Manchester, as a few plotted against Brown's leadership, fringe meetings were celebratory in tone, 'The left's time has come,' said Neal Lawson at a meeting of his highly influential leftish Compass group.

Brown had already started to use a more overtly interventionist language, arguing that the government would do whatever it took to prevent the collapse of the banking system. Crucially his confidence was bolstered by the fact that he was not alone as a leader facing the nightmare. Once a Republican administration in the US was starting to prepare a big rescue package, he had doctrinal collateral. No one could accuse him of acting like an Old Labour statist, always his big neurotic fear, when President George W. Bush was spending trillions to prop up the banking sector. Brown had been much more frightened by the collapse of Northern Rock the year before.

But a moment of crisis for followers of the light regulatory touch was not an entirely liberating one for Brown. He had been Chancellor when the City had boomed, cutting their taxes and hailing their contribution to the economy. Brown had even opened the London headquarters of Lehman Brothers in Canary Wharf. He was so proud of his friendship with Alan Greenspan, the architect of America's freewheeling economy now spectacularly crashing, that he cited the world's most powerful banker in his book of speeches published shortly before he became Prime Minister – one of the few public figures with whom Brown sought association. He had sheltered behind a banker, Derek Wanless, when he wanted a respectable figure to endorse his tax rise for the NHS. Above all he had been Chancellor for ten years, and now the economy was heading for a deep and dangerous recession. Such a sequence could never be unmixed good news for Brown and was bound to raise big questions about his approach during the previous decade, his regulatory changes, the substantial increase in public spending during the final years as Chancellor (failing to fix the roof when the sun was shining, as Cameron/Osborne simplistically put it) and his blanket adulation of the City.

To prove he was not 'Old Labour', Brown showed that he could be an ally of the bankers, allowing the Tories no space to claim they were the party for the City. Fearful of raising a series of taxes overtly, he became a cheerleader for the financial markets as they provided him with an alternative source of revenue. There were many differences between Blair and Brown, but both were products of Labour's defeats in the 1980s and 1992 when their party was perceived as anti-American, soft on defence, anti-business and hostile to the City. Like horror-film characters, they backed away from one threat, only to walk into a worse one. In the early years of the new century there was less appetite for war, wary suspicion of the US and fuming hatred of bankers. The duo had not only been trapped by their past, but had become victims of their indiscriminate desire to be 'new'.

Nonetheless at first voters appeared to give Brown a fresh chance. His speech to the Labour conference at the end of September was confidently delivered in the light of the highly charged context. If it had been a flop the rebels might have been emboldened. As it was he managed to dismiss both David Cameron and David Miliband with his famous proclamation of experience: 'This is no time for a novice.' The speech had a slightly lighter touch than previous pedestrian efforts, helped by Alastair Campbell, who was becoming more actively involved. On Monday night before his speech the following day I was talking to Campbell in the main conference hotel. Brown appeared with Sarah and his entourage of advisers and detectives. 'Will you come up and look at the speech later?' Brown pleaded with Campbell, who was at the hotel with one of his children. Campbell sighed after Brown had strolled out for a round of parties: 'My heart sinks when I see him at the moment. He is always asking about the speech.' It was billed as the biggest of Brown's career and the crisis gave it a focus.

Miliband, who had a poor conference trying too hard to be someone he was not, failed to look anything close to a credible challenger. He seemed to be playing at being a public figure and the act was too obvious. When Straw, Hoon and Purnell held their self-important meeting shortly after the speech they were no longer potential slayers of Brown. He had moved on and they trailed tamely after him.

The following week, as the scale of the crisis grew even more ominously clear, the Conservatives met in Birmingham. In the US there were doubts whether Congress would back Paulson's rescue package. Back in London British banks were on the brink of collapse. Cameron and Osborne were thrown by the course of events and made an uncertain pitch throughout the week. This happens when the paradigms change; even sure-footed politicians lose their grip. Osborne made a speech in which he blamed Brown for the emergency. In the middle of the week the two of them offered a bipartisan approach, and Osborne went to London with a flourish to hold a meeting with a suspicious Darling at the Treasury. By the end of the conference Cameron was attacking Brown again.

Cameron and Osborne were showing early signs of political awkwardness in relation to complex policy making and in their reaction to unpredictable events. They had been gleeful in opposing the nationalization of Northern Rock and were not sure now whether to affect a non-partisan approach or to blame Brown for virtually the entire crisis. They tried both and were exposed for the first time as gauche opportunists.

Still neurotically alert to any perception that he had vacated New Labour terrain, there was a part of Brown that was entirely relaxed about government intervention. He was much more disconcerted by the fallout from the non-election, even though it was a relatively trivial event compared with the collapse of the financial markets.

Even the placid Darling had been shaken by the collapse of Northern Rock, but now he knew what to expect. Mervyn King, the governor of the Bank of England, had learnt from Northern Rock too. King had behaved like an ideological academic at first, resistant to saving the bank and then slow to grasp the urgency for action when he came to recognize that a rescue package was essential. This was not especially surprising. King was an academic with ideas. He too was trapped by his past, but he was learning fast, having no choice but to do so.

Senior Treasury officials were at their very best in this latest crisis. One relative newcomer told me she was in awe of the selfless efforts of officials working around the clock to come up with a package. The crisis in the US had heightened the drama but given them all a sense that they were not alone. Brown in particular felt emboldened by the global reach of the emergency.

The subsequent £500 billion rescue package was far more ambitious than Paulson's equivalent in the US. The package came in three parts, mind-boggling in scale and ambition. £50 billion of taxpayers' money was offered to banks to rebuild their capital reserves. £200 billion of liquidity was made available as short-term loans in an attempt to thaw the frozen interbank lending markets. A further £250 billion would underwrite lending between banks – another attempt to shore up their balance sheets. In the mid-1990s when seeking power New Labour had been scared about pledging to spend a few pennies. The five early pledges that defined its first election-winning campaign did not cost an additional penny in total spending. Now Brown and Darling thought nothing of sums in the hundreds of billions. A year earlier Darling had fretted about paying for the partial abolition of inheritance tax. The cost of that proposal was the equivalent of worrying over buying a second-hand car when you are about to borrow the cash for a flight to the moon. The sums were crazy, surreal in their scale. Yet there was no alternative to epic intervention. The banks could not fail without taking an even bigger leap into the unknown.

The Treasury announced that seven precarious banks and one building society would take part: Abbey, Barclays, HBOS, HSBC, Lloyds TSB, Nationwide Building Society, Royal Bank of Scotland and Standard Chartered. Brown hailed the package as a 'bold and far-reaching solution' to the crisis, one that would help every family and business in the country. The term 'bold' had been often deployed in the New Labour era. This time the claim had substance. On the morning of the announcement Brown told his close ministerial ally, Shriti Vadera, that he feared he would have to resign by the end of the day.

'This is not a time for conventional thinking or outdated dogma but for fresh and innovative intervention that gets to the heart of the problem,' Brown declared with a public display of bravado. He also promised that taxpayers would be protected and would earn 'a proper return', although he could not have been sure.

The scheme was the product of intensive work for several weeks. Senior figures were involved from the Treasury and the Bank of England. Ministers with specialist knowledge, such as the newly ennobled Paul Myners and Brown's old ally Shriti Vadera, were at the heart of the operation, more involved in the detail than Brown or Darling.

Brown's role was central for two reasons. As Prime Minister he could have vetoed the scheme or called for a package that was less costly and more in line with the US. He did not do so, not least because he recognized that Paulson's package failed to match the severity of the situation. He had also been actively involved in the international response, encouraging the central banks to cut interest rates. The package was by no means perfect. It failed to resolve the precise relationship between the banks and the government that had become their partial owner. As a result the banks continued to behave almost as if nothing had happened, and the government was unsure how prescriptive it should be, never having had a clear sense of what form of state ownership was desirable and in what circumstances.

Ownership had always been a policy area that terrified Brown and Blair, so they avoided the issue altogether. Brown declared vaguely: 'In reaching agreement on capital investment the government will need to take into account dividend policies and executive compensation practices and will require a full commitment to support lending to small businesses and homebuyers.' There was no edict insisting that the banks should begin to lend more, or to cut their exorbitant bonuses.

Nonetheless the package saved the banks and the deposits held within them. There were no Lehmans-style closures, and at a point when Brown was used to reading in British newspapers that he was useless and mad he received, in November 2008, the endorsement of the Nobel prize-winning economist Paul Krugman in the *New York Times*, an almost comical contrast to his media coverage in Britain.

Gordon Does Good
By PAUL KRUGMAN

Has Gordon Brown, the British prime minister, saved the world financial system?

O.K., the question is premature – we still don't know the exact shape of the planned financial rescues in Europe or for that matter the United States, let alone whether they'll really work. What we do know, however, is that Mr. Brown and Alistair Darling, the Chancellor of the Exchequer, have defined the character of the worldwide rescue effort, with other wealthy nations playing catch-up ... the Brown government has shown itself willing to think clearly about the financial crisis, and act quickly on its conclusions. And this combination of clarity and decisiveness hasn't been matched by any other Western government, least of all our own.

Brown was ecstatic. He had been used to reading what bad news he was. Now a distinguished economist was suggesting that he had saved the world – quite a leap. Inadvertently Brown claimed to have 'saved the world' during a subsequent Prime Minister's Question Time, when he had meant to refer slightly more modestly to rescuing the banks. Tory MPs split their sides at the gaffe, seeing monstrous arrogance. They were witnessing the opposite, an insecure Prime Minister clinging to a public endorsement as if it were a life raft. But the Krugman article demonstrated again that what we see in Britain is what we choose to see and not always what is in front of our eyes. From the American perspective Brown was leading the way. In Britain he was still viewed largely with disdain. Neither was entirely correct. On this occasion there was a third way that most voters chose not to see: Brown dared to lead when he felt it was safe to do so.

The defensiveness of Brown and his Chancellor was vividly reflected in Darling's Mais Lecture delivered at the end of October, a prestigious platform in which a leading economist or public figure makes his pitch. Predictably Brown was becoming anxious that the government's policies were being associated with Keynes and a return to Keynesianism. Darling was similarly minded, although his pragmatism was more determined. He believed in sound managerial administration as a guiding idea rather than as a cover for more rooted ideological objectives.

After conversations with Brown the Chancellor stressed in his lecture that his approach to the economy was not inspired by a single economist who was suddenly back in fashion. Instead he was doing what it would be 'perverse' not to do, which was to borrow more in a recession. He promised that the government would return in the medium term to a course of prudence, although he did not explain what that would mean in policy terms. In hailing a prudent course and at the same time putting the case for spending and borrowing, Darling got into an unavoidably contorted position: Yes, the government's famous fiscal rules had brought about stability in the past. Nonetheless it was necessary to drop the rules in order to achieve stability in the medium term.

Brown and Darling's ambivalence over linking their response to the crisis to any set of defining values, combined with the erratic nature of the Cameron/Osborne dance, fuelled a period of dizzying politics. Three of Brown's key allies urged him over the autumn and winter to become more overtly ideological. Ed Balls, Ed Miliband and Douglas Alexander were not especially close. In particular Miliband and Alexander viewed Balls with wary suspicion. But all three shared a similar outlook. They were the social democrats in the cabinet, along with Brown. Separately Balls, Miliband and Alexander told Brown that he needed to be more open about the reasons why a left-of-centre government was better suited to respond to the crisis, with its belief in intervening in markets and its support for Keynesian economics. Balls was adamant that the government's economic policies had always been in line with Keynes, his hero. All of them were frustrated that Brown still worried about the reaction of the *Daily Mail* and therefore opted for the language of an apolitical manager a lot of the time.

The quest for a guiding theme was reflected in the frenzied build-up to the pre-budget report in 2008. The stakes could not have been

381

higher. For the first time since Brown had called off the election a year earlier, polls suggested he was back in the game. All of them recorded a substantial narrowing of the Tory lead. For three weeks in the prelude to the report Brown, Darling, Balls and Mandelson met each morning to discuss options. They all agreed on the need for an additional fiscal stimulus, but there were intense discussions about what form it should take. Balls was especially keen on a cut in VAT, because the money went straight back into the economy and would have a sustained impact for a year. Darling put forward other options for consideration, but accepted that most of them would not have the same theoretical impact, although he had his private doubts about whether the VAT reduction would make very much difference. Balls was particularly keen on a rise in income tax on higher earners, as was Ed Miliband in his separate discussions with Brown. Darling agreed to raise taxes on earnings above £150,000 from 2011, along with a national insurance increase, in effect another rise in income tax. Brown was worried about all the options, but characteristically was swayed emphatically in favour of the VAT cut when he heard Ken Clarke advocating it. He saw it as a way to split the Tories.

Brown worried a little about the tax rise and yet agreed instinctively with Balls that the two of them had wanted to have a high rate for top earners since the mid-1990s. Here was their chance. I saw Ed Miliband at a conference on the weekend after the pre-budget report and he declared excitedly: 'How about the new top rate of tax? After all the years of agonizing, in the end we just did it and the early feedback suggests it is popular.'

But in their neurotic attention to detail, Brown and his small band at the top of the government ignored an element of policy making that had always been central in their early days in the Treasury. They forgot to tell a story about what they were doing and to prepare the voters in advance. When Darling announced that borrowing was to rise to £118 billion there was a sharp intake of breath in the Commons. Several newspapers and BBC's *Newsnight* proclaimed 'The Death of New Labour'. Columnists reached a similar verdict. Brown was furious and phoned several newspaper editors directly to complain.

Mandelson toured the studios in a damage-limitation operation, arguing that he was the personification of New Labour and supported the package.

It was too late. On the Saturday after the pre-budget report the left-of-centre Progress pressure group held its annual conference in London. Once again minister after minister argued that the economic crisis was a left-of-centre moment. As they were doing so news seeped through of a poll in the next day's *Sunday Times*. It gave the Conservatives a fourteen-point lead. Brown's mini-bounce in the polls had ended with the economic statement in which he had tried so hard to reinforce his fleeting semi-popularity. Darling lacked the will or the guile for a political fight. He delivered his pre-budget report as if it were a report on the state of the M4 motorway, and then disappeared to leave the field to the Tories, who briefed very effectively against the measures for the rest of the week. From Darling there was no act of explanation or advocacy. Brown, Balls and Mandelson had been too busy worrying about the precise measures to bother about their overall effect.

As far as voters were concerned the package looked bleak. Britain was heading for a recession and was in debt at a level that was almost impossible to contemplate.

Did this period mark the death of New Labour? The question implies that the project was a clearly defined entity in the first place. It was never as solid a construct as that. The project was shapelessly expedient. As New Labour was partly an illusion, it could not die. There was nothing there to run out of breath. The Blairite version of New Labour would have almost certainly avoided the tax rise on high earners. The Brownite version had always wanted to make such a move and now seized the opportunity. Brownite New Labour did not die with the pre-budget report. In a limited way it discovered room to breathe.

In January 2009 the IMF issued a report arguing that Britain was the least well equipped of the bigger countries to deal with the crisis, a conclusion leapt on by the Conservatives and much of the media. Soon Britain was officially in recession under the leadership of a

Prime Minister who had declared as Chancellor the end of boom and bust.

Brown's response was to work harder than ever. His public performances were dismal, the product of exhaustion, a continuing failure to prioritize his time and a curious carelessness about the way he sought to project himself. With a schedule packed with meetings and the economy on the edge of a cliff, Brown had less time to prepare for interviews or planned doorsteps in which he would utter a sound bite. As a result he sounded more wooden than ever. 'I'm getting on with the job' was often his dreary reply to questions.

Mandelson watched the interviews with some alarm, comparing them with Blair's, which were always polished and elegant. Mandelson complained of what he regarded as Brown's amateurishness in his public demeanour and about his inability to focus on essentials. At the height of one crisis Mandelson strolled into Brown's office to find him writing a long, intellectual paper for Obama's senior advisers, worthy and worthwhile, but not necessarily what a Prime Minister should be doing as his government appeared to be falling apart.

Amidst the political vortex, Brown at least had a strategy once more by the beginning of 2009, a clear and highly ambitious one that had multiple objectives. He looked ahead to the G20 summit in London scheduled for March with an acute awareness of political and economic opportunities. In the weeks leading up to the summit Brown hoped to appear like an international statesman who could make things happen across the globe and to convey a more parochial message, that the entire international community was planning another fiscal stimulus while the Conservatives in Britain were isolated in opposing one for their country.

What followed was another example of epic politics. For someone accused of being too cautious, Brown was staking all on persuading the world to act together by the time of the summit, or at least being seen to do so. As ever, the risk was a calculated one. He knew that the US administration led by the newly elected President Obama was dancing to the same tunes. Brown had close ties with senior Democrats in the administration who had plotted economic policy regularly with him since the early 1990s. Conveniently, Brown and Obama, still in his early spell-binding phase, genuinely agreed on doing whatever it took, two social democrats at ease with the idea of governments intervening.

Indeed one of the striking disparities about the situation in early 2009 was the deification of Obama and the loathing of Brown when they had similar views and followed similar policies. On one level of course the explanation was obvious: Obama was fresh, new and charismatic. Brown was old and knackered, and had lost any of the charisma he once possessed. Nonetheless the yawning gap in the way the two were perceived pointed to a heightened irrationality in politics, in the US and Britain.

Obama's pre-presidential book *Audacity of Hope* was the key, nearly one hundred thousand words in which the aspiring President articulated precisely what Brown had thought but did not dare express. Written before the global recession, it became a guide as to how to get out of it.

Obama put the case for active government in ways that even the most anti-statist reader would find difficult to refute. First he made the broadest argument: 'In every period of great economic upheaval and transition we've depended on government action to open up opportunity, encourage competition and make the market work better.' The words were a statement of the obvious, but were rarely expressed with such clarity. There were agonies in Downing Street about the two words 'government action', and worries too about publicly arguing that governments can make markets work better. Would that appear too left-wing? Would such an endorsement of government action lead to another rise in the polls for the smaller-state views of David Cameron?

Obama was untroubled by such thoughts. Instead he developed his case, arguing that active government was necessary to 'build the infra-structure, train the workforce and lay the foundations for economic growth'. He wrote of 'the vast potential of a national economy' and proceeded to give specific examples, indispensable when politicians make abstract points: 'The Hoover dam, the Tennessee Valley

Authority, the interstate highway system, the Internet, time and again government investment has helped pave the way for an explosion of private economic activity.'

We did not hear such a robust defence of government investment in Britain until the 2010 election moved into view. Instead when New Labour invested from 1999 onwards, which it had done bravely and necessarily, we heard about the pivotal role of the private sector and the need for the government to be more self-effacing, to stand back and do less. The Blairite version of New Labour took hold. In policy terms this did not mean the British government was in a different place to Obama, as Brown was pulling strings in the Treasury that challenged depoliticized Blairism, but in making a case robustly and clearly, both Blair and Brown were miles away in a state of tortured insecurity.

Pronouncing before the credit crisis, Obama was equally strong about the role of the state in such precarious economic situations. He wrote: 'Active national government has also been indispensable in dealing with market failures.' What a shame that no British minister uttered that sentence with a triumphant flourish after a range of voices, many of them on the right, called for the public ownership of Northern Rock. For New Labour the shadow of the 1970s continued to make its destructive mark.

Unburdened by the past, Obama again offered precise examples: 'Roosevelt after the stock market crash in 1929 engineered a series of government interventions that arrested further economic contraction ... he set up a regulatory structure that helps limit the risk of economic crisis.' What was that, a defence of regulation? It was a defence that chimed with the popular mood after the chaos caused by the lightly regulated banks, but again in the UK we rarely heard such a case, in contrast to the relentlessly uncritical stress on the virtues of markets.

Obama put his case for government in a much wider context. He made it clear that markets could work better than government intervention. In some cases, he pointed out, there were unforgivable inefficiencies in government activity. He was a fan of the private sector and saluted that old Blairite formula that what matters is what works.

But his clarity and self-confidence about the role of government gave him the space to demolish the disastrous domestic record of President Bush: 'Without a clear governing philosophy President Bush has responded by pushing the conservative revolution to its logical conclusion – even lower taxes, even fewer regulations, and an even smaller safety net.'

Cameron and the ultra-Blairites were fans of Obama as a symbol of potent change, but they would not make the case he made for government. Instead they emphasized the opposite, putting the case for the smaller state with a bigger role for lower taxes, the private sector and charities. Blair did not use the pulpit of Downing Street to put the case for government activity either. Yet in the end it marks the great divide between the centre left and centre right, the former seeing government as capable of being in some circumstances a benevolent force, the latter instinctively suspicious. Gordon Brown, his well-known ministerial allies, and others such as David Miliband would almost certainly agree with every word in *Audacity of Hope*. Indeed Brown's views about the constructive role for government in helping people to fulfil their potential, and the value of markets in many situations, chime directly. Barack was a Brownite. Blair and Cameron were further to the right. Only when the recession took hold did Brown start to deploy language more boldly, once he had the protective cover of Obama making the same case as an international superstar.

In the build-up to the G20 Brown also had to persuade Germany and France to sign up to a new international package. Equally significant, he had to find the space for a further fiscal stimulus in the UK. This was proving almost impossible, with even the governor of the Bank, Sir Mervyn King, arguing that Britain could not afford to borrow more. The increasingly self-confident and publicly assertive King made this case when Brown was in the US putting the argument for international action. King was part of a new pattern in British politics, non-elected figures acquiring more power than the elected ones. Reluctantly Darling had announced that King would serve another full term as governor of the Bank, meaning that he would still be in place when Brown and Darling faced the prospect of being out of power within a year or so. King was not a deft political operator, but power without electoral accountability is a dizzying combination and the excitement went to his head.

The subsequent G20 Summit in London was one of the most extraordinary events hosted by a British government in recent times, an unpopular Prime Minister cajoling other world leaders to sign up to a new agreement in the face of the international crisis. The end result was not what Brown had hoped for originally. There was no coordinated economic stimulus plan, and regulation, although global in principle, was still to be applied by national regulators who could take different approaches. Any help to poor countries was limited in scope, and there seemed little prospect of a global trade deal that could lift their prospects in the long term. There was plenty of ammunition for Brown's critics to dismiss the event as spin.

But there were hints in the rhetoric and in substantive measures that a new way of running the world economy was emerging from Brown's relentless focus. Obama said as much when he acknowledged that the 'Washington consensus' of unfettered globalization and deregulation was now outmoded, and called for a more balanced approach to regulating markets rather than letting them run free. There were some specific funding pledges: $500 billion for the IMF to lend to struggling economies, $250 billion to boost world trade, $250 billion for a new IMF 'overdraft facility' countries could draw on, $100 billion that international development banks could lend to poorest countries. It was the shift in the stance of the US, previously the strongest opponent of international regulation, that had opened the way for a much broader attempt to regulate the financial sector. Obama had unlocked the door, but without Brown's exertions the world might not have cautiously shoved it open.

The measures went far beyond banks' capital requirements to include the global regulation of hedge funds, tax havens and executive pay, something that would have been unthinkable before the crisis broke. And in the new Financial Stability Board, which would now incorporate all G20 members, there was the potential for a powerful new global financial regulator. Even more significant was the increased power given to the international financial institutions, the World Bank and the International Monetary Fund, who had been subcontracted by the G20 to monitor and run many of their policies.

The IMF managing director, Dominique Strauss-Kahn, was jubilant after the meeting, saying that the IMF 'is now truly back'. The IMF's image had been tarnished during the Asian financial crisis and, until the current crisis came to a head, there had been fears that the organization was losing its relevance. Strauss-Kahn was particularly enthusiastic about the plan for the IMF to issue $250 billion worth of its own currency, the SDR, saying this was the first step towards the IMF issuing its own liquidity as well as being a lender of last resort – the two key functions of a world central bank. The IMF was also being made more representative, with China and India getting a bigger say, and its top job opened to all comers, not just Europeans, in the future.

For a few days Brown led the bulletins surrounded by the glitter of foreign leaders, a flattering context. He got reasonable press coverage too, although it was punctuated by a fair amount of scepticism. Quite a few disapproving pundits commented patronizingly that 'Gordon must be like the cat that got the cream' after the summit, an evocation of a pathetic figure on a fleeting high.

Coincidentally I had an appointment to see Brown on the Monday after the summit. It was fascinating reading similar newspaper columns on the way into Downing Street, so many writers asserting authoritatively that Brown would be euphoric. When I saw him he was low, almost as down as after the non-election in 2007. Already he realized that the summit had not produced much of a bounce in the polls. The issues seemed distant from the concerns of frightened voters, even though there was a deep and direct connection. The reform of the IMF was not a policy area that got voters going when some had lost their jobs or were about to do so.

But the other reason Brown was gloomy was because he was not daft. He knew the economic prospects were unremittingly nightmarish and told me that the politics of the forthcoming budget were awful, with higher borrowing figures due to be announced. As I left my meeting with Brown, Neil Kinnock came bouncing into his office, the next guest. 'Hello Gordon … How are you mate?' Brown put his arm around Kinnock like a son needing the support of a solicitous father.

On every front politics was in a state of flux, not just in relation to seismic economic events. A communications revolution was taking place at the same time, in which the Internet was becoming the vibrant mediator of politics. The changes were as wildly unpredictable as those raging through the global economy. Political leaders could not tell quite what to make of it. In Labour's case they had only recently mastered the art of conveying a coherent message through the orthodox media. Now a new beast appeared on stage, almost literally from nowhere.

Some of Brown's more assertive advisers urged him to pay less attention to the newspapers in the age of the Internet. One or two of them dared to point out that the media had moved on from the 1980s and 1990s when the mighty newspapers held sway. They carried some hope that this new and shapeless stage would allow them to project their ideas unmediated, an optimism that faded when Brown appeared on YouTube at the start of the scandal over MPs' expenses and looked like a deranged criminal on the loose. But their hopes were not unjustified. Suddenly communication was anarchic and less controlled by a few mighty proprietors. An artful politician could take command as Obama managed to do during the US presidential campaign, building up support and cash on the Web.

But in Britain the right-wing dominance in the press was replicated on the Internet. The sites that managed to be entertaining, provocative and at times informative were almost entirely prompted by innovative individuals who loathed the government. One in particular personified their energetic anarchism. Guido Fawkes broke stories, tormented Brown, and in his libertarian crusade openly loathed elected politicians. This gave him quite a lot of leeway, but his malevolent focus was on Labour. He became more influential than newspaper columnists in shaping the agenda. The BBC's *Today* programme once ran four items that had been inspired by Guido's website in a single show. When deciding on their running orders, BBC producers seemed to turn to his site as much as to any of the newspapers.

A former Labour party adviser to Peter Mandelson, Derek Draper, had resurfaced after Brown became leader. Draper had disappeared from public view for a few years after facing accusations in an early lobbying scandal, but he had retained a fascination with the latest developments in the media and how to present a case.

The resurfacing and energetic commitment was noteworthy. Draper had been close to Mandelson and, even though the two had fallen out, had been seen as being on the Blairite wing. In fact his hero was Roy Hattersley and he had come to despair of Blair's timid expediency and right-wing leanings. For a time at least he had more hope of Brown. After Brown became leader Draper set up a left-of-centre website to counter the explosion of Tory-supporting blogs. Almost immediately the site was hammered by the Tory-supporting blogs for being too loyal to Labour, although its loyalty gave it a distinctive novelty, more or less the only media outlet that pointed out anything positive the government was doing. But Draper worried about the unequal battle on the Web and was in particular alarmed by the impact of Guido Fawkes.

His basic assessment was correct. Guido Fawkes was running rings around orthodox media outlets and almost entirely to Labour's disadvantage. Draper got in touch with Damian McBride, Brown's erratic adviser, who had more time on his hands after being removed from his formal post of press secretary the previous autumn. There was method in Draper's thinking. McBride had good contacts in the newspapers and had kept up with the gossip about leading Tories. Increasingly bored, McBride made the mistake of responding to Draper's requests for trouble-making stories by emailing rumours relating to senior Tories, and in one case to a shadow cabinet member's wife. Neither had thought through whether such malicious material might harm them rather than the intended Tory victims. If they had gone ahead with the site, I suspect it would have seemed too contrived and desperate. McBride's involvement would almost certainly have been traced. The whole project was misconceived.

But the project never got off the ground. With a neat symmetry Guido Fawkes obtained the emails and published them with the relish of someone lighting a fuse in the wholly confident knowledge that a massive explosion would follow. A weak attempt by Labour's supporters to emulate Guido Fawkes was destroyed by the man himself.

After McBride's departure Brown's media coverage got even worse. At least McBride had kept one or two influential political editors more or less neutered. Brown was also worried about another consequence of the affair. It would make it much harder to attack the Tory leadership in the future. He felt that their privileged backgrounds should be an issue, but after this there was no obvious way to proclaim it.

From the left to the right, commentators weighed in to analyse Brown's ugly side. Brown's cabinet colleagues were relieved at the departure of McBride, but felt the circumstances were so damning that they became even more critical of Brown's seemingly wayward leadership.

The sequel could not have been worse. A non-elected prime minister at the height of a recession, publicly awkward, losing an ally for acting malevolently against colleagues then faced the MPs' expenses scandal, day after day of terrible headlines beginning with his expenses laid bare on the front page of the *Daily Telegraph*. It looked terrible.

Contrary to another myth, Brown was prepared for the eruption. When I spoke to him on the Monday after the G20 summit, when he was supposed to be the cat that had got the cream, he cited the forthcoming publication of MPs' expenses as another reason why the summer would be bleak. The clumsiness of his response is explained partly because his heart was not in it. He continued to declare privately that people went into politics to serve and not to make money. In public he had to appear tough in what became a competition with the other party leaders over who could crack the whip most ruthlessly.

The public mood was violently angry. The BBC Five Live presenter Simon Mayo told me he was so shocked by some of the emails from listeners calling for MPs to be lynched that he had problems reading them, let along broadcasting them. The populist producers of BBC One's *Question Time* could not believe their luck. They did not have to whip up the audience into an anti-politics frenzy. Voters were ready to throw stones at the panel of politicians.

The *Daily Telegraph*, the newspaper that had obtained exclusive access to all the MPs' expenses, had the politicians in its thrall. Each night the main party leaders would await to hear who had been earmarked for the following day's front page. The symbolism demonstrated the shift in the balance of power from elected politicians to the non-elected media.

Brown's ambivalence brought out the worst in him. He was furious at the *Daily Telegraph* for its coverage of his expenses claims and extracted an apology. He did not share the growing view that most MPs were crooks and yet he knew he had to respond to the frenzy of anger in the country. Typically, as the frenzy mounted he also wondered if there was a political opportunity in being seen to act. Out of the collision of contradictory thoughts came a predictably muddled response. Attempting to look tough, Brown commissioned a series of independent reviews, one to deliver a verdict on the expenses and another to outline a future regime.

Brown liked to commission independent reviews only when he had already arranged the outcome. On this subject the level of public anger was so great that he had to relinquish control and hand it over to former civil servants who would act as they saw fit, with calamitous consequences. At more or less the same time he sought to make some capital out of the situation by outlining his own immediate plans on a YouTube video without consulting the other party leaders. The performance became notorious as he smiled in the wrong places and put forward a series of measures that were never likely to command support from his own MPs, let alone opponents.

Next he hosted a meeting with the other party leaders in which his behaviour was so determinedly uncooperative that Cameron and Clegg left in genuine as well as partisan despair, united in their antipathy to Brown (a fleeting liaison that was to acquire much greater significance after the 2010 election result).

Brown's fruitless initiatives followed on from an embarrassing U-turn after MPs had inflicted a surprise defeat on the government. Twenty-seven Labour MPs voted with the Liberal Democrats and the Tories to back a demand for all former Gurkhas to be allowed to live in the UK, not just those who retired after 1997. Brown appeared out of touch once more, no finger on the public pulse as he initially refused to make concessions and then faced the might of the actress Joanna Lumley in alliance with ageing Gurkhas, an alliance more powerful than any elected politician.

Brown felt desperate once again, and had plenty to be desperate about. Some of what happened was self-inflicted. Drained of self-confidence, his public performances were as bad as they had been after the non-election in 2007, and Number Ten was as weak and underpowered as it had been when he first moved there as Prime Minister. No one apart from Balls and Mandelson, who had other preoccupations, dared to challenge him on any front. He had no senior adviser whom he rated and trusted in the way that Blair had Alastair Campbell and Jonathan Powell.

There was no attempt from anyone within Number Ten to woo the media or explain to editors and columnists what they were trying to do. The open-plan war room in Number Ten in which Brown, his senior press team and advisers sat together stoked a sense of panic and was not in itself a solution to the organizational chaos that marred the Brown regime.

There was much talk at the time that Brown was slower to respond to the expenses crisis than Cameron and that when he did so he was cack-handed. One of the labels that stuck ever more firmly was that he was a ditherer, a figure who could not make his mind up what to do. This was another cliché that obscured a more complex reality. So-called dither was preferable to rushed decisions made without thinking through the consequences, an occasional characteristic of Tony Blair's. Brown was quite good at taking long-term decisions. He was hopeless at those that called for quick thinking on the spot.

Another cliché applied at this point was that Brown was never cut out to be a prime minister because he could not deal with a multiplicity of issues. But no human being could deal with an unusually potent combination of an economic crisis and a parliamentary scandal and emerge with his or her reputation enhanced.

The expenses scandal was especially damaging. Brown had to vie with Cameron in being tough, and yet there had to be a degree of fairness in the way MPs were dealt with. As it turned out Brown was damned by some of his MPs for being too tough and by the public for being too soft. Only a new prime minister on a honeymoon could have managed such a crisis without alienating virtually everyone.

Not surprisingly, Labour was mauled in the European elections, a poll that took place in the midst of the various unrelated eruptions, securing a puny 15.3 per cent of the vote. In the days leading up to the elections and in the immediate aftermath Brown faced the second attempt to get rid of him. Several cabinet and junior ministers resigned. The biggest departures were the Home Secretary, Jacqui Smith, and the Communities Secretary, Hazel Blears. But they were far from heroic resignations. The rolling news coverage on TV gave a sense of heightened drama, another relatively new media phenomenon that had taken control of the agenda and our minds. Both these ministers, although disillusioned with Brown, were embroiled in the expenses drama and would have probably had to leave in any case. They were not part of a synchronized coup and lacked the authority to lead a revolt because of the allegations whirling around them about their expenses. Yet the impression was conveyed of a government that was falling apart because of Brown's leadership.

In reality the small group of insurrectionists from the previous September had failed to recruit many more MPs with the weight to make a mark in the second attempted coup. As the polls closed on the night of the European elections they produced the chairman of the Education Committee, Barry Sheerman, who gave an interview on the Ten O'Clock News. He was their new recruit, a fresh voice. But his main complaint was the way Brown had handled the expenses issue.

He felt that Labour MPs should have been treated more fairly – not a message likely to go down well with the wider electorate. Once more the disparate rebels conveyed varying messages.

Their weakness was highlighted by what should have been their ultimate show of strength, the sudden resignation of the Welfare Secretary, James Purnell, a figure revered by the Blairite/Cameronian orthodoxy that pervaded much of the media. In a statement issued after the polls had closed, Purnell declared that he did not believe Labour could win under Brown's leadership. He offered no analysis as to how Labour might win because he did not have one.

Purnell had not bothered to liaise with the rebels although he had told David Miliband about his intentions, but did not know whether the Foreign Secretary would follow suit. In fact Miliband did not take much persuading to stay put. A short phone call from Peter Mandelson did the trick.

Miliband enjoyed being Foreign Secretary too much to risk all on a resignation of uncertain consequence. If he had followed Purnell he would have brought down Brown, but there was a part of Miliband who was still thrilled to be in the cabinet. When he was first mooted as a possible leader in 2007 he told me: 'It's quite an honour to be Environment Secretary. I still can't believe it when I look around the cabinet table that I am there.' This was endearingly modest, but not the mindset of someone ready to knife a prime minister. He was still not ready as coup number two took shape in the summer of 2009.

More substantially, Miliband was far from certain what would follow the act of regicide. A leadership contest might make matters worse for a chaotic government in the midst of a recession. Purnell strolled off the political stage and was hailed as a hero by Brown-haters in the media, but his act was pointless. Miliband was dismissed as a coward, but he remained a player with a future. He took the more sensible, less glamorous path, but he was troubled by the consequences. 'We are a really poor government at the moment,' he told allies over the summer, knowing he had kept the government in place.

The other potential leader showed no interest in leadership. Alan Johnson had been mooted as a possible leader for a couple of years.

Unlike Brown he was an entirely relaxed media performer and had an authentic public voice, the self-deprecating and efficient administrator. His greatest strength was his past: from a poor upbringing he went on to become a postman and would joke that the nearest he got to Chequers was delivering the mail. His background was the perfect counter-narrative to the privileged Etonians who were running the Conservative party. But Johnson had never said or done much of interest in his political life. No one quite knew where he stood because he never felt inclined to spell out his wider outlook. He insisted at least once a day that he did not want to become leader. In case there was any doubt, he would also point out that he had lost the deputy leadership contest in 2007. He made the defeat seem like an achievement, vindication for lack of ambition. Johnson was the most reluctant dauphin in the history of those waiting for the crown.

An astute reader of the rhythms of politics, Mandelson had made the correct analysis. As he pointed out afterwards to anyone who asked, his support for Brown was not an act of sentimentality but of ruthless calculation. There was no one else ready to do the job. Throughout the hours and days of the second coup, Brown was safer than he seemed.

But the cabinet reshuffle that accompanied the crisis highlighted his weakness. Once more Blairites were promoted. In some cases those who might have resigned in protest at his leadership were elevated as a reward for reluctant loyalty. The new Defence Secretary was Bob Ainsworth, a solid, unspectacular minister. He had indicated to some rebels that he was on their side and would resign. Brown was aware of the danger that he might go, and promoted him. Johnson was elevated to Home Secretary.

Most significantly, Brown was too weak to make Ed Balls his new Chancellor. For a few days preceding the reshuffle Brown had decided to place Balls in the Treasury, and Darling never forgave him for what he regarded as an act of betrayal by a former friend.

As was nearly always the case in these raging dramas, the situation was more complicated than Darling recognized, or than the wider media expressed when they took his side. The first and basic factor was that at some point Brown was always going to make a move to place Balls in the Treasury. Darling must have known when he accepted the post in the first place that the issue was bound to be a running theme. Contrary to mythology, Balls was ambivalent about making the move to the Treasury too early and still had a few doubts in the immediate approach to the reshuffle. There was no question that he wanted to be Chancellor at some point, but he was more flexible about the timing than Darling realized.

Up until the last moment Mandelson was on Brown's side about the virtues of the change. Then on the Thursday afternoon, the day before the reshuffle, Mandelson had a meeting with Darling in which he explored the possibility of the Chancellor switching post.

The trigger for the move in the week leading up to the reshuffle had been Darling's expenses claims as an MP. It had become a major story, and he suspected Balls or an ally in Number Ten of stirring it up. This was not the case. The *Daily Telegraph* chose to give it prominence because it was an irresistible juxtaposition, a Chancellor in trouble over expenses.

Brown was genuinely frustrated with Darling and was not acting out of malevolence. He had made Darling Chancellor at a time of relative economic calm and thought him an ideally solid administrator to steer the ship towards a general election. The economic crisis, Brown felt, required a Chancellor who could control the Treasury, was an economist, and was highly political.

Darling's sense of being betrayed was understandable. He had worked around the clock seven days a week since the collapse of Northern Rock, and this was his reward. He was one of the most decent and dedicated figures in British politics at a time when the anti-politics culture was reaching a dangerously hysterical level. None of these admirable qualities meant that he was suited to be Chancellor in the midst of the gravest economic crisis for at least sixty years, as he had famously put it the summer before. Still, he knew that Brown was in no position to move him and stood his ground. As a result he became unsackable and discovered a new assertiveness to accompany his suddenly much higher profile. For Darling the metamorphosis from publicity-shy administrator to media-friendly and muscular politician was complete, one of the more extraordinary political journeys.

Brown's political year ended as it had begun, with an attempted coup and a reshuffle carried out in a position of extreme weakness. But at the end of it he was still at the top of politics, as he had been since 1992. He had no constituency in the media, little support in the cabinet, many Labour MPs were wondering whether they should have joined the half-hearted insurrection, and his closest allies admitted openly that they had never dreamed that Brown would be as poor as he had been at times over the last eighteen months. But he was Prime Minister, still in the battle. Stamina was a factor and experience was another. His various rivals and critics had felt little heat in the past and did not know what to do when it scorched them. The only other figure who knew what it was like in the furnace was Mandelson, and he had decided to stick with Brown.

There was another underestimated factor, utterly perverse though it seems. On one level Brown was in hell, but on another, as one close ally observed to me, 'Gordon enjoys being Prime Minister. He likes the intensity of the work, the global dimension, and wielding power.'

Brown could cope with hell and almost enjoy it. His response to being in hell is proof that no matter what the pressures, being Prime Minister is not easy to give up.

THIRTEEN

Whatever It Takes

Political leadership is an art. The great political artists can generate a mood of excitement around what they are doing, even if they are not doing very much. By the summer of 2009 the story of the Labour government since 1997 and the limited revival of the Conservatives could only be explained in terms of the capacity of various leaders to mesmerize and the failure of others to do the same, or to do it for very long.

The mesmeric powers of the best political artists are so potent that quite often what is happening in front of our eyes is not what we choose to see. These skills have little to do with making policy, even though it is the policies that impact on our lives and not the magician's conjured image.

Tony Blair had a genius for making the humdrum seem exciting. Between 1994 and 1999, if Blair had announced he was going for a short walk around the garden of Number Ten, the world would have hailed a revolution in transport policy. So imagine the excitement if Blair had declared in 1997 that a Labour government would take over greedy train operators, high earners would pay more tax, the free market in energy was over, and that we must all plan to pay for care for the elderly, with the well-off paying more.

Brown's government had announced policies along these lines in the spring and summer of 2009 and quite a few more besides. Yet it was loathed by voters from left and right. It had no support in the media and was accused of lacking purpose. The government had come to loathe itself as it moved fearfully towards a general election in 2010.

The disparity was striking, the transition from New Labour's seemingly never-ending honeymoon to its prolonged decline. When Blair was cautiously dumping the referendums on electoral reform and the Euro, ruling out any tax rises, keeping to the previous Tory government's spending plans and refusing to touch the privatized railways, he and Labour were hailed for their energetic, radical crusade. The euphoric front pages of still mighty newspapers suggested we were living through a revolution when not very much was happening at all. Throughout most of 2009 Brown looked pale and miserable while some of his ministers hid away in a state of detachment. Yet in policy terms his government displayed an erratic boldness. In comparison with Blair's era it was being more radical.

Policies are easily lost if they do not fit the prevailing narrative. The only story that anyone wanted to write or read in the summer of 2009 was of a crumbling administration. Privately senior ministers spoke of little else. Yet in his 2009 budget the Chancellor, Alistair Darling, put up taxes for high earners by a substantial amount, an enormous step from the early timidity about laying a finger on income tax. The papers screamed their disapproval, but polls suggested the move was by far the most popular the government had made for some time – a vivid example of the disconnect between the lives of voters and those who mediate politics. The government published a Green Paper on care for the elderly that was more daring still, finally accepting that voters would have to put aside substantial sums for care and proposing some precise solutions. Brown agonized over this one with all his old caution, rightly predicting that there would be more loud headlines about Labour and stealth taxes. He still gave it the go-ahead and got no credit for doing so.

Ed Miliband's White Paper on the route map towards lower carbon emissions, published in the summer, was also innovative. Even the normally sceptical environmental groups hailed it as a significant step forward. One told me that the document was 'historic' in its determined interventionism. Miliband had always seen the state as a potentially benevolent force, and to some extent his approach to green issues reflected his faith in active government. The same applied to Ed Balls, whose proposals to guarantee training or education for all sixteento eighteen-year-olds were aimed at enhancing the prospects of children in poorer areas. When David Miliband became an MP in the North East he told me that what struck him more than anything else was that if kids in his constituency left school at sixteen, most would be doomed to a life of low income and unreliable employment. Balls presented his policy as a 'guarantee', a reassuring term, yet he was compelling teenagers to train. He was right to do so, but in Britain a clamorous army of rightist libertarians portrayed any compulsion, however liberating in the long term, as the act of a sinister, interfering nanny state.

More revolutionary, the Transport Secretary, Andrew Adonis, focused on the railways with an energy that had long been absent in this important policy area. When National Express went begging for a more generous contract, Adonis nationalized the East Coast main line. Imagine the agonized internal debates over such a move in 1997. After nationalizing a bank or two, this seemed like small beer. Adonis had shown similar resolve in initiating moves towards a high-speed rail network.

Of course the chaotic government was at times being adventurous in spite of itself, or because it had no choice, or because the more daring proposals applied to a safely distant future. Comically, the policy for care for the elderly came in the form of a Green Paper, no more than a consultative document, as if the government had the time to consult and act. The White Paper on carbon emissions set tough targets that would come into force conveniently after the next election. Gordon Brown intervened with a hangdog reluctance in dealing with the banks, towards which his government was still pathetically timid, pleading with them to lend to small businesses even though it was in many cases the biggest shareholder. The banks possessed the power they still retained because the government chose to keep a distance.

Politics has countless dimensions. There are always reasons specific to their time for governments acting in the way they do. The mild-mannered Attlee could transform Britain partly because the context after the Second World War gave him the space to do so. Thatcher made her moves only after a winter of discontent under Labour gave her the ammunition and cause to act. Cameron and Osborne proposed to cut the size of the state by 25 per cent in the summer of 2010, but could only follow their ideological crusade by blaming Labour for Britain's deficit. The expedient motives matter, but so do the subsequent policies, and on the whole the ones announced under Brown's leadership hinted at a coherent outlook that would certainly enhance the quality of most voters' lives.

No one noticed in the summer of 2009. Brown had lost the artist's gift to cast a spell. He managed it briefly when he became Prime Minister in the summer of 2007. Indeed, he created the ultimate work of political art, projecting himself as the apolitical, consensual father of the nation while planning for an early election that would smash the Conservatives to pieces. Then he was tempted to hold an even earlier election, but after much toing-and-froing failed to do so, and the spell was broken. Now voters saw only the obvious flaws.

Brown became a more hopeless communicator during most of 2009. When questioned he looked tetchy at best, woeful at worst. In public he could not resort to humour, a powerful weapon in the political artist's armoury. The veteran MP Gerald Kaufman once told me that Harold Wilson 'learned' to have a sense of humour. Wilson was an underestimated artist. Brown had a sense of humour, but chose not to deploy one of the most powerful weapons in politics.

Mistakenly, in the summer of 2009 Brown thought that he could play one of his oldest tricks of all, his favourite dividing line about investment versus cuts. But as ever the real story was more complicated than orthodoxy allowed. Across the media the summer narrative insisted that a deranged Brown and a deluded Balls were insanely insisting on a political argument in which they would in effect lie about Labour's future spending plans and compare fantasy figures with the Tories' spending cuts. In contrast the noble Chancellor, Darling, was supposedly fighting an internal battle with the support of Mandelson for a more credible message. This narrative was only partially correct.

In terms of framing the debate, Brown was on to something. Pre-election battles capture the essence of a divide between two parties. Policy details are always scarce and evasive. In the run-up to an election policies are often symbols rather than part of a detailed programme for power. Desperate for an audience, to get back into the debate, Brown articulated what he genuinely believed, that Labour would protect public services as assiduously as possible, whereas the Conservatives would cut them as a matter of ideology as much as expediency.

He had plenty of evidence to support this view. Cameron had declared openly that he wanted a smaller state and that he had 'entered politics to cut taxes'. Brown had increased investment in public services close to the level of equivalent countries in Europe. More recently Cameron and his shadow chancellor, George Osborne, had called for spending cuts at the height of the recession. Labour was planning to continue to invest beyond the election, in line with the US, Germany and France. In this debate at least Cameron and Osborne were on the Thatcherite right. But in Britain they were still being widely hailed as reforming modernizers and Labour was perceived as reckless.

Brown wanted to reframe the debate and had grounds to do so. He was strongly encouraged by the cabinet minister Sean Woodward, a Tory defector who had been an architect of John Major's victory in 1992. Woodward told Brown consistently in the summer that the Conservatives won in 1992 by exaggerating the scale of the threat posed by Labour and by playing up their tax-cutting proposals even though they knew that taxes would have to rise after the election. He convinced Brown that Labour could do this in reverse by placing a similar emphasis on its commitment to public spending compared with the Tories' cuts.

Brown pounced on the advice. He knew from his experience as shadow chancellor and Chancellor that the economic debate had to be politicized accessibly, and in a way that presented the choice in a favourable light for Labour. His mistake was to get carried away at a point of maximum public cynicism about British politics, claiming repeatedly in his clashes with Cameron during Prime Minister's Question Time in the summer that there would be overall year-on-year increases in public spending if Labour was elected, as if the need to repay the growing debt was a minor diversion. His distortion was no greater than John Major's during the 1992 election, but he did not have the authority or support, internally and externally, to get away with it. Fragile claims were no longer possible in the age of round-the-clock scrutiny, at least it was not possible for Brown.

In particular Darling was having none of it. Feeling betrayed, and no longer willing to be loyal as a matter of course, he was privately contemptuous of Brown. He was starting to enjoy the approval of columnists, especially the Conservative-supporting ones, for his 'realism'. He did not stop to wonder whether he was being hailed in the media partly because his technocratic, non-political style was helping the Conservative cause as much as Brown's too overtly partisan projection of the economic debate.

At this point, the summer of 2009, Mandelson and Balls were working well together, an alliance even more unlikely than the one that Mandelson re-formed with Brown. In a spirit of fleeting creativity the two of them worked out a more credible formula on tax and spend, a third way between Brown and his Chancellor. Mandelson delivered the words at a House of Commons' press gallery lunch in July:

> Of course there will be pressures on spending after 2011 and constraints for the next decade. But this depends on our success in preventing short-run unemployment turning into long-term joblessness, and on our investments in those sources of future employment.
>
> This is why maintaining spending and investment in our underlying strengths throughout the recession is vital. The Conservatives are focusing on the exit strategy of current policies before these have had the chance to work.

This was an intelligent, modest and true portrayal of the political divide, although not as vivid as Brown wanted it to be. The Conservatives had created the divide by opposing a fiscal stimulus during the recession and calling instead for cuts in public spending, creating a genuine opportunity for Labour and the Liberal Democrats. But Brown wanted to make bigger claims. Mandelson had a theory as to why he persisted: 'When you have no constituency in the media I suppose you feel the need to shout very loudly in order to be heard,' he observed privately. Brown shouted so loudly that more voters turned away amidst talk of noisy divisions in government. Most cabinet ministers left for their summer holidays in despair for the second successive year. 'We've thrown away the summer because of Gordon,' declared one cabinet minister to me, someone who was once close to him.

But once more the critics failed to offer alternative rallying cries. Brown had half a point in insisting that Labour could not win an election in a thousand years by merely echoing the Conservatives' message. 'Give us a fourth term. We will cut in the same way as the Conservatives!' was not exactly a slogan to galvanize a long-serving government towards victory. There were no obvious routes towards victory and not much in the way of slogans.

Indeed, Brown started to revive the old slogan from the 1990s. He stood for the many and not the few, he claimed, like the leader of an ageing rock group returning to a long-ago hit. The Conservatives started to deploy the same words too, just as Heath/Wilson/Callaghan had done in the 1970s. They looked back for policies and language, repeating the same corporatist errors when the world had moved on.

Towards the end of the summer term David Cameron bumped into Charles Clarke. The full-time mutineer looked up at the Conservative leader and said: 'Don't worry, we'll get rid of Gordon before the election.' Cameron responded: 'That's exactly what I'm worried about.' The rebels went off on their summer holidays planning vaguely to strike again. Cameron went away in a more commanding position

407

than at any point in his leadership, fearing only the removal of the Prime Minister. Brown headed back to Scotland wondering what levers to pull after another traumatic year.

When a prime minister is in trouble a familiar sequence plays out each summer and early autumn, a recurrent pattern in the unpredictable rhythms of British politics. Over the summer break there is some speculation that the unpopular prime minister will return refreshed. When he or she returns the situation now gets worse rather than better. After 1992 the sequence became darkly comical under John Major. At the end of each July he would disappear, battered and exhausted. At the start of September he would be back for another relaunch, one that lasted around ten seconds before the party's civil war erupted on an even more intense level. To a degree the pattern applied to Blair in his later years. With Brown the precision of the repetitive nightmare was almost too much for him to bear.

At the end of August the Scottish justice minister, Kenny MacAskill, allowed the so-called Lockerbie bomber Abdelbaset Ali Mohmed al-Megrahi to be released on compassionate grounds. He had been found guilty of the bombing of Pan Am flight 103 above the Scottish village of Lockerbie in December 1988, in which 270 people were killed. Megrahi had always insisted on his innocence and was supposedly dying of cancer.

The story of his release caused as much of a media frenzy as Darling's interview the year before. Various ministers insisted that the issue was a matter for the Scottish government in Edinburgh, conveniently led by the SNP. But in the confused devolution settlement the British government remained responsible for foreign policy and was bound to have been involved at some level in the release. What did Brown know about it all? That was the question raging as politicians returned for the pre-election fray in September. Brown was at Chequers and at first he tried silence as a form of evasion. The question was toxic. Of course he was indirectly complicit in such a move, and yet to acknowledge as much in the media hysteria would have destroyed his attempt to set the post-holiday agenda. He opted for silence and got into even more trouble as a result.

The row had little to do with substance, but reflected a revolutionary change in the political and media culture, as profound as the economic changes erupting around the globe. It was more about what we as a country expect from a prime minister in the modern era, or at least what the media expect. The new culture was entirely at odds with Brown's political style and explained why he had failed to engage with the electorate as Prime Minister. The drama was a sequel to the Damian McBride affair, a disaster brought about as a nervy, insecure government sought to address the might of the Internet. Brown's attempt to deploy silence as a way of killing a story exposed a naivety about the demands of the media in the post-Blair era.

Tony Blair was the architect of the new culture, and not the journalists who demanded that Brown must step forward to account for his role in the release. As far as policy was concerned, Blair was the most cautious prime minister in modern times, fearful of acting in ways that might alienate his so-called middle England supporters. In terms of communication he was a genuine revolutionary. Blair chose to be our guide around the clock, responding within seconds to every event, from the death of Princess Diana to the imprisonment of Deirdre in *Coronation Street*. He was a rolling commentator on his leadership and an eternal advocate, flexible as to what he was talking about and willing at all times to be held to account.

The revolutionary impact is underestimated still. Margaret Thatcher never gave prearranged interviews to the *Today* programme. She hardly appeared in public in the build-up to the Falklands War or during the conflict itself beyond delivering a few statements calling on us all to 'rejoice'. Her low media profile meant that a single subsequent engagement with an angry voter in which she was questioned about the sinking of the *Belgrano* became a historic event.

The contrast with Blair in the build-up to Iraq – when he gave a daily press conference and chose to appear in front of angry voters – was like entering two different worlds, and incidentally challenges the view that he was a 'liar'. If Blair had something to hide, he could have hidden it.

Brown developed an entirely different approach to leadership, which was less ostentatious but sometimes effective. Whereas Blair tended to advocate first and develop policies second, Brown opted for the reverse. He implemented some courageous policies, but it was not till after their implementation that he became a public advocate on their behalf.

Some in the media purported to despise Blair for his presentational skills, but they did not really do so. They loved the ubiquity and the self-deprecating advocacy, which is why a lot of them turned later to David Cameron, who modelled his leadership style on Blair.

If Blair had been Prime Minister, Alastair Campbell would have phoned within twenty-four hours to tell him that his silence over the prisoner's release had become the story and that the only way to change the narrative was to speak out. Brown had no equivalent to Campbell. Only Peter Mandelson or Ed Balls would have had the authority or courage to make such a call, and they had big departments to run.

For Brown, breaking the silence would have been difficult over an issue as complex as one involving Libya, Lockerbie and relations with the US, and at a time when he was, as Mandelson had noted, without a constituency in the media. But as one of Blair's former senior advisers told me: 'As Prime Minister you face a decision every hour which comes down to one question – do you want to cut your throat or slit your wrists?' In opting for silence Brown sought to avoid the question and predictably it became the strident story.

By the time of Labour's conference the 'Lockerbie bomber' affair had faded, but it had damaged Brown and the operation around him, one that was not quick enough on its feet to deal with a media storm. His party conference speech was the next big moment, again an event in which he had an audience without having to fight to be heard, one of the last such occasions before the election.

He blew it by trying too hard. Drafts of the conference speech were doing the rounds in Number Ten by the beginning of August. One adviser told me it went through more than forty drafts. At one point the speech was going to be a personal address about his extraordinary journey in Number Ten, one that he had never envisaged: the collapse of the banks, the nationalizations, the income-tax increases on high earners. He was planning to acknowledge openly that he was unpopular, that his personality had become an issue and to admit to faults and some mistakes. It was going to be an attempt at a game-changing speech, one that surprised, a cathartic moment that took the breath away.

But in the end Brown could not face delivering such a personal account. 'It's not me. I can't do it,' he told his closest advisers. He was also worried about headlines proclaiming: 'It's all my fault – Brown'. Instead he churned out a spate of supposedly new policy announcements, on the naive assumption that voters paid as close attention to politics as he did. The announcements mattered little, and most were not implemented, but they had the impact of making the speech too dense, as if he was delivering one of his budget speeches.

For the second year running he spoke against the background of heightened speculation that he would not lead Labour into the next election, and also for the second year running he had the kernel of an argument about the recession: that the Conservatives had faced the 'economic call of the century' and had called it wrong. The powerful argument was lost in the mountain of disparate policy announcements.

At least as significant, the tensions at the top of the government were rising. To the great unease of Darling and Mandelson, Brown made virtually no reference to spending cuts. He said merely that the government would raise tax 'at the very top, cut costs ... and make savings where we know we can' to protect front-line services, hardly the prelude to discussions about that autumn's pre-budget report.

The pre-budget report was a mess, as all Darling's budgets and pre-budget reports had been for different reasons. Mandelson had hoped that the message in the report and the policy details would be decided by the late summer and every message honed to prepare for its unveiling. The key players could not agree on what the message should be.

Yet again the bulk of the columnists in the newspapers blamed Brown and Balls. Darling was portrayed as the noble hero arguing for a Calvinistic message about public spending cuts. Balls in particular wanted to highlight that the government would continue to invest in education. This was seen as blasphemous in most of the media.

The orthodox media narrative went along these lines:

> The Chancellor, Alistair Darling, had a tough time of it at the hands of the reckless Brown and his sidekick Balls. Darling was increasingly assertive, an economically realistic and politically attuned Chancellor. Sadly he was hampered by his neighbour, who was disastrously obsessed about dividing lines with the Tories.
>
> Balls wanted to spend more on education in order to improve his chances of becoming the next leader of the Labour party. Quite sensibly the Treasury wanted to increase VAT rather than put up national insurance contributions. Equally sensibly Darling wanted to spell out in more detail how the cuts would fall. He had the full support of Peter Mandelson, who has fallen out fatally with the Brownite entourage. As a result of this calamitous pre-budget report, the government will not dare to have a budget next spring. Therefore the election will be held in March and Labour will be slaughtered.

But this assessment did not add up.

Part of the gap arose from the internal contradiction in the accounts. How could Darling have become both more assertive and yet hugely disappointed with his own pre-budget report because Brown and Balls prevailed over him?

There were other elements of the orthodox account that did not quite make sense. Most fundamentally the participants had a background, a past history, that did not tally in this new narrative. When Brown and Balls were at the Treasury they managed to deliver economic policy in ways that were electorally popular and at least credible at the time. Of course, they were operating in an almost comically more benevolent climate, but Labour chancellors tended to be persistently unpopular whatever the economic weather.

Brown and Balls had not been politically illiterate and had not suddenly become so. Conversely, it would have been surprising if Darling had acquired so quickly all the formidable skills required to meet the immediate challenge and would therefore be flourishing were it not for the lunacy of the Brownite entourage. Darling's genius in previous ministerial assignments was to keep his policy area out of the news altogether. The collapse of the economy could not go unnoticed in quite the same way.

There was another twist, involving the reporting of political dramas. The source of a revelation tended to be treated by journalists as authoritative and those on the other side of the source's argument as wrong. Would a further Treasury-inspired rise in VAT have been more popular or wiser economically, as some reports implied? Similarly all parties agonized about whether giving more details of spending cuts was the right pre-election move.

Away from the media glare there was a broad agreement between Brown, Balls, Darling and Mandelson about the overall strategy, protecting front-line services, putting up taxes as part of the package, and making clear that the deficit would be cut. Most specifically there was no argument about the need to maintain spending levels for another year. Darling had also agreed several months before that spending on education would go up slightly in real terms.

His dispute with Balls was over the presentation of this decision. The Treasury wanted the focus of the pre-budget report to be on the stringency of its approach, rather than to highlight the increase in spending. Balls thought it was ridiculous to hide a decision that showed how the government was prioritizing education in an otherwise bleak set of plans. He had a conversation with Darling on the Sunday before the pre-budget report and his officials were engaged in discussions with their Treasury equivalents until the final moments to ensure that what Balls regarded as a positive message was not underplayed or ignored entirely. There was no row between Balls and Darling about the principle of an increase in spending on schools.

At several meetings with Brown, Darling also made it clear that the Treasury preferred a VAT rise to an NIC increase and that it wanted to spell out in more detail where future cuts would fall. But some ministers believe that this was not necessarily Darling's own firmly settled view, and that as an MP representing a relatively marginal seat he was aware of the downside of an even tougher approach in a statement that already included more overt tax rises than any government had introduced for decades.

The actual strategy was less timid than most reports conveyed. The decision to put up taxes again, with a further increase in NI contributions, was one that caused angst beyond the Treasury. Brown had his doubts at one point, not surprising for someone who became Chancellor in 1997 convinced that it was politically impossible to make the outright case for any tax rises. Now he contemplated an election with VAT going back up, income-tax rises for high earners, and a phased NIC increase, which was another income-tax increase for all but low earners.

That decision was made partly to give some credibility to the limited spending objectives and to signal that the government was willing to make unpopular decisions in order to repay debt over time. Electoral calculations played their part too. Would the Conservatives put up VAT in their emergency budget? How would they pay for their schools programme if they did not commit to Labour's increase in spending? Such questions were widely dismissed as those tired old 'dividing lines', as if disagreement was unhealthy, but politics was partly about a divide based on values and expedient judgement connected with those core beliefs. The fuss over dividing lines was a red herring.

Other highly charged issues were much more significant, although they were not directly connected with specific economic policies. Darling continued to feel a deep sense of personal grievance that Brown had contemplated ditching him for Balls the previous summer, and was at the very least relaxed if the media hailed once more his supposedly more prudent approach. Brown still rated Balls's judgement on economics and politics more highly than any other figure – not easy for a chancellor to swallow.

Meanwhile, some Brownites complained that Darling was not a robust enough advocate at pivotal moments, such as in the delivery of budgets and pre-budget reports. Other cabinet ministers fumed to journalists about the largesse accorded to Balls as they contemplated heavy cuts in their departments. Peter Mandelson was furious at Brown's manoeuvring in Europe that had resulted in the relatively obscure Baroness Ashton securing the foreign affairs portfolio.

At a key moment ministers were at war, but they could not agree what they were at war over. There were echoes of the two attempted coups, when rebels were not sure what it was precisely they were trying to do and yet their muddled scheming was enough to cause confusion. Now at the very top ministers fumed over disparate matters, all of them unavoidably linked to Brown.

The range of voices widened dramatically towards the end of the year. In particular, and against character, the deputy leader, Harriet Harman, joined the band of discontented cabinet ministers. Her disaffection was highly significant because, to her considerable credit, she had displayed a dignified loyalty to Blair when he sacked her early in Labour's first term and had behaved with tolerance when Brown treated her with tactless thoughtlessness after she had won the deputy leadership contest. But by the end of 2009 even she had had enough.

She was motivated partly by the broader altruistic factor. Reading the polls, she despaired of Labour recovering under Brown. More specifically she was furious about what she perceived as Number Ten briefing against her, a resentment heightened by her exclusion from key meetings about the forthcoming election. In the build-up to the first attempted coup and to some extent during the second she had been wholly loyal to Brown. By the end of 2009 she had ceased to feel any loyalty at all. Like Darling she felt betrayed. The third attempted coup was taking shape.

But Darling and Harman were not close. Darling shared Brown and Mandelson's doubts about her strategic abilities. She viewed Mandelson with even more wariness than she did Brown. Her closest ties were with women on the centre left, the former cabinet minister Patricia Hewitt and the *Guardian* columnist Polly Toynbee, who had been calling on Brown to go for eighteen months. Her husband was the trade unionist Jack Dromey, a senior figure in the mighty Unite union, widely regarded as a Brownite fiefdom. But the union, a product of several mergers, was incapable of embodying any one single strand in the Labour party. Dromey had become as disillusioned with Brown as his wife, partly because of her treatment at the hands of first Blair and then Brown.

Meanwhile David Miliband was more convinced than ever that he was part of a very poor government and had come closer to concluding that his leadership would be part of a solution. But he was not especially close to Harman, even though she had decided that Labour would have more chance of avoiding a slaughter if Miliband became leader.

Here were the seeds of a coup and also the seeds of total failure. Harman did not trust Mandelson. Darling did not rate Harman highly. Miliband was close to Mandelson but not to Harman or Darling.

Towards the end of the year and over the Christmas break, Charles Clarke planned his final strike against Brown. This time he was determined to succeed and thought he could do so. The general election was only months away. The issue of a new leader being forced to call an early election did not apply as it would have done during the previous summer when Labour was even lower in the polls. Crucially, Clarke knew there was more tangible discontent in the cabinet than during previous insurrections. He had held meetings or conversations with virtually every senior minister and was convinced they would make a move if Labour MPs displayed their discontent too.

As Clarke conducted his ministerial tour, this is what he found. Mandelson was moodily despondent, protesting about what he regarded as Brown's amateurishness compared with the smooth public performances of Blair, as well as still fuming that Brown had failed to secure a post in Europe for a big figure that might even have included himself. Darling despaired about Brown's 'investment versus cuts' dividing line and wanted to reframe economic policy. He was dreading the build-up to the budget. Douglas Alexander saw chaos and defeat heading Labour's way under Brown, who he felt had failed to establish himself as a national leader and a leader of a team. David

Miliband thought the government was hopeless. Straw was more ambivalent, but felt excluded from strategic meetings in which he believed, like so many others, that he had an indispensable contribution to make. Harman had had enough.

Clarke knew that the key to any success was securing new voices to the cause, not the 'usual suspects'. At which point for once the disparate motives and tactics of the rebels coalesced. Clarke was close to another former cabinet minister, Patricia Hewitt. The two of them had worked together in Neil Kinnock's office in the 1980s, stormy days in opposition, harder to take than those in government that seemed to have more point to them. Hewitt was also close to Harman. The two of them had been senior figures in the National Council for Civil Liberties in the 1970s and early 1980s. Hewitt had been dropped from the cabinet by Brown when he became Prime Minister in 2007, one of the few so-called Blairites not to have benefited from his neurotic balancing act. Like nearly all those closer to the former Prime Minister her response to demotion was to leave politics altogether. Already she had announced she was standing down from parliament at the election.

Geoff Hoon was also handily disenchanted. Brown had indicated that he would get the Foreign Affairs portfolio in Europe. Like Mandelson he was furious about the appointment of Baroness Ashton.

Brown spent Christmas and the New Year in a state of considerable anxiety, knowing that there would be one final attempt to remove him. This time he was especially worried because he feared that the disenchanted Mandelson, his saviour in the summer, was directly involved. Mandelson was not in fact at the centre of things for once. He knew that the rebels were stirring and felt less inclined to come to Brown's rescue. That was more or less the limit of his engagement, although he remained in constant contact with David Miliband. Charles Clarke had told Miliband that one hundred and fifty Labour MPs would declare their support for a leadership contest, a figure so overwhelming that Brown would be doomed.

The third coup looked the most pathetic of the lot. In fact Brown was in real danger this time, in a way that he had not been in the previous two. Leading cabinet ministers were almost ready to wield the dagger. But the qualification is important. None of them were unequivocally willing to do so. Once more there was no great coordination. On the day before the insurrection Darling knew something big was about to kick off, but he had not decided what to do in response.

Halfway through the first Prime Minister's Question Time of the year, in which Brown performed with some of his old verve and wit, news circulated that Hewitt and Hoon were calling for a leadership contest. But very quickly the two of them revealed the limits of their political subtlety when they behaved in a way that was laughably disingenuous. Over lunchtime they gave a series of interviews in which they insisted that they were calling for a leadership contest, but not for the removal of Brown. They would not say how they would vote in a contest, but argued that the exercise would clear the air.

The rebels' attempt at an act of catharsis was stifled by their transparent scheming. Hewitt and Hoon were both standing down at the election showing the limits of their commitment to the party's future. Labour MPs were deeply unimpressed by the manoeuvre and felt no inclination to join a risky crusade under a dodgy leadership. Instead they rushed to condemn their botched initiative.

Brown was not to know at first the scale of the dismissive condemnation and nor were the cabinet ministers wondering whether this was the moment when they would finally dump their leader. After Prime Minister's Question Time Brown rushed to his office in the House of Commons to hit the phones in one more attempt to rescue his leadership. This time there was no Mandelson by his side. He was alone with a few aides contacting cabinet ministers in order to secure their support. There was an extraordinary few hours in which Brown did not get the public declaration of loyalty he needed. Ed Balls arrived at a reception in Number Ten and dismissed the coup loyally as he did so. Ed Miliband toured the studios in defence of Brown. At first that was more or less it.

I spoke to Stewart Wood, one of Brown's longest-serving advisers, at lunchtime on the day the coup was staged. He was with the PM in his office. Wood tried to put a brave face on the absence of cabinet support, telling me that he thought it valuable that ministers were saving their fire in case the rebels had more surprises to come. In truth he knew that some members of the cabinet were contemplating turning their fire on Brown.

In a brief conversation Mandelson told Brown he would issue a statement of support. The subsequent words were extraordinary:

> No one should overreact to this initiative. It is not led by members of the government. No one has resigned from the government. The prime minister continues to have the support of his colleagues and we should carry on government business as usual.

Note the lack of any personal endorsement from Mandelson. He was keeping options open. What if someone were to resign from the government? Should colleagues carry on government business as normal rather than rush out and buttress the position of a precarious Prime Minister? There was also no outright condemnation of the initiative. At the very least this was laid-back Mandelson compared with his hustle in defence of Brown during the late evening the previous June after Purnell had resigned.

Meanwhile from David Miliband, Harman, Darling and Straw there was silence. That was not the case with most Labour MPs. They rushed to the microphones to attack the move. No additional rebel stepped forth beyond the hard core.

This was a dramatic reverse from the first coup in the autumn of 2008 when cabinet ministers, Harman in particular, were loyal and expressed their concern about restless Labour MPs. I saw Harman early that autumn and she told me: 'The cabinet is loyal. The members are loyal. The parliamentary Labour party is a problem but they have got to calm down. There will not be a change of leader.' By January 2010 Labour MPs had calmed down. They realized it was too late to make a switch. But Harman and the cabinet had become the restless ones.

419

Brown was calm, as oddly he tended to be at times of high crisis. He was often in a state of panic-stricken fury over routine matters such as where a story was placed in the running order on a news bulletin, or whether it was placed at all. Facing a cabinet revolt, he told his advisers that he sensed Labour MPs had no appetite for another insurrection, and with a solid focus arranged to meet senior ministers.

The ministers were quickly revising their objectives. Indeed the objectives were never clear. Harman wanted at the least a negotiating ploy in order to strengthen her position. Similarly Darling sought a context where he could assert more control over economic policy. Aware that Labour MPs were not responding in the way that Charles Clarke had suggested, several ministers aimed to weaken Brown but not to kill him off.

Brown was focused and engaged as Harman, Straw and Darling met him in Number Ten early in the afternoon. Harman and Straw met Brown together. Harman told him that as the party's deputy leader she had a right to be involved in the planning for the election and complained that she had been the subject of too many hostile briefings. Brown told her that she must attend all relevant election meetings. She would join Mandelson and Alexander in planning the election and fronting it. He said with a degree of sincerity that he knew nothing about briefings against her.

Harman was casually dismissed sometimes in discussions between Downing Street advisers and political journalists. Such exchanges are common in politics when journalists and advisers become close. The journalist offers an anecdote exposing the apparent weakness of a cabinet minister. The adviser reciprocates with a despairing sigh and an alternative anecdote. A story appears subsequently. Sometimes the adviser is a little taken aback to see the exchanges in print. I saw Harman and Dromey one evening in November when she had been criticized in *The Times* by unnamed advisers. They were upset and furious. I suggested that some of it was unintentional, with no coordinated media operation against her. They did not believe me. But she emerged from her meeting in January with Brown satisfied about the newly clarified arrangements. Straw was similarly reassured.

Making the most of Brown's fragility, Darling insisted that he have complete freedom to speak out about the government's intentions to cut public spending in order to reduce the deficit. He also told Brown that he did not want Ed Balls to take part in future pre-budget meetings as he had done in the build-up to all previous economic statements. Brown agreed to all of this. He had no choice. Shut away from the rolling television news, he was not entirely sure that the revolt had petered out while he was speaking to his restive cabinet ministers.

He was reluctant to bend to Darling's pressure, although he did not show this when they met. Once more he was battling for his job and affected agreement, saying that he recognized the need to achieve a balance in the projection of the economic message and that cuts were part of it. Of course Darling could speak out. After all he was Chancellor. Darling left his meeting satisfied. He arranged three newspaper interviews in the next four days in which he emphasized the need for sweeping spending cuts once the recovery had been secured. He was like a liberated prisoner and could not control himself. Even Mandelson got fed up with reading Darling stating yet again how awful it was going to be. 'I think a bit of light is required as well as darkness,' he observed after reading the third Darling interview in the immediate aftermath of the attempted coup. Darling's message was to Brown and Balls as well as the markets, media and the electorate: 'Finally I'm in charge.'

Straw, Harman and Darling declared their belated loyalty. This left only David Miliband. By mid-afternoon Miliband should have realized the game was up and rushed out a declaration of loyalty. He opted for silence and then later he issued only an ambiguous statement. Not used to being exposed politically, the Foreign Secretary moved too slowly. He was a man of ideas and at this stage of his career he was more than a quick-thinking schemer. He was also isolated in the Foreign Office, as the drama unfolded.

Mandelson was not at the centre of the drama either, excluded by Harman, and therefore of limited use, although he spoke to David Miliband several times during the afternoon. Later he surfaced to give a remarkably candid interview on BBC's *Newsnight* where he stated:

'The simple truth is that Labour party members did not want to change their leader.' During the *Newsnight* interview Mandelson did not utter a word of praise for Brown. Miliband told friends later that if Labour's poll ratings had not improved slightly after the turn of the year Brown would have been removed, but the slight narrowing of the gap had given him a degree of momentum.

The third coup, failing as spectacularly as the previous two, marked another moment of extreme ambiguity in Brown's eternally precarious career. On one level Brown was hugely relieved and curiously liberated. Ironically he was safer as Prime Minister than he had been since the calamitous non-election in the autumn of 2007. There would not be a fourth coup, with an election so close. He knew now for sure that he would lead Labour into the election and would not be removed humiliatingly in advance. Some Blairites told me at around this time that Brown would look for an excuse to resign, as he would not want to fight the election. Once more they wilfully misread him, their loathing leading them to reach the wrong conclusions. He was utterly determined to fight on and still thought the election was winnable. Brown was no coward, as they had chosen to believe. If anything he was too driven, failing to recognize that there was more to life than the relentless quest for personal political success. At this phase of his career, the harder he pursued it, the more elusive his still unfulfilled ambition became. He wanted to win an election as a leader, the missing laurels in his long career at the top. He would do whatever it took in order to win, or at least to get a chance to do so.

In the immediate aftermath, advisers to Brown noted a surprising calm, an echo of the period when he knew that Blair was finally leaving Number Ten. It was as if another heavy sack of coal had been lifted from his creaking back. Brown had been Prime Minister for more than two years during which he feared a coup might erupt at any time. This additional pressure was another burden. A leader who was instinctively suspicious and wary he lived in fear of his colleagues, wondering who might betray him and when. At least Margaret Thatcher was taken by surprise when her cabinet rebelled against her in November 1990. Brown was afraid of such an event, holding meetings with the likes of Mandelson, Miliband and Darling at one moment, and at the next moment wondering whether they would call on him to go. Suddenly, at the end of a day in which he was fleetingly in extreme danger, the prospect was gone for ever.

Yet the damage was immense on three different levels. Voters might not pay much attention to politics, but even the most distracted would have noticed that not even Brown's colleagues seemed to have faith in him. If they were not supportive, why should the electorate give him backing? The accumulated impact of the coups was to convey a sense that Brown was only just clinging on, to the despair of many in his party. This was hardly an attractive image as he prepared to lead Labour towards a challenging election.

Equally important, Brown was weakened and not reinforced by the failed coup, even if he felt free from further internal threats. Most significantly Darling seized almost total control of economic policy and preparations for the budget. Tory-supporting columnists lauded him for his prudence compared with the alleged recklessness of Brown and Balls. Darling became increasingly assured the more he was praised in the media. He was discovering how intoxicating it could be to read that you are the star of the government, saving it from a wayward Prime Minister. But Darling still lacked the political cunning and presentational gifts that Brown and Balls at their best had displayed at the Treasury.

Instead he walked into a near-fatal trap. Striding on to the Tories' terrain that the debt was the overwhelming issue, he insisted that Labour would be ruthlessly prudent. He wanted no upbeat message about increased investment, even though the government was planning to spend more in the short term. Although cuts were unavoidable, Darling never pointed out that they would take place from a much higher base than in the 1980s. Instead, on the eve of the general election he happily agreed that the cuts would be deeper than those imposed by Thatcher in the 1980s. Then, as the election campaign began, George Osborne became less prudent, announcing a cut in the planned increase in national insurance. The same columnists who praised Darling for insisting that Labour did not have a penny to spare now hailed Osborne as a genius for, in effect, spending billions of pounds on a tax cut rather than repaying debt. Labour was in the worst of all worlds, preaching gloom without a clear positive message. The Tories also shamelessly began to make spending commitments in the way that Brown and Balls had wanted to do. Once more the commentators who approved of Darling's managerial austerity praised the Tories for achieving momentum. A stronger Brown would never have let this happen, but he was less in control of the election campaign as Prime Minister than he was as Chancellor for the previous three.

One instance of his weakness related to VAT. Brown and Balls wanted to include a manifesto pledge not to increase VAT for the next parliament. Darling vetoed the move on the grounds that it would appear irresponsible. Senior Treasury officials were fans of VAT increases as one way of tackling the deficit. Darling spoke increasingly for the Treasury and for his own reputation with the Conservative-dominated media. As a result Osborne made hay, announcing good-news policies as if the economy was booming and getting away with it.

But the Conservative duo was also showing signs of fragility in the early pre-election manoeuvres. Two days before the attempted coup Labour published extensive details of the Conservatives' tax and spending plans, showing how they did not remotely add up. To the surprise of Brown and his entourage, Cameron and Osborne were thrown by the onslaught, behaving as if they had not expected such an attack, as if their words and those of their shadow cabinet colleagues had no rigorous meaning beyond a headline for the following day or perhaps following hour. Cameron gave a BBC interview in which he said that the marriage tax allowance was an aspiration and not a pledge. An hour later he confirmed that the proposal was a firm commitment, but he did not know the precise details. Neil Kinnock had been lambasted in the media for his woolly comments on Labour's tax plans in the run-up to the 1992 election. The army of Conservative supporters in the British media made little of Cameron's gaffe. Nonetheless the Conservatives conveyed a sense that they were not quite ready for the fray. Their slogans were confusing and contradictory. Their posters featuring Cameron were immediately mocked on the Internet. The polls started to show a narrowing of the Conservatives' lead. Brown was in good form at Prime Minister's Question Time, finally cracking the occasional joke. He had almost found a prime-ministerial voice now that the election was moving into view, partisan and cunning, closer to the old Brown than the cumbersome attempt to project a Churchillian one-nation gravity.

Brown told his inner entourage that he was almost excited about the forthcoming election. Finally it was in sight. There were no more agonies over timing. It was happening on 6 May, the same day as the local elections. Brown had been a sceptic about 'choice' in public services. He proved to be one about choice over election dates. He was much more content when he had no choice, although he neurotically checked out the possibilities of going earlier when it appeared that Labour had acquired some momentum. It was never going to happen. The party was broke and needed the impetus of the local elections to maximize turnout, rather than contest two campaigns in the space of a few weeks, as happened in 1992 when John Major opted for an election in April.

Only one major event was in store before the general election: what was to be Darling's final budget. In effect he delivered his second budget in the space of a few months. The pre-budget report had become a budget, one of the many innovations Brown introduced when he was Chancellor. Darling complained with good humour that he had made so many announcements back then, at the end of the year, that there were not many left. He had no room politically or economically for any game-changing moves. Instead in the budget speech he made a strong case for the role of government, in the recession and in sustaining recovery. In policy terms it was a non-event, and yet the policies he had introduced since becoming Chancellor, sometimes reluctantly, were those that Brown had sometimes yearned to present as Chancellor but concluded were politically impossible. Labour ended its third term with higher tax rates for top earners and an overall tax take closer to those of other equivalent countries in

Europe. The tragedy for Brown, Labour and the country was that nearly all the additional cash would be spent on repaying debt. The argument about higher taxes being an investment that improved the quality of all our lives, rich or poor, was lost in an economic emergency. Nevertheless, amidst seething discontent on the centre left, conditioned for disillusionment, as well as on the right, by the end the government had become radical almost in spite of itself.

The Labour election campaign was darkly ineffective from the beginning. A big part of the problem was Brown himself. Across the country voters told tired Labour activists that they were turning away because of their leader. Conscious of how he was perceived, Brown became an even less confident public performer. He had been told to look more cheerful and so he smiled, but he smiled by numbers, and nearly always at the wrong moment, when a deadly serious question was being posed. He was not listening to the words, but thinking suddenly of what Mandelson and Campbell had told him about his public demeanour: cheer up! So he smiled like a demented mourner misreading the mood of a funeral. This is what can happen to public performers when they are drained of confidence. Performance becomes self-parody, pieces of well-meant advice a source of torment. Mandelson and Campbell were too aware of Brown's presentational problems and limited his appearances to the most controlled situations. Brown was emotionally drained. His gruelling itinerary sapped him further.

Part of him wanted to set the campaign alight with a grand gesture. He drafted a speech on the eve of the election setting out his plans to stand down within a year of the poll. He wanted to make clear that a vote for Labour did not mean a full term of Brown. But after such a long period in power, New Labour's past became a guide. Balls, Mandelson and Alexander were all opposed to the move, citing what happened when Blair had pre-announced his departure, a move that became destabilizing on several different fronts. The speech he never delivered would probably not have made a great deal of difference either way. By then the course was set.

At a time when Labour needed to take some risks in terms of policy and message, the architects of the campaign played it safe. Brown and Mandelson in particular were conditioned to be cautious after the defeats in the 1980s and early 1990s that had defined their politics. They wanted to convey a single message: Do not risk the recovery by letting in the Conservatives. After thirteen years in power Labour needed more than a timid warning to inspire voters disillusioned by economic and political turmoil. Mandelson had banned Whelan from Labour's HQ. Darling had banned Balls from Number Ten for key economic meetings. Brown had acquiesced. He had no choice. He had grown weak.

Halfway through the campaign Brown and Mandelson agreed that he needed to be seen in slightly less controlled circumstances. There were limits to the excitement that could be generated from an appearance at a supermarket by someone who looked as if he could do with a good night's sleep. The entirely correct decision to loosen things up a bit led to the most famous event of the campaign, one of the most bizarre episodes in any general election of modern times.

Instead of another photo charade in a shopping centre or hospital, Brown stopped off in Rochdale to meet real voters. One of them was Gillian Duffy, a lifelong Labour supporter, who had popped out to buy a loaf of bread.

Brown had been visiting a community re-offender project in Rochdale when Duffy called out to him and asked why he was not addressing the debt crisis. As part of the new 'real voters' strategy, she was ushered by an aide to speak directly to the Prime Minister.

She asked him politely about a range of issues including the national debt, education and immigration.

At this point she said: 'You can't say anything about immigrants ... all these eastern Europeans are coming in, where are they flocking from?' Brown answered her questions and, as they parted, Duffy praised Labour education policy, describing Brown as a 'nice man' and telling reporters she had already filled in her postal ballot, voting Labour. As he got into his ministerial Jaguar, the Prime Minister complimented the former council worker for coming from 'a good family' and said: 'It's very nice to see you. Take care.'

The discussion was destined to get little coverage on the day's election broadcasts, but Brown was still wearing a microphone provided by Sky News, which recorded him turning to his aide Justin Forsyth and growling: 'That was a disaster.'

'Whose idea was that?' he continued, and then blamed 'Sue' – Sue Nye, his longest-serving aide and friend.

The aide asked what Duffy had said.

He replied: 'Everything, she was just a sort of bigoted woman who said she used to be Labour.'

The comments were relayed to Duffy, who was aghast that Brown – 'a man who is going to lead this country, an educated person' – would make such an accusation. She protested: 'I'm very upset. What was bigoted in what I said?' Later she told journalists that she would 'rip up' her postal vote.

Minutes later Brown arrived for a BBC radio interview with Jeremy Vine. While he was live on air, Vine played the Prime Minister his comments. Once again incapable of hiding how he felt, he held his head in his hand as he listened. His apology was stuttering and couched in equivocal language.

With the row dominating the afternoon, Brown was forced to abandon plans to prepare for the following day's TV debate. He telephoned Duffy to say sorry and then went to her house to make another apology.

Elections are based on an illusion that political leaders like and respect every single voter they meet. Voters are allowed to harangue leaders, but never the other way around. In private, no doubt leaders across the world despair of voters that they meet, but they never do so in public. In being recorded unawares by a microphone that should have been switched off, Brown had smashed the illusion to pieces.

Some such sequence had been bound to happen sooner or later. Because Brown was obsessed with the media he assumed that he was media-aware. He was not. Ever since Brown became leader, indeed from the day he launched his campaign to replace Blair, when the autocue blocked the cameras' view of his opening speech, he had shown little awareness of how television works.

Brown's reaction highlighted the dangers of being at the top of politics for such a long time. Even his closest allies despaired, pointing out that they met the likes of Duffy every time they left Westminster and returned to the real world. Brown had not done so for ages. He also had a heightened sense of how the media might report the exchange. This was more understandable. Desperate to highlight Labour's policies, such as the re-offenders project he had visited in Rochdale, he assumed that the bulletins would now focus on his exchange with a voter that he decided had gone badly. He saw the imagined headlines: 'Voter takes on Brown ... Labour's campaign in crisis!' Not for the first time, his fear of a bad headline generated much worse.

Until his encounter in Rochdale, Brown was still opting for controlled situations, meeting reliable Labour supporters in carefully chosen locations. Even the televised debates were governed by comforting rules that made too much spontaneity impossible. But in his exchange with Gillian Duffy he was, almost for the first time in twenty years, exposed in a public context. For a few minutes he did not know what would happen next. Wisely, Labour's strategists had decided their lifeless campaign needed some sparks, even if they did not have this particular explosion in mind. Brown was also keen, in theory, to meet so-called ordinary voters, but unused to conversing authentically in public, he assumed that his few minutes with Gillian Duffy were a disaster.

He felt he was drowning because he was not entirely in control. Once one of the sharpest readers of politics, he read his own dismal forebodings into an innocuous exchange, as if nothing but total control of a public encounter could yield success.

Trailing in third place, Brown lived in fear of anything that could make matters worse. In releasing his fearful frustration about an incident that had gone well, he managed to make matters much, much worse. He could not read political situations any more.

In looking back at his three years as Prime Minister, one of his closest allies reflected that by the time Brown finally acquired the top job in 2007 he had 'run out of juice'. He kept going for another three years until so many of his ideas and strategic assumptions tentatively formed when he became shadow chancellor in 1992 were challenged by a pensioner shopping for bread in 2010.

The election result transported him onto entirely new terrain: a hung parliament with Labour in second place in terms of votes and seats. If Labour had won a few more seats, a Lib/Lab coalition might have been possible. Senior pollsters argued after the election that such a result would have been achievable under a different leader. Yet during Brown's leadership no poll suggested that a specific alternative candidate would improve the party's ratings. It is possible that under a different leader, ill-equipped to face the economic crisis, Labour might have fared worse still. We will never know. All we know for sure is that after the election Labour surfaced from a third term of deranged politics still breathing, something of a miracle in itself.

FOURTEEN

New Labour to New Politics

Shortly after Brown stepped down I asked one of those who had worked with him at the Treasury and in Number Ten whether it was as bad as we had assumed, the temper eruptions and moody gloom. At times it was, he confirmed. But then he cited the case of Brown's diary secretary, Leanne Johnson, who had worked with him in the Treasury and asked to move with him to Number Ten when Brown became Prime Minister. 'She got more of his temper than anyone else because he was often angry about his diary.' Why did she stay with him, I asked. 'Because she knew that basically he was a good man and that the tempers were never really aimed at anyone other than himself.' On the whole Brown was at odds with himself, and was unquestionably the chief victim of that unstilled anger.

The rest of the New Labour story will start to make more sense too over time. For now, one narrative of sorts is already in place. It relates that Tony Blair was on a journey in which he set out to please everyone at the beginning and ended by doing what was 'right', even though this made him unpopular. Blair is the main propagator of the story and has come to believe it fervently. Brown is seen widely as someone who blocked the way as Blair sought to complete his noble journey.

The reality is far more complicated. Throughout his career as leader and Prime Minister, Blair sought solutions that would either be popular, or else the least unpopular that his extensive skills could contrive. The truth is that while Blair regarded his early popularity as vindication for his actions, he managed to take his later unpopularity as a form of vindication too.

A key moment that highlights the flaws in the current mythology took place in the autumn of 1996, a few months before Labour took power in 1997. Blair wanted to announce that the tax burden would not rise under a Labour government. Brown and Balls held their ground and took the bolder course. Balls said to Blair that if he made the pledge he would be lying, and it would be seen as a lie when the government put up taxes after the election. Mandelson stormed out of the meeting, appalled by Balls's rudeness and, in his view, misjudged approach to 'tax and spend'. But the blunt assertion was necessary. Even the more sensible among the Conservatives were privately admitting at the time that the tax burden would have to rise as they surveyed the dilapidated public services that scarred the UK.

That was the largely forgotten backdrop in 1997. Another myth much repeated was that the Labour government had inherited a booming economy. In reality the inheritance was an unbalanced one, with an urgent need for investment in public services, the crumbling schools and hospitals and creaking trains. The coming together of a duopoly shaped by four successive election defeats with the decay of the public services was a challenging one. Over time Brown found the money without threatening Labour's electoral appeal and at times enhancing it. He should have invested more evenly over his period in the Treasury, but he too was on a journey, and one that Blair nearly blocked at the very beginning.

For Labour in the future, and the coalition that is modelled in many ways on early New Labour, lessons erupt from this elusive era. Great political leaders make the most of the tiny political space available to them. At times Blair and Brown had more space than they realized – in the mid-1990s when the Tory party collapsed and in 2001 after they had secured a landslide second term for Labour. Margaret Thatcher's genius was to recognize when space opened up, as it did for her with the schism in the Labour party after the 1979 election. She moved faster than some of her colleagues thought would be politically safe because she knew there was no credible alternative government at least for the first half of the 1980s. Blair and Brown had less space than Thatcher, largely because the still powerful media in Britain leans to the right, but they could have been much bolder at times.

After Brown had lost the 2010 election there was immediate critical revisionism amongst his closest allies. One told me that Brown should have contested the 1994 leadership contest and encouraged a contest in 2007 when he won by a walkover. Another said that the Brownite paradigm of allowing the City to boom in order to pay for public services was a disaster: regulation should have been much tougher from the beginning. Someone else who had worked closely with him for years said that it was only towards the end that they realized Brown had needed Blair all along as a leader with compelling presentational gifts whom the Chancellor could hide behind. An even closer ally condemned his caution in the Treasury. 'He could have made the story about Laura Spence [the brilliant student who was rejected by Oxford] a defining one for his entire career, making fairness, access and breaking class barriers his themes. But he ran a mile the moment the media attacked the story.' These are observations from very close colleagues. They are also all plucked neatly out of context and applied to the new one in which the defeated Brown licks his wounds and his disciples seek to move on.

When the leadership contest in the Labour party began, almost immediately after Brown's departure in the summer of 2010, the closest Brownites went their separate ways. The two Eds stood against each other and Douglas Alexander backed David Miliband. There were no Brownites then, except as defined by a common desire to formalize their divergence. Most of the Blairites had left the stage altogether, lacking the will and political dexterity to last the course. The Brownites battling it out and the exiled Blairites were a final reminder that a party controlled by a handful of individuals is subject to the same level of turbulence as one held to account by the wider membership.

The divide between the two sides was difficult to capture because the two dominant individuals left so many false trails, starting with that deceptively vague adjective 'new' placed beside the name of an existing party with a turbulent history.

Blair was agile and skated on thin ice when it came to policy detail. Hence he could readily argue for a big increase in public spending at one moment and for tax cuts the next.

Blair told me towards the end of his period as Prime Minister that 'In England a Conservative government can govern from the right. A Labour government can only govern from the centre ground.'

This was a revealing observation, confirming that Labour's most electorally successful leader regarded England as an instinctively Conservative-supporting country. His response at first was to steer a third way through every challenge or crisis. He was pro-European but an ardent pro-American as well. He wanted to cut taxes, but sometimes to put up spending. The third way was not merely a tentative philosophy but a guide for a Prime Minister who projected boldness but sought compromise almost as an end in itself.

By the third term Blair lost the anchorage of his third way and became more determinedly energetic in relation to 'reform', but in ways little different from the Conservative party's approach. When David Cameron became Conservative leader in 2005 he declared his support for Blair's public service reforms, and in doing so made a tactically astute move that also was an act of conviction. Both Cameron and Osborne revered Blair, as did quite a few of their senior staff. That idolatry, with its capacity for heightened misunderstanding of the subject, is an important ingredient in the story of Cameron's leadership. In the build-up to the 2010 election, whenever there were doubts about tactics, the reassuring words went around the open-plan offices shared by the Cameron and Osborne courts: 'It's OK. Blair did the same thing in 1996.'

Blair, the self-proclaimed political cross-dresser, made it easier for the Conservatives to claim him as one of their own and cleared the way for the coalition formed without great ideological trauma after the 2010 election. Blair could be attractively self-deprecating and yet was capable at times of the ultimate act of egotism: extrapolating from his own personal rootless politics an entire historic sweep. If he personally felt attracted by ideas usually associated with the right, then we were all in an era of cross-dressing – the entire Western world was. If he was uneasy with approaches identified with the centre left and felt more affinity with, say, President Bush, then we were all living through a phase where terms such as left and right were redundant. One of his favourite themes was the disappearance of a left and right. This was because he, Tony Blair, had long since disappeared from the left. The Con/Lib coalition is in many ways the natural extension of Blairism.

The term 'Blairite' obscured what Blair had come to espouse, which was a form of compassionate Thatcherism, a contradiction in terms that he never resolved. Specifically Blair was suspicious of the state in most of its manifestations and developed what became an indiscriminate faith in the private sector. From the middle of the second term there was virtually nothing he said or did that could not have been said or done by a Conservative leader, as Cameron recognized. Not surprisingly this made Blair popular with the intelligent Tory-supporting columnists. His electoral success and spell-binding presentational gifts also made him liked for a time by his confused party. His calm, good-humoured decency made his close colleagues unswervingly loyal. By the end a lot of them were devoted to Blair and had ceased to have any affinity with their party. When he left Number Ten quite a few 'Blairites' more or less gave up too. This was Brown's inheritance when he became leader.

Blair found a way of dealing with this strange mutation, a Labour leader espousing policies closer to those supported by the Conservative party and right-wing columnists. Whenever Labour figures called for a policy that was on the left of centre, Blair warned them about returning to their 'comfort zone'. What he really meant was that it was not easy for a left-of-centre party to accept right-wing solutions, or what he termed 'radical' policies. Terms such as 'Blairite', 'comfort zone' and 'radical', all of them conveniently apolitical, disguised the fact that by the end of his leadership Blair's own comfort zone was on the well-intentioned right of politics, small state, laissez-faire, pro-President Bush, pro-deregulation.

Brown had a monstrous ego too, determined to do whatever it took to secure the leadership. All the competitive instincts that might have been purged on the sporting fields before he lost the sight in one eye went into politics.

But he was much less confident than Blair that his own personal views represented a historic tide. In some ways he functioned from the opposite starting point. As I observed him closely and spoke to him occasionally, and a lot more regularly to the two Eds, Balls and Miliband, I discovered that his closest aides were cautious social democrats, although they never used the term. In the apolitical era this was the equivalent of discovering a politician was gay in previous less tolerant decades. They did not dare to come out fully, but they had a belief in the state as a benevolent force, in contrast to Blair's instinctive and more fashionable wariness. When I spoke to them at the height of their run-ins with Blair, they always used to pause at some point in the conversation and declare: 'It all comes down to a view of the state.' Brown sought progressive ends by more recognizably left-of-centre means: higher public spending on NHS and schools (transport took him longer, but like a train to Blackpool he got there in the end), redistribution and specific measures aimed at helping the poor. He was more alert to issues of accountability, the great raging unanswered question of the New Labour era and one that will torment future governments: to whom are public services accountable and in what form? The question was posed at various meetings held by centre-right think tanks after the 2010 elections. They too recognized its tantalizing centrality.

Brown had no faith that left-of-centre arguments would command wide support in England, so his false trails took a very different form from Blair's. All the individuals and devices with which he became associated were aimed at giving him the space to introduce the policies he cared about. His informal alliances with bankers, leaders of the CBI, the editor of the *Daily Mail*, his mischievous flirtation with Margaret Thatcher, and the appointment when he was Prime Minister of ministers from outside the Labour party, were all instruments or deliberately misleading signals as he got on with the main task. The lectures in Britishness, prudence and courage were also deceptively apolitical. They were all framed with the intention of moving Britain on from the previous more right-wing assumptions that drove debates on such accessible and yet vague themes. Similarly the tax cuts, the light regulatory touch, the authoritarian support for detaining suspects without charge and the lectures about the importance of low public spending (in the early years at least) were all deployed in the hope of winning broader support for the need to invest in public services and to help the poor – Brown's two big causes. He hoped, but was never sure, that some of his more progressive instincts would come to be shared by what he called the mainstream majority, a favourite phrase.

What made the task so challenging was that Brown needed to act often against the instincts of the Treasury, Tony Blair, the Conservative party and most newspapers – a daunting array of opponents. He was the rebel in New Labour's big tent of support while affecting to be its leading spokesman. The journalist Simon Jenkins wrote a stimulating book arguing that Blair and Brown were the sons of Thatcher, following her ideas and policies. Jenkins was only half right, and even Blair was more complicated than Jenkins suggested. Brown was never a disciple of Thatcher, but he would have been relaxed about the book, another false trail.

In the spring of 2010 I asked Peter Mandelson why he thought Brown had such problems talking about spending cuts when, between 1992 and 1999, he gloried in his reputation as an iron chancellor or iron shadow chancellor. Mandelson confirmed what Ed Balls and others had told me at the time. The early public narrative was never the whole story. Brown was planning to spend and was already doing so discreetly after the 1997 election, targeting additional spending on poorer areas and discreetly putting up taxes. Mandelson said that in 2010 Brown's instincts were to challenge Treasury orthodoxy again as he had done when he arrived as a new Chancellor. He did not want his election campaign determined by an institution he had never trusted. In 2010 such obstinacy in the face of the gaping deficit had driven Mandelson and Darling to despair. But there was something rebelliously endearing in the prime-ministerial defiance. As happened to Thatcher in the late 1980s, he was now a rebel in the government that he led.

As I wrote that last sentence a thousand conversations whirled around my head, discussions with ministerial colleagues of Brown who loathed him, regarding him as a bullying lightweight, treacherous, incapable of making a decision, acting only for self-advancement. These accusations became a big theme during Brown's leadership, again all of them curiously apolitical. By the end of his leadership it was almost impossible to find anyone who had a good word to say for him anywhere. Senior Blairites told me of shocking acts of betrayal as Brown plotted to remove Blair. When he became Prime Minister officials, advisers and cabinet ministers who were once admirers turned away as they despaired of his behaviour, disloyalty, inability to lead a team, lack of deftness, absence of long-term strategic thinking. Sympathetic columnists were more scathing. The best of the left-of-centre columnists, Polly Toynbee, was convinced that she had been misled when he was Chancellor as Brown and his allies promised a more progressive government when they took over.

I had those conversations with the Brownites too, the 'Just you wait and see' exchanges in which a revolutionary paradise was implied. Cameron was also expecting something big. In the summer of 2007 he asked me when I thought 'it' would be coming, the game-changing package. It never came.

But that does not mean Brown had no plan when he got in to Number Ten. This cliché is as simplistic as the one about Blair lying in order to take us to war. It does not make sense. How could Brown, who planned for his arrival at the Treasury as if he was fighting a solo military campaign on the Western Front, have strolled into Number Ten without giving serious thought to what he would do there? The answer is that he had not metamorphosed from a control freak to a dilettante, but his prime-ministerial plan went catastrophically wrong and he never recovered. The attempt at a recovery brought out the worst in him, as well as a dogged resilience that was both awesomely formidable and ugly at times.

Before the 2010 election Andrew Rawnsley wrote a revealing and well-sourced book that made headlines for its depiction of Brown as a prime minister with a bullying, volcanic temper. Politics is a human vocation and, as Rawnsley asserted, voters have a right to know about the character of a prime minister. But Brown did not go into politics to vent his temper.

In Brown's case the political vocation is too easily overlooked and is at least as interesting as the eruptions of anger. Whereas Blair regarded England's instinctive Conservatism as a reason for clinging to the centre ground, Brown had a bolder project, or at least he did between 1992 and 2002, his peak decade. He feared that most voters in England did not share his social democratic instincts, but he sought ways in which England could become more social democratic in spite of itself.

The differences between Blair and Brown are more important than the soap opera of volcanic tempers, betrayal and frustrated ambition. If their successors in the Labour party do not understand what really happened they will not be able to move on from the fog of the last two decades. The Tories have their own fog to contend with. They are an important part of the story. Blair and Brown were neurotically obsessed about the Tories, even when Labour was twenty points ahead in the polls. In that respect they were as one.

In the spring of 1998 when Tony Blair was still on his seemingly never-ending honeymoon and the new Conservatives' leader William Hague was the subject of ridicule at best, I had a cup of tea in Blair's office. Suddenly an adviser came rushing in to the office in a state of panic, as if a war had broken out. He announced that Hague had changed his party's policy on rural post offices. Number Ten was a fever of activity as advisers worked out how to respond. Hague was thirty points behind Blair in the polls at the time. From the Euro to Iraq, Tory policy continued to influence Labour policy.

Cameron was right when he described himself as the heir to Blair. There are differences between the two of them. Blair was a pro-European, although an erratic one, and had the wit to realize that public spending needed to rise. Cameron would not have done so, and instictively opposed the increases in spending on the NHS in 2002. His hostility towards the state was too deep-seated. But there is a direct line that connects Thatcher, Blair, Cameron and Clegg. In some ways Clegg is the more direct heir to Blair, while quite a few of Clegg's senior colleagues in the Liberal Democrats share an outlook closer to Brown's, at least in terms of economic policy.

We are back to where we began. Our changing views of Brown are partly explained by the contradictions in his character and his attempts to create so many false trails. He was the cautious risk taker, sweating neurotically over incremental moves and yet presiding over a revolution at the Treasury. He was hated by some of his colleagues, while others were so devoted they would have died for him. He was the greatest bibliophile in Downing Street since Gladstone and yet struggled to write a decent speech. He entered politics with a desire above all to alleviate poverty and yet became an admiring ally of Alan Greenspan, the evangelist for the lightly regulated marketplace. He wanted Blair's job with an ambition that tortured him and yet he waited more than a decade before he made his move.

But as future governments struggle to combine the unavoidably expensive provision of civilized public services with electoral popularity, and struggle over how to reform them effectively, distancing from the New Labour era will make way for renewed curiosity. For the two antagonists who seized control of a party there will be many more bumpy rides to come as their distinct roles move in and out of focus. At some point the picture will resolve, and Brown's epic journey will be seen as much more than one loud, angry scream.

ACKNOWLEDGEMENTS

Many thanks to my editors at Fourth Estate, Louise Haines and Michael Upchurch, Robin Harvie, Steve Cox and Anthony Hippisley, and to my agent, Andrew Gordon. Even in the relatively short time since the book was conceived, Brown's position and reputation changed several times. They were supportive and encouraging whatever the political context. Equally, thank you to the politicians who appear in this account. The book is based on notes from conversations with them that took place from 1992 to 1996 when I was a BBC political correspondent, from 1996 to 2000 when I was Political Editor of the *New Statesman*, and from 2000 as a political columnist for the *Independent* and as presenter for GMTV, when many discussions took place over coffee in the green room before and after interviews. Some of the later sections are also based on interviews I conducted for the BBC Radio 4 series *The Brown Years*, broadcast in the autumn of 2010. All the interviews for the series took place after the 2010 election. My thanks to the producers of the series, Martin Rosenbaum and Paul Twinn.

The long and stimulating discussions over the years convince me that the politicians who appear in these pages from across the political spectrum act for many reasons, but above all because they want to enhance lives and not diminish them.

Many books on New Labour have helped to form my impressions. The ones cited in these pages are: *The Third Man* by Peter Mandelson; *1 Out of 10* by Peter Hyman; *The End of the Party* by Andrew Rawnsley; *The Unfinished Revolution* by Philip Gould; *The Unconventional Minister* by Geoffrey Robinson.

INDEX

GB indicates Gordon Brown.

Rock and 283; partnership with GB 59–61;
pre-budget report, 2008 and 382, 383;
pre-budget report, 2009 and 412, 413, 414,
415; redistribution and fairness,
importance of 92, 137; refuses GB's request
to relinquish role as Schools Secretary and
return to Number Ten 318–19; resists
Blair's call to pledge not to raise taxes, 1997
131, 432; 'respect agenda', outlook on 218;
role of state in individuals lives, on 219–20;
Schools Secretary 266, 277, 318, 403; social
democrat 381; Southwold summer
meeting with GB, 2008 351–6, 357; starts
to work for GB 58–9; 10p tax and 240, 331;
terrorism, doubts over GB's approach to
225; Wanless NHS review and 150; Welfare
to Work and 60; windfall tax and 93
Bank of England 59, 102, 103, 106–13, 215,
281, 377, 379, 387–8
BBC 25–6, 50, 71, 117, 151, 174, 176, 180,
194, 197, 213, 227, 237, 238, 252, 269, 300,
301, 304, 307–8, 311, 318, 322, 333, 334,
341, 351, 360, 362, 369, 382, 390–1, 392–3,
421–2, 424, 428
Bear Stearns 373
Beckett, Margaret 46, 86, 354
Benn, Hilary 310
Benn, Tony 80
Bercow, John 262
Black, Ann 329
Blair, Cherie 100, 101, 195
Blair, Tony 1, 3, 5, 9, 13, 18, 23, 25, 37, 41, 58,
342, 415; accountability, argues with GB
over public service delivery and 107;
arguments/fallings out/disagreements with
GB 73–86, 96, 99, 103–4, 107, 123–46,
163–78, 183–242; big tent 20, 33; bind
successor to policies, attempts to 235,
239–40; budgets and 114, 116–17; 'cash for
honours' 307, 308, 309, 311; challenges GB
over economic policy 90–1; Cherie Blair's
relationship with GB and 101; child
poverty, pledge to abolish 136–7; 'choice'
agenda and 106, 147, 148, 163, 219, 223,
259, 273, 325, 425; close working
relationship with GB, 1992–4 67–71;
coalition negotiations, 2010, GB speaks to
concerning 27, 34; compartmentalisation
of time 87, 102, 232; Conservatives,
closeness to 7, 221–2, 223, 434–5; David
Miliband and 347; departs as Prime
Minister 235, 243, 244–7, 263; Euro and
87, 147, 178–80; European constitution,
u-turn on referendum on 195–6;

evangelical/messianic zeal 161–2, 180, 187,
224, 235; farewell tour 235, 245–7, 263; GB
as Prime Minster, contact with 27, 34, 278;
GB introduces media tactics to 70–1; GB,
admiration for 69; GB's temper, outlook
on 62–3; GB's influence over 86; GB's
separate power base, attempts to break up
102, 103–4; GB worries about as leader
74–6; General Election campaign, 2005
199–200, 203–5, 206, 207, 208–10; Granita
deal and 76–80, 103, 128, 184; heart
operation 201, 202; Hutton report and
194; 'I do not have a reverse gear' 1; ID
Cards and 217, 218; income tax, outlook
on 31–3, 131–3, 152, 161, 163, 432;
independent state schools 220–3; inherits
policies from Smith era 87; Iraq and 15, 68,
113, 159, 161, 165, 178–9, 180, 186–7, 191,
193, 194, 201, 204, 205, 209, 210, 212, 213,
246, 248, 270, 409–10; Israel's bombing of
Lebanon, 2006 and 230; Labour as a
governing force lost in focus on 187–8;
Labour Conference, 2004 200–1; Labour
Conference, 2006 235, 246; Labour leader,
becomes, 1994 5–6, 49, 66–7, 72–3, 85; lack
of focus/detail on policy 70, 75–6, 434;
Liberal Democrat alliance negotiations,
1997 87, 141–4; local elections, May, 2006
and 227–8; Mandelson and 14, 60; media
and 50, 102–3, 118, 131, 213, 217, 409–10;
NEC seat 62; negotiations with GB over
departure 73–80, 85, 184–242; NHS and
138–41, 158–9, 161–71; 9/11 and 6, 152,
154; ninety days detention and 218;
Olympic Games bid, 2012 217, 218, 317;
outlook on second term 147, 148; policy
disagreements with GB 3, 5, 116–17,
131–45, 148, 161–80, 201, 218–23;
popularity 161, 191, 431; presentation,
importance of 102–3, 118, 131, 433, 435;
Presidential 186; pro-Americanism 147,
178–9; public spending, complacency over
levels of, 2001 151–2; 'reform'/'anti-reform'
debate, creates 7, 110, 162, 164, 434;
reshuffle, summer, 1998 128–9; resignation
statement, 2006 29; 'respect agenda' 217,
218; Routledge GB biography and 125–8;
7/7 London terrorist attacks 217–18;
Scottish Devolution and 87, 92; scrutinizes
policy before 1997 election 87; shares
office with GB, 1983 70–1, 101; tactically
bold, strategically cautious 154; terrorist
legislation 217, 218; third way 119, 434;
timing of departure as Prime Minister 77,

outlook on 45–6, 165–9, 171–3, 201, 216,
232, 281, 366, 374–5, 376, 381, 385–9, 422,
437, 440; minimum wage 12, 58, 62, 87,
135, 145, 189, 217; national insurance
contributions 57, 135, 150, 151, 160, 363,
382, 412, 413–14, 423; NHS *see* NHS;
ownership 120–1, 379–80; pensions/
pensioners 46, 117, 118, 135–6, 138, 206,
217, 220, 241, 330, 333; PFI 92–3; political
philosophy 45; potential and 44, 45, 75, 89,
159, 236, 237–8, 258, 327, 387; poverty and
3, 12, 44, 56, 59, 75, 92, 110, 135–8, 140,
151, 152, 153, 203, 204, 206, 220, 260, 261,
331, 342, 440; as Prime Minster 252, 258,
259, 264, 272–3, 284; prudence 3, 92, 94,
95, 98, 114, 117, 146, 152, 189, 297, 381,
423, 437; redistribution 42, 43, 46, 48, 92,
104, 115–19, 120, 121, 145, 159–60, 323,
330, 332, 436; scheming becomes detached
from policy-making 263, 274–5; spending
increases/investment, 1997–2010 3,
138–41, 148, 150, 153, 154–71, 274, 436,
440; stamp duty 118, 206; stealthy
approach to 76, 94, 104, 117, 118, 119, 150,
159, 188, 256, 402; tax credits 12, 43, 117,
118, 119, 135, 137, 139, 140, 151, 159, 189,
206, 329–30, 331, 332, 333; tax rises to
increase spending 141, 148, 150–60, 153,
154–7, 158–60, 161, 171; terrorism and
334–5; Tory spending plans, promise to
stick to 1997 90–1, 149; unemployment 44;
university funding 171–7; VAT 382,
413–14, 424; Welfare to Work 60, 62, 93–4,
133; windfall tax 62, 93
POPULARITY/REPUTATION 5–6, 9–10,
98; Chancellor, first term 6, 105;
Chancellor, second term 6, 160, 191,
206–7; Chancellor, third term 6, 228;
Shadow Chancellor 6, 55, 61–4, 98; Prime
Minster 6, 9–10, 283, 305, 313, 326, 335,
337, 340, 353, 383, 401
PRIME MINISTER: accession/inheritance,
difficulties of 211, 235, 239–40, 244, 256–7;
as agent of change, attempts to project
image of 258, 260, 264, 269; Alistair
Campbell, considers return of 354–5;
appointment of non-Labour figures to
government 20, 260–2, 268; advisers in
Number Ten, lack of senior 277–8, 394,
410; bankers and 3, 54, 150, 375, 376, 436;
becomes Prime Minister 56, briefings
against other Labour figures and 3, 303–4,
325–6, 359, 415, 420; 'Britishness', concept
of 259–60, 293, 437; budget, 2009 and 402;

budget, 2010 and 423, 425–6; Bush/U.S.,
constructs distance between UK and
273–4, 284; cabinet meetings/government,
stresses importance of 269–70; cabinet,
formation of first 250–1, 264–8; 'cash for
honours' and 307, 307–8, 309, 310, 311;
coalition negotiations and 16–18, 23–35;
consensus, attempt to build a national
225–6, 235–9, 250–1, 259–68;
constitutional reform 270, 271–2, 274, 284;
'conviction politician', attempts to project
image of 258, 284; Crewe-and-Nantwich
by-election, 2008 335–8; Davies defection,
role in 261–3; depression, appearance of as
304–5, 312–13, 314, 316–17, 389–90;
deputy Labour leadership contest and
255–6; Downing Street operation,
problems with 278–80, 317–22; Downing
Street, chaotic move/transition into
277–81; Economic Council 366, 372–3;
electoral reform 270–1; ends ability to
'declare war without a vote' 270; expenses,
MPs 390, 392–5, 396, 398; failings, admits
to personal 319–20; final cabinet meeting
30; financial crisis, 2008 281–4, 341, 362–6,
372, 373–90, 398, 411; finds logistical
step-up to Prime Minister tougher than
expected 277–81; first statement as Prime
Minster, Downing Street, 2007 262–4;
fiscal stimulus 382, 384–9, 407; flooding,
2007 and 276, 282; foot-and-mouth, 2007
and 276, 280, 281, 282; forty-two days
detention without charge and 334–5; G20
summit 384, 387, 388–9; General Election,
aborted 2007 and 283, 284–5, 287–307;
General Election, 2008 257, 268, 303;
General Election, 2010 9–14, 18–19,
426–30; 'getting on with the job' 384;
Glasgow East by-election, 2008 339, 340–1;
government as a benevolent force, views
220, 360, 361, 362, 374, 375, 385–9, 402,
436; government of all the talents 251, 268,
436; Gurkhas and 394; honeymoon period
275–80; identity as, attempt to establish an
211–12, 224–6; inability to focus on
essentials 384; inheritance tax proposals
302; investment versus cuts dividing line,
2009 404–7, 411–15, 416, 421, 423–4, 437;
Iraq and 260, 274, 295–6, 297, 334; Iraq,
flies to during Tory conference, 2007 297;
Labour conference, 2007 283, 292–5;
Labour conference, 2009 410–11; Labour
leadership victory speech, 2007 258–61;
Lisbon Treaty signing 313; Lockerbie

bomber affair 408–10; loss of authority as 18, 19; lost data discs, 2007 312, 313; luck, bad 335; media and 17, 245, 248–9, 252, 269, 273, 274, 279, 300–2, 303–4, 321, 322–3, 324, 332, 334, 350–1, 354–5, 356–60, 370, 379–80, 384, 390–2, 393, 394, 399, 401, 404, 408–10, 426, 427–9, 433; Miliband threat and 345–53; national insurance increase 413–14; NHS 272–3, 274, 284; Northern Rock 281–3, 284, 322, 323–4, 331, 363, 377, 386, 398; *Observer* article, February, 2008 326–8; Parliament Square, proposes change to right to demonstrate in 271; personal trainer, uses 350, 353; plan/strategy for 3, 257–64, 270, 313, 315–16, 438; plots/coups/rebellions against 315, 316, 326, 332, 334, 345–53, 359, 365–70, 375, 376, 395–8, 407–8, 415–23; PMQs 273, 302, 380, 402, 418, 425; police investigations into Labour Party deputy leadership campaign funding 309–12; popularity as 9–10, 283, 305, 313, 326, 335, 337, 340, 353, 383, 401; poverty, attempts to address issue of 260; pre-budget report, 2007 303; pre-budget report, 2008 381–3; pre-budget report, 2009 411–15; stand down within a year of 2010 general election, drafts a speech setting out plans to 426; rebelliousness as 437–8; recession and 383–4, 411; recession and 383–4, 411; re-launch, September, 2008 360–1; reshuffle, 2008 354, 370–2; reshuffle, 2009 397–9; resignation, 2010 27–30, 33–6; scheduling cock-ups 313–14; self-confidence dives 304–5, 312, 316, 394; self-interested deviousness, image of 302–3; sense of mission as 326–8; sleaze and 307–12; Southwold holiday, 2008 350–6, 357, 360, 361, 371; Stringer calls for GB to go 336–7; stubbornness 332; summer statement on autumn legislative programme, introduces 271, 275; super casino, scraps planned Manchester 273, 275; tax system, deliberately makes complicated 332–3; tax on higher earners, raises 2008 382, 383, 402; 10p tax 240, 289, 328–34, 335, 336, 355; team splits in 2010 leadership election 433; team fractures in light of 2007 non-election 303–4; temper/fragile mental state 280–1, 308, 309, 315, 316–17, 431, 439; terrorism and 276, 281, 282, 334–5; Thatcher visits No. 10 284; tries to restore trust in Labour on becoming 56; U.S. and 273–4; VAT and

382, 413–14; willingness to dump on anyone facing allegations of any sort 310–11
SHADOW CHANCELLOR: becomes, 1992 36, 37; Campaign for Recovery 56–7; City, relationship with 89; competence, makes the main dividing line between Labour and Conservative 46–52, 61, 88, 149; Conservative spending plans, promises to stick to for two years 90–1, 149; 'endogenous growth theory' 88–9; golden fiscal rules 94–5, 113, 189, 381; Granita meeting with Blair 76–80, 98, 103, 128, 184, 185, 193, 207, 232; Labour leadership 1992, considers standing for 68–70; Labour leadership contest, 1994, steps aside in 72–80, 433; markets and 45, 89; media and 38; minimum wage and 58, 62; NEC, fears for seat on 62–3; obsessed with preparing the ground 58; popularity dives as 38–40, 55, 61, 62–4; potential of people, aims to unlock 89, 159; public persona, develops evasive 42–50; rewrites left-of-centre policy making, 1992–4 38; shadow budget 56, 57, 61, 70, 86, 183; tax, resists Blair's call to pledge not to raise, 1997 432; tax and spend, attempts to ditch previous perception of Labour on 42, 45–7, 57, 60–1, 62, 89–91, 432; Thatcherite moves as 57, 60–1; top rate of income tax, promises not to raise 90–1; Welfare to Work 60, 62; windfall tax 57, 62, 93–4
SPEECHES AND LECTURES: 3; anthology of (*Moving Britain Forward*) 236–7; CBI, 2008 361–2; first statement as Prime Minster, Downing Street, 2007 262–4; General Election count, 2010, Kirkcaldy, Scotland 11–13; Labour conference, 2001 152–4; Labour conference, 2003 188–90; Labour conference, 2004 200–1; Labour conference, 2007 293; Labour conference, 2008 376; Labour conference, 2009 410–11; Labour leadership victory speech, 2007 258–61; lecture to Charter 88, before 1992 election 45; Mansion House, 2006 226–7; NFT business leaders gathering, September, 1994 87–9; plans to stand down within a year of 2010 general election, drafts a speech setting out 426; Policy Forum, 2008, Warwick University 341, 342–3; pre-budget report, 2001 155–8; resignation speech, 2010, Downing Street 35–6; Social Market Foundation, 2003 165–9; statement announcing later

INDEX

374, 375, 377; inheritance tax, promise to abolish 296–7, 298, 302; lack of experience 266; little interest in policy detail, 2010 election 92; Mandelson return, reaction to 372; national insurance, cut in planned increase 423–4; Northern Rock, reaction to collapse of 323; public relations, obsession with 51, 283, 294; tax and spend policies, 2010 424
ownership 120–1, 379–80

Parker, Alan 319, 320
Paulson, Hank 373, 377, 378, 379
pensions policy 46, 117, 118, 135–6, 138, 206, 217, 220, 241, 330, 333
Peston, Robert 7, 73, 196, 204
Portillo, Michael 40, 65, 147, 149, 183, 226
Powell, Jonathan 278, 394
Prescott, John 61, 105, 127, 142, 184, 191, 192, 193, 196
Price, Lance 151
Private Finance Initiative (PFI) 92–3
Progress 383
Public Private Partnership (PPP) 120
Purnell, James 266, 363, 368–9, 370, 376, 396

Question Time 393

Rawnsley, Andrew 127, 439
redistribution 42, 43, 46, 48, 92, 104, 115–19, 120, 121, 145, 159–60, 323, 330, 332, 436
Reid, John 32, 164, 169, 170, 195, 199, 250–1
'respect agenda' 217–19
Robinson, Geoffrey 92, 93–4, 95, 99, 108, 115, 129, 184, 318
Robinson, Nick 233, 237, 301
Robson, Steve 109, 120
Roosevelt, Theodore 386
Routledge, Paul 7, 73, 125–6, 128, 129, 175, 204
Royal Bank of Scotland 373

Scholar, Tom 317
Scotland 87, 92, 144, 408
SDP 41
SDP/Liberal alliance 18
Seldon, Anthony 115, 196
7/7 London terrorist attacks, 2005 217–18
Sheerman, Barry 395–6
Sherlock, Neil 27
Short, Clare 84, 179–80
Shrum, Bob 115, 247, 279, 289, 290, 291, 299
Simon, Siôn 231
Sinclair, Paul 350–1, 352

single currency *see* Euro
Sixsmith, Martin 134
Sky News 197, 245, 280, 301, 428
Smith Institute 308–9
Smith, Jacqui 276, 317, 334, 394
Smith, John 40, 42, 49, 53, 55, 56, 57, 58, 61, 65–7, 69, 70, 72, 73, 80, 87, 246
SNP 32, 339, 340, 408
Spectator 274, 374
Spence, Laura 172, 433
stamp duty 118, 206
stealth taxes 104, 117, 118, 119, 124, 130, 146, 150, 159, 188, 256, 402
Steel, David 26–7, 32
Stelzer, Irwin 195–6
Stevenson, Wilf 236, 309
Strauss-Khan, Dominique 389
Straw, Jack 30, 32, 230, 232, 326, 343, 351, 363, 368, 370, 376, 417, 419, 420, 421
Stringer, Graham 336–7
Summers, Larry 58
Sun 127, 151, 195–6, 198, 205, 213, 248, 294, 334
Sunday Telegraph 160, 204, 292
Sunday Times 66, 67, 383
Sure Start 137

tax and spend policies: budget, 1997 115–17, 125; budget, 1998 117–19; budget, 2002 159–60; budget, 2003 6, 160–1; budget, 2004 203, 205–6; budget, 2007 239–42, 328–31; budget, 2009 402; budget, 2010 423, 425–6; competence, GB makes dividing line between Labour and Conservative 46–52, 61, 88, 149; financial crisis and *see* financial crisis; golden fiscal rules, GB's 94–5, 113, 189, 381; inheritance tax 57, 296–7, 298, 302; investment versus cuts dividing line, 2009 404–7, 411–15, 416, 421, 423–4, 437; Labour Party dilemmas over, 1987–1992 45–6; markets *see* markets, financial; national insurance contributions 57, 135, 150, 151, 160, 363, 382, 412, 423; perception of Labour on, GB attempts to ditch previous 42, 45–7, 57, 60–1, 62, 89–91, 432; pre-budget report, 2001 155–8; pre-budget report, 2007 303; pre-budget report, 2008 381–3; pre-budget report, 2009 411–15; 381, 423, 437; prudence 92, 94, 95, 98, 114, 117, 146, 152, 189, 297, redistribution 42, 43, 46, 48, 92, 104, 115–19, 120, 121, 145, 159–60, 323, 330, 332, 436; spending increases/ investment, 1997–2010 138–41, 148, 150,

455